Organization of Memory

CONTRIBUTORS

GORDON H. BOWER

ALLAN M. COLLINS

JAMES G. GREENO

WALTER KINTSCH

PETER H. LINDSAY

GEORGE MANDLER

DONALD A. NORMAN

LEO POSTMAN

M. ROSS QUILLIAN

DAVID E. RUMELHART

ENDEL TULVING

JAMES F. VOSS

GORDON WOOD

ORGANIZATION
OF MEMORY

Edited by
Endel Tulving

Department of Psychology
Yale University
New Haven, Connecticut

and

Wayne Donaldson

Department of Psychology
University of Pittsburgh
Pittsburgh, Pennsylvania

ACADEMIC PRESS   New York and London   **1972**

253643

BF
371
074
1972

ACADEMIC PRESS, INC.
111 Fifth Avenue, New York, New York 10003

United Kingdom Edition published by
ACADEMIC PRESS, INC. (LONDON) LTD.
24/28 Oval Road, London NW1 7DD

LIBRARY OF CONGRESS CATALOG CARD NUMBER: 73-182647

This volume is a collection of papers prepared for a symposium made possible through financial support provided under a contract with the Personnel and Training Branch, Psychological Sciences Division, Office of Naval Research.

Contents

Part I

1. A Pragmatic View of Organization Theory
Leo Postman

2. Organizational Processes and Free Recall
Gordon Wood

3. A Selective Review of Organizational Factors in Memory
Gordon H. Bower

4. Organization and Recognition

George Mandler

5. On the Relationship of Associative and Organizational Processes

James F. Voss

Part II

6. A Process Model for Long-Term Memory

David E. Rumelhart, Peter H. Lindsay, and Donald A. Norman

7. Notes on the Structure of Sematic Memory

Walter Kintsch

8. How to Make a Language User

Allan M. Collins and M. Ross Quillian

9. On the Acquisition of a Simple Cognitive Structure

James G. Greeno

Part III

10. Episodic and Semantic Memory

Endel Tulving

List of Contributors

Numbers in parentheses indicate the pages on which the authors' contributions begin

GORDON H. BOWER (93), Department of Psychology, Stanford University, Stanford, California

ALLAN M. COLLINS (309), Bolt Beramek and Newman, Inc., Cambridge, Massachusetts

JAMES G. GREENO (353), Department of Psychology, University of Michigan, Ann Arbor, Michigan

WALTER KINTSCH (247), Department of Psychology, University of Colorado, Boulder, Colorado

PETER H. LINDSAY (197), Center for Human Information Processing, Department of Psychology, University of California, San Diego, La Jolla, California

GEORGE MANDLER (139), Department of Psychology, University of California, San Diego La Jolla, California

DONALD A. NORMAN (197), Center for Human Information Processing, Department of Psychology, University of California, San Diego, La Jolla, California

LEO POSTMAN (3), Department of Psychology, University of California, Berkeley, California

M. ROSS QUILLIAN (309), Department of Social Science, University of California at Irvine, Irvine, California

ix

DAVID E. RUMELHART (197), Center for Human Information Processing, Department of Psychology, University of California, San Diego, La Jolla, California

ENDEL TULVING (381), Department of Psychology, Yale University, New Haven, Connecticut

JAMES F. VOSS (167), Department of Psychology, University of Pittsburgh, Pittsburgh, Pennsylvania

GORDON WOOD (49), Department of Psychology, Michigan State University, East Lansing, Michigan

Preface

The swing of the pendulum back toward psychology as a study of the structure and function of the human mind is nowhere more apparent than in the current reevolution of the interest in memory. The study of human memory is one of the most rapidly expanding problem areas in psychology. While the total number of psychological publications and publications in experimental psychology increased by a factor of approximately two and a half in the decade from 1960 to 1970, the number of publications dealing with human memory jumped almost sixfold in the same interval. This impressive growth has been accompanied by an equally striking change in the nature of experimental work and theoretical speculation. Especially in the language researchers use in describing their problems and in discussing the deeper meaning of their findings do we find a clear break with the earlier traditions. While only a decade ago psychologists interested in verbal learning searched primarily for empirical relations governing acquisition, transfer, and extinction of habits, contemporary students of memory are seeking an understanding of how the mind works in registering and storing mnemonic information and in the utilization of that information in a great variety of situations.

This book is about organizational processes in memory. It grew out of a two-day conference held at the University of Pittsburgh in March 1971. The conference was sponsored by the Personnel and Training Research Programs, Psychological Sciences Division, Office of Naval Research, under Contract Nonr-624(18). It was held under the auspices of the Learning Research and Development Center of the University of Pittsburgh, which is one of the research and development centers of the National Center for Educational Research and Development of the Office of Education.

As is usually the case, this conference, too, began with only its general topic firmly fixed. Everything else—participants, the nature of their contributions, the exact coverage of various possible topics, and the overall format of the organization of the conference—evolved almost spontaneously and, in a sense, inexorably. The book, therefore, is what it is, not because of careful planning on anyone's part but, rather, because of how the different authors of its chapters interpreted and executed their mission.

The purpose of the conference, as we somewhat vaguely communicated it to prospective participants when we first invited them to contribute to its proceedings, was to examine and evaluate the state of the art in the study of memory and learning from the organizational point of view through a detailed analysis of extant empirical data and their relation to theoretical notions, as well as to point out and define problems in need of further study and thought. Each participant, however, was encouraged to pursue these general objectives from his own personal vantage point in any way and form that he deemed appropriate in light of the general topic of the conference.

The organization of the book, owing to its peculiar genesis, is somewhat adventitious, but it is not entirely contrived. There are ten chapters grouped into three parts. Chapters 1 through 5 of Part I are concerned with recent developments in laboratory research on remembering of verbal materials by normal human adults. These chapters review experimental findings and theoretical thinking with respect to a number of problems of current interest. These problems include the nature and significance of organization in free recall, detection and measurement of organization, organization and limited capacity of memory, organization and recognition memory, retrieval processes and retrieval plans, the nature of encoding processes, attributes and dimensions of memory, and the relationship between organization and association. All of these chapters are especially concerned with the relationship between experimental data and their theoretical implications. Chapters 6 through 8 of Part II look toward the future and foretell vigorous activity in the very recently created problem area of semantic memory. Semantic memory is concerned with storage and utilization of knowledge about meaning of words, concepts, relations among them, and rules for the use of such knowledge. Chapters 6 through 8 delineate a number of basic problems having to do with the structure and functioning of semantic memory and outline possible solutions to these problems. Much of this work is theoretical rather than experimental, representing initial attempts at, as one of the authors put it, "modeling of the mind." Chapter 9 of Part II describes methods of studying acquisition of mental structures, elementary building blocks of semantic memory, together with experimental findings from several initial experiments. Finally, Part III contains a single chapter, Chapter 10, that was originally not a part of the conference but represents an afterthought to one interesting aspect of the coverage of the conference. It suggests a possibly useful heuristic distinction between episodic and semantic memory. According to this distinction Part I of this book is primarily about episodic memory, while Part II is primarily about semantic memory.

We hope that the book is useful and of interest to all serious students of memory. It should help them to keep track of and to organize the multitude of experimental problems and theoretical puzzles, together with the wealth of empirical evidence, that have occupied the central position in a good deal of recent research, and to direct their attention to new vistas that have recently opened up in the form of the study of broader aspects of human memory.

Endel Tulving
Wayne Donaldson

PART   I

1 | A Pragmatic View of Organization Theory[1]

Leo Postman

My comments will be directed toward two related objectives. The first of these is an assessment of major developments in organization theory during the last decade. While the time span is brief, the theory

[1] The preparation of this report was facilitated by grant **MH 12006** from the National Institute of Mental Health.

has had a profound impact on research in verbal learning and memory. Thus, a preliminary historical appraisal may not be premature. The second aim is an examination of the extant empirical base of organization theory. The focus will be on the relation between hypothetical processes and experimental facts. Such an inquiry will of necessity entail the juxtaposition of organization theory and alternative conceptions of the basic conditions of acquisition and retention, notably those of contemporary associationism. A question permeating all these considerations will be whether and in what ways organization theory represents a fundamental departure from the mainstream of prior thought about learning and memory. It was recently stated that "a modest revolution is afoot today within the field of human learning, and the rebels are marching under the banner of 'cognitive organization'" (Bower, 1970, p. 18). Would it have been more appropriate to speak of evolution, reform, or, perhaps, even Restoration?

Development of Organization Theory

ANTECEDENTS IN GESTALT THEORY

When we think of organization processes in memory, we are naturally reminded of an earlier revolution launched under the banner of Gestalt. It was a basic tenet of Gestalt psychology that memory is governed by principles of organization and, more particularly, the laws of perceptual grouping. The perceptual configuration that constitutes the original experience of an event is preserved in the memory trace. Thus, "whatever factors favor organization in primary experience must at the same time favor association, retention, and therefore recall" (Köhler, 1941, pp. 492 f). The major focus of Gestalt experiments was on progressive changes in the memory trace over time. Free of the constraints imposed by external stimulation, the temporal evolution of the memory trace was expected to bring out in bold relief the principles of neural interaction that determine organization. We need not concern ourselves here with the discouragingly complex and inconclusive history of the experiments carried out under these auspices (cf. Riley, 1962). It will be useful, however, to bring to the fore certain features of the Gestalt approach to memory for purposes of comparison with contemporary views of organization.

There are four points in the Gestalt argument that are worthy of emphasis. First, mnemonic organization is established largely, if not entirely, by the initial perception of the events to be remembered. The properties of the trace reflect the neural events which accompany the primary perceptual experience. Second, the form of the organization is determined by the relations among the component units, such as proximity and similarity. Thus, for any set of units there is a natural or optimal organization. The processes by which such organization is achieved represent, for the most part, innate dispositions of the organism. Third, the long-term availability of prior experiences for recall depends on the temporal stability of the memory traces laid down by these experiences. For example, the availability of an association is governed by the continuing cohesiveness of the underlying unitary trace. Fourth, the accessibility of available traces for recall is a function of the similarity between these traces and current stimuli. As Köhler put it, "Whenever in the midst of present mental processes a step is taken back into the past, the specific direction of this step appears to be determined principally by kinship between the processes of the moment and particular traces of the past. This holds for recognition, for recall by similarity as such, and for recall on the basis of an association" (Köhler, 1940, p. 134).

As will become apparent shortly, current developments in organization theory have been converging upon a set of parallel propositions, although the conceptual framework and some of the underlying assumptions are clearly different: (1) The organization imposed by the learner on a set of items depends on his perception of the structure of the list. Thus, the presence of taxonomic, semantic, or conceptual categories must be discovered before it can be utilized (Mandler, 1967a, pp. 334 f). (2) For any list of items presented to a particular subject there is an optimal organization that will maximize recall. This assumption is, for example, the point of departure for the experiments investigating negative transfer from part to whole learning (Tulving, 1966). In contrast to the Gestalt position, no appeal to innate forces of organization is implied. The bases of organization for verbal units are obviously attributable to prior linguistic experience. It is interesting to note, however, that such classical determinants of perceptual grouping as the distribution of pauses during the presentation of a string of elements have once more been invoked to demonstrate the power of organizational processes in recall and recognition (Bower & Winzenz, 1969). (3) The view that the level of recall reflects the stability of higher-order units is, almost by definition, a basic tenet of any organizational account of memory. Consequently, long-term retention is seen as dependent on the integrity of the structure developed during acquisition (Mandler, 1967a; Mandler, Pearlstone, & Koopmans, 1969). (4) The distinction between availability and accessibility of stored information (cf. Tulving & Pearlstone, 1966) is assuming central importance in current analyses of retention. The thrust of the evidence is that success in recall depends on the reinstatement of the specific retrieval cues established during original learning (e.g., Thomson & Tulving, 1970; Tulving & Osler, 1968). Such findings can be readily related to the problem of process-trace similarity with which Köhler was concerned, and Höffding before him. If organization aids recall by generating potent retrieval cues, then the continuity of the theoretical issue becomes apparent.

One or the other of the analogies between the concerns of Gestalt theory and of present-day analyses of organization may be legitimately questioned as being formalistic or farfetched. Nevertheless the parallels are clearly discernible. The motivation for dwelling on them is not primarily antiquarian. Recognition of the historical continuities helps to identify the issues that must be faced when memory is viewed as governed by organizational processes. These issues, then, concern the relation between event perception and mnemonic organization, the identification of normatively optimal high-order groupings, the dependence of recall on the temporal persistence of the products of organization, and the conditions determining the accessibility of available units.

ORGANIZATION AND THE LIMITED CAPACITY OF MEMORY

Within the framework of Gestalt theory the concept of organization often lacked specificity and tended to be invoked in a post hoc fashion. The theory never gained decisive empirical support and gradually lapsed into virtual oblivion. The spectacular revival during the last decade of an organizational approach to memory is attributable to a new formulation which had the virtues of both precision and objectivity. In Tulving's (1962) classical paper, in which this new formulation was developed, the concept of subjective organization was firmly anchored to the operations of information measurement. Theoretically, the aim was to extend to free recall the ideas of recoding and chunking which Miller (1956) had introduced in his analysis of the immediate memory span. Thus, organizational processes were seen as critical if not essential because of the limited capacity of the memory system. At the same time the postulation of such processes promised to make sense of the entrenched but theoretically empty principle of improvement through repetition. "Repetition does not change the basic storage capacity of memory. Rather, organizing processes accompanying repetition lead to an apparent increase in capacity by increasing the information load of individual units" (Tulving, 1962, pp. 344 f).

This analysis added an important new dimension to the concept of organization, namely, that of functional utility. It is through organization that the organism's inherently limited capacity for storing information can be overcome. Given the rapidly accumulating evidence for the effectiveness of recoding and chunking, the assertion clearly had face validity but the full implications for the role of organizational processes in memory remained to be explored.

In assessing this role, one may choose to adopt either a strong or a weak principle of limited capacity. According to the strong form of the principle, the limits of the system are those observed in the measurement of the immediate memory span, and the development of higher-order units is always and inescapably required if these limits are to be exceeded. That is the position explicitly advocated by Mandler: "Organization is absolutely necessary if memory is to exceed the limit of individual items that the system can deal with at any one time. This process of organization involves recoding the input material into new and larger chunks. Memory consists of the recall of a limited number of chunks (that is, about seven) and retrieval of the contents of these chunks" (1967a, p. 331).

The key words in Mandler's statement, which deserve careful attention, are "absolutely necessary." If the principle is accepted as valid, one is forced to infer that higher-order units have been formed whenever an individual succeeds in reproducing significantly more than seven items. Since it is known that such levels of recall are easily attained, the assertion that recall is a function of organization acquires the status of an axiom and is not in need of empirical verification. Those espousing the strong principle have, however, to assume the burden of proof for two propositions: (a) that the storage capacity of the memory system is, in fact, limited under all circumstances (and, in particular, outside the special conditions under which the immediate span is measured) to about seven functional units, and (b) that chunking is the only way in which these limitations can be overcome.

A weak principle of limited capacity takes its point of departure from the fact that there is, indeed, a ceiling on the amount of information that can be processed and stored during any one period of time. (This fact has, of course, been in clear evidence ever since the length-difficulty relationship was first demonstrated by Ebbinghaus.) It is not assumed, however, that the ultimate limits of the system are indexed by the span of immediate memory. Quite apart from the development of higher-order groupings there may be a cumulative increase in the number of functional units stored as a result of repeated exposures to the same set of materials. The possibility is thus left open that repetition may have effects other than unitization: for instance, changes in the "strength" of the neural representation of individual units. Even though the bounds of capacity are considered as indeterminate, the system is still viewed as limited, and the establishment of higher-order groupings may serve significantly to reduce the degree of limitation. Thus, according to the weak principle, organization enhances the amount retained after a given period of learning time. Organization is not, however, accepted as "absolutely necessary" for the recall of more than about seven items.

It would be difficult to guess which conception of limited capacity would receive wider acceptance today. The strong principle has been advocated vigorously by Mandler (1967a) and documented by experimental findings which will be discussed below. Recently, the problem of limited capacity has been discussed most extensively in the context of the distinction between short-term and long-term memory. It has been argued that in free recall the terminal items are retrieved from a short-term store and those from the earlier part of the list from a long-term store (e.g., Craik, 1970; Glanzer & Cunitz, 1966; Raymond, 1969). The short-term system is viewed as strictly limited, with earlier presented items subject to displacement by incoming new ones, whereas the capacity of the long-term system is not specified (Atkinson & Shiffrin, 1968; Glanzer, Gianutsos, & Dubin, 1969). Taking his point of departure from the dual-process hypothesis, Glanzer (1969) has suggested that the mnemonic structure of a list, for example, the presence of associative relations, has its critical effects while the relevant items are in the short-term system, presumably by permitting rehearsal of the appropriate groupings. If this assumption is accepted, then the implication is that the scope of mnemonic organization is severely constrained by the limited capacity of the system in which the higher-order groupings must be established in the first place.

As the theoretical models multiply, the relationship between memory capacity and organization becomes more and more uncertain. As we have seen, one influential position is that organization helps to eliminate the bottleneck of limited capacity; another asserts that the development of organization is held in check by the limitations of the system in which the higher-order units must be formed. A resolution of these centrifugal arguments is clearly in order.

The experimental facts bearing on the relation between mnemonic capacity and organization are not extensive. One line of evidence comes from the finding that the number of functional units recalled and the size of these units vary independently. The relevance of this observation to the problem of capacity becomes apparent when we consider results such as Cohen's (1963) showing that after a constant amount of study time the number of chunks recalled from lists of unrelated words and from categorized lists is the same (for comparable findings see also Bower, 1969; and Tulving & Patterson, 1968). The categorized chunks comprised a larger number of nominal units than did the noncategorized ones. The implication is, of course, that the number of chunks recalled reflects the subject's constant mnemonic capacity which is not affected by changes in the informational content of the individual chunks. Such results parallel those obtained for the immediate memory span whose invariant capacity can be specified in terms of the magical number seven plus and minus two.

The picture becomes less clear, however, when it is shown that the number of chunks recalled varies as a function of such task variables as length of list, even though the size of each of these units remains invariant (e.g., Tulving & Pearlstone, 1966). If mnemonic capacity remains constant, then it must be assumed that the apparent chunks have been grouped hierarchically into "superchunks" (Mandler, 1967a). Such an assumption must be made if the strong principle of limited capacity is to be maintained but, at the present time, must be regarded as entirely conjectural (cf. Tulving & Patterson, 1968, p. 245). The fact that the number and the size of functional units in recall vary independently lends obvious support only to the weak principle of limited capacity.

In developing his argument for the strong form of the principle, Mandler placed considerable emphasis on the positive correlation between the number of categories used by a subject in sorting a list of words and the amount of recall (Mandler, 1967a; Mandler & Pearlstone, 1966; Mandler, Pearlstone, & Koopmans, 1969). He assumes that the sizes of individual chunks and the number of different chunks that can be accommodated are subject to comparable limits (5 ± 2). On this assumption, an increase in the number of categories up to about seven permits an optimal utilization of the available storage capacity, that is, serves to maximize the amount of information that can be handled by the system. The category-recall relation was, indeed, shown to be dependable under a variety of experimental conditions. Once more, however, the facts appear to be consistent with the weak principle of limited capacity, but do not compel acceptance of the strong version. It has not been demonstrated, for example, that the apparent limits on the size and number of chunks cannot be overcome under conditions of protracted practice.

The basic difficulty with the strong principle of limited capacity is that the extremely high levels of recall for nominal units, of which the human learner is obviously capable, force the theorist to pyramid superchunks within the hypothetical organizational schema, and then to proceed to a multiplication of schemata. It is difficult to envisage how firm empirical support for such a conceptualization might be obtained. Moreover, and perhaps equally important, as a general theoretical framework such a model of organizational processes appears to be too closely tied to the operations of span measurement and free-recall learning. It is not clear how applicable the hierarchical model of chunking is to other phenomena. An organizational schema growing with about five units per level does not appear to provide a convincing account of memorization of long passages of prose and poetry. The fact that subjects can acquire large vocabularies of discrete paired associates may not be directly relevant because the hierarchical principle was formulated with reference to memory in the absence of external retrieval cues. Nevertheless, it is far from satisfactory to dispose of such evidence by postulating a discontinuity between the laws governing memory in the absence and in the presence of external cues. Limited capacity must surely be a fundamental property of the memory system which transcends particular experimental arrangements.

We conclude that the weak principle of limited capacity constitutes an important argument for the functional utility of organizational processes. There is good evidence that unitization can help to overcome the inherent limitations of the memory system, whatever they may be. No compelling evidence has been adduced, however, that the limits are such as to make unitization a necessary, and the only sufficient, condition for the retention of materials exceeding in length the span of immediate memory. Adoption of the strong principle of limited capacity places an unnecessary burden of proof on the organization theorist.

As for the question of whether organizational units are initially formed in the short-term or in the long-term store, any definitive answer would be premature at this time. Inferences about the temporal locus of organization have been based primarily on the relation between serial position in input and unitization in output. With respect to semantic organization, the experimental findings are inconsistent: Grouping effects have been found to be independent of serial position in some investigations (Glanzer, 1969; Glanzer & Meinzer, 1967) but not in others (Tulving & Patterson, 1968). Since acoustic encoding is assumed to occur primarily if not exclusively in the short-term system, grouping on the basis of acoustic features should be limited to items in the terminal positions, but this expectation has not been borne out; the necessary condition for acoustic grouping is massed presentation regardless of whether it occurs early or late in the list (Bruce & Crowley, 1970). It is possible, as these investigators suggested, that acoustic similarity becomes effective in retrieval when the traces of the relevant items overlap in primary memory. Other explanations are, of course, possible. For example, massed presentation may be required to make acoustic as distinct from semantic similarity a functional basis of organization. The capacity for organization does not appear to be effectively limited by the narrow bottleneck of a quickly overloaded short-term system.

THE FUNCTIONAL LOCUS OF ORGANIZATION: STORAGE OR RETRIEVAL?

There is another more fundamental question that has been asked about the locus of organizational processes. Does organization enhance storage, facilitate retrieval, or both? When the concept of unitization or chunking was first extended from the immediate memory span to free recall, the emphasis was clearly on organization as a means of overcoming the limitations of storage capacity: "Organizing processes . . . lead to an apparent increase in capacity by increasing the information load of individual units" (Tulving, 1962, pp. 344 f). It was not long, however, before attention came to center increasingly on the functional significance of organizational processes for retrieval. This shift in emphasis is theoretically important, and it will be useful to bring out clearly the considerations underlying it.

Another quotation from Tulving will help to bring the issue into focus: ". . . It is not the fact of 'storage' of list items that is at issue in the FR experiment, but rather the form of storage, or accessibility of items. . . . The list items have been 'stored' in the subject's memory for a long time . . . and the input list serves simply as a set of instructions as to which of the stored items the subject has to retrieve" (1964, p. 222; see also 1968, p. 29). To the extent that the learning materials consist of items in the subject's vocabulary, the problem of storage per se is essentially bypassed, and success in remembering depends on the effectiveness of the retrieval operations at the time of test. The efficiency of retrieval is in turn determined by the rearrangement of items in storage. Higher-order groupings increase the probability of retrieval of nominal items because they now become accessible not only as individual units but also via other items with which they are joined. Moreover, if a label such as a category name is attached to a higher-order unit, then that label can serve as a potent retrieval cue for the individual components of the unit.

According to this conceptualization, what is limited is not the amount of input that can be accommodated without overtaxing storage capacity but rather "the number of units that can be retrieved in succession without intervening external instructions" (Tulving, 1964, p. 234). That is, retrievable units are limited in number.

It is true, of course, that familiar words in the learner's vocabulary may be assumed to be stored in the sense of being available as potential responses before the experiment begins. However, in the context of a recall experiment, storage may be legitimately taken to imply more than that: What has to be stored is information that serves to segregate the set of prescribed items from the rest of the subject's vocabulary. Such information may include a variety of attributes characteristic of the input material—nonverbal (e.g., temporal or spatial) and verbal, associative and nonassociative (cf. Underwood, 1969). These attributes presumably mediate the retrieval of the nominal units at the time of test. It is reasonable to suppose that there are limitations on the storage of such attributes; if so, then the development of higher-order units may serve to mitigate the storage load. In order to be effective in recall, retrieval information must be stored at the time of input (Thomson & Tulving, 1970; Tulving & Osler, 1968). Given that basic principle, it may not be possible or advisable to separate sharply the influence of organization on storage and on retrieval.

The most impressive experimental evidence for the effects of organization on retrieval per se comes from studies of cuing. In the recall of categorized lists, supplying the names of the categories at the time of test enhances recall (e.g., Tulving & Pearlstone, 1966; Weist, 1970) and serves largely to eliminate retroactive losses (Tulving & Psotka, 1971). Cuing increases the accessibility of higher-order units but does not influence the recall of words within categories; the latter are recalled in an all-or-none, or, rather, some-or-none, fashion (Cohen, 1966). The invariance in the number of items per category, which has been taken to reflect the fixed retrieval power of subject-generated and externally provided cues, may well be peculiar to the familiar taxonomic categories used in these experiments. The interitem relations that permit the formation of chunks and the associations between the categorical cues and the individual instances represent highly overlearned preexperimental habits. In the input phase, the category names are provided to the subject or are rendered salient by blocking of the instances. Thus, the subject is in effect instructed to divide the total list into a series of sublists, each anchored to its category label. Under given conditions of practice there are limits on the length of the sublists that can be recalled. Consequently, there is little variation in the number of instances that are reproduced provided the category name is recalled or supplied as a cue. By the same token, strings of letters that form a word are recalled in an all-or-none fashion. If the word is recalled at all, the entire string of letters is reproduced. This analogy may overstate the case, but it calls attention to the special characteristics of the cuing studies which constrain the inferences that may be drawn regarding the effects of organization on retrieval. These constraints apply not so much to the conclusion that cuing increases the accessibility of interrelated nominal units as they do to the some-or-none characteristics of the process. When the categories differ in saliency, or organization is subjective, the picture may be expected to be different because the groupings will vary in size and cohesiveness and the potency of implicit and explicit retrieval cues may not be the same.

The cuing experiment is of basic theoretical importance because it provides an operational basis for differentiating between the availability and accessibility of materials in memory (Tulving & Pearlstone, 1966) and permits inferences about retrieval processes with the conditions of storage held constant. As we have seen, the major supporting evidence has come from studies using categorized lists. Thus, the functional groupings were established prior to the experiment and reinforced during the presentation of the learning materials. Do groupings newly established by the learner in the course of memorization likewise facilitate retrieval? It appears to be a tenet of organization theory that such is, indeed, the case; however, the evidence for this assumption is becoming increasingly ambiguous. The studies of cuing recently initiated by Slamecka (1968, 1969) have contributed substantially to the growing uncertainty. Before the implications of this evidence are evaluated, it is necessary to examine the theoretical rationale of Slamecka's studies which bears directly on the question of the locus of organizational processes.

Slamecka was interested in reexamining the prevailing assumption that organization is a characteristic of trace storage. The alternative possibility is that traces are stored independently, and that the organized features of recall are entirely the result of retrieval strategies. On the latter assumption, "traces are functionally isolated, so that the fate of one does not influence the fate of any other" (1968, p. 505). Recall is organized because the subject "perceives or detects" the structure of the list during input, encodes and stores a general representation of this structure, and on this basis forms a retrieval plan to guide his search through the independent item traces.

Such a formulation suffers from intrinsic ambiguities if not internal contradictions. The first of these concerns the defining operations for the establishment of independent traces. Independence of traces must be assumed to reflect independence of perceptual events. But what are the independent perceptual events during the presentation of a list of words? It would be hazardous to define them in terms of the nominal E-units, that is, the individual words. It has been shown that during the presentation of a given item previously seen words are likely to be rehearsed, and the composition of such rehearsal sets changes from one input occasion to the next (Rundus & Atkinson, 1970). Thus, if the subject is thinking of the sixth and eighth words while the ninth is being presented, do their traces still remain independent? Given the facts of short-term memory and of rehearsal, the problem of the relation between E-units and S-units cannot be avoided. If one wishes to hold that there is no interaction of traces, then the issue is simply shifted back to the delimitation of the perceptual events that are represented by the independent traces.

A related difficulty comes to light when one examines the assumption that the learner detects and stores a general representation of the structure of the list, thus developing a framework for subsequent retrieval. How can the structure of the list be detected? In one way or another, there has to be juxtaposition of the representations of related or similar items: if APPLE appears in the third position, PEAR in the seventh, and ORANGE in the tenth, the subject somehow has to think of them together if he is to perceive or detect the presence of the fruit category. Some "process-trace communication" or interaction of traces seems to be required. Thus, the hypothesis of storage independence does not appear to be readily amenable to experimental test because the basic premises are not stated with sufficient precision. However, the empirical findings obtained under the auspices of this hypothesis are of considerable interest and pose important problems of interpretation.

In Slamecka's (1968) studies of cuing in free recall, the experimental subjects were supplied with a set of list items at the time of test; their ability to recall the remaining items was compared with that of control subjects who were not cued. Over a variety of materials (including categorized lists) and conditions, the results were uniformly negative: the context provided by the cue words failed to facilitate the recall of the remainder of the list. The situation did not change when a constant order of presentation was used and serially ordered cues were supplied (Slamecka, 1969). On the face of it, the results militate against the conception of associative or organized storage. Subsequent investigations using the same or similar techniques confirmed Slamecka's basic findings, although some cuing effects were demonstrated for normatively related items (Allen, 1969; Wood, 1969a).

The method of contextual cuing introduced by Slamecka, while straightforward at first glance, turns out to be quite complex upon closer scrutiny, and is probably to some extent biased against the detection of cuing effects. The major problems of measurement and interpretation have been discussed by Allen (1969) and need not be restated here. Granted that there may be a measurement bias, the null results must nevertheless be taken very seriously. One would expect the effects of contextual cuing to be sufficiently robust to become clearly apparent even when the conditions of observation are less than optimal.

Several explanations of these negative findings warrant consideration. It is possible, first of all, that under the conditions of these experiments most of what is available is also accessible and is, therefore, recalled. If so, recall would exhaust the storage (cf. Cofer, 1967; Freund & Underwood, 1969). The contextual cues are designed to promote retrieval from higher-order units, but if such units have been adequately developed they are likely to be recalled, and there would be no targets left for cuing. The fact that Slamecka's results were just as negative for categorized as for noncategorized lists is consistent with this speculation. Powerful cuing effects have been observed under other conditions with the former type of materials (although category names rather than individual instances have typically been used as the cues). Second, if there is a retrieval plan guiding recall, then that plan could be seriously disrupted by the presentation of a random selection of items in a haphazard sequence. (Prior instructions about the cuing procedure were used by Slamecka with a view to mitigating the disruption caused by the novel testing procedure. However, such instructions would not necessarily prevent the degradation of the retrieval plan.) Thus, it may be necessary to recognize the existence of a basic indeterminacy: It may not be possible to tap the positive effects of organization by procedures that themselves interfere with the organized characteristics of recall.

In light of these considerations it becomes important to go beyond the manipulation and analysis of free-recall performance itself to seek information about the characteristics of storage. The answer to the question of what has been learned (or stored) is most likely to be found in analytic tests of transfer. Such tests can be designed to focus directly and sensitively on the hypothesized effects of prior learning. Thus, if traces are not functionally isolated and higher-order groupings are a property of storage, then free-recall learning of a list of words should be a significant source of transfer in the subsequent mastery of an associative task composed of the same elements. Evidence to be further considered later on leaves little doubt that such is indeed the case. It is useful to note that a test of associative transfer minimizes the difficulties inherent in the method of contextual cuing: It is known that the subject has learned the materials which are expected to function as sources of transfer, in contrast to the critical items in the contextual cuing procedure whose availability is uncertain. Moreover, the performance requirements in the successive tasks are sufficiently different to remove the disruption of retrieval plans as a condition of interference.

The results obtained in studies of transfer argue strongly for organization in the sense of interdependence of items as a property of storage under conditions of free-recall learning. On the other hand, the unexpected ineffectiveness of contextual cuing implies that in the free-recall situation itself retrieval is not usually a matter of simple associative chaining.

ENCODING SPECIFICITY AND ORGANIZATION

The apparent failure of contextual cuing procedures brings to the fore the importance of specifying precisely the conditions under which retrieval cues may be expected to be effective. A general theoretical answer to this question has been proposed by Tulving in the form of a principle of encoding specificity. The principle asserts that "no cue, however strongly associated with the TBR [to-be-remembered] item or otherwise related to it, can be effective unless the TBR item is specifically encoded with respect to that cue at the time of storage" (Thomson & Tulving, 1970, p. 255). Information to be used in retrieval must be stored at the time of input. This principle is supported by the finding that associative cues to the TBR items aid recall only if they were present at the time of input (Freund & Underwood, 1970; Tulving & Osler, 1968). The hypothesis was subjected to a very exacting test in an experiment by Thomson and Tulving (1970) in which there was a shift from weakly associated cues at input to strongly associated ones at output. As predicted, performance in this case was no better than under conditions of noncued recall. (It should be noted, however, that facilitation by cues presented at output only has been reported by Bahrick, 1969, 1970.) If the principle of encoding specificity is valid, what are its implications for the relationship between organization and recall?

Before this issue is considered in general terms, it is of interest to note that for purposes of assessing the role of encoding specificity the experimental operations have focused on the recall of individual nominal units. Thus, in the studies mentioned above, a different associative cue was presented along with each item in the list, and under the appropriate conditions the same cues were employed as prompts at the time of recall. These arrangements shade into those of paired-associate learning. This continuity of procedures emphasizes the point that the conditions of retrieval are seen as specific to individual items. To the extent that the item-specific cues are critical at the time of output, recall would appear to be independent of the membership of the items in higher-order groupings.

Consider now the more general case of the free-recall experiment in which the retrieval cues are not provided, item by item, on the input trials, but, rather, are assumed to be generated by the learner. Extrapolating from the experimental findings mentioned above, we are led to assume that on any given trial the encoding of item n will be significantly influenced by the cumulative context provided by items $n-1$, $n-2$, $n-3$, etc. Now, when the order of presentation changes from trial to trial, the context for any given nominal item changes likewise. Consequently, the specific way in which each item is encoded may be expected to vary as practice continues. Such a state of affairs will obviously not be conducive to the development of fixed higher-order units. Rather, as the encodings vary and multiply, a given item is likely to become incorporated into more than one higher-order unit. Exactly such a process has been proposed to account for the advantage of distributed over massed repetition of items within a list (Madigan, 1969). Thus, if there is variable encoding of nominally identical items, the organization that develops should comprise a network of higher-order units, or a complex network of associative groupings. Such a process of structuration can be seen to be fundamentally different from the formation of cohesive, rigidly ordered chunks. One of the urgent tasks of organization theory would appear, therefore, to be the systematic exploration of the relationship between the principle of encoding specificity and the concept of unitization.

These considerations lead to some interesting questions about the similarities and differences between categorized and noncategorized lists. Variable encoding of nominally identical items is likely to be at a minimum in the case of the former. Once the presence of taxonomic categories is detected by the learner, successive instances will be coded accordingly and probably rehearsed together (Rundus, 1970). Consequently, category names should be potent retrieval cues, and there is ample evidence that they are. When the list is noncategorized, variable encoding on successive trials becomes a possibility, and it becomes difficult to specify effective retrieval cues on any a priori basis. If multiple overlapping groupings are formed, then more than one nominal item may be required to establish a distinctive context and to provide a useful prompt at the time of recall. On this assumption, the absence of cuing effects in Slamecka's experiments may be understandable. More generally, it will be useful to recognize that in the analysis of organizational processes, and in particular of the conditions of retrieval, it is not safe to assume that the same principles govern the processing and recall of categorized and of noncategorized lists. One speculation that comes to mind is that unitization with the original connotation of chunking may be a process that is applicable primarily to the recall of categorized lists. On the other hand, the development of aggregates of overlapping groupings may represent a better approximation to the products of free-recall learning when the materials are noncategorized.

WHO OR WHAT DOES THE ORGANIZING AND RETRIEVING?

One of the sources of appeal of the concept of organization is undoubtedly that it implies an active learner who imposes structure on the materials to which he is exposed. The subject is credited with discovering and utilizing the systematic features introduced into the materials by the experimenter, and also with inventing idiosyncratic bases of organization. And he is seen as adept at taking advantage of a rich variety of cues in making stored information accessible to recall. To say that the subject does all these things is, of course, just a descriptive statement; naturally the theorist is moved to specify the mechanisms that control the organizing activity and the retrieval efforts. Within the framework of an information-processing approach, computer methodology readily suggested a mode of operation for the control mechanisms. Thus, Mandler's (1967b) model of rule-governed behavior in learning and memory is clearly rooted in the concepts and language of computer programming. Such models may well prove to have heuristic value although their power to generate truly new predictions remains to be demonstrated. There is, however, also a danger inherent in the postulation of elaborate control mechanisms within the framework of information-processing models: the disposition to build into specialized components of the hypothetical system the mechanisms of organization and of retrieval. Whatever the necessary operations are conceived to be, the specialized components are preprogrammed to carry them out, and thus the most difficult theoretical questions are begged. Two examples from recent theoretical discussions of organizational process in memory will serve to illustrate this point.

We shall consider first the reallocation hypothesis which has been proposed to account for the systematic effects of perceptual grouping on the recall and recognition of strings of digits, and, in particular, for the finding that repetition produces little or no learning when the group structure is changed on successive presentations (Bower & Winzenz, 1969). The gist of the hypothesis has been lucidly summarized by Bower (1970) as follows:

> As a grouped string arrives, the perceptual coder first decides whether it has been heard before by trying to match the first one or two groups of the string to the traces of past strings it has stored at various "locations" in memory. If this match succeeds, then the input string is allocated or shunted to the location of the matching trace, thus to contact or strengthen the trace residing there. If the match fails, then the incomplete string is shunted to a

new location and stored as a new trace. . . . A string repeated with the same group structure will often be shunted to the same storage location, is likely to signal a high matching score with respect to the trace residing there, and so it will be recognized. . . . To handle immediate recall, it must be assumed that recall consists in reading out the information in the trace in the most *recently* activated storage location, with better recall from stronger traces (pp. 28 f).

The fact that grouping influences recognition can be seen to be built into the system on an a priori basis. Ultimate recognition of identity depends on prior recognition of partial identity by a specialized component, the perceptual coder, which has the property of trying to match the first one or two groups of the incoming string with the traces of previously heard strings. To the extent that the mode of operation of the perceptual encoder is inferred from the results of the memory tests, the argument becomes, of course, circular. Not only is recognition proper made dependent upon prior partial recognition (itself unexplained) by the perceptual encoder, but the completion of the process also appears to require the intervention of additional, specialized control units: on the basis of the decision of the perceptual encoder the input has to be shunted to a particular trace location, which implies some agent cognizant of the incoming pattern searching through the field of traces to locate the appropriate one. A matching score of a particular magnitude is then "signalled" and is presumably monitored and evaluated by still another agent. When it comes to recall, some unit in the system has to (a) identify the most recently activated storage location, and (b) read out the information from that location.

Bower recognizes, of course, that the language of the model is heavily metaphorical and suggests that it could be restated in other terms. The problem at issue is not, however, the reliance on metaphors, but the reification of organizing processes, and the multiplication of specialized control mechanisms. Given information about the accomplishments and the limitations of memory, logical analysis permits the construction of a multiplicity of systems with appropriate control units and specialized components which are capable of these accomplishments and subject to these limitations. Decisions among the alternative systems are likely to be difficult, at least insofar as they involve a choice among different kinds of "theoretical hardware." There remains the question of the heuristic value of the models. The answer to this question is complicated, primarily because it is often unclear how essential the role of a particular model is in generating a given set of useful empirical hypotheses. In the case of the allocation model, for example, the implications that were tested experimentally were the following: (a) constancy of the initial group in a segmented string is critical for improvement as a function of repetition; (b) subject-imposed as well as experimenter-imposed groupings can be effective in influencing recall; (c) repetition of an ungrouped string is more likely after two than after one exposure to a grouped version of the same string. It is probably fair to say that none of these predictions is particularly novel or compellingly tied to the reallocation model. Nevertheless, the fact remains that the investigators were led to pursue these empirical questions in an attempt to test the implications of that particular model.

Our second example of built-in organizing mechanisms is provided by a tentative model recently proposed by Kintsch (1970) to account for organization in free recall. The model is a marker theory: each word is assumed to be encoded in memory as a list of markers representing its semantic-syntactic, sensory, and phonetic properties. The meaning of a word is defined in terms of the relationship of its semantic markers with those of other words. When a word is presented in a free-recall experiment, the appropriate marker list is "tagged" to store the information that the item has occurred. Tagging a marker increases its "familiarity value." If there is room, the item enters the short-term rehearsal buffer, and as long as it is held there, "cognitive work is performed on it." New associations are formed, including associations with a starting symbol such as "List I." In addition, meaningful relations among the items are utilized in the following manner: "The markers of the words held in short-term memory are scanned. If a marker X is found that is in common to two (or more) words A and B, A and B are tagged in the marker list of X. Thus a system of cross-references is built up. Whenever a marker, or a set of markers is being worked with its familiarity value receives an automatic updating." In retrieval, after reproduction of the items available in short-term memory and of those associated with the starting symbol, "a word is chosen at random and its markers are scanned. The marker X with the highest familiarity value is selected and the system now moves to inspect the entry corresponding to that marker. The familiarity values of the markers of X are determined and if they are above criterion, X is produced as an overt response. The search process is renewed with one of the already recalled words as its starting point. If the recognition check of X is negative, the markers of X are now scanned in turn, and the whole process recycles" (p. 362).

The implication is, of course, that semantically related items should cluster in recall! The author admits that the model is not stated explicitly enough to be testable, and that the heavy emphasis on control processes (choice of markers, rules, search strategies, etc.) gives the model great flexibility and thus makes it difficult to test. True enough;

what is open to question is the author's evaluation of this state of affairs. It can be argued, he suggests, "that recall is a very complex process and that this kind of flexibility is just what is needed in a model." One cannot help but ask what explanatory or predictive power is envisaged for a highly flexible model whose rules of operation can presumably be specified with precision only on the basis of the observed facts of recall. If the principles of control have to be induced empirically, or postulated on the basis of linguistic analysis, what is left of the *memory model* per se is an armamentarium of devices, charged with scanning the store, deciding on markers to be tagged, applying redundancy rules, adopting search strategies, judging the familiarity values of markers, and so on. How can such rational reconstructions of the mechanisms of memory be validated, and, in the meantime, what is their pragmatic usefulness? In the absence of convincing answers to these questions, one has to agree with Tulving and Patterson that "In the long run, nothing much can be gained by postulating a homunculus searching through one or more types of memory store for desired mnemonic information" (1968, p. 247).

This digression to memory models was undertaken with a view to disassociating as sharply as possible organization theory in a general sense from the commitment to largely metaphorical models of information processing. A perusal of the current literature suggests that there is a correlation, and probably an increasing one, between these approaches to the problem of memory. It is useful to emphasize, therefore, that the correlation is not a necessary one. It is my guess that in the foreseeable future the elaboration of metaphorical models will do little to advance the systematic analysis of organizational processes in memory. Again, in agreement with Tulving and Patterson, I see as the most pressing problems for the organization theorist the identification of functional units of memory and the identification of the retrieval cues that make these units accessible in recall.

The Nature of the Empirical Evidence for Organization

In the preceding section we have reviewed some of the orienting attitudes and theoretical assumptions that have guided the analysis of organizational processes in memory. While the discussion necessarily considered relevant experimental findings, it remains for us to focus directly on the nature of the empirical evidence from which inferences about organizational processes are drawn. In the present section we shall consider a few selected issues under this general heading. The selection was made in the hope of pinpointing problems of method and interpretation that appear to require continuing attention.

OUTPUT CONSISTENCY AS AN INDEX OF ORGANIZATION

As Tulving recognized (e.g., 1962, 1968), a discrepancy between E-units and S-units provides prima facie evidence for the occurrence of organizational processes: the subject's output reveals a structure that was not present in the input. For this reason, measures of subjective organization (SO) and intertrial repetition (ITR) have been used widely as indices of the degree of structure imposed by the learner on a group of apparently unrelated items. (They are complemented by measures of clustering which presumably reflect the degree to which the subject is making use of the structure provided by the experimenter.) We shall not concern ourselves with the strictly quantitative questions that arise in the use of these indices, but will focus instead on some problems of interpretation.

Under standard conditions of free-recall learning with unrelated words as the materials, the indices of pairwise repetition typically remain rather low. It is recognized that there are no definite criteria for evaluating the absolute level of output consistency, but a few examples will serve to illustrate this point. In Tulving's (1962) original study introducing the SO measure, the mean value of the index, which can vary from 0 to 1, reached a value of .30 after 16 trials on a list of 16 words. At that point recall performance was nearly perfect. In a recent study of learning to learn in free recall (Postman, Burns, & Hasher, 1970), subjects had six trials on each of three successive lists of 20 unrelated words. Under one of the experimental conditions the subjects were given standard free-recall instructions; under another condition they were urged to group the words in output and to maintain the groupings from one test to the next. The degree of output consistency increased over lists, and to obtain maximum readings we will consider the ITR scores for the terminal pair of trials on the third list. At this point in practice, approximately 17 items were recalled under both conditions. The mean ITR scores (obtained minus expected) were 5.5 and 6.4 under standard and grouping instructions, respectively. These scores were based on repetitions of pairs of items in either the same or the reverse order. Thus, even for well-practiced subjects explicitly instructed to maintain a consistent order of output, the index reached only about 40% of the maximum possible value. During the acquisition of the first list, the corresponding percentage was about 20. Comparable results may be readily found in other studies.

On the basis of the observed absolute levels of output consistency, one may arrive at one of two alternative conclusions: either the development of higher-order groupings plays a relatively modest role in free-recall learning or the measures of output consistency provide a highly fallible and partial index of the degree of subjective organization. We favor the second alternative, partly in light of other evidence to be discussed below and partly on a priori grounds. As was suggested elsewhere (Postman, 1971), there are good reasons to suppose that organization, in the sense of the establishment of systematic interitem dependencies, will in many cases not be reflected in a high degree of output consistency. As a network of multiplex interitem relations develops, there is a corresponding increase in the number of equivalent pathways leading from one response to another. It is only when the groupings are based on a sequential rule, as in the case of an alphabetical schema, that a one-to-one relation between degree of organization and output consistency is to be expected.

In the context of the present discussion, the difference between categorized and noncategorized lists once more warrants consideration. At comparable levels of recall, the degree of output consistency is substantially higher for the former than for the latter. In one of our experiments (Postman, 1971), for example, both types of list were learned to a criterion of 16/20 and were then presented for three additional trials. Averaged over the three terminal pairs of trials, the mean ITR score was 2.4 for the noncategorized lists and 6.1 for the categorized lists. In the case of the latter, the ITRs reflected a high degree of categorical clustering. The mean number of categorical repetitions per trial was 9.3. It should be noted that, of the two indices of output adjacency, the clustering measure was substantially higher than the ITR score. Such a difference is, of course, to be expected since the criterion of clustering is not the adjacent recall of specific nominal items, as it is in the case of ITRs, but rather the recall of members of the same category.

The implication of this pattern of results is that the concept of unitization or chunking, as it was originally derived from Miller's analysis, is pertinent primarily to the organization of categorized materials. For noncategorized lists, the most adequate representation of the structure developed in the course of acquisition appears to be in terms of a network of overlapping higher-order groupings with multiple connections converging on individual items. The picture is that of an associative network or aggregate of networks (cf. Deese, 1959, 1960), although it is not implied that the interitem connections necessarily reflect normative associative probabilities.

The question of whether it is useful to distinguish between categorical and noncategorical groupings has been discussed previously (Mandler, 1968; Postman, 1964; Tulving, 1968). No argument is being made, of course, for a basic discontinuity of processes. It is easy enough to demonstrate that cohesive chunks are sometimes formed during the acquisition of noncategorized lists. The distinction that has been made is directed toward a specification of the modal products of free-recall learning. The empirical evidence does seem to point to the usefulness of some such distinction. It is a fact that at comparable levels of recall the degrees of output consistency differ drastically for the two kinds of material. The results of some studies of retention are also pertinent here. Investigations of retroactive inhibition in the free recall of categorized lists indicate that at least some categorical groupings are forgotten in an all-or-none manner, and that such losses can be eliminated by appropriate cuing in the test stage (Strand, 1971; Tulving & Psotka, 1971). In the latter study, the cuing effects were, in fact, so powerful as to eliminate virtually all retroactive effects under conditions of potentially heavy interference. By contrast, no clear relation was observed between membership in stable output units and resistance to retroactive interference for lists of unrelated words (Postman & Keppel, 1967). For such materials, long-term retention was likewise found to be unrelated to stability of output order (Postman, 1970).

There is a further finding that bears directly on the interpretation of indices of output consistency that should be mentioned here. While there is generally a positive correlation between such indices and the speed of free-recall learning, it is possible, by the use of appropriate instructions, to effect a disassociation between these measures of performance. Specifically, instructions to adhere to a consistent output order bring about substantial increases in the measures of intertrial repetition without at the same time producing reliable gains in recall (Mayhew, 1967; Postman et al., 1970; Puff, 1970). Order of output is a characteristic of performance which, to some extent at least, is under the subject's control, and hence can be significantly influenced by instructions. It appears that such subject-controlled changes in the characteristics of output do not significantly affect the efficiency of either storage or retrieval.

It is of interest to contrast the instructional manipulation of output order with Mandler's (1967a) procedure of having subjects sort a list of apparently unrelated words into a limited number of categories of their own choice. Mandler recognized that measures of intertrial repetition do not permit an assessment of the kind of organization that has occurred (or, we might add, has not occurred). In order to evaluate fully the relation between type of subjective organization and recall, it is desirable to make the entire structure generated by the learner accessible to inspection. In the analysis of the results, the emphasis then shifts from the correlation between degree (scaled unidimensionally) of organization and recall to the consequences of different types of organization, for example, number of different categories used in sorting, and performance. (In studies using taxonomically categorized materials, the importance of the pattern of groupings, as determined by the number of categories and of items per category, has of course been clearly demonstrated, e.g., Tulving & Pearlstone, 1966; Weist, 1970.) The shift in emphasis from sheer amount to quality or pattern of subjective organization is methodologically important and points away from intertrial repetition as a basic measure of organization. We agree with Mandler (1967a, p. 337) that such measures do not tell us much more than that some organizational activity has occurred which is reflected in the output.

ORGANIZATION AS A SOURCE OF TRANSFER

The measurement of output regularities can be only a first step in the experimental analysis of organizational processes. The obvious next move is to manipulate the assumed conditions of organization and to evaluate their effects on recall. When we consider the implementation of this strategy, we note that the distinction between categorized and noncategorized materials once more becomes important, for practical if not for theoretical reasons. When the potential basis of higher-order groupings is known, for example, taxonomic categories or normative associative relations, the independent variables can be specified and the results evaluated with reference to these groupings. That is done when such factors as the number and size of categories are varied. When the TBR items are ostensibly unrelated, only the conditions of presentation can be manipulated, and the basis of organization has to be inferred from output regularities or the subjects' post hoc identification of higher-order units (e.g., Rosner, 1970).

If one wishes to assess the functional significance of the subjective organization that has been achieved, the most obvious experimental avenue is provided by tests of transfer. Such tests are conventionally used to answer the question of what has been learned; they can be formulated so as to focus on the characteristics of the higher-order groupings that have been developed in the course of prior practice. It is convenient to divide the relevant studies into two classes according to whether transfer is investigated between successive free-recall tasks or between free-recall and controlled associative learning. This methodological division reflects a difference in theoretical objectives. The former have been concerned primarily with the relative effectiveness of different

kinds of subjective groupings, and the latter with the relationship between organization and association.

Studies of transfer between successive free-recall tasks bring into focus
the assumption that speed of learning depends on the particular structure
that is imposed on the materials during acquisition. To sharpen the
prediction, it becomes useful to add the further assumption that for
each subject learning a given list of items there is an optimal organization that will serve to maximize his performance. Prior practice that
establishes groupings inconsistent with the optimal structure should,
therefore, be a source of interference. One important implication of this
hypothesis is that there should be negative transfer from part-list to
whole-list learning when the items are drawn from a pool of unrelated
words: the higher-order units established during part learning should
be less than optimal for the mastery of the total list (Tulving, 1966).

Because the logic of the theoretical argument leads to the prediction
of a counterintuitive empirical result, the part-to-whole transfer effects
are of considerable importance for the hypothesis of optimal organization. The predicted negative consequences of prior part learning have
been observed in several experiments (Bower & Lesgold, 1969; Novinski,
1969; Tulving, 1966). The origin of the interference in the persistence
of inappropriate higher-order units remains, however, to be conclusively
demonstrated. There are other mechanisms that may be responsible for
the retardation of whole-list learning. It has been found that the differentiation between old and new items is maintained throughout the acquisition of the test list and systematically influences the distribution of
rehearsal time and the order of output. In one experiment, about half
the subjects reported that they used the strategy of learning and recalling
new items before old ones (Roberts, 1969).[2] Whichever component of

---

[2] In Roberts' experiment, the items in the part list were classified as old, and
those added in the test stage as new. Oldness and newness were thus confounded
with differences in time of original presentation and conditions of practice. While
the results are clearly relevant to the analysis of part-to-whole transfer, they
bear only very indirectly on the question of output priority of new items under
conventional conditions of free recall. Evidence for the latter phenomenon was
obtained by Battig, Allen, and Jensen (1965), but the question was later raised
of whether it was largely a function of serial position biases (Baddeley, 1968;
Postman & Keppel, 1968; Shuell & Keppel, 1968). The latest investigation (Battig
& Slaybaugh, 1969), which controlled for such biases, yielded positive evidence
for a priority effect, but the results must be regarded as of very limited generality:
the materials were CVCs; the effect was found only in the second half of the
trials to criterion; and fast learners who had recalled each item at least once
during the first half of the trials were excluded from the analysis. The generality
and robustness of the phenomenon remain to be established.

the test list is neglected is, in effect, subject to retroactive inhibition during input and to output interference at the time of recall. Thus, a deficit in performance may be produced by the subject's failure to give an adequate amount of attention to all items during both input and output. Some credence is given to this possibility by the finding that, relative to a control treatment, prior part learning depresses recall of old words much more than that of new words (Bower & Lesgold, 1969; Novinski, 1969). In this connection it is important to note the finding of Wood and Clark (1969) that part-to-whole negative transfer appears to be reduced when subjects are explicitly informed about the composition of the test list. To the extent that performance factors play a significant role in the test stage, the explanation of the negative transfer effects cannot be sought entirely in the conflict between successive modes of organization.

It is important to recognize that the original interpretation of the negative transfer effects cannot be substantiated by demonstrations of test-stage facilitation when the experimenter imposes the same structure on the part and on the whole list. In the experiment of Bower and Lesgold (1969), for example, the expected positive effects were obtained when items paired during part learning continued to be paired during whole learning; Birnbaum (1968, 1969) has shown that whole-list learning benefits when taxonomic groupings can be carried over intact from part-list learning. Such findings do not tell us anything decisive about the sources of part-to-whole interference when the learning tasks consist of unrelated words and the higher-order groupings must be generated, on a more or less idiosyncratic basis, by the subject. There is still no direct evidence that in such cases the development of optimal subjective units is, in fact, delayed in the test stage. An analogy from paired-associate transfer will serve to bring out the methodological point at issue. It would be misleading to draw inferences about the mechanisms of interference under the A-B, A-D paradigm from the phenomena of facilitation observed under the A-B, A-B' paradigm. Positive and negative transfer effects are not necessarily complementary manifestations of the same underlying process.

The problems of interpretation become even more complex when transfer from whole to part learning (Tulving & Osler, 1967) is considered. The test task may be viewed as requiring the establishment of a new organization that may be partly incompatible with the original one. On the other hand, recall of the part list may be seen as being dependent primarily on the subject's ability to discriminate between a recently presented subset of items and the remainder of the list. Failures of discrimination could lead to the erroneous rejection of correct responses and thus depress performance. This interpretation is supported by Ehrlich's (1970) finding that recall of the whole list was unimpaired after a series of interpolated trials on subsets of items for which recall was far from perfect and showed little improvement as a function of practice. Ehrlich's conclusion was that destructuration of the original list reduced recall on the interpolated test, but it is difficult to conceive of a process of destructuration that is momentary and fully reversible.

Results such as Ehrlich's do call attention to the importance of determining the relations between transfer and retention under conditions of free recall. It is interesting in this connection to note Hasher's (1970) recent finding that learning by the pure part method (acquisition of individual parts followed by a combination stage) results in better long-term retention than learning by the whole method. The relatively short-range associations established during part learning may not be optimal for immediate reproduction of the total list, but may be more resistant to extraexperimental interference than groupings drawn from the entire list.

We have dwelt on the part-whole paradigm at some length because of the potential theoretical significance of the results: as originally formulated, the design centered attention on the important concept of an optimal subjective structure. This conception of the conditions of maximal learning efficiency is well worth pursuing. It receives some additional support from the fact that both free-recall and serial learning are facilitated when the order of presentation represents common rather than uncommon output sequences of other subjects (Earhard, 1967; Tulving, 1965). The emphasis appears to have shifted recently to demonstrations of positive transfer when there is forced identity of organization in the successive stages of practice, that is, from optimal subjective units to normative groupings imposed by the experimenter. As we have suggested, the original observation of negative transfer is not substantially clarified by such findings; the efficacy of different subject-generated structures is no longer at issue. It is precisely in focusing on subjective groupings that organization theory is likely to make its essentially new contribution. The problem of interference between subjective units warrants renewed consideration.

TRANSFER BETWEEN FREE AND ASSOCIATIVE RECALL

We turn now to studies of transfer between free recall and associative learning. The basic concern here is with the continuity of the processes that come into play under the two conditions of practice. Transfer effects can be investigated in both directions, that is, from associative learning to free recall and vice versa. A continuity of processes can, of course, be inferred from significant transfer effects in either direction. However, the choice of design has by no means been haphazard, but has clearly been determined by the theoretical orientation of the investigator. Transfer from paired-associate to free-recall learning has been examined with a view to demonstrating (a) the relevance of principles of organization to associative learning, and (b) the significance of interitem associations for the development of higher-order units. Transfer from free-recall to paired-associate learning, on the other hand, bears primarily on the question of whether the interitem dependencies established under the two conditions of practice are functionally equivalent. In order to focus on the differences in theoretical emphasis, we shall discuss some illustrative examples of both types of design.

Studies of transfer from paired-associate to free-recall learning will be considered first. An experiment by Segal and Mandler (1967) exemplifies the use of this design for purposes of exhibiting the role of organizational processes in paired-associate learning. The question of interest was whether, in addition to the horizontal organization of the items into prescribed pairs, there also developed separate vertical organizations of the stimulus and of the response terms. The results of the transfer tests confirmed this expectation: after unidirectional paired-associate learning, free recall was higher when all the items were drawn from the same vertical set than when the list was mixed. This difference was eliminated when paired-associate learning was bidirectional and, hence, not conducive to vertical organization. There was little evidence, however, for the formation of interitem associations among the members of vertically organized sets. It should be noted, moreover, that relative to a control condition in which an unrelated paired-associate list is learned, there is negative transfer in the acquisition of vertically organized items (Wood, 1969c). That is, the facilitation produced by vertical organization is only relative. As for horizontal organization, recall was relatively high when the test list was composed of a subset of previously paired items. The measures of intertrial repetition indicated that the pairwise associations were transferred to the free-recall phase.

In interpreting the beneficial effects of vertical organization on recall, Segal and Mandler noted the apparent absence of interitem associations and attributed the facilitation of recall to a process of coding that took place during unidirectional practice on the paired-associate list. They suggested that "right-side" and "left-side" cues were probably attached to each vertical set which aided retrieval in the transfer stage. (Along rather similar lines, Battig, 1966, has presented evidence that items are coded or categorized according to their difficulty or the degree to which they have been mastered.) The conclusion that the items in a paired-associate list are classified according to position is entirely reasonable. The fact that stimulus terms rarely intrude as response errors is in accord with this assumption. An interpretative question that warrants attention, however, is whether the use of such coding devices should be subsumed under the heading of organizational processes. That is, is the attachment of distinctive classificatory labels an instance of organization? If so, there is an extension of the concept that patently unties it from the establishment of higher-order units in recall as a defining criterion. This is not a purely semantic question. In the interest of preserving the explanatory power of the concept of organization, it is important not to define it in a "residual" fashion, that is, to apply it to all systematic dispositions that cannot be attributed to sheer association by contiguity.

More generally, agreement remains to be reached on the implications of the assertion that organizational processes play a significant role in paired-associate learning. Within the framework of Gestalt psychology, the meaning of such a statement was, as we have seen, unambiguous: pairwise association was considered a special case of perceptual organization (Köhler, 1941). From the point of view of modern organization theory, it would be reasonable to consider each of the prescribed associations as a two-item chunk. Whether such a formulation leads to new and testable consequences is still uncertain. As for the grouping of pairs on the basis of such attributes as difficulty or state of learning, the theoretical implications become even more uncertain. Battig (1966) has suggested that learning to group or relate subsets of items serves as a means of reducing interpair interference. But how? It is not immediately apparent that the formation of "higher-order multiple-pair chunks" (p. 180) would indeed be a source of facilitation under conventional conditions of paired-associate learning. To the extent that chunking implies a loss of differentiation among the components of the higher-order unit, an argument could be made for the opposite prediction.

As was noted earlier, studies of transfer from paired-associate to free-recall learning have shown that interitem associations constitute a potential basis for unitization. The apparent persistence of pairwise groupings observed by Segal and Mandler (1967) has already been mentioned (see also Wood, 1969c). In one of our recent experiments (Postman, 1971), free-recall learning of a list of words was significantly facilitated by the prior acquisition of a paired-associate list in which the same words served as stimuli and responses. Moreover, the pairs from the previously learned list appeared as clusters in the subjects' output throughout free-recall learning. The number of such clusters increased as a function of trials along with the level of free recall. The transfer effects become negative when only one member of each paired-associate unit is represented in the free-recall list (Wood, 1969b,c). What Wood calls "inappropriate higher-order units" are established during the paired-associate phase; it is possible that the elicitation of the missing associate serves as a source of interference. The latter findings are consistent with the hypothesis of optimal organizational units discussed above. However, some reconsideration of this assumption is indicated when prior paired-associate learning produces a significant amount of facilitation, with improvements in free recall accompanied by increases in the number of pairwise clusters.

We turn now to transfer from free-recall to paired-associate learning. Does subjective organization in free recall lead to the establishment of interitem linkages that share the functional properties of pairwise associations? If so, the transfer effects should be predominantly negative because the arbitrary arrangement of the items in the paired-associate test stage should, in the large majority of cases, be in conflict with the subjective groupings established in the course of free-recall learning. In a series of experiments reported in detail elsewhere (Postman, 1971), the evidence has consistently supported this expectation. The design was extended to measure proactive interference in the recall of the paired-associate test list. The question of interest was whether the earlier subjective groupings would recover to become a source of interference at recall. Significant proactive effects were found when the lists were categorized, but not when they consisted of unrelated words. In the case of the latter, the interitem dependencies developed during free-recall learning were sufficiently stable to produce negative transfer, but they were not strong enough to recover over time and to produce proactive losses in long-term recall. Once more, an important functional difference between the two types of material is in evidence.

These findings serve to bolster the argument that the subjective units established in free recall and the products of controlled associative learning share common functional properties. A helpful conclusion is that the question of what is learned need not be an issue dividing exponents of association and of organization. Clearly the results do not argue for the primacy of the explanatory principles of either theoretical position. As noted earlier, there are also apparent implications for the question of whether organization influences storage as well as retrieval. Given the sharp discontinuity between the "retrieval plans" (cf. Slamecka, 1968) that might be conceived as appropriate to the free-recall and the paired-associate phase, the source of the negative transfer effects must be sought primarily in the stored products of prior learning. At this point, mention should also be made of Earhard's (1969) finding that a change in output requirements (specifically, a shift from free to alphabetical recall) is less disrupting if the relevant instructions are given to the subject prior to the input rather than at the time of recall. The accumulating evidence clearly makes it more and more difficult to argue for a principle of independent storage.

ALTERNATIVE BASES OF ORGANIZATION

In considering the bases for the establishment of organizational units we have focused primarily on the semantic characteristics of words. There are, of course, other features of the input material which may give rise to systematic groupings; among these the serial order of input has received special consideration. To the extent that the subject groups or chunks the items according to their order of presentation, the criterion of organization becomes the correspondence rather than the divergence of input and output sequences. There are three experimental arrangements under which the tendency toward serial ordering has been evaluated: (a) single-trial free recall; (b) multiple-trial free recall with a constant order of input; and (c) the method of incremental list presentation used by Mandler and Dean (1969) in which a new item is added to the list on each trial. In all these cases substantial evidence for input-output correspondence has been obtained.

The fact that higher-order units may be based on the order of input was recognized early by Tulving and Patkau (1962) when they introduced the concept of an adopted chunk. They defined an adopted chunk as any group of items for which the sequence in recall is the same as in input. Measuring performance after a single input trial, they were able to show that such variables as frequency of word usage and the level of approximation to English had little or no effect on the number of adopted chunks. The variations in recall associated with these variables were attributable primarily to the sizes of adopted chunks. Serial ordering was thus seen as a potentially important and effective basis of organization. Grouping on the basis of contiguity occurs in the absence of any normative dependencies between items. For example, when randomly selected pairs of items are presented repeatedly during a single input trial, the recurrent pairings are reflected in a substantial amount of clustering at the time of recall (Wallace, 1969). It is important to note that adjacency of input is readily used as a basis of grouping under conditions of single-trial free recall. Such a strategy can obviously not be pursued with profit when there are multiple trials with randomly changing orders of input; to the extent that serial ordering is a preferred mode of unitization, the subject is forced to adopt nonpreferred group-ings. In that respect, the standard free-recall task may impose a rel-atively unfamiliar and difficult mode of memorization on at least some individuals. Some of the results obtained under conventional multiple-trial conditions lend support to this possibility.

In spite of some early findings to the contrary (Waugh, 1961), there is by now substantial evidence that free recall is higher when the order of input is constant than when it varies from trial to trial (Jung & Skeebo, 1967; Lachman & Laughery, 1968; Mandler & Dean, 1969; Post-man et al., 1970). When the items are presented in a constant order, the input-output correspondence is high, and the same is true when the incremental procedure is used (Mandler & Dean, 1969). On the basis of their results, the latter investigators were led to conclude that "seria-tion is the preferred method of organizing lists, with serial order adopted by Ss whenever possible" (p. 215). The corollary of this conclusion would seem to be that grouping on the basis of semantic relations is a non-preferred method. The bias in favor of seriation was convincingly demon-strated in a further study by Mandler (1969) in which the incremental procedure was used with categorized lists. Even under these conditions, close to 40 percent of the subjects recalled the items in serial order and, hence, showed no categorical clustering. For the remaining subjects, the level of clustering was high and input-output correspondence declined to a chance level as a function of trials. Closely related is Kintsch's (1970) finding that for categorized as well as for noncategorized items there is a clear correlation between the adjacency of items in input and in output.

The fact that seriation appears to be a preferred mode of output, sometimes even in the presence of compelling categorical relations among the items in a list, poses both a methodological and an interpretative problem. Since seriation and categorical groupings are incompatible, the usual measures of intertrial organization are likely to be attenuated, especially on the early trials. Subjects will be disposed to order their recall serially on the first test, especially when the words are unrelated, and it may take some time before they abandon this approach and shift their attention to the semantic relations among the items. When both seriation and categorical clustering are possible, as in Mandler's (1969) experiment, the divergence of preferences makes the average measures of output consistency unrepresentative of the behavior of indi-vidual subjects. In short, when there are competing modes of grouping the items, the normative assessment of the degree of organization by any one index becomes difficult. Many of the extant analyses have, of course, relied on a single index.

The interpretative problem is similar to the one raised above in our discussion of coding. It is possible to argue that seriation is a basic organizational process (Mandler, 1969). However, input-output correspondence is also grist to the mill of the contiguity theorist. It is precisely on the basis of the evidence for seriation and related findings that Wallace (1970) has recently made a case for an associationistic explanation of the phenomena of subjective organization and clustering. These particular empirical facts appear to serve both theoretical positions equally well.

There are other principles of groupings that have been identified. One of these is the tendency to recall newly learned items before old ones, which would reflect a categorization according to the state of learning. While there is still some room for disagreement about the occurrence of this phenomenon under conventional conditions of free-recall learning (see footnote 2, p. 26), Roberts (1969) has presented convincing evidence for such effects in the test stage of part-to-whole transfer. A grouping of items on the basis of relative recency of acquisition obviously cuts across semantic categories and serial orders. The operation of the principle of priority for new items would thus detract from the potency of the other two forms of organization.

As the evidence for multiple and divergent modes of organization accumulates, it will become increasingly important to specify their necessary and sufficient conditions and their relative weights in the performance of a given memory task. So far, the main thrust of experimental analysis has been directed toward the identification and measurement of the separate processes; the manner of their interaction now requires explicit attention. There is a parallel here to the development of research on transfer. In early systematic formulations, attempts were made to relate the direction and amount of transfer to a single underlying process, such as stimulus differentiation (e.g., Gibson, 1940). These proved inadequate and were followed by analyses of net transfer effects into subprocesses, each of which is characterized by a different set of functional relations. The interaction of the subprocesses, for example, of the transfer of response learning and that of forward and backward associations, has posed a difficult analytic problem. The time appears to have come for a component analysis of organizational processes, and the analytic complexities are likely to be comparable.

EXPERIMENTAL ISOLATION OF ORGANIZATIONAL PROCESSES

To conclude this discussion of methodological problems, we shall comment briefly on the boundaries of the experimental operations that permit conclusions about organizational processes in memory. Going back to Tulving's (1962) original analysis, we would agree that a subject-generated organization can be inferred when the input is apparently unstructured and a stable structure can be discerned in the output. However, when a known structure is imposed on the input by the experimenter and is reflected in the subject's output, it becomes far less clear what inferences can be legitimately drawn about the role of organizational processes. In many cases it is reasonable to conclude that the subject has utilized the mode of organization provided to him. But is also becomes necessary to entertain the logically tenable alternative that the conservation of structure is brought about not by organizational activities on the part of the subject but by the operation of other mechanisms, for instance, association by contiguity. In principle, an organized input can be learned in many different ways, even by "rote."

A few examples may help to clarify the problems of interpretation that are at issue here. First, we refer back to our earlier suggestion that seriation is as readily attributable to association by contiguity as to organization on the basis of temporal or spatial order. The same alternative explanations apply to the finding that recall suffers when subjects are forced to change their word groupings from trial to trial (Bower, Lesgold, & Tieman, 1969). Second, consider the commonly used procedure of blocked presentation of instances in a categorized list. These instances are already linked by preexperimental associations. (It does not matter for present purposes how these interitem linkages were established.) Each of the instances is also associated with the appropriate category name which will presumably serve as the retrieval cue. It is plausible to assume that these various associations are strengthened or primed by the presentation of the blocked material. Success in recall (including categorical clustering) will depend in the first instance on the availability of the appropriate retrieval cues, and then on the accuracy of differentiation between intralist and extralist instances (cf. Bower, Clark, Lesgold, & Winzenz, 1969). If this account is reasonably correct, it is not clear that much can be inferred about organizational processes in memorizing. The essential implications are rather that (a) the subject brings to the experimental situation an associative or categorical structure that can be specified normatively, and (b) correct recall depends on the activation of preexisting associations by appropriate retrieval cues and discrimination between prescribed and extraneous responses.

In order to press the interpretative problem, let us assume that the following list of blocked letters of the alphabet is presented to a subject for free recall: ABCDHIJKPQRSWXYZ. Perfect recall of the list can be predicted after one trial, provided the subject remembers the starting points of the successive four-letter blocks (retrieval cues); the problem of differentiating between appropriate and inappropriate responses has been minimized by the use of blocks of fixed length. It may be argued that the recognition of the list structure and the identification of the anchor points A, H, P, and W represent organizational activity on the part of the subject. Perhaps so. However, the essential antecedent events that lead us to predict perfect recall after one exposure occurred in the subject's childhood: the integration of the alphabet into a highly available sequence, probably by virtue of frequent rote repetition. When a sophomore reproduces our list after one presentation, we are safe in concluding that the subject has noted the discontinuities in a familiar sequence and the number of items per block. But that is at best relatively weak evidence for organization.

Our example may be contrived, but it does call attention to the limited implications of some recent experiments on organization which lean heavily on the recall of familiar groupings presented to the subject. Consider, for example, a recent study by Bower et al. (1969). The major new feature of this experiment was the presentation of nested category lists in the form of hierarchical trees. The structure of such trees is defined by the principle of class inclusion such that instances of a high-level category serve as superordinates for lower-level instances. In one experiment four such lists were learned concurrently. Recall was far higher when each list was presented separately in the form of a complete conceptual tree than when the arrays of words comprised random selections of items from all four hierarchies. A similar difference was obtained when the method of presentation was incremental, with words at progressively lower levels of the hierarchies added on successive trials. When the hierarchies were presented intact, analysis of the recall protocols revealed a high degree of input-output correspondence, indicating that the subjects "were essentially using the structural information in the blocked input as a retrieval plan for generating their recall" (p. 327). In a control experiment it was shown that successful guessing could account for only a fraction of the difference between the two conditions of presentation. Clearly, however, the prior knowledge of the conceptual structure of the lists was decisive. To account for their results, the authors propose a modified hypothesis of reconstruction: the presentation of the items in the form an an hierarchical tree "enables S to directly strengthen particular category-instance associations and it also provides him with a systematic (hierarchic) plan for cuing these candidates for recall, which candidates are recalled only if they pass a recognition test for list membership" (p. 340).

The interpretation is entirely plausible, but in light of our previous discussion it becomes reasonable to raise the question of how much the results really tell us about the role of organizational processes in memory or, for that matter, the development of retrieval plans. Obviously the conceptual hierarchies in question had to be thoroughly overlearned prior to the experiment to permit the orderly reproduction of more than 100 words after less than 8 minutes of learning time. The subject's task was, in effect, to draw selectively from well organized and accessible structures which he brought to the experiment. Neither a new organization nor a new retrieval plan was needed. As the authors indicate, the requirements specific to the experiment were to strengthen or prime some of the preexisting associations and to differentiate between intralist and extralist instances. The nature of the task must have been clearly apparent under the blocked but not under the random method of presentation. It is interesting to note, in this connection, that under the random incremental procedure recall was no better for the categorized materials than for lists of unrelated words. (The latter finding by itself would entail the conclusion that conceptual hierarchies do not provide an effective basis for organization!) Now, it is a very interesting fact that subjects are as efficient as they apparently are in utilizing their prior knowledge in the performance of a recall task. However, when both the groupings and the nature of the retrieval plan are given pre-experimentally, the results cannot be readily generalized to either the acquisition or recall of less well structured materials.

We conclude that for purposes of assessing the power of organizational processes in memory the use of highly structured familiar material has limited utility. As far as the establishment of the higher-order units and the development of effective retrieval plans are concerned, all the critical events have occurred prior to the experiment. It is possible to assume that these preexperimental dispositions are the product of organizational processes, but we do not know whether or not such is the case. The experiment itself bears largely on the question of how these products of past learning are utilized in a given test situation. The problem is important in its own right, but it is tangential to the main issues before organization theory which are concerned with the processes that make possible the storage and retrieval of higher-order units.

These comments will be considered irrelevant by those who agree with Mandler's (1967a, p. 370) suggestion that "any memory experiment with words (that is, with units that are in the vocabulary) is just one way of tapping already existing organizations." If this position is adopted, the problems toward which such experiments can be directed become very limited in scope. Organization per se is taken as already given;

one can do no more than explore the ways in which it is utilized. I would prefer to say, instead, that new organizations are never entirely independent of those the subject brings to the experiment. Language habits influence the mastery of all new verbal tasks. Given recognition of this fact, however, the process of organizing as well as the utilization of prior organizations appears to be subject to experimental analysis.

Organization and Association

THE DEFINITION OF ORGANIZATION

We have deliberately avoided discussing the definition of organization up to this point. It seemed best to postpone this question until some of the current theoretical and experimental issues had been considered. In many recent studies, the definition of the concept is implicit or confined to a single operational criterion, for example, the presence of a significant degree of output consistency in recall or the occurrence of negative transfer under the part-to-whole paradigm. The implied usage of the concept conforms for the most part to what Tulving (1968, p. 16) has called a definition of organization in the strong sense: "Such organization occurs when the output order of items is governed by semantic or phonetic relations among items or by the subjects' prior, extraexperimental or intraexperimental acquaintance with the items constituting a list."

Two features of this definition require attention: first, it focuses on a particular dependent variable, viz., output order which is assumed to reflect the existence of high-order groupings. However, if the systematic groupings are already present in the input, as in some of the studies discussed above, then the same results are predicted on the basis of association by contiguity and by the principle of secondary organization. The power of the definition thus appears to hinge on whether or not there is a discrepancy between input and output order. Second, organization defined in the strong sense excludes discrepancies between input and output orders that are "independent of the subjects' prior familiarity with a set of input items" (p. 15). Such discrepancies, as, for example, those reflecting the priority of the most recently presented items in output, are considered to be instances of organization in the weak sense. Seriation would presumably fall under this heading as well. The heuristic value of the distinction between primary and secondary organization may warrant further discussion. This distinction gives central importance to the basis on which items are grouped, sharply contrasting spatiotemporal and semantic features of the input materials.

If it is the activity of imposing structure on the materials which is at the heart of the concept, then the specific bases on which items are grouped or a retrieval plan is formulated may not have to be included among the defining criteria of organization. However, it will be important to maintain the distinction between primary and secondary organization if the two types of grouping turn out to reflect disparate mechanisms and have different consequences for performance. Such would be the case, for example, if improvement over trials were dependent on secondary, but not on primary, organization.

A definition of organization proposed by Mandler focuses on the products of organizational processes rather than on the characteristics of recall performance: "A set of objects or events are said to be organized when a consistent relation among the members of the set can be specified and, specifically, when membership of the objects or events in subsets (groups, concepts, categories, chunks) is stable and identifiable" (Mandler, 1967a, p. 330). In short, organization has occurred when stable interitem relations have been established such that the material can be partitioned into specifiable subsets. This definition is neutral with respect to the basis of the higher-order groupings, nor does it prescribe any performance characteristics by which organization is to be indexed. As has become clear in our discussion of seriation, application of these defining criteria leaves open the question, at least in some important cases, of the mechanisms responsible for the development of the observed stable units.

The activities and strategies of the learner were emphasized by Bower (1970, p. 19) in a recent discussion of the implications of the concept of organization: "The ideas of interest to me can be formulated in terms of the notions of groups (or classes) and relations (or relational rules). . . . Grouping and relating are basic cognitive processes, and I think they are inevitably involved in specifying what is learned and how it is learned by the adult human subject." To say that such processes are inevitably involved could not, of course, become part of an ultimate formal definition since such an assertion would beg the question at issue. The testable implication of this approach is that performance should be some increasing function of the opportunities for grouping and relating items afforded by the experimental task. Success in the implementation of this approach will depend on the investigator's ability to specify the rules and relations the subject is expected to utilize and the exact consequences of these cognitive operations for the observable characteristics of performance.

Organization is a term that carries a considerable amount of surplus meaning (both cognitive and affective). It will be important, therefore, to work toward a consensus on the definition of the term and then to apply it consistently in the analysis of learning and memory. Since organization is a theoretical construct, it is reasonable to suggest that the concept needs to be securely anchored to both antecedent conditions and observable consequences. The statements cited above appear to provide the basic ingredients for such a formulation. The description of the antecedent conditions will have to specify the extent to which the learning materials incorporate groupings previously acquired by the subject and a normative assessment of the opportunities that appear to exist for the development of new interitem relations. (Here the "unrelated" list becomes an important special case because the normative basis for higher-order groupings is presumably negligible.) A complete specification of hypothetical intervening events would encompass assumptions about both processes and products: the activity of grouping as well as the nature of the units that are established. These events need not, of course, remain altogether hypothetical. For example, grouping of items in rehearsal can be observed directly, and information about the composition of higher-order units can be obtained from the subject. The choice of the critical dependent variables must obviously depend on the assumptions made about the nature of the intervening processes. Clearly, inferences about organization have not remained tied to the measurement of output consistency. When interest centers on the question of what is learned, measures of transfer are likely to provide a more definite answer than internal analyses of the characteristics of performance.

RELATIONSHIP BETWEEN ORGANIZATION AND ASSOCIATION

With these problems of definition in mind, I would like in conclusion to comment briefly on the relationship between organization and association. The concept of association has many connotations and usages (cf. Postman, 1968). The core of the concept remains, however, the same as it has been historically, viz., that the sequential dependencies in output reflect in a lawful and predictable manner the order of events in input. Thus, contiguity is a necessary condition of learning. However, the contiguities that are critical for learning need not be between directly observable events. Modern association theorists have leaned heavily, probably too heavily, on implicit mediators to account for the establishment of linkages between apparently remote events.

As far as the specification of the products of learning, and in particular free-recall learning, is concerned, the difference between exponents of association and of organization appears to reduce largely to matters of language. However it is stated, the major endproduct of practice is the establishment of interitem dependencies (cf. Postman, 1971). One theorist prefers to think in terms of the development of associative chains and networks, the other in terms of higher-order units and chunks. The organization theorist is likely to stress discrepancies between input and output order, only to see them referred by the associationist to contiguities during rehearsal and on successive tests of recall (Wallace, 1970). Nor does one have to stretch such hypothetical processes as implicit associative responses unduly to account for the dispositions of relating and grouping nominal units (e.g., Wood & Underwood, 1967).

We thus return to our earlier suggestion that there is no necessary disagreement between exponents of organization and of association about what is learned. Nor do they need to disagree about how items are reproduced at the time of test. Retrieval cues are, after all, implicit stimuli that fit well into the traditional armamentarium of the associationist. It is fair to say that neither position has generated precise and rigorously testable hypotheses about the mechanisms responsible for the establishment of stimulus-response connections, interitem dependencies, higher-order units, or chunks. An associationist's cell assemblies dwell as much in the realm of metaphor as do trace aggregates, storage bins, and marker systems. In short, in spite of the apparent opposition between the two points of view, it is not difficult to make translations from one language to the other, and there are many shared weaknesses. While it is useful to stress the continuities, it is also clear that the differences in language and in conceptualization have been of considerable pragmatic importance. During the last decade, organization theorists have asked many important and imaginative questions about the conditions of learning and recall that association theorists had not asked. Whether the best in both approaches can be melded productively remains to be seen.

Summary

This paper has presented a critical review of major developments in organization theory and has examined the current status of the empirical evidence for organizational processes in memory. The relationship between theoretical constructs and empirical findings was emphasized throughout. Attention was also focused on the similarities and differences between the principles of organization and of association.

The survey of historical trends began with a discussion of the antecedents of contemporary approaches to organization in Gestalt theory. There has been a continuity of concern with a number of basic issues, including the relation between event perception and mnemonic organization and the conditions determining the accessibility to recall of the products of organization. Recent analyses have centered on the role of organization in overcoming the individual's limited capacity for storing and retrieving information.

In assessing the functional utility of organizational processes, one can adopt either a strong or a weak principle of limited mnemonic capacity. According to the strong principle, the limitations of the system are such that organization is always required if the span of immediate memory is to be exceeded. A weak principle holds that the development of higher-order groupings serves to increase mnemonic capacity but makes no firm assumptions about the limits of the system. It was argued that the existing evidence is consistent with the weak form of the principle but gives no conclusive support to the strong version.

Granted that organization increases mnemonic capacity, a fundamental question arises concerning the locus of organizational processes, viz., whether they serve to enhance storage, aid retrieval, or both. Recent studies of cued recall have served to place increasing emphasis on the facilitation of retrieval. After review of some of the relevant evidence it was suggested that organizational processes are likely to have correlated effects on both storage and retrieval. In this connection, the recently advanced hypothesis of independent trace storage was examined, and apparent internal inconsistencies in this theoretical position were pointed out. Attention was also called to the need for systematic exploration of the relationship between the principles of organization and encoding specificity. Finally, the heuristic value of formal memory models in the analysis of organizational processes was discussed.

The section concerned with the empirical base of organization theory considered first the validity of measures of output consistency as indices of organization. It was concluded that such measures provide only a fallible estimate of the degree of organization and yield little information about the quality and pattern of subjective groupings. The value of tests of transfer for purposes of assessing the products of organizational activity was stressed. Three types of relevant transfer designs were discussed: (a) studies of transfer between successive free-recall tasks focus on the effects of a prior organization on the development of a new one. Experiments on part-to-whole transfer were reviewed under this heading. Attention was called to some of the remaining uncertainities about the sources of interference in this situation. (b) Transfer from paired-associate to free-recall learning has been investigated from two points of view—to demonstrate the applicability of principles of organization to associative learning, and to assess the significance of interitem associations for the development of higher-order units. The explanatory value of conceptualizing paired-associate learning as a special case of organization remains to be established. The presence of significant transfer effects under this paradigm indicates that pairwise connections, even though chosen arbitrarily, provide an effective basis of grouping in free recall. (c) Investigations of transfer from free-recall to paired-associate learning bear on the question of whether subjective organization leads to the establishment of interitem linkages that share the functional properties of pairwise associations. The subjective groupings formed in the course of free-recall learning should, for the most part, be in conflict with the arbitrary pairings in the test stage. The expected negative transfer effects have been obtained in a number of experiments. The subjective units established in free recall and the products of controlled associative learning thus do appear to share common functional properties.

Some general methodological problems in the experimental analysis of organizational processes were considered next. One of these concerns the identification of alternative bases of organization. While attention has centered primarily on the semantic characteristics of words, there is evidence that other features of the input materials may give rise to systematic groupings, for example, the serial order of presentation. When there are competing modes of grouping, measures of organization based on any one index are likely to be attenuated. Difficulties of interpretation also develop when a known structure is imposed on the input and is reflected in the subject's output. In such cases there is no assurance that the conservation of structure reflects organizational activities rather than the operation of other mechanisms such as association by contiguity. For this reason, the use of highly structured materials is seen as having limited utility for the assessment of the effects of organizational processes on memory.

The final section of the paper discussed the definition of organization and the relationship between organization and association. After a review of currently accepted connotations of the concept, it was pointed out that a general definition of organization needs to be securely anchored to both antecedent conditions and observable consequences. A complete explication of the hypothetical intervening events would encompass assumptions about both processes and products; that is, it would specify the nature of the organizing activity and the characteristics of the resulting higher-order units. As for the relationship between organization and association, there is a basic agreement that the major end product of practice is the establishment of interitem dependencies. To that extent, the differences between the two positions appear to reduce largely to matters of language. Nor is there any essential divergence in the analysis of retrieval processes. It is recognized, however, that, in spite of these continuities, the differences in language and conceptualization have had significant consequences for the development of research on memory.

References

Allen, M. M. Cueing and retrieval in free recall. *Journal of Experimental Psychology,* 1969, 81, 29–35.

Atkinson, R. C., & Shiffrin, R. M. Human memory: A proposed system and its control processes. In K. W. Spence and J. T. Spence (Eds.), *The psychology of learning and motivation,* Vol. 2. New York: Academic Press, 1968.

Baddeley, A. D. Prior recall of newly learned items and the recency effect in free recall. *Canadian Journal of Psychology,* 1968, 22, 157–163.

Bahrick, H. P. Measurement of memory by prompted recall. *Journal of Experimental Psychology,* 1969, 79, 213–219.

Bahrick, H. P. Two-phase model for prompted recall. *Psychological Review,* 1970, 77, 215–222.

Battig, W. F. Evidence for coding processes in "rote" paired-associate learning. *Journal of Verbal Learning and Verbal Behavior,* 1966, 5, 177–181.

Battig, W. F., Allen, M. M., & Jensen, A. R. Priority of free recall of newly learned items. *Journal of Verbal Learning and Verbal Behavior,* 1965, 4, 175–179.

Battig, W. F., & Slaybaugh, G. D. Evidence that priority of free recall of newly learned items is not a recency artifact. *Journal of Verbal Learning and Verbal Behavior,* 1969, 8, 556–558.

Birnbaum, I. M. Free-recall learning as a function of prior-list organization. *Journal of Verbal Learning and Verbal Behavior,* 1968, 7, 1037–1042.

Birnbaum, I. M. Prior-list organization in part-whole free-recall learning. *Journal of Verbal Learning and Verbal Behavior,* 1969, 8, 836–838.

Bower, G. H. Chunks as interference units in free recall. *Journal of Verbal Learning and Verbal Behavior,* 1969, 8, 610–613.

Bower, G. H. Organizational factors in memory. *Cognitive Psychology,* 1970, 1, 18–46.

Bower, G. H., Clark, M. C., Lesgold, A. M., & Winzenz, D. Hierarchical retrieval schemes in recall of categorized word lists. *Journal of Verbal Learning and Verbal Behavior,* 1969, 8, 323–343.

Bower, G. H., & Lesgold, A. M. Organization as a determinant of part-to-whole transfer in free recall. *Journal of Verbal Learning and Verbal Behavior,* 1969, 8, 501–506.

Bower, G. H., Lesgold, A. M., & Tieman, D. Grouping operations in free recall. *Journal of Verbal Learning and Verbal Behavior,* 1969, 8, 481–493.

Bower, G. H., & Winzenz, D. Group structure, coding, and memory for digit series. *Journal of Experimental Psychology Monographs,* 1969, 80, No. 2, Part 2, 1–17.

Bruce, D., & Crowley, J. J. Acoustic similarity effects on retrieval from secondary memory. *Journal of Verbal Learning and Verbal Behavior,* 1970, 9, 190–196.

Cofer, C. N. Does conceptual organization influence the amount retained in immediate free recall? In B. Kleinmuntz (Ed.), *Concepts and the structure of memory.* New York: Wiley, 1967.

Cohen, B. H. Recall of categorized word lists. *Journal of Experimental Psychology,* 1963, **66,** 227–234.

Cohen, B. H. Some-or-none characteristics of coding behavior. *Journal of Verbal Learning and Verbal Behavior,* 1966, **5,** 182–187.

Craik, F. I. M. The fate of primary memory items in free recall. *Journal of Verbal Learning and Verbal Behavior,* 1970, **9,** 143–148.

Deese, J. Influence of inter-item associative strength upon immediate recall. *Psychological Reports,* 1959, **5,** 305–312.

Deese, J. Frequency of usage and number of words in free recall. The role of association. *Psychological Reports,* 1960, **7,** 337–344.

Earhard, M. Subjective organization and list organization as determinants of free recall and serial recall memorization. *Journal of Verbal Learning and Verbal Behavior,* 1967, **6,** 501–507.

Earhard, M. Storage and retrieval of words encoded in memory. *Journal of Experimental Psychology,* 1969, **80,** 412–418.

Ehrlich, S. Structuration and destructuration of responses in free-recall learning. *Journal of Verbal Learning and Verbal Behavior,* 1970, **9,** 282–286.

Freund, J. S., & Underwood, B. J. Storage and retrieval cues in free recall learning. *Journal of Experimental Psychology,* 1969, **81,** 49–53.

Freund, J. S., & Underwood, B. J. Restricted associates as cues in free recall. *Journal of Verbal Learning and Verbal Behavior,* 1970, **9,** 136–141.

Gibson, E. J. A systematic application of the concepts of generalization and differentiation to verbal learning. *Psychological Review,* 1940, **47,** 196–229.

Glanzer, M. Distance between related words in free recall: Trace of the STS. *Journal of Verbal Learning and Verbal Behavior,* 1969, **8,** 105–111.

Glanzer, M., & Cunitz, A. R. Two storage mechanisms in free recall. *Journal of Verbal Learning and Verbal Behavior,* 1966, **5,** 351–360.

Glanzer, M., Gianutsos, R., & Dubin, S. The removal of items from short-term storage. *Journal of Verbal Learning and Verbal Behavior,* 1969, **8,** 435–447.

Glanzer, M., & Meinzer, A. The effects of intralist activity on free recall. *Journal of Verbal Learning and Verbal Behavior,* 1967, **6,** 928–935.

Hasher, L. The whole versus part problem: Acquisition and retention. Doctoral dissertation, University of California, Berkeley, 1970.

Jung, J., & Skeebo, S. Multitrial free recall as a function of constant versus varied input orders and list length. *Canadian Journal of Psychology,* 1967, **21,** 329–336.

Kintsch, W. Models for free recall and recognition. In D. A. Norman (Ed.), *Models of human memory.* New York: Academic Press, 1970.

Köhler, W. *Dynamics in psychology.* New York: Liveright, 1940.

Köhler, W. On the nature of associations. *Proceedings of the American Philosophical Society,* 1941, **84,** 489–502.

Lachman, R., & Laughery, K. R. Is a test trial a training trial in free recall learning? *Journal of Experimental Psychology,* 1968, **76,** 40–50.

Madigan, S. A. Intraserial repetition and coding processes in free recall. *Journal of Verbal Learning and Verbal Behavior,* 1969, **8,** 828–835.

Mandler, G. Organization and memory. In K. W. Spence and J. T. Spence (Eds.), *The psychology of learning and motivation.* Vol. I. New York: Academic Press, 1967. (a)

Mandler, G. Verbal learning. *New directions in psychology: III.* New York: Holt. Rinehart and Winston, 1967. (b)

Mandler, G. Association and organization: Facts, fancies and theories. In T. R.

Dixon and D. L. Horton (Eds.), *Verbal behavior and general behavior theory*. Englewood Cliffs, New Jersey: Prentice-Hall, 1968.

Mandler, G. Input variables and output strategies in free recall of categorized words. *American Journal of Psychology*, 1969, **82**, 531–539.

Mandler, G., & Dean, P. J. Seriation: Development of serial order in free recall. *Journal of Experimental Psychology*, 1969, **81**, 207–215.

Mandler, G., & Pearlstone, Z. Free and constrained concept learning and subsequent recall. *Journal of Verbal Learning and Verbal Behavior*, 1966, **5**, 126–131.

Mandler, G., Pearlstone, Z., & Koopmans, H. S. Effects of organization and semantic similarity on recall and recognition. *Journal of Verbal Learning and Verbal Behavior*, 1969, **8**, 410–423.

Mayhew, A. J. Interlist changes in subjective organization during free-recall learning. *Journal of Experimental Psychology*, 1967, **74**, 425–430.

Miller, G. A. The magical number seven, plus or minus two: Some limits on our capacity for processing information. *Psychological Review*, 1956, **63**, 81–97.

Novinski, L. Part-whole and whole-part free recall learning. *Journal of Verbal Learning and Verbal Behavior*, 1969, **8**, 152–154.

Postman, L. Short-term memory and incidental learning. In A. W. Melton (Ed.), *Categories of human learning*. New York: Academic Press, 1964.

Postman, L. Association and performance in the analysis of verbal learning. In T. R. Dixon and D. L. Horton (Eds.), *Verbal behavior and general behavior theory*. Englewood Cliffs, New Jersey: Prentice-Hall, 1968.

Postman, L. Effects of word frequency on acquisition and retention under conditions of free-recall learning. *Quarterly Journal of Experimental Psychology*, 1970, **22**, 185–195.

Postman, L. Organization and interference. *Psychological Review*, 1971, **78**, 290–302.

Postman, L., Burns, S., & Hasher, L. Studies of learning to learn: X. Nonspecific transfer effects in free-recall learning. *Journal of Verbal Learning and Verbal Behavior*, 1970, **9**, 707–715.

Postman, L., & Keppel, G. Retroactive inhibition in free recall. *Journal of Experimental Psychology*, 1967, **74**, 203–211.

Postman, L., & Keppel, G. Conditions determining the priority of new items in free recall. *Journal of Verbal Learning and Verbal Behavior*, 1968, **7**, 260–263.

Puff, C. R. Free recall with instructional manipulation of sequential ordering of output. *Journal of Experimental Psychology*, 1970, **84**, 540–542.

Raymond, B. Short-term storage and long-term storage in free recall. *Journal of Verbal Learning and Verbal Behavior*, 1969, **8**, 567–574.

Riley, D. A. Memory for form. In L. Postman (Ed.), *Psychology in the making*. New York: Knopf, 1962.

Roberts, W. A. The priority of recall of new items in transfer from part list learning to whole list learning. *Journal of Verbal Learning and Verbal Behavior*, 1969, **8**, 645–652.

Rosner, S. R. The effects of presentation and recall trials on organization in multi-trial free recall. *Journal of Verbal Learning and Verbal Behavior*, 1970, **9**, 69–74.

Rundus, D. An analysis of rehearsal processes in free recall. Doctoral dissertation, Stanford University, 1970.

Rundus, D., & Atkinson, R. C. Rehearsal processes in free recall: A procedure for direct observation. *Journal of Verbal Learning and Verbal Behavior*, 1970, **9**, 99–105.

Segal, M. A., & Mandler, G. Directionality and organizational processes in paired-associate learning. *Journal of Experimental Psychology*, 1967, **74**, 305–312.

Shuell, T. J., & Keppel, G. Item priority in free recall. *Journal of Verbal Learning and Verbal Behavior*, 1968, **7**, 969–971.

Slamecka, N. J. An examination of trace storage in free recall. *Journal of Experimental Psychology*, 1968, **76**, 504–513.

Slamecka, N. J. Testing for associative storage in multitrial free recall. *Journal of Experimental Psychology*, 1969, **81**, 557–560.

Strand, B. Z., Further investigation of retroactive inhibition in categorized free recall. *Journal of Experimental Psychology*, 1971, **87**, 198–201.

Thomson, D. M., & Tulving, E. Associative encoding and retrieval: Weak and strong cues. *Journal of Experimental Psychology*, 1970, **86**, 255–262.

Tulving, E. Subjective organization in free recall of "unrelated words." *Psychological Review*, 1962, **69**, 344–354.

Tulving, E. Intratrial and intertrial retention: Notes toward a theory of free recall verbal learning. *Psychological Review*, 1964, **71**, 219–237.

Tulving, E. The effect of order of presentation on learning of "unrelated" words. *Psychonomic Science*, 1965, **3**, 337–338.

Tulving, E. Subjective organization and effects of repetition in multitrial free-recall learning. *Journal of Verbal Learning and Verbal Behavior*, 1966, **5**, 193–197.

Tulving, E. Theoretical issues in free recall. In T. R. Dixon and D. L. Horton (Eds.), *Verbal behavior and general behavior theory.* Englewood Cliffs, New Jersey: Prentice-Hall, 1968.

Tulving, E., & Osler, S. Transfer effects in whole/part free-recall learning. *Canadian Journal of Psychology*, 1967, **21**, 253–262.

Tulving, E., & Osler, S. Effectiveness of retrieval cues in memory for words. *Journal of Experimental Psychology*, 1968, **77**, 593–601.

Tulving, E., & Patkau, J. E. Concurrent effects of contextual constraint and word frequency on immediate recall and learning of verbal material. *Canadian Journal of Psychology*, 1962, **16**, 83–92.

Tulving, E., & Patterson, R. D. Functional units and retrieval processes in free recall. *Journal of Experimental Psychology*, 1968, **77**, 239–248.

Tulving, E., & Pearlstone, Z. Availability versus accessibility of information in memory for words. *Journal of Verbal Learning and Verbal Behavior*, 1966, **5**, 381–391.

Tulving, E., & Psotka, J. Retroactive inhibition in free recall: Inaccessibility of information available in the memory store. *Journal of Experimental Psychology*, 1971, **87**, 1–8.

Underwood, B. J. Attributes of memory. *Psychological Review*, 1969, **76**, 559–573.

Wallace, W. P. Clustering in free recall based upon input contiguity. *Psychonomic Science*, 1969, **14**, 290, 292.

Wallace, W. P. Consistency of emission order in free recall. *Journal of Verbal Learning and Verbal Behavior*, 1970, **9**, 58–68.

Waugh, N. C. Free versus serial recall. *Journal of Experimental Psychology*, 1961, **62**, 496–502.

Weist, R. M. Optimal versus nonoptimal conditions for retrieval. *Journal of Verbal Learning and Verbal Behavior*, 1970, **9**, 311–316.

Wood, G. Retrieval cues and the accessibility of higher-order memory units in multitrial free recall. *Journal of Verbal Learning and Verbal Behavior*, 1969, **8**, 782–789. (a)

Wood, G. Higher order memory units and free recall learning. *Journal of Experimental Psychology*, 1969, **80**, 286–288. (b)

Wood, G. Whole-part transfer from paired-associate to free recall learning. *Journal of Experimental Psychology*, 1969, **82**, 532–537. (c)

Wood, G., & Clark, D. Instructions, ordering, and previous practice in free-recall learning. *Psychonomic Science*, 1969, **14**, 187–188.

Wood, G., & Underwood, B. J. Implicit responses and conceptual similarity. *Journal of Verbal Learning and Verbal Behavior*, 1967, **6**, 1–10.

2 | *Organizational Processes and Free Recall*[1]

Gordon Wood

[1] The author's research is supported by Grant MH 16991 from the National Institute of Mental Health. Thanks are due to Joyce Pennington, Benton J. Underwood, David S. Gorfein, Joan E. Wood, Joanne Dafoe, and the participants in the Pittsburgh Conference. Special thanks are due to Endel Tulving for his numerous helpful comments and criticisms. The author is solely responsible for any misinterpretations or instances of faulty logic which the chapter may still contain.

The basic problem for students of learning and memory is to understand how the human mind processes information. Memory researchers are concerned with how organisms record events and use the record of that event at a later point in time. Some of the authors of chapters in this book have been investigating the "intelligent" use of event memory. The "intelligent" use of event memory includes computing new information from stored information, seeking and evaluating new relations among stored events, etc. These investigators agree that understanding the nature of semantic memory is necessary in order to explain the "intelligent" use of information. Other contributors have attempted to understand memory processes without considering the "intelligent" use of event memory. Although there are differences in the strategies used to study memory processes, the contributors appear to agree that any adequate theory of memory processes will have to account for both "intelligent" and "nonintelligent" processing. Clearly, most of us do a great deal of both. Although the reader may prefer "intelligent" uses over "nonintelligent" uses, most of our knowledge of memory processes has been obtained by studying the recording and "nonintelligent" use of events. Also, the reader should not interpret "nonintelligent" too broadly. "Nonintelligent" refers to the fact that verbatim recall is used to study memory processes. There is considerable evidence that subjects make "intelligent" use of their semantic memory in order to encode events for subsequent verbatim recall (cf. Adams, 1967).

The investigation of the recording and "nonintelligent" use of events has usually involved list learning procedures (i.e., the verbatim recall of a list of words). The reason for this is simply convenience. The verbatim recall of a single word is an event which can be easily measured. Also, there is little reason to doubt that the processes involved in simple-event memory are any different from the processes involved in complex-event memory. For example, if subjects are asked to study a prose passage, the number of "idea" units (complex events) that are recalled is highly correlated with the number of words from the passage (simple events) that are recalled (Howe, 1970).

Organizational processes in free recall are studied because this approach has been and continues to be a useful vehicle for understanding memory processes. More specifically, a knowledge of grouping (organizing) operations may be necessary in order to understand the recording and use of events. Although the free recall task has been used for other reasons, many investigators, myself included, have used it primarily because it is a convenient way to study organizational processes. The free recall task has been popular with students of organizational processes because it is possible to assess the organization that subjects impose on the to-be-recalled material.

During the last decade students of memory processes have studied extensively the effect of organizational processes on free-recall learning. The purpose of this chapter is to evaluate their progress and to indicate directions for further research. The chapter is divided into three main sections: the effect of organization on learning and retention, storage and retrieval processes, and the nature of memory. In the first section, the importance of organizational processes for event memory is assessed by evaluating the relationship between subject-imposed organization and recall, the evidence for and properties of higher-order memory units, and the effect of organization on retention. The issues of whether there is a disparity between events that are stored (available) and events that are accessible, whether the kind of processing depends on the size (level) of the event, and the organization of the memory store are considered in the second section. The nature of memory (properties of an event which are stored) and the relationship between organizational factors and the properties of an event are considered in the last section.

Organization, Learning, and Retention

The rapid upsurge in the number of studies of organizational processes can be traced in large part to the development of new measures for assessing organization. Prior to the last decade, the customary procedure was to measure organization by determining the amount of clustering according to experimenter-defined categories. It can be argued that this procedure is not particularly useful because there is probably a discrepancy between what the subject stores as a single unit and what the experimenter defines as a single unit. Since the experimenter has no way of knowing what the subject will store as a unit, measures of organization based on experimenter-defined organizational units such as categories probably do not accurately reflect the organizational structure that the subject imposes on the to-be-recalled material. What the subject defines as a unit is believed to be reflected in the organization the subject imposes on recall, measured by the consistency of output orders over trials (Tulving, 1962). Since the organization measure does not depend on the use of experimenter-defined organizational units or the consistency of input order over trials, Tulving labeled the measure subjective organization (SO). Another measure of organization based on the comparison of recall orders from trial to trial was developed by Bousfield and Bousfield (1966). They labeled their measure intertrial repetitions (ITRs).

Although the SO measure and the ITR measure are usually highly related, the ITR measure has been favored by investigators since it is considerably easier to compute. In addition, Tulving has unpublished data which indicate that when the ITR and SO measures are not highly correlated, the ITR measure is more useful. In this chapter the term subjective organization is used to describe organization measured by comparing recall orders from trial to trial regardless of whether Tulving's SO measure or Bousfield and Bousfield's ITR measure was used. The subjective organization measures were devised to assess organization imposed on recall by the subject. Therefore, these measures are "appropriate" only when the input order is varied for successive trials. If a constant input order is used, the organization measures are likely to reflect experimenter-imposed as well as subject-imposed organization. In this chapter, the adjective subjective will not be used when the subjective organization measures are used to assess output consistencies in the absence of varied input. The subjective organization measures have been criticized for being deficient in that they do not reflect categorical organization or the occurrence of units larger than two words (Mandler, 1967). Yet, in spite of these limitations, and in the absence of more suitable measures, investigators have made extensive use of subjective organization measures. For more information about organization measures see Shuell (1969).

SUBJECTIVE ORGANIZATION AND RECALL

There have been numerous attempts to determine the relationship between organization, as assessed by subjective organization and clustering measures, and recall. The results of these investigations are equivocal. If organization and recall are causally related, then the variables which influence the amount of organization should have a similar effect on recall. Organization is higher following constant input order than varied input order (Mandler & Dean, 1969; Wallace & Nappe, 1970), and constant input order has generally been found to result in higher recall than varied input order. However, manipulating the number of test trials influences organization more than recall (Rosner, 1970). Thus, the variables which influence output consistency do not necessarily have a similar effect on recall.

If organization and recall are causally related, then subjects who are high organizers should also have high recall. If subjects are separated on the basis of their organization scores, high organizers tend to have better serial and paired-associated performance than low organizers (Earhard, 1967; Earhard & Endicott, 1969). Yet, it is questionable whether subjective organization, as an individual difference variable, is an important determiner of performance. Significant correlations are obtained between free recall and paired-associate performance when subjective organization is controlled (partial correlations), indicating that organization is not the common factor responsible for free recall and paired-associate performance. Also, if subjects are asked to learn multiple lists composed of different events (e.g., nonsense syllables, words) in an unmixed list design, relatively high correlations across materials are obtained for recall scores but not for subjective organization scores. This finding also indicates that organization, as assessed by subjective organization measures, is not the common individual difference factor determining level of performance (Gorfein & Blair, 1971).

The studies in which organization and recall were correlated have yielded conflicting results. A number of investigators have reported moderately high correlations between subjective organization and recall scores (e.g., Allen, 1968; Mayhew, 1967; Tulving, 1962, 1964), but other investigators have been unable to obtain significant correlations. In some cases subjects had considerable recall before attaining high levels of organization. In other cases, substantial recall was accompanied by little organization (Carterette & Coleman, 1963). In one study, significant correlations were obtained between subjective organization and recall measures for high organizers only. The subjects who were moderate or low organizers were eventually able to recall most of the words, but their organization scores were low throughout learning (Shapiro & Bell, 1970).

The failure to find consistent high correlations between recall and subjective organization measures may mean that organization and recall are not related, or that the subjective organization measures are inadequate. Postman (1970), who was also unable to obtain significant correlations between subjective organization and recall measures, suggests that a high degree of consistency of output may not be an optimal way to process the to-be-recalled material. He indicates that interitem associations may be an important determiner of amount recalled. A recent study by Bousfield and Rosner (1970) gives some support to Postman's view that multiple associations are established during free recall. They gave one group standard free recall instructions and a second group instructions to be uninhibited during recall. If a subject in the uninhibited condition thought of a word, he was to write it down regardless of whether the word was from the list or a repeated word. The uninhibited subjects gave many item repetitions, supporting the view that subjects form multiple interitem associations during free recall. If subjects establish multiple associations during free recall, then the subjective organization measures are not accurate assessments of the organization the subjects impose on the list. The experimental procedures may encourage subjects to form multiple associations and, consequently, mitigate against finding a high correlation between subjective organization measures and recall.

Subjective organization measures may be inadequate because the experimental procedure results in the pitting of experimenter-imposed organizations (varied presentation orders) against subject-imposed organization. Since the to-be-recalled lists usually consist of "unrelated" words, there are many different ways the list can be organized. By using a varied order of presentation the experimenter discourages the formation of a single organization. Since the subjective organization measures are designed to assess the extent to which subjects use a single organization, it follows that the correlation between subject organization and recall may not be very high. By using a constant order of presentation, the experimenter is more likely to encourage the formation of a single organization. In this case, the organization and recall measures should be more highly related. Wallace (personal communication) provided the correlations between organization and recall for the Wallace and Nappe (1970) study in which order of presentation was manipulated. The correlations were computed on the total number of words recalled and the total organization score (inter-trial repetitions) for all trials combined. As expected, the correlations were higher for the constant-presentation order conditions. For the first experiment, the correlations ranged from .46 to .83 for the four constant-presentation conditions, and the correlations were .11 and .26 for the two varied-order presentation conditions. For the second experiment, the correlation was .63 for the constant-order condition and .30 for the varied-order condition.

In sum, there is little choice but to conclude that either the organization measures are inadequate or organizational factors have little effect on recall. My preference is to question the adequacy of the organization measures. In addition to the criticisms offered by Mandler (1967), the organization measures are suspect because they are obtained by placing experimenter-imposed organization in conflict with subject-imposed organization. The relationship between organization measures and recall should be considerably higher if subjects were free to control the input order for successive trials (i.e., have their input orders consistent with their preferred organization). Also, evidence from transfer experiments supports the view that organizational factors are important for free-recall learning.

HIGHER-ORDER MEMORY UNITS

A basic issue in understanding the storage and subsequent utilization of events is whether the events are processed independently or dependently. If events are processed independently, the recall of one event should not influence the recall of other events. For example, if you believe the probability of recalling an event is determined solely by the number of times you "experience" the event, regardless of context, then you are accepting the independence view. If you believe that subjects group events into larger-than-single-event units, then you are accepting the dependency position. Theorists who argue for the importance of organizational processes for free recall view recall as dependent (cf. Tulving, 1968).

The first firm evidence for the dependency position was obtained by demonstrating that prior part-list learning can retard subsequent whole-list free-recall learning (Tulving, 1966). The experimental subjects were given half of the List 2 words as List 1. The List 1 words for control subjects were unrelated to the List 2 words. List 2 was identical for all subjects. If recall is independent, the experimental subjects should have been superior to the controls since they received half of the List 2 words in List 1. The fact that there was negative transfer for experimental subjects for the later stages of List 2 learning (see Figure 1) is consistent with the dependency position. Or, stated differently, the results support the view that subjects form higher-order memory units (two or more mutually associated items) during free-recall learning. Since subjects are believed to be limited in the number of memory units they can recall (cf. Tulving, 1968), it was expected that experimental subjects would have to reorganize or enlarge their List 1 memory units in order to learn List 2. That is, the organization that the experimental subjects imposed on List 1 was believed to be inappropriate for List 2. The fact that negative transfer was obtained supports the view that the List 1 organization was inappropriate. Other investigators have replicated and extended the part-whole transfer effect (Birnbaum, 1968, 1969; Bower & Lesgold, 1969; Novinski, 1969; Ornstein, 1970). Prior part-list learning can facilitate subsequent whole-list learning if the lists are designed in such a way that the List 1 organization is "appropriate" for List 2 learning.

Although the results of the part-whole transfer studies are, in general, consistent with the view that subjects form higher-order memory units during free recall, it is difficult to obtain clear evidence for negative transfer with this design. The evidence for negative transfer is based largely on the finding that the experimental subjects do not maintain their initial superiority over controls for the later trials of List 2 learning. The problem of relying on differences obtained in the later stages of List 2 learning can be avoided by using a whole-part transfer design. Tulving and Osler (1967) assessed transfer from an 18-word, free-recall list to a 9-word, free-recall list in a further attempt to determine whether the free recall of a word is dependent upon the recall of other words in the list. Since the experimental subjects had poorer performance on

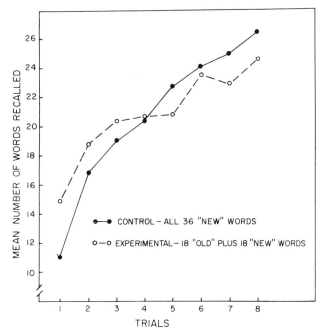

Fig. 1. Learning curves for the experimental and control groups for List 2 (whole list) learning. (After Tulving, 1966.)

List 2 than the control subjects, the authors asserted that the memory units formed by experimental subjects during List 1 learning were inappropriate for List 2 learning. The authors also manipulated the number of trials on List 1 (6, 12, 24), but the number of List 1 trials did not affect the amount of negative transfer. Wood (1969a) used a procedure very similar to the one employed by Tulving and Osler (1967), except that serial rather than free-recall learning of List 2 was required. There was no negative transfer for experimental subjects who received one free recall trial (List 1), weak evidence of negative transfer for subjects who received three free recall trials, and clear evidence of negative transfer for subjects who received 6 or 10 free recall trials (see Figure 2).

It is unclear why the number of List 1 trials did not influence the amount of negative transfer in the Tulving and Osler study. If the amount of organization increases over trials (Tulving, 1962), and the organization established during List 1 learning of a whole-part transfer design is inappropriate for List 2, there is little choice but to predict

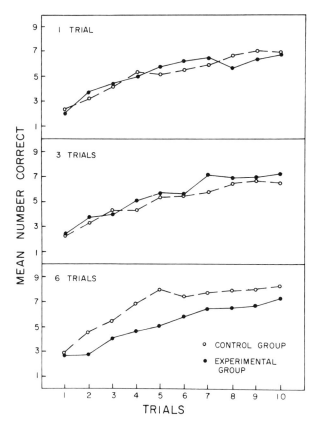

Fig. 2. Mean number of words correctly recalled for the 10 serial learning anticipation trials (List 2) for subjects who received either 1, 3, or 6 trials on List 1. (After Wood, 1969a.)

that the amount of negative transfer will increase with degree of List 1 learning. There are several explanations that might account for the fact that the number of List 1 trials did not influence the amount of negative transfer. Perhaps the amount of organization does not increase, appreciably, as a function of trials. This view is supported by the fact that some investigators (e.g., Puff, 1970) find very little change in subjective organization scores as a function of trials. Also, recent evidence suggests that the to-be-recalled material is organized very rapidly and the organization is relatively resistant to change (Howe, 1970). Perhaps subjects tend to form multiple organizations with repeated trials, and multiple encoding (representation) does not result in greater negative effects than single encoding. Perhaps, as Mandler (1962) suggested, a high level of learning results in a structure which reduces interference effects. Also, it may be that the effect of degree of learning on transfer is different for a free recall to free recall transfer design than for a free recall to serial transfer design. In one study the number of List 1 free-recall learning trials (5, 10, 15) influenced subsequent serial learning. The subjects who had the greatest number of free recall trials had the poorest serial learning (Shapiro, 1970). Yet the control groups were not comparable to those used by Tulving and Osler (1967) and Wood (1969a), so it is difficult to make meaningful comparisons of these studies. In short, the effect of List 1 learning on whole-part transfer remains to be explained.

A disadvantage with a free recall to free recall or free recall to serial transfer design as a means of studying organization is that it is difficult to control the number of inappropriate higher-order memory units formed during List 1 free-recall learning. However, it is possible to manipulate the number of inappropriate higher-order memory units for free-recall learning by using a paired-associate to free recall transfer design (Wood, 1969b). The number of words in List 2 (0, 6, 12, 18) that belonged to a memory unit formed during List 1 learning was manipulated. Only one word from any two-word unit was presented in List 2. The amount of negative transfer increased as the number of words in List 2 that belonged to a List 1 paired-associate pair increased (see Figure 3). In a subsequent study (Wood, 1969c), negative transfer also occurred when subjects were given one word from each paired-associate pair for free recall. Thus, there is ample evidence for the view that recall is dependent. The associations established during paired-associate learning have a marked effect on subsequent free-recall learning.

The evidence from the transfer studies can be interpreted in terms of associations or organization. A theorist who prefers to explain the evidence in terms of associations can argue that associations between to-be-recalled items and not-to-be-recalled items retard free-recall learning. Therefore, negative transfer is obtained with a whole-part transfer design. Negative transfer is obtained with a part-whole transfer design because the associations formed during part learning interfere with the associations to be found during whole learning. The part-whole transfer evidence gives clear support for the importance of the particular associa-

tions formed (higher-order memory units), not the mere number of associations, as the important determiner of free-recall learning. Thus, I am
at least in partial disagreement with Postman's comments elsewhere
in this volume regarding the importance of inter-item associations. As
long as specific associations are considered, there does not appear to
be any evidence which dictates that investigators use organizational
instead of associationistic terminology when interpreting the transfer
design studies. My preference is for organization terminology (higher-

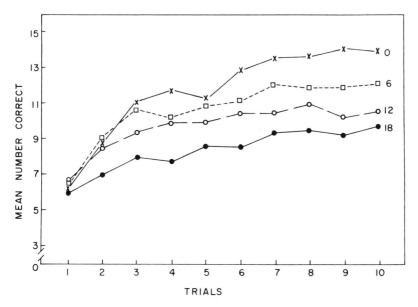

Fig. 3. Mean number of words correctly recalled for the List 2, free recall trials
for subjects who received 0, 6, 12, or 18 List 1 words in List 2. (After Wood,
1969b.)

order memory units) because this view encourages one to consider questions that would probably not be asked if free recall were considered
solely in terms of associations. For example, Postman, as an association
theorist, suggests that we do a component analysis of organization. My
preference, as a believer in organizational processes, is to attempt to
study organizational processes involving more complex events (larger
units, manipulating organization independently of the to-be-recalled
events, etc.). Obviously, the eventual worth of the two approaches can
be assessed only in terms of the degree to which they increase our understanding of the recording and use of events.

NUMBER AND SIZE OF HIGHER-ORDER MEMORY UNITS

Given that recall is dependent, one can consider the nature of the dependency relations that are established during free recall. That is, given that subjects form higher-order memory units, what are the characteristics of these units? The prevalent view is that subjects can recall only a limited number of higher-order memory units on each trial; the increase in performance over trials reflects an increase in the size, not the number, of higher-order memory units (Miller, 1956; Tulving, 1968). There is support for the view that only a fixed number of memory units can be recalled regardless of the size of the units. In one study, the recall of four word units (e.g., north, south, east, west) was compared with the recall of single word units (Tulving & Patterson, 1968). In another study, the recall of three word units (e.g., birth control pill, ice cream cone, fair-weather friend) was compared with one word units (Bower, 1969). In both studies, recall was independent of size of the units. One could argue that the investigators did not use very large memory units, and therefore the view that subjects recall a fixed number of memory units regardless of the size of the unit has not been tested adequately. However, this criticism is valid only if it can be demonstrated that subjects do, in fact, form large memory units. If subjects form memory units of five, plus or minus two, items (Mandler, 1967), then the above studies adequately sample the range of possible memory-unit sizes.

There is ample evidence that both the number and size of the higher-order memory units are important determiners of recall. One way to investigate the effect of the number and size of memory units on free recall is, of course, to simply vary the number and size of the conceptual categories present in the free recall list. Yet, if list length is held constant, it is impossible to manipulate the number of categories without varying the size of each category. The early studies of the effect of the number of categories on free recall performance resulted in equivocal findings (e.g., Bousfield & Cohen, 1956; Dallett, 1964; Mathews, 1954). If there are more categories (units) than the subjects can spontaneously recall, the amount of recall tends to decrease as the number of categories increases. If retrieval cues are provided, the cues are effective only when more categories are presented than the subjects can spontaneously recall (Dallett, 1964; Tulving & Pearlstone, 1966). Thus, the question of the optimal number of categories is complicated by the fact that subjects have to "move" within higher-order memory units and between higher-order memory units at recall. To eliminate the confounding effect of "moving" between memory units, it is necessary to provide retrieval cues or limit the number of higher-order units to a number that subjects can spontaneously recall. Also, since investigators have used different word lists to assess the effect of number and size of memory units, the manipulation of the characteristics of the memory units may have been confounded with list variables such as interitem associative strength. This problem can be avoided by using the same word lists for all subjects.

Another way to investigate the effect of the number and size of memory units is to present the same materials to all subjects and have them organize the material into categories. Mandler and Pearlstone (1966) and Mandler (1967) required subjects to sort lists of "unrelated" words into categories. For some of the experiments, the subjects were free to use as many categories as they desired, but in most cases they were instructed to use from two to seven categories. Subjects were asked to recall as many of the words as possible following the sorting task. The major finding was that the recall of words is a linear function of the number of categories used in sorting. The relationship between the number of categories used and recall was still obtained when the total sorting time and the number of sorting trials was held statistically and experimentally constant. The effect is not attributable to slow-learning subjects choosing fewer categories for the sorting task, since the relationship was still obtained when the number of categories was specified. In the experiments in which the subjects were allowed to use more than seven categories for the sorting task, the linear relationship did not hold beyond seven categories. If from two to seven categories are used, the amount of recall is increased by about four words for every additional category (Mandler, 1968). Although the relationship between the number of categories and recall is a reliable finding for college students, the relationship does not appear to hold for younger children (Mandler & Stephens, 1967). The authors suggest that the disparity in the findings with young children and adults is probably due to a developmental change from syntagmatic to paradigmatic responding. It appears that younger children simply do not categorize material in the same way as adults.

The finding of a linear relationship between number of categories and recall is strong support for the importance of grouping operations. Yet, it does not necessarily follow that subjects normally group the to-be-recalled events into categories during free recall. Sorting the to-be-recalled material into discrete categories may be just one of the many strategies (see Bower's chapter) that subjects use to encode events. If categorizing items is the preferred free recall strategy, then a significant relationship between the number of categories and recall should be obtained when recall precedes categorization. The sole purpose of the sorting task would be to determine how many categories each subject used when studying the material. Higgins and Basden (1968) reversed the Mandler procedure and found that when recall of words preceded categorization there was no significant relationship between the number of categories used in sorting and the amount of recall.

The fact that no significant relationship was found between the number of sorting categories and recall when recall preceded sorting suggests that subjects may not categorize material during learning unless they are explicitly instructed to do so. Or, as Mandler (personal communication) suggested, the failure to obtain a significant relationship between number of categories and recall when recall precedes categorization may be due to the failure of subjects to perceive the recall and sorting tasks as related. If the tasks are perceived as unrelated, the sorting task is not a useful way to determine the number of categories subjects used during learning. Higgins and Basden (personal communication) conducted experiments in which they asked the subjects to use any rules that they used in remembering the words to sort the words into piles. That is, the sorting task was to reflect the rules they used to memorize the words. The subjects only sorted words that they had recalled. When subjects were not restricted in the number of categories to be used for the sorting task, a significant positive relationship was obtained between recall and number of categories, supporting the view that subjects categorize the to-be-recalled events during free recall. When subjects could use no more than seven categories for the sorting task, the correlation between recall and number of categories was essentially zero. Thus, the effect of placing a restriction on the number of categories used in sorting is different when recall precedes categorization than when it follows. Higgins and Basden conducted an additional experiment in which sorting preceded recall and no limit was placed on the number of categories subjects could use in sorting. The correlation between the number of categories and recall was not significant, but a significant correlation was obtained between the number of categories recalled and amount of recall.

Higgins and Basden suggest that amount of recall is dependent on the number of categories recalled rather than the number used for sorting. This view is in essential agreement with Mandler's position. The relationship between the number of categories and recall holds when seven or less categories are used because subjects can generally recall all the categories. If more categories are used, then the number of categories that subjects can retrieve should be the more accurate predictor of recall. Since the amount of recall increases linearly with the number of categories (higher-order memory units), the optimal number of memory units is the largest number that a subject can "spontaneously" recall. If more memory units are formed than can be spontaneously recalled, the amount of recall will be influenced by whether the subject can develop a means to retrieve the higher-order memory units.

There appears to be agreement (cf. Mandler, 1967; Tulving & Pearlstone, 1966) that the recall of categories and the recall of items within categories can best be understood by treating the two as independent processes. Although it is reasonable to separate the recall of categories and the recall of items within categories when considering the recall of conceptually related words or the recall of words that subjects have sorted into discrete categories, it is not clear whether the same approach is appropriate for explaining the free recall of "unrelated" words. In order for the separation of the recall of memory units from the recall of items within units to have general validity, subjects should form discrete higher-order memory units during the free-recall learning of "unrelated" words. The issue of the separability of recall between and within memory units is considered in greater detail later. Basically, the problem is to determine whether the mechanism underlying the recall of higher-order memory units is different from the mechanism underlying the recall of items within memory units.

Finally, the discussion of the number and size of the higher-order memory units formed during free-recall learning would be incomplete without mentioning Mandler's extension of Miller's theory. Although Mandler (1967) agrees with Miller (1956) that subjects can only recall a limited number of higher-order memory units, he disagrees with Miller with respect to the number of items subjects can recall within a higher-order memory unit. Miller argues that subjects increase their recall by increasing the size of the limited number of memory units they can recall. Mandler argues that subjects are only able to recall a limited number of items within a memory unit. The optimal size of each memory unit is believed to be about five. Given a limit on both the size and the number of higher-order memory units formed, some mechanism is needed to enable subjects to learn long lists. Mandler's mechanism is hierarchical organization. Each higher-order memory unit can be represented by one item, such as a category name. Then the category names can be grouped into higher level, higher-order memory units. This process can be continued until there are about five different levels of higher-order memory units. Assuming the size of each unit is about five, the number of words that can be encoded by a single unit increases by a multiple of five for each higher level in the hierarchy. The evidence for hierarchical organization is considered in the storage and retrieval processes section.

ORGANIZATION AND FORGETTING

There is ample evidence that organizational factors can have a marked influence on the amount of forgetting. The effect of organization on retroactive inhibition depends on whether conditions favor the forgetting of whole categories (i.e., subjects are asked to recall many categories), or portions of categories (i.e., subjects are asked to recall a small number of large categories). As long as the number of memory units to be re-called is relatively small, there is greater retroactive inhibition when successive lists have similar organizations. The organization effect is obtained if organization is manipulated by constructing the interpolated lists so that they contain words from the same categories used in List 1, or different categories (Shuell, 1968; Thompson & Poling, 1969; Watts & Anderson, 1969; Winograd, 1968). The organization effect has also been obtained by presenting the same lists to all subjects and mani-pulating organization by instructing subjects as to how to organize their lists, by having subjects sort the words into designated cate-gories, or by manipulating the presentation order of the lists (Wood, 1970, 1971b).

An issue of some importance is whether it is theoretically useful to make a distinction between cue dependent and trace dependent forgetting (Tulving & Madigan, 1970). It has recently been demonstrated that if subjects are provided with retrieval cues for the to-be-recalled memory units, there is very little forgetting. Without the retrieval cues there is marked forgetting. The forgetting that occurs when retrieval cues are not provided is attributed mainly to a state in which memory units are available but not accessible (Tulving & Psotka, 1971). The effective-ness of retrieval cues in minimizing forgetting may be limited to cases in which highly related words are used in each category (see Postman's chapter). Unfortunately, there does not appear to be any way to demon-strate the importance of cue dependent forgetting for the "general case." Given that a retrieval cue has to be encoded along with the to-be-recalled event to be effective (Thomson & Tulving, 1970), there is little choice but to assess the importance of cue dependent forgetting by using a procedure which encourages subjects to encode the designated retrieval cue along with the to-be-recalled event. If the retrieval cue is not encoded along with the to-be-recalled event, the cue will be ineffective. In this case, the failure to obtain a cueing effect can be attributed to trace dependent forgetting or the use of "inappropriate" retrieval cues. Thus, assessing the relative importance of cue and trace dependent forgetting for the "general case" will probably have to await a more complete understanding of the nature of the encoding process.

SUMMARY

There is evidence to support the role of organizational processes in free-recall learning. More specifically, there is some support for the view that subjects can recall only a fixed number of memory units. The increase in performance over trials reflects an increase in the size, not the number of memory units. The organizational view is supported by evidence from transfer, sorting, and retroactive inhibition studies, but other interpretations are also possible. For example, the evidence can be interpreted within an associationistic framework. Unfortunately, the relationship between recall and organization has not been clarified very much by the studies in which subjective organization measures and recall scores were correlated. This is probably because the subjective organization measures are inadequate. The measures do not reflect categorical organization or the occurrence of units larger than two events, and the measures are obtained by experimental procedures which pit experimenter-imposed organization against subject-imposed organization. The belief that subject-imposed organization should be an accurate predictor of amount of recall follows from the view that subjects attempt to impose a single organization on the to-be-recalled material. This view appears to be incorrect. If the experimenter-imposed organizations (varied presentation orders) encourage subjects to use multiple organizations to encode the to-be-recalled events, it seems that subjects will do so.

There are still problems to be solved before we will have an adequate understanding of the role of organizational processes for learning and retention. For example, we need to develop more adequate measures of organization, or change our procedures for assessing organization. There seems to be little point in pitting experimenter-imposed against subject-imposed organization. Given adequate measures of organization, it may be possible to clarify how organization changes over trials. In addition, we need to extend the range of organization theory by determining the extent to which organization theory accounts for the memorization of different kinds of events.

Storage and Retrieval Processes

AVAILABILITY VERSUS ACCESSIBILITY OF INFORMATION

An issue of great importance for any adequate theory of memory is whether it is necessary to distinguish between the processes involved in the storage and utilization of events. In a classic study by Tulving and Pearlstone (1966), subjects were presented lists of words belonging to categories together with the category names and asked to recall the category instances. The major finding was that cued recall (presenting category names as cues) was better than noncued recall. The superiority of cued to noncued recall indicates that there is a discrepancy between information that is accessible and information that is available. Information may be stored (available), but not accessible unless appropriate retrieval cues are provided. This study gives firm support to the view that it is necessary to distinguish between the storage and utilization of events.

Numerous studies have replicated and extended the Tulving and Pearlstone finding. Retrieval cues facilitate recall when they are presented during both learning and recall. Retrieval cues do not facilitate recall when they are presented only for the recall trial unless the preestablished association between the cue and the to-be-recalled word is of considerable strength (Thomson & Tulving, 1970; Wood, 1967b). It is likely that a retrieval cue is effective only if the information about its relation to the to-be-recalled item is stored at the same time that the item is stored. This view is supported by the fact that, in general, the presence of a retrieval cue having a strong preexperimental association with the to-be-recalled item has little influence on the recall of the item if the item has been studied in the presence of a weak associate (Thomson & Tulving, 1970).

The crux of the encoding specificity hypothesis is that the effectiveness of a retrieval cue depends primarily on the nature of the encoding process, and not on preestablished language habits. In order for a word to be an effective retrieval cue for another word, information about the two words must be stored at the same time. Given that two words are encoded at the same time and one can serve as a retrieval cue for the other, it does not necessarily follow that the two words are stored together. Words may be stored independently. The fact that related words are frequently recalled consecutively could be due to the subject's use of a retrieval plan to link the related words. That is, by making a storage-retrieval distinction, one can attribute the dependency of words at recall to retrieval, not storage, processes. Evidence for the independence of items in storage comes from studies in which subjects were provided list words as retrieval cues for other list words.

RETRIEVAL OF HIGHER-ORDER MEMORY UNITS

If words are stored together, then list words should, according to Slamecka, serve as effective retrieval cues for other list words. Slamecka (1968a,b, 1969) tested this view by conducting a series of studies in which he presented subjects with a free recall list and then provided half of the subjects with some of the list words as cues for the recall of other list words. Since cued subjects did not recall more words than noncued subjects, Slamecka concluded that the storage of items is probably independent. Freund and Underwood (1969) also provided list words as retrieval cues and found that cueing had essentially no effect. However, other investigators (Allen, 1969; Hudson & Austin, 1970; Wood, 1969d) have demonstrated that under certain conditions providing list words as cues results in greater recall. If subjects are encouraged to form many small memory units during the learning trial, providing list words as retrieval cues can have a strong facilitative effect. The effectiveness of list words as retrieval cues for other list words can be explained by making a distinction between the availability and accessibility of higher-order memory units.

It has been suggested that subjects can recall only a limited number of higher-order memory units on each trial; the increase in performance over trials reflects an increase in the size, not the number, of higher-order memory units. However, it is possible that both the size and the number of higher-order memory units increase over trials, but subjects can retrieve only a limited number of the higher-order memory units. If memory units are available but not accessible at recall, the presence of retrieval cues to remind subjects of the available memory units should facilitate performance. Since Tulving and Pearlstone (1966) have demonstrated that words may be available in store but not accessible unless appropriate cues are provided, it seems reasonable that higher-order memory units may be available in store but not accessible unless appropriate cues are provided.

If the words of the list are formed into higher-order memory units, each list word should be an effective cue for the memory unit of which it is a member. One problem with the Slamecka studies is that the lists contained only 30 words. Therefore, the fixed number of memory units subjects can recall may have been equal to or greater than the number of memory units formed. If all the memory units formed during learning were accessible at recall, there is little reason to expect that providing list words as retrieval cues should facilitate recall. In the Freund and Underwood (1969) study, the subjects were only given one trial on a 40 item list. It seems unlikely that subjects could form more memory units than the fixed number they can recall if they are only given one study trial. In the studies in which subjects were given longer lists, multiple trials, and "encouraged" to form many memory units, providing list words as retrieval cues facilitated recall. In short, Slamecka's evidence for the independence of storage can be explained by making a distinction between the availability and accessibility of higher-order memory units. The effectiveness of list words as retrieval cues for other list words does not appear to be an indication of the independence or dependence of items in storage. Postman gives additional reasons for rejecting Slamecka's independence interpretation in his chapter.

RETRIEVAL OF MEMORY UNITS AND ITEMS WITHIN MEMORY UNITS

The distinction between the recall of higher-order memory units and the recall of items within memory units has been useful for explaining many phenomena of free recall (e.g., Slamecka's data, independence of item recall and category recall). Although the distinction is useful, it is still not clear whether free-recall learning actually involves two distinct organizational processes. One organizational process is believed to be the groupings of items into higher-order memory units, such that all the members of each unit are recalled or none is recalled. The second process is believed to involve the development of a retrieval plan to allow the subject to move from one higher-order memory unit to another during recall (cf. Bower, 1970a; Tulving & Pearlstone, 1966). The question of interest is whether the organizational processes involved in forming memory units are, in fact, any different than the processes involved in moving from one higher-order memory unit to another.

There is some evidence to suggest that the same mechanism may be responsible for the two organizational processes. Mandler (1967) re-analyzed some of Tulving and Pearlstone's (1966) data to determine if the relationship between set size (number of categories or number of items within a category) and recall was similar for the recall of categories and the recall of items within categories. Mandler noted that the size-recall functions for category recall for the Tulving and Pearlstone data were similar to the size-recall functions that he obtained for recall of items within categories. In addition, Mandler indicated that Cohen's (1966) data on category recall are consistent with the size-recall functions for recall within categories. The finding that the number of categories recalled is about equal to the recall of unrelated words is also consistent with the view that one mechanism underlies the recall of categories and recall of items within categories (Cohen, 1963).

Another way to investigate whether the same mechanism is responsible for recalling memory units and recalling words within memory units is to investigate organizational processes involving large memory units. Assuming that subjects do form large memory units, it may be that subjects form large memory units by combining two or more small memory units. Thus, the organizational processes involved in forming large memory units may be similar to the processes which enable a subject to move from one memory unit to another during recall. If the process of forming a large memory unit does not differ from the process of moving from one memory unit to another, and the process of forming a large memory unit does not differ from the process of forming a small memory unit, then it follows that free-recall learning may involve only one kind of organizational process. Wood (1971a) investigated whether the process of forming large memory units is similar to the process of forming small memory units. More specifically, the study investigated whether forcing subjects to reorganize large memory units produced the same negative effect as is obtained when subjects are forced to reorganize small memory units. Numerous studies have demonstrated that forcing subjects to reorganize small memory units impairs free recall performance.

A whole-part transfer paradigm was used to assess the effect of forcing subjects to reorganize large memory units. List 1 contained 18 categories of three words each, and List 2 contained 9 categories of three words each. The experimental subjects received all 27 List 2 words in List 1. Even though the within-category organization established during List 1 learning was appropriate for List 2 learning, the negative effect due to the inappropriate between-category organization offset or overpowered the positive effect of within-category organization. The effect of forcing subjects to reorganize memory units does not depend on the size of the memory unit. Thus, the view that subjects develop discrete higher-order memory units and a retrieval plan to move from one higher-order memory unit to another lacks support. There is no evidence that the process involved in moving from one memory unit to the next is any different than the process involved in increasing the size of a single unit. It is true that subjects may form more memory units than they can recall, but only when they are encouraged to form a large number of small memory units. There is no evidence that subjects form more memory units than they can recall when "unrelated" words are presented consecutively during the study trials. The fact that subjects form more memory units than they can recall when related words are presented consecutively does not necessarily mean that subjects attempt to form discrete memory units during free recall. The subjects may be attempting to form one large memory unit, but they fail in this attempt because linking words between categories is considerably more difficult than link-ing words within a category. In short, the grouping operations involved in forming a higher-order memory unit may be identical to the grouping operations involved in "moving" from one unit to another. Therefore, it may be more accurate to conceptualize free-recall learning as the process of forming one large higher-order memory unit.

Even though the same mechanism may be responsible for forming memory units and moving between memory units, it is still likely that subjects form discrete memory units during free recall, particularly during the early stages of learning. The number of discrete memory units formed should be influenced by the nature of the to-be-recalled material. If the to-be-recalled material includes words from many different categories, discrete memory units are likely to be formed. The discrete memory units are likely to be formed early in learning since it is easier, in general, to encode words from the same category than between categories. At the later stages of learning, the subjects should link the discrete higher-order memory units. Even though the words may be formed into a single higher-order memory unit at the later stages of learning, it could be argued that, in one sense, the organization consists of two or more discrete units. That is, since the recall of items belonging to the same category is likely to be more dependent (more resistant to interference) than the recall of items from different categories, one could argue that more than one discrete unit is formed. Also, if one considers all the events that a normal adult stores, there can be little question that memory processes involve a great many discrete memory units. Although we have the capacity to generate links between any two stored events if we are *given* both events, the differential effectiveness of retrieval cues for *recall* indicates events are stored or retrieved in discrete units.

The notion that the same mechanism is responsible for the recall of memory units and items within memory units has an implication for theories which postulate multilevel storage systems. Namely, the mechanism responsible for the storage and retrieval of an event is probably the same regardless of the level of the event in the hierarchy. Given that the same mechanism is involved, it may not be theoretically useful to postulate a multilevel storage system. On the other hand, the view that the same mechanism is involved at different levels in the hierarchy does not provide any support or refutation of the assertion that the storage of events involves multiple levels. Evidence for a multilevel view of memory storage must come from other sources.

Free-recall learning can be viewed as involving a two-level storage system. The to-be-recalled material is organized into clusters and stored at one level, and labels for the clusters are stored at a different level. Retrieval from storage is accomplished by using the stored labels. The argument for the storage and use of labels is based on the subjective reports of subjects. Subjects were asked to give a one word label for each associative category that they used to organize the to-be-recalled material. The subjects tended to form larger clusters for the easier-to-learn lists (high interitem associative strength) and reported less ambiguous labels for the word clusters of the easier lists (Matthews & Manasse, 1970). This evidence, although correlational, gives some support for a two-level storage system. Other evidence supports the view that subjects can give labels for the memory units they form, and the presence of these labels at recall facilitates recall (Dong & Kintsch, 1968). However, it does not follow, necessarily, that the storage of clusters and labels involves two different storage levels. Associating the labels with the clusters may occur after the subject has stored the clusters, or the labels may be stored at the same level as an element of each cluster. That is, the process involved in storing labels may not be any different than the process involved in storing words in a cluster. The label may be stored along with the "appropriate" cluster, but, at recall, the subject deletes the category label. Regardless of the "location" of the label in storage, there is no evidence that category labels are more effective retrieval cues for stored clusters (memory units) than elements of memory units (Hudson & Austin, 1970).

PROVIDING A RETRIEVAL PLAN

Although providing subjects with a hierarchical organization (Bower, Clark, Lesgold, & Winzenz, 1969), a pegword mnemonic (Wood, 1967a), or retrieval cues (Tulving & Pearlstone, 1966) can have a powerful effect on recall, attempts to provide subjects with a means to link "unrelated" memory units during the study trial have been only partially successful. Bower, Lesgold, and Tieman (1969) attempted to facilitate the retrieval of higher-order memory units by arranging for structural linkage between memory units via a common element. The control list was identical to the linked list except that no two clusters shared a common element. The subjects who received the linked list were superior to the subjects who received the control list for the first trial, only. Thus, providing a means to move between units had only a small effect on recall. The present author and Joyce Pennington conducted three experiments in an attempt to demonstrate that providing a retrieval plan can have a marked facilitative effect on recall.

Experiment I

The presentation order of the list was manipulated in an attempt to assess the effects of providing subjects with a means to move from one higher-order memory unit to another. Alternately, if the reader prefers to consider the linking of memory units as a means of increasing the size or decreasing the number of units, this experiment investigated the effect of varying the size or the number of experimenter-defined memory units on free-recall learning. All subjects received the same list of 55 words. For the 5 E-Unit Group, the list of 55 words was divided into five units of 11 words each. Each 11-word unit contained four pairs of related words (e.g., aunt, cousin; nun, pope) and three ambiguous words to link the pairs of related words. The ambiguous words were presented in all capital letters when they were expected to be used as links between memory units. For example, one 11-word unit was comprised of the words: aunt, cousin, SISTER, nun, pope, CARDINAL, robin, bluejay, LARK, spree, frolic. For the 10 E-Unit Group, each 11 word unit was divided into two units by changing the presentation order (e.g., aunt, cousin, SISTER, nun, pope, cardinal; spree, frolic, LARK, robin, bluejay). For the 20 E-Unit Group, related words were presented consecutively, but ambiguous words were not expected to be used as links between memory units (e.g., aunt, cousin, sister; lark, spree, frolic; robin, bluejay; nun, pope, cardinal). For the Random Group, the presentation order was random with the restriction that obviously related words were not presented consecutively.

Each subject was given a booklet which contained an instruction page, study pages, and test pages. The list of 55 words was printed on each study page. There were spaces between experimenter defined units, and the ambiguous words were printed in all capital letters when they were expected to be used as links between memory units. The subjects in the experimental conditions were told that the ambiguous words (in all capital letters) could be used to link groups of related words. There were six alternating study and test trials. Each study trial was 55 seconds, and each test trial was 165 seconds.

The mean number of words correctly recalled for Experiment I (see Figure 4) gives little support for the view that providing ambiguous words as links between memory units has much effect on free-recall learning. There was only a small, nonsignificant difference in the recall of the three experimental groups. The fact that the Random Group had slightly lower performance than the three experimental groups is of little interest since numerous studies have revealed that a constrained presentation order results in higher performance than a random order. The failure of the ambiguous words to serve as effective links between memory units may be due to separate encoding of the two meanings of each ambiguous word. If the two meanings are encoded separately, there is little reason to expect the ambiguous words to serve as effective links between memory units. The problem of separate representations of a "single" event is discussed in greater detail in the nature of memory section.

Experiment II

The effect of providing a retrieval plan was assessed further by giving experimental subjects a retrieval plan prior to the presentation of the

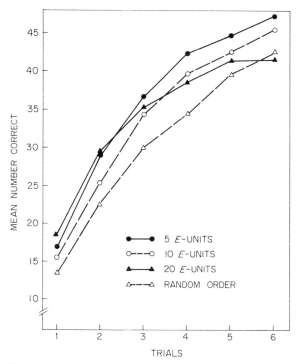

Fig. 4. The mean number of words correctly recalled for the six free recall trials in Experiment I.

free-recall list. All subjects learned a list of 18 category names, and then a list of 54 category instances, three instances per category. The List 1 category names for the experimental subjects were appropriate for the List 2 category instances. The List 1 category names for the control subjects were unrelated to the List 2 category instances. List 2 was identical for all subjects. The experimental subjects were told that the first list (category names) was an outline for List 2, and that List 2 would consist of three words from each of the List 1 categories. The category names were presented along with the category instances for the List 2 study trials, but the subjects were instructed that they would only be asked to recall the category instances.

Each subject received a booklet containing instruction pages, study pages, and test pages. For List 1 learning, the experimental subjects received study pages on which 18 category names were printed. There were three blank lines below each category name. The experimental subjects were told that the first list was an outline for List 2 since List 2 would consist of three words from each of the categories listed. The control subjects received a different list of 18 category names for List 1. All subjects were given four alternating study and test trials on List 1. Each study trial was 54 seconds, and each test trial was 54 seconds. For List 2, the study pages consisted of 18 category names printed in all capital letters and three instances from each of the categories printed in lower case letters below the appropriate category name. The subjects were instructed that they would only be asked to recall the category instances (words printed in lower case letters). All subjects were given five alternating study and test trials on List 2. Each study trial was 72 seconds, and each test trial was 270 seconds.

The mean number of words correctly recalled for the last trial of List 1 and the five trials of List 2 is presented in Figure 5. The experimental subjects were only slightly superior to the control subjects for the recall of List 2 category instances. The List 2 differences were not significant. However, if one assumes that the two lists of category names were of equal difficulty, the significant Conditions by Lists (List 1 versus List 2) interaction indicates that the increase from List 1 to List 2 was greater for the experimental than for the control subjects. Yet, the support for the importance of providing subjects with a retrieval plan is weak since the magnitude of the effect was small and dependent on the assumption that the two lists of category names were of equal difficulty.

The failure to find a marked superiority for experimental subjects was quite surprising. Since it is well established that providing category names as retrieval cues can markedly facilitate recall, we expected that having subjects learn the appropriate category names prior to learning the category instances would also have a powerful effect. The failure to obtain a powerful effect by providing a retrieval plan and the previous failure to support the view that free recall involves two distinct organizational processes led us to believe that the directness of the retrieval plan was an important consideration. If recall depends upon one kind of organizational process, then retrieval plans which involved the direct linking of to-be-recalled items should be more effective than plans which link items by using extra-list items (e.g., category names).

Experiment III

The purpose of this experiment was to demonstrate that retrieval plans which involve a direct linking of "unrelated" memory units can have a powerful facilitative effect on recall. All subjects were told to study the same 36 words for List 1. The experimental subjects received the 36 words in the context of four sentences. The nine words to be recalled

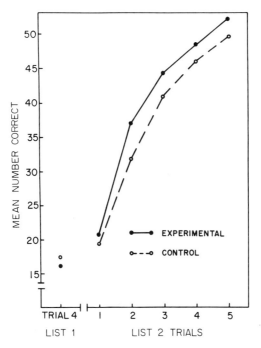

Fig. 5. The mean number of words correctly recalled for the last trial of List 1 and the five trials of List 2 for the experimental and control subjects in Experiment II.

in each sentence were printed in all capital letters; the filler words and "inappropriate" suffixes were printed in lower case. The sentences were not particularly well integrated semantically. For example, one sentence was: "The SCOTCH RULER WATCHed the BLUE CARDINAL TIE the BASS to the FLY ROD." There were two blank lines below each of the 36 to-be-recalled words for the experimental subjects. The experimental subjects were instructed that the sentences presented during List 1 would provide an outline of List 2 in that, for List 2, each line under the List 1 capitalized words would be replaced with a word related to the capitalized word. All subjects received 36 groups of three words each (e.g., Scotch, Dutch, German; Ruler, King, Prince) for List 2. Since the experimental subjects were given four sentences which contained one word from each List 2 category for List 1, they were provided with a direct means to move from one higher-order memory unit to another during List 2 recall. The control subjects were not told about the List 1-List 2 relationship, and their List 1 presentation order consisted of four columns of nine words each. The words in each column were identical to the capitalized words in one of the sentences, and were in the same order given to the experimental subjects. Each subject received a booklet containing instruction pages, study pages, and test pages. There were four alternating study and test trials on List 1. Each study trial was 72 seconds, and each test trial was 108 seconds. There were also four alternating study and test trials for the 108 words of List 2. Each study trial was 108 seconds. The test trials were 3, 4, 6, and 6 minutes for trials 1–4 respectively.

The results support the view that providing subjects with a retrieval plan can facilitate recall in that the experimental subjects were clearly superior to the control subjects on List 2 learning (see Figure 6). The magnitude of the effect for Experiment III (mean of about 20 items) is somewhat greater than the magnitude of the effect for Experiment II (mean of from 2–4 items). Obviously, there are many possible interpretations of the results for Experiments II and III since the experimental procedures differed in many respects. My preference is to interpret the two experiments as support for the view that a retrieval plan which directly links memory units is more effective than a plan which links units by using extra-list items. Assuming that the relationship between the directness and effectiveness of a retrieval plan is reliable, the process of developing an effective retrieval plan is similar to the process of forming a large memory unit. Thus, there is little support for the view that noncued free-recall learning involves two distinct organizational processes.

RETRIEVAL PLANS AND HIERARCHICAL ORGANIZATION

The purpose of a retrieval plan is to provide the subject with a set of retrieval cues for the to-be-recalled material. Retrieval schemes such as mnemonic systems involving the use of a well-memorized list of cues are very effective high-level retrieval plans. Although there is ample evidence that the use of mnemonic systems can markedly facilitate recall (cf. Bower, 1970b; Bugelski, Kidd, & Segmen, 1968; Senter & Hauser, 1968; Wood, 1967a), mnemonic systems are not effective for all kinds of material. Bower (1970a) indicates that forming higher-order memory units is a low-level retrieval plan; associating two higher-order units is a slightly higher-level retrieval plan. Although these retrieval plans are considered to be low level, they are more general than the mnemonic system type in that they can be used to recall many kinds of verbal material. Moreover, in some cases at least, the memory units may be

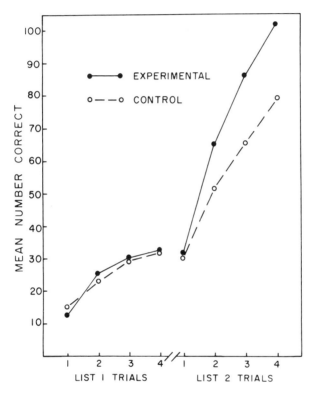

Fig. 6. The mean number of words correctly recalled by experimental and control subjects for Lists 1 and 2 in Experiment III.

organized in such a way that the subject has an excellent retrieval plan. If the to-be-remembered material is organized in a hierarchical fashion, then the hierarchical order provides the means for subjects to move from one memory unit to the next, or a way to form one large memory unit. Bower et al. (1969) and Cohen and Bousfield (1956) found that recall was better for hierarchically organized material. In the Bower et al. study, recall was 2–3 times better for the hierarchical organization than for the random presentation. Other investigators (Preusser &

Handel, 1970; Segal, 1969) have demonstrated that subjects use the hierarchical arrangement inherent in the to-be-recalled material.

The higher recall of material presented in a hierarchical order and the tendency to recall material in a hierarchical order suggests that hierarchical retrieval plans are effective, but the evidence does not necessarily mean that retrieval or storage processes are hierarchical. If one presents ten sentences of ten words each and asks subjects to recall the ten sentences, it is likely that recall will be higher and more sentence-like than if one presents the same 100 words in a random order. However, it does not follow that storage and retrieval processes are sentence-like. It is clear that more evidence is needed to establish the importance of hierarchical processes. Perhaps other approaches such as the investigation of retrieval time from semantic memory (cf. Collins & Quillian, 1969, 1970) or different analyses of sorting data (cf. Miller, 1969) will provide this evidence.

The Nature of Organization and the Storage-Retrieval Distinction

The importance of cues for recall supports the need to make a distinction between storage and retrieval processes, but it is not clear whether organization influences storage, retrieval, or both. The attempts to assess the influence of organizational processes on storage and retrieval have not been particularly successful partially because there does not appear to be any way to directly assess storage. (Recent evidence indicates that retrieval processes are involved in recognition learning.) The criticisms of Slamecka's studies in this chapter and in Postman's chapter also suggest that it may be impossible to determine whether storage is independent (i.e., whether organization influences retrieval only). An additional problem is a lack of consensus regarding what is meant by organizational processes.

Organizational processes can be viewed as grouping operations which result in the direct linking of the to-be-recalled events. In this case, organization can be considered as nothing more than a label for a specific set of associations which link the to-be-recalled events. An alternate position is to view organization as a "frame of reference" which affords subjects a basis for processing new information. For example, organization may involve the formation of a retrieval plan, the success of which is independent of the characteristics of the to-be-recalled material. There is no compelling evidence to support either view. If subjects memorize a list of retrieval cues (pegword mnemonic), the "presence" of retrieval cues is likely to result in facilitated recall. Yet, pegword systems are effective for only limited kinds of material, and it is necessary to spend considerable time memorizing the retrieval cues. Besides, a pegword mnemonic can be viewed as a "grouping operation" to link the to-be-recalled events. Obviously, if one selects one's materials carefully, one can facilitate recall by informing subjects about the "appropriate" organization, but this finding only supports the view that some arrangements of events are easier to learn than others. In some studies, subjects provided with advanced organizers were able to perform better than control subjects not given the advanced organizers (Ausubel & Fitzgerald, 1962). However, these studies can be criticized because the control subjects were not given extra time on the to-be-recalled material to compensate for the time the experimental subjects spent on the advanced organizer (Peeck, 1970). In short, there does not appear to be any evidence, nor does there appear to be any way to obtain evidence, which would demonstrate, conclusively, that organization is better considered as a "frame of reference" than as a specific set of associations. Given the lack of agreement regarding the nature of organization and the difficulty of directly assessing storage, it will be extremely difficult, if not impossible, to reach agreement concerning the relationship of organizational processes to storage and retrieval.

The Nature of Memory

There seems to be agreement among the contributors to this book that attributes of the to-be-recalled material are encoded. If attributes are processed, then it follows that the same event can be represented in two or more ways. If there is multiple representation of events, then memory theorists need to consider the nature and number of attributes encoded, the factors which influence the attributes encoded, the relative importance of various attributes, the relationship between organizational processes and attributes of memory, etc. Given multiple representations of events, the number of ways events can be organized should be markedly increased. And it is expected that the organization of the to-be-recalled events (experimenter-imposed organization) should be an important determiner of the attributes of memory and the relationship between organizational processes and attributes of memory. The discussion of attributes of memory is limited primarily to acoustic and semantic attributes and emphasizes research in which the to-be-recalled material is the same for all subjects. For a detailed discussion of attributes of memory see Underwood (1969).

ATTRIBUTES OF MEMORY

There is ample evidence for the view that attributes of events are encoded. The studies in which the to-be-recalled material was held constant and subjects were encouraged to encode different attributes of the material are particularly convincing. Bower (1970a) reported an unpublished study by Bobrow and Light in which ambiguous words were used. Each ambiguous word (e.g., cardinal) could be classified according to two categories (e.g., clergy and birds). If the context was such that subjects classified the word according to one category (e.g., cardinal, priest, minister) the category label appropriate to the context (e.g., clergy) was an effective retrieval cue; the other category label (e.g., birds) was not an effective retrieval cue. Bobrow (1970) used ambiguous noun pairs (e.g., bark-pitcher) as the subject and direct object of sentences. The major manipulation was the context in which the noun pairs were placed (rest of the sentence). For recall, subjects were presented the subject of the sentence and asked to give as much of the sentence as they could. The main finding was that the effect of a repeated presentation of the noun pairs had little effect on recall when the context was changed so that subjects would be likely to encode different semantic attributes on successive presentations. The effect of changing the sentence context without "changing" the semantic attributes of the nouns had about the same effect as keeping the context constant for successive repetitions. Thus, there is strong evidence that context can influence the attribute encoded.

The view that attributes are stored and that context manipulations are important determiners of the particular attributes stored has implications for two issues. Slamecka's evidence for the independence of items in storage is based on the results of studies in which subjects were provided list words as retrieval cues for other list words. Although it was asserted earlier that the results of the cueing studies can be accounted for by making a distinction between the availability and accessibility of higher-order memory units, the results can also be assigned to the effect of context on attributes stored. Let us assume that there are two or more attributes of each word that can be encoded, and that the context of each word (e.g., adjacent words in the list) is an important determiner of the attribute(s) encoded. Thus, each word in the list is, at least to some extent, like an ambiguous word (e.g., cardinal). If the attribute encoded (cardinal as a member of the clergy) is not the attribute that is "generated" (cardinal as a bird) when the word is presented as a retrieval cue, then there is little reason to expect the list word to serve as an effective retrieval cue for other list words. Theorists who argue that list words should serve as retrieval cues for other list words if storage is dependent, implicitly assume that subjects store the to-be-recalled material or the dominant attribute of the material. This assumption does not appear to be valid. Voss makes a similar argument in his chapter. Another issue related to attribute and context effects is whether constant encoding or varied encoding results in better recall. The present author recently investigated the effect of "multiple" versus "single" encoding of ambiguous words on free-recall learning.

Experiment IV

The purpose of the study was to investigate the effect of context on the amount and ordering of recall. The list for all subjects consisted of 11 ambiguous words and two words from each of 22 categories for a total of 55 words. Each ambiguous word (e.g., cardinal) could be classified according to two categories (e.g., clergy and birds). For one group, the ambiguous words were always presented in the same context (e.g., PRIEST, CARDINAL, MINISTER; or, ROBIN, CARDINAL, SPARROW). For the other group, the ambiguous words appeared in one context (e.g., PRIEST, CARDINAL, MINISTER) on the even-number study trials, and in a different context (e.g., ROBIN, CAR-DINAL, SPARROW) for the odd-numbered study trials. Words belonging to the same category were presented consecutively on the study page, and there were blank spaces between categories. Each category contained either two or three words. For example, if cardinal was presented in the clergy category (priest, cardinal, minister), then robin and sparrow were the only instances of the bird category. The presentation order of the categories was random, with the restriction that categories which could be linked by one of the ambiguous words (e.g., clergy and birds) were not presented consecutively. Except for the limitation imposed by the design, the presentation orders were identical for the constant- and varied-context subjects. Each subject received a booklet which contained an instruction page, study pages, and test pages. All subjects received six alternating study and test trials. Each study trial was 55 seconds, and each test trial was 165 seconds. Standard free recall instructions were given to all subjects.

Although the constant-context subjects recalled slightly more ambiguous words (mean of 43.5 versus 42.0) and total words (mean of 214.2 versus 193.9) for the six free recall trials, the differences were not significant. However, there was a strong context effect on the order of recall. The extent to which the context manipulation influenced the ordering of recall was assessed by counting the number of ambiguous words used as links between categories. Each ambiguous word could be an instance of two of the 22 categories. The question is whether the instances of the two categories to which each ambiguous word could be classified were recalled consecutively. If the instances from the two categories were recalled consecutively and the appropriate ambiguous word was one of the instances recalled, then the ambiguous word was considered to be the link between the two categories. For the constant-context subjects, the mean number of ambiguous words which served as links did not exceed one for any of the six recall trials. For the varied-context subjects, the mean number of ambiguous words which served as links was .28, 1.57, 1.57, 3.00, 4.07, and 5.43 for Trials 1–6, respectively. In short, the ambiguous words were used as links between categories in the varied-context condition only. Yet, the linking of categories with ambiguous words did not influence the amount of recall. This study provides further evidence that order of output and recall are not necessarily related. More important, the results indicate that recalling an event is not influenced particularly by whether there is "single" or "multiple" encoding. The latter finding has to be interpreted with caution, however, because other evidence suggests that context effects can influence the amount of recall.

Given that context manipulations influence the attributes encoded, the superiority of constant over varied presentation orders for free-recall learning may be due to the encoding of the same attributes of the to-be-recalled material on successive trials. Since it is unlikely that subjects attempt to encode words singly, it is probably better to ask whether forming unique, nonoverlapping memory units (each event represented in only one memory unit) results in better performance than forming overlapping memory units (each event represented in more than one memory unit). The Bower et al. (1969b) study provides strong evidence that forming unique, nonoverlapping memory units results in higher recall. The authors used a list of 24 words presented in six groups of four each. Each subject was given cards on which four words were printed. The subjects were instructed to construct a visual image which included the four objects named. One group received the same grouping of the words for successive trials. The other group received an order such that no two words were on the same card more than once. The performance of subjects who received the same four tuples for successive trials was markedly superior to that of subjects who were given changed groupings. In some cases, however, a variation in encoding may be responsible for improved recall.

The crux of the encoding-variation hypothesis is that subjects are likely to encode the same event differently if there is a change in context between the first and second presentation (Melton, 1967). If there is a lag between the presentations of a repeated word, then the context for the second presentation and presumably the attributes encoded should differ for the two presentations. Madigan (1969) assessed whether the encoding-variation hypothesis accounts for the finding that the probability of recalling a repeated word increases as the number of intervening words (lag) increases. Madigan varied the cue word (same versus different) for the two presentations of a repeated word. The cue words were presented for both study and test trials. In general, having a different cue word eliminated the lag effect, but the cue effect (same versus different) did not influence amount recalled.

In sum, it is not clear how encoding variation influences free-recall learning. The fact that constant presentation orders result in higher recall than varied orders indicates that constant encoding is superior to varied. Yet, the lag effect phenomenon, the lack of a context effect on recall in Experiment IV, and the lack of a correlation between output order and recall suggest that we have much to learn about the effects of multiple representation. Having failed to provide an adequate solution to the problem of encoding variation, we will now consider different types of attributes.

There is evidence to support the view that many different attributes of the to-be-recalled material may be stored (see Underwood, 1969). The importance of a particular attribute is believed to be dependent on the nature of the to-be-recalled material and the memory task. For example, as the meaningfulness of the to-be-recalled material increases, associative verbal attributes are believed to become more important and acoustic attributes less important. Also, the problem of assessing the relative importance of various attributes is complicated by the fact that different kinds of attributes may not be independent. .For example, Underwood points out that if a subject remembers the acoustic attributes of the to-be-recalled material he may be able to reconstruct the orthographic attributes. Thus, assessing the relationships among the attributes of the to-be-recalled material is likely to be a very difficult problem. Fortunately, it may not be necessary to study the relationships among attributes. If all or most attributes can be "computed" from one or two basic attributes (e.g., semantic, acoustic), then it may only be necessary to study the basic attributes. The first issue to be considered is whether semantic attributes are the basic attributes of long-term memory.

Until recently, the popular view of memory was that acoustic coding was a temporary phenomenon limited to short-term memory, and semantic attributes were important for long-term memory (see Norman, 1969). It is becoming increasingly apparent, however, that acoustic properties can play a role in retrieval from long-term memory. Bruce and

Crowley (1970) varied whether words were semantically related (e.g., bean, carrot, corn, potato), acoustically related (e.g., gain, cane, reign, vein), or unrelated acoustically and semantically. The critical words were presented consecutively in early input positions, late input positions, or distributed throughout the list. The semantically similar words were recalled better than the control words, regardless of the order of presentation. The acoustically similar words were recalled better than the control words at the early and late input conditions, but not for the distributed conditions. Thus, acoustic coding can occur in long-term memory. The fact that the acoustically similar words were not better recalled than control words when they were distributed in the list may mean that subjects are unlikely to recognize acoustic similarity unless the acoustically similar words are presented consecutively. Other investigators have reported evidence consistent with the view that acoustic encoding can be important for long-term memory (e.g., King & Forrester, 1970; Wickens, Ory, & Graf, 1970). The present author has investigated the effects of acoustic versus semantic encoding on free-recall learning by presenting the same to-be-recalled material to all subjects.

Experiment V

All subjects were presented with a list of the same 40 words and asked to sort the words into categories. The words were selected so that they could be sorted into semantic categories (animal, transportation, weather, etc.) or rhyming categories (e.g., bale, nail, pail, gale, ale; lane, chain, vein, brain, crane). The words to be sorted were printed in four columns on the top part of the sorting page. All subjects received the same random orders of the words. The semantic-sort subjects were given the category names and told to sort the words by writing each word under the appropriate category name. The acoustic-sort subjects were told to sort the words into categories of words that rhyme. All subjects sorted the words twice. Following the sorting task, all subjects were asked to recall the list words. The acoustic-sort subjects clustered their recall according to acoustic categories; the semantic-sort subjects clustered their recall according to semantic categories. The semantic-sort subjects recalled significantly more words (26.18 versus 19.53) than the acoustic-sort subjects. Yet, the fact that the acoustic-sort subjects recalled a substantial number of words is consistent with the view that subjects can encode acoustic attributes in long-term memory. The results can be interpreted as support for the importance of semantic attributes relative to acoustic attributes in long-term memory. Or, if one prefers to account for differences in performance in terms of organization, it could be argued that semantic grouping results in a better organization than acoustic grouping.

The fact that events can be stored in long-term memory by acoustic representation argues against the separation of short-term and long-term memory on the basis of the type of attribute encoded. In addition to the evidence for acoustic encoding in long-term memory, there are logical grounds for rejecting the view that different attributes are encoded for long-term and short-term memory. Namely, the view of direct and complete intercommunication between the short-term and long-term stores is inconsistent with the assertion that there are different modes of representation in the two stores (Gruneberg & Sykes, 1969). Thus, there is little reason to expect that the memory processes involved in acoustic representation are any different than the processes involved in semantic representation. Another way to determine if the processes for acoustic and semantic representation are similar is to determine if the effect of grouping operations depends on the type of attribute subjects are encouraged to encode.

ORGANIZATION AND ATTRIBUTES OF MEMORY

Experiment VI

The study was designed to test the notion that grouping related items is more important for acoustically than semantically related items. Bruce and Crowley (1970) found that semantically related words were recalled better than control words regardless of order of presentation. However, this was not the case for acoustically related words. This finding suggests that the effect of grouping related words should be greater if acoustic properties are encoded than if semantic properties are encoded. It may be that acoustically related items must be presented consecutively for subjects to recognize the "common" attribute, or that grouping is more important for the storage of acoustic than semantic attributes.

All subjects received the same list of words. The words could be organized according to semantic properties (e.g., parole, jail, kidnapping, trial), or sound properties such as a long O-sound as in foam and open or a K-sound as in cake and kitchen. The design was a 2×2 factorial in which the basis for processing (semantic versus acoustic) and the type of activity (classification versus grouping) were the variables manipulated. All subjects were given either the semantic categories or the sound categories into which they were to classify or sort the words. The sort subjects were instructed to write the words under the appropriate category labels (either sound labels or semantic labels). The classification subjects were given the 36 words in three columns of 12 words each. There was a blank line beside each word for the subjects to write the sound category (e.g., O-sound, K-sound), or the semantic label (e.g., law, medicine). It was expected that the sort-subjects would be more likely to group related words than the classify-subjects. The subjects classified or sorted the words twice. Following the sorting or classifying task, all subjects were asked to recall the words.

The mean number of words correctly recalled was 23.50, 11.67, 18.83, and 8.83 for the semantic-sort, acoustic-sort, semantic-classify, and acoustic-classify subjects, respectively. The effect of activity and attribute processed were both significant, but the interaction was not significant. Since the effect of attribute processed did not depend on the extent to which the words were grouped, it is not necessary to formulate additional theoretical notions to account for the effect of kind of attribute processed. It can be argued that the type of attribute effect is due to the ease of forming words into higher-order memory units and retrieving these memory units. Encoding semantic attributes probably results in greater recall because much of our long-term verbal processing involves semantic rather than acoustic grouping.

Epilogue

The last decade of research on organizational processes in free recall has resulted in increased understanding of the storage and use of events. The view that subjects increase the amount of their recall by increasing the size of a limited number of memory units seems to adequately account for the processing of certain kinds of events. It is useful to make a distinction between the availability and accessibility of events, and a distinction between the recall of memory units and items within memory units. The same mechanism is probably involved in the recall of memory units and items within memory units. With respect to the nature of memory, there is general agreement that individuals encode attributes of the to-be-recalled materials, and there is some evidence to suggest that the effect of grouping operations does not depend on the particular attributes encoded. The presentation order of the material can have a marked effect on the kind of attribute encoded.

Although organization theory is consistent with much of the evidence from free recall studies, there are many unresolved issues. It cannot be claimed that organization is the only viable theory because the evidence can also be interpreted within an associationistic framework. There does not appear to be general agreement regarding the nature of organization, and the general range of organization theory has not been determined. There is a need to develop more adequate measures of organization or procedures which will allow a more accurate assessment of the role of organizational processes in event memory. Finally, students of memory must be cognizant of the fact that our present techniques may limit the kinds of problems we can solve. For example, I believe it is unlikely that our current procedures will enable us to assess the relative importance of cue dependent and trace dependent forgetting, or to determine whether organization influences storage or retrieval processes. Hopefully, our present techniques will enable investigators of "intelligent" uses of event memory to understand the nature of semantic memory. Then it should be possible to formulate and test theories of memory which account for both "intelligent" and "nonintelligent" uses of event memory. This promises to be an exciting endeavor.

References

Adams, J. A. *Human Memory*. New York: McGraw-Hill, 1967.
Allen, M. M. Rehearsal strategies and response cueing as determinants of organization in free recall. *Journal of Verbal Learning and Verbal Behavior*, 1968, **7**, 58–63.
Allen, M. M. Cueing, and retrieval in free recall. *Journal of Experimental Psychology*, 1969, **81**, 29–35.
Ausubel, D. P. & Fitzgerald, D. Organizer, general background and antecedent learning variables in sequential verbal learning. *Journal of Educational Psychology*, 1962, **53**, 243–249.
Birnbaum, I. M. Free-recall learning as a function of prior-list organization. *Journal of Verbal Learning and Verbal Behavior*, 1968, **7**, 1037–1042.
Birnbaum, I. M. Prior-list organization in part-whole free-recall learning. *Journal of Verbal Learning and Verbal Behavior*, 1969, **8**, 836–838.
Bobrow, S. A. Memory for words in sentences. *Journal of Verbal Learning and Verbal Behavior*, 1970, **9**, 363–372.
Bousfield, A. K., & Bousfield, W. A. Measurement of clustering and of sequential constancies in repeated free recall. *Psychological Reports*, 1966, **19**, 935–942.
Bousfield, W. A., & Cohen, B. H. Clustering in recall as a function of the number of word categories in the stimulus word list. *Journal of General Psychology*, 1956, **55**, 95–107.
Bousfield, W. A., & Rosner, S. R. Free vs. uninhibited recall. *Psychonomic Science*, 1970, **20**, 75–76.
Bower, G. H. Chunks as interference units in free recall. *Journal of Verbal Learning and Verbal Behavior*, 1969, **8**, 610–613.
Bower, G. H. Organizational factors in memory. *Cognitive Psychology*, 1970, **1**, 18–46. (a)
Bower, G. H. Analysis of a mnemonic device. *American Scientist*, 1970, **58**, 496–510. (b)
Bower, G. H., Clark, M. C., Lesgold, A. M., & Winzenz, D. Hierarchical retrieval schemes in recall of categorized word lists. *Journal of Verbal Learning and Verbal Behavior*, 1969, **8**, 323–343. (a)

Bower, G. H., & Lesgold, A. M. Organization as a determinant of part-to-whole transfer in free recall. *Journal of Verbal Learning and Verbal Behavior*, 1969, **8**, 501–506. (b)

Bower, G. H., Lesgold, A. M., & Tieman, D. Grouping operations in free recall. *Journal of Verbal Learning and Verbal Behavior*, 1969, **8**, 481–493.

Bruce, D., & Crowley, J. J. Acoustic similarity effects on retrieval from secondary memory. *Quarterly Journal of Experimental Psychology*, 1970, **9**, 190–196.

Bugelski, B. R., Kidd, E., & Segmen, J. Image as a mediator in one-trial paired-associate learning. *Journal of Experimental Psychology*, 1968, **76**, 69–73.

Carterette, E. C., & Coleman, E. A. Organization in free recall. Paper presented at the meeting of the Psychonomic Society, Bryn Mawr, Pennsylvania, August, 1963.

Cohen, B. H. Recall of categorized word lists. *Journal of Experimental Psychology*, 1963, **66**, 227–234.

Cohen, B. H. Some-or-none characteristics of coding behavior. *Journal of Verbal Learning and Verbal Behavior*, 1966, **5**, 182–187.

Cohen, B. H., & Bousfield, W. A. The effects of a dual-level stimulus word list on the occurrence of clustering in recall. *Journal of General Psychology*, 1956, **55**, 51–58.

Collins, A. M., & Quillian, M. R. Retrieval time from semantic memory. *Journal of Verbal Learning and Verbal Behavior*, 1969, **8**, 240–247.

Collins, A. M., & Quillian, M. R. Does category size affect categorization time? *Journal of Verbal Learning and Verbal Behavior*, 1970, **9**, 432–437.

Dallett, K. M. Number of categories and category information in free recall. *Journal of Experimental Psychology*, 1964, **68**, 1–12.

Dong, T., & Kintsch, W. Subjective retrieval cues in free recall. *Journal of Verbal Learning and Verbal Behavior*, 1968, **7**, 813–816.

Earhard, M. Subjective organization and list organization as determinants of free recall and serial recall memorization. *Journal of Verbal Learning and Verbal Behavior*, 1967, **6**, 501–507.

Earhard, M., & Endicott, O. Why are there individual differences in subjective organization during free-recall memorization? *Journal of Verbal Learning and Verbal Behavior*, 1969, **8**, 316–319.

Freund, J. S., & Underwood, B. J. Storage and retrieval cues in free recall learning. *Journal of Experimental Psychology*, 1969, **81**, 49–53.

Gorfein, D. S., & Blair, C. Factors affecting multiple trial free recall. *Journal of Educational Psychology*, 1971, **62**, 17–24.

Gruneberg, M. N., & Sykes, R. N. Semantic and acoustic coding in short- and long-term memory. *Psychological Reports*, 1969, **25**, 849–850.

Higgins, J., & Basden, D. Memory and organization. *Proceedings of the 76th Annual Convention of the American Psychological Association*, 1968, **3**, 75–76.

Howe, M. J. A. Repeated presentation and recall of meaningful prose. *Journal of Educational Psychology*, 1970, **61**, 214–219.

Hudson, R. L., & Austin, J. B. Effect of context and category name on the recall of categorized word lists. *Journal of Experimental Psychology*, 1970, **86**, 43–47.

King, D. J., & Forrester, W. E. The influence of semantic and acoustic similarity on retention of short sentences. *Psychonomic Science*, 1970, **20**, 222–223.

Madigan, S. A. Intraserial repetition and coding processes in free recall. *Journal of Verbal Learning and Verbal Behavior*, 1969, **8**, 828–835.

Mandler, G. From association to structure. *Psychological Review*, 1962, **69**, 415–427.

Mandler, G. Organization and memory. In K. W. Spence & J. T. Spence (Eds.), *The Psychology of Learning and Motivation.* New York: Academic Press, 1967. Pp. 327–372.

Mandler, G. Organized recall: Individual functions. *Psychonomic Science,* 1968, 13, 235–236.

Mandler, G., & Dean, P. J. Seriation: The development of serial order in free recall. *Journal of Experimental Psychology,* 1969, 81, 207–215.

Mandler, G., & Pearlstone, Z. Free and constrained concept learning and subsequent recall. *Journal of Verbal Learning and Verbal Behavior,* 1966, 5, 126–131.

Mandler, G., & Stephens, D. The development of free and constrained conceptualization and subsequent verbal memory. *Journal of Experimental Child Psychology,* 1967, 5, 86–93.

Mathews, R. Recall as a function of number of classification categories. *Journal of Experimental Psychology,* 1954, 47, 241–247.

Matthews, W. A., & Manasse, K. Associative factors in free recall. *Quarterly Journal of Experimental Psychology,* 1970, 22, 177–184.

Mayhew, A. J. Interlist changes in subjective organization during free-recall learning. *Journal of Experimental Psychology,* 1967, 74, 425–430.

Melton, A. W. Repetition and retrieval from memory. *Science,* 1967, 158, 532.

Miller, G. A. The magical number seven plus or minus two: Some limits on our capacity for processing information. *Psychological Review,* 1956, 63, 81–97.

Miller, G. A. A psychological method to investigate verbal concepts. *Journal of Mathematical Psychology,* 1969, 6, 169–191.

Norman, D. A. *Memory and Attention.* New York: John Wiley, 1969.

Novinski, L. Part-whole and whole-part free recall learning. *Journal of Verbal Learning and Verbal Behavior,* 1969, 8, 152–154.

Ornstein, P. A. Role of prior-list organization in a free recall transfer task. *Journal of Experimental Psychology,* 1970, 86, 32–37.

Peeck, J. Effect of prequestions on delayed retention of prose material. *Journal of Educational Psychology,* 1970, 61, 241–246.

Postman, L. Effects of word frequency on acquisition and retention under conditions of free-recall learning. *Quarterly Journal of Experimental Psychology,* 1970, 22, 185–195.

Preusser, D., & Handel, S. The free classification of hierarchically and categorically related stimuli. *Journal of Verbal Learning and Verbal Behavior,* 1970, 9, 222–231.

Puff, C. R. An investigation of two forms of organization in free recall. *Journal of Verbal Learning and Verbal Behavior,* 1970, 9, 720–724.

Rosner, S. R. The effects of presentation and recall trials on organization in multitrial free recall. *Journal of Verbal Learning and Verbal Behavior,* 1970, 9, 69–74.

Segal, E. Hierarchical structure in free recall. *Journal of Experimental Psychology,* 1969, 80, 59–63.

Senter, R. J., & Hauser, G. K. An experimental study of a mnemonic system. *Psychonomic Science,* 1968, 10, 289–290.

Shapiro, S. I. Serial organization and prior free recall. *Canadian Journal of Psychology,* 1970, 24, 57–63.

Shapiro, S. I., & Bell, J. A. Subjective organization and free recall: Performance of high, moderate, and low organizers. *Psychonomic Science,* 1970, 21, 71–72.

Shuell, T. J. Retroactive inhibition in free-recall learning of categorized lists. *Journal of Verbal Learning and Verbal Behavior,* 1968, 7, 797–805.

Shuell, T. J. Clustering and organization in free recall. *Psychological Bulletin,* 1969, **72,** 353–374.

Slamecka, N. J. An examination of trace storage in free recall. *Journal of Experimental Psychology,* 1968, **76,** 504–513. (a)

Slamecka, N. J. Testing for associative storage in multitrial free recall. *Proceedings of the 76th Annual Convention of the American Psychological Association,* 1968, **3,** 71–72. (b)

Slamecka, N. J. Testing for associative storage in multitrial free recall. *Journal of Experimental Psychology,* 1969, **81,** 557–561.

Thompson, C. P., & Poling, D. R. Free recall of successive lists: Effect of category size and category repetition. *Psychonomic Science,* 1969, **16,** 201–202.

Thomson, D. M., & Tulving, E. Associative encoding and retrieval. *Journal of Experimental Psychology,* 1970, **86,** 255–262.

Tulving, E. Subjective organization in free recall of "unrelated" words. *Psychological Review,* 1962, **69,** 344–354.

Tulving, E. Intratrial and intertrial retention: Notes towards a theory of free-recall verbal learning. *Psychological Review,* 1964, **71,** 219–237.

Tulving, E. Subjective organization and effects of repetition in multitrial free-recall learning. *Journal of Verbal Learning and Verbal Behavior,* 1966, **5,** 193–198.

Tulving, E. Theoretical issues in free recall. In T. R. Dixon and D. L. Horton (Eds.), *Verbal Behavior and General Behavior Theory.* Englewood Cliffs, New Jersey: Prentice-Hall, 1968. Pp. 2–36.

Tulving, E., & Madigan, S. A. Memory and verbal learning. *Annual Review of Psychology,* 1970, **21,** 437–484.

Tulving, E., & Osler, S. Transfer effects in whole-part free-recall learning. *Canadian Journal of Psychology,* 1967, **21,** 253–262.

Tulving, E., & Patterson, R. D. Functional units and retrieval processes in free recall. *Journal of Experimental Psychology,* 1968, **77,** 239–248.

Tulving, E., & Pearlstone, Z. Availability versus accessibility of information in memory for words. *Journal of Verbal Learning and Verbal Behavior,* 1966, **5,** 381–391.

Tulving, E., & Psotka, J. Retroactive inhibition in free recall: Inaccessibility of information available in the memory store. *Journal of Experimental Psychology,* 1971, **87,** 1–8.

Underwood, B. J. Attributes of memory. *Psychological Review,* 1969, **76,** 559–573.

Wallace, W. P., & Nappe, G. W. Subjective organization following constant input order in multitrial free recall. *Psychonomic Science,* 1970, **18,** 115–117.

Watts, G. H., & Anderson, R. C. Retroactive inhibition in free recall as a function of first- and second-list organization. *Journal of Experimental Psychology,* 1969, **81,** 595–597.

Wickens, D. D., Ory, N. E., & Graf, S. A. Encoding by taxonomic and acoustic categories in long-term memory. *Journal of Experimental Psychology,* 1970, **84,** 462–469.

Winograd, E. List differentiation, recall, and category similarity. *Journal of Experimental Psychology,* 1968, **78,** 510–515.

Wood, G. Mnemonic systems in recall. *Journal of Educational Psychology,* 1967, **58** (6, Pt. 2), 1–27. (a)

Wood, G. Category names as cues for the recall of category instances. *Psychonomic Science,* 1967, **9,** 323–324. (b)

Wood, G. Whole-part transfer from free recall to serial learning. *Journal of Experimental Psychology*, 1969, **79**, 540–544. (a)

Wood, G. Higher order memory units and free recall learning. *Journal of Experimental Psychology*, 1969, **80**, 286–288. (b)

Wood, G. Whole-part transfer from paired associate to free recall learning. *Journal of Experimental Psychology*, 1969, **82**, 532–537. (c)

Wood, G. Retrieval cues and the accessibility of higher order memory units in multitrial free recall. *Journal of Verbal Learning and Verbal Behavior,* 1969, **8**, 782–789. (d)

Wood, G. Organization, retroactive inhibition, and free-recall learning. *Journal of Verbal Learning and Verbal Behavior,* 1970, **9**, 327–333.

Wood, G. Organization, large memory units, and free recall. *Journal of Verbal Learning and Verbal Behavior,* 1971, **10**, 52–56. (a)

Wood, G. Activity, organization, retroactive inhibition, and free recall. *Journal of Verbal Learning and Verbal Behavior,* 1971, **10**, 116–122. (b)

3 | A Selective Review of Organizational Factors in Memory[1]

Gordon H. Bower

Organization in Perception and Learning

It is a truism that we only remember our mental acts, our perceptions, thoughts, and imaginings. We do not remember events in the world,

[1] The author's research is supported by grant MH13950-04, from the National Institutes of Mental Health.

but rather our encoding or interpretation of those events. Our interpretation of stimulus events depends not only upon stimulus variables but also upon subjective factors such as our attitude, and our expectation or mental set established by the prior psychological context. Interest in organization and memory had its historical roots in Gestalt psychology, as Postman (this volume) notes. The Gestalt position was that the interpretation of an event results from certain organizational processes operating upon the sensory input. In vision, with which we will be mainly concerned, these processes are characterized by the so-called "Gestalt laws" of grouping and figure-ground segregation. These were pointed out by Wertheimer almost 50 years ago, and they formed a strong prong in the attack of Gestalt psychology (with its emergent wholes, field forces, nativistic organizing tendencies, structural meanings, and similar constructs) upon elementarism in stimulus-response psychology.

Memory can do little more than record the products of perception and thinking and thereby, perhaps, reshuffle its prior contents. But the implication follows, as Köhler (1940) clearly saw, that insofar as Gestalt laws of organization apply to the description of immediate perception, so do they also apply to delayed recall of earlier perceptions—to our memories of earlier stimuli. So far as I am aware, Solomon Asch (1969) is one of the few contemporary psychologists whose research has followed out these implications, on the "natural coherence" in memory of elements and properties of a (nonverbal) stimulus field. My research group has also done a few studies on verbal stimuli to which I shall refer presently.

Gestaltists, whether studying perception or memory, were addressing themselves to the "structure" of psychological elements. The terms structure or organization refer to the totality of relations holding among the elements in the set under consideration. Thus the basic terms of analysis are the *relation* between two or more elements, and the *group*, the latter refering to a collection of items connected by a common relation or sharing a common property. The Gestalt psychologists attempted to specify various physical bases for grouping of psychological elements in perception. The usual assumption has been that perceptual coherence and perceptual groupings of elements determines what is remembered about a stimulus field.

Laws of Grouping

Psychological elements customarily get grouped (classified, categorized, chunked) on the basis of common properties or relations. Grouping occurs at several different levels, from simple perceptual groupings (e.g., figure-ground segregation) through multiple-unit groupings (e.g., Nixon,

Agnew, and Humphrey, Muskie fall into two well-known groups) up to propositional groupings (e.g., arguments pro versus con an issue). The reason for discussing groupings is that these appear to be the basic units in memory. People's recall of sets or series of elements has characteristics predictable from the way they have grouped together subsets of the elements.

The main laws of grouping as they operate in memory experiments will be illustrated with recall of serially presented strings of elements. The illustrative experiments employ the immediate memory span procedure, in which elements such as letters or numbers are presented to the subject, following which he tries to recall them in their correct serial order. In such serial presentations, the strongest determinate of perceptual grouping is *proximity* in space or time. Elements are likely to be assigned to the same group if they occur closely together in space or time. If S sees the series ABC DEF GHI . . . , with a blank space between triplets, he will organize and recall that as a series of triplets (Bower & Winzenz, 1969). Similar grouping occurs with a *temporal* pause between visually or acoustically presented triplets.

These perceptual groupings affect serial recall in at least three ways. First, groupings produce a characteristic pattern of transition error probabilities or TEPs across serial positions in recall. The TEP at position n in the series is the conditional probability of an error in recalling the element in position n, given correct recall of element n-1 of the series. If elements within a group are highly interassociated, then the group will tend to appear as an all-or-none unit in recall; therefore, TEPs for adjacent elements within a group will be much lower than TEPs for adjacent elements separated by a group boundary. In concrete terms, for a series presented as ABC DEF . . . , the probability of an error in recalling C, given recall of B, will be much less than the probability of an error in recalling D, given recall of C. Figure 1 shows a typical example of a TEP profile for immediate recall of a string of 12-digits presented acoustically and segregated by temporal pauses into groups of sizes 23232. The figure illustrates the tell-tale saw-toothed profile, of low TEPs within each functional group and a sharp increase in TEP going across the boundary between successive groups. So, that type of profile is one characteristic outcome in memory resulting from grouping of elements.

Another objective trace of grouping is a failure of accumulative serial learning with repetition of a series if its group structure is altered afresh each time it is presented. Using the experimental design made famous by Hebb, a series like 83 592 746 9157 will be readily learned (its immediate recall will improve) if it is presented the same way every other trial with a totally new item between repetitions. However, im-

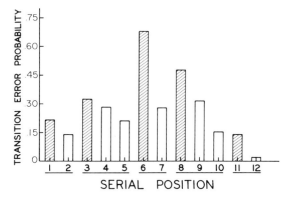

Fig. 1. Transition error probabilities for digit series presented with a 23232 group structure. Over Serial Position 1 is the error probability of item 1. For a later position n, the bar indicates the conditional probability of an error on Element n given correct recall of Element n-1. The initial transition into each group is cross-hatched.

mediate recall will not improve if the series of digits is regrouped in a new way at each presentation, e.g., 835 9274 691 57 on the second presentation, then 8 359 27 469 157 on the third presentation, and so on (Bower & Winzenz, 1969).

A third implication is that many serial lists can be devised for which there are clearly optimal versus nonoptimal groupings. For example, a string of letters such as ICBM PHD CIA FM is grouped in an optimal way, whereas IC BMP HDC IAFM is not optimal. When spacers mark off meaningful units (acronyms or words) or pronounceable compounds, then these perceptual units make contact with their representations in long-term memory, and ease the load on short-term memory for the string. As a result, when perceptual units induced by groupings correspond to "meaningful" units, recall of that string of elements is optimal (Bower & Springston, 1970).

So, to briefly summarize, perceptual groupings in a serial string become recall units, and three outcomes for assessing this fact were listed: the sawtoothed TEP profile, absence of cumulative learning with changed groupings, and optimal recall when perceptual groups correspond to meaningful groups. With these symptomatic indices aside, let us return to our discussion of the laws of grouping.

In the cases mentioned above, the series is a string of letters or digits segregated by a homogeneous "spacing character," either a blank visual space or a soundless pause. But any distinctive element could serve as a spacer—a sound, a word, a special visual character. In experiments in my laboratory by Winzenz (1970), with recall of digit strings, the word "zero" was inserted as a spacer, as in the auditory series "eight, three, zero, five, nine, two, zero, seven, four, six, zero, nine, one, five." The subject was instructed to ignore and not recall the zero-spacer. However, the recall results showed the zero-spacer to be a completely effective grouping device. It produced the typical TEP pattern of Figure 1, and variation across trials in the location of the spacer in the same digit string caused a complete failure of accumulative learning.

The next law of grouping to be discussed is "similarity": elements are more likely to be grouped together the more similar they are in respect to relevant properties. A student of mine, Fred Springston, has investigated several different bases for similarity groupings, using the "optimal correspondence" effect in memory as his index of grouping. One of these cases was with acoustic presentations of letters of acronyms over headphones to the two ears, with some letters assigned to the left ear only and some to the right. Evidence was obtained indicating that ear-of-arrival could serve as a basis for grouping, and recall was best overall when successive letters of an acronym arrived at the same ear rather than having a shift in ears during presentation of the acronym (cf., Yntema & Trask, 1963).

Another experiment on similarity as a grouping factor used visual letters presented in different colors. Each twelve-letter string consisted of four acronyms, one of four letters, two of three letters, and one of two letters. These acronym sizes were presented in the left-to-right order 4-3-3-2 or 2-3-3-4. Adjacent letters within the acronym were printed in either the same color (which should facilitate optimal groupings) or different colors (which should hinder optimal groupings). Using a switch from capital to lower-case letters to signify a switch to a different color, examples of optimal groupings are ICBMphdCIAfm and IDfdrCBSymca. Examples of unoptimal color groupings are ICbmpHDCiafm and IDFDrcbSYMca. (As these examples illustrate, grouping of adjacent letters into acronyms is also promoted or hindered by their having the same or different *sizes*.) A card containing such a twelve-letter string was shown to the subject for five seconds, then his immediate serial recall of the string was requested. As expected, Springston found that immediate recall was better when the color groupings corresponded to the acronym than when these groupings conflicted. Correct serial recall averaged 8.3 letters (out of twelve) for the optimal strings compared to 7.1 letters for the nonoptimal color groupings. Thus, the successive spatial letters of an acronym were readily grouped into the meaningful unit if they were the same color; such grouping into units by spatial proximity was hindered if the successive letters of the acronym appeared in different colors.

A final grouping principle to be mentioned is "good figure." Some of Wertheimer's (1923) demonstrations of this principle involved organization of an ambiguous portion of a figure by extrapolation of a smooth curve or some other regularity apparent in an unambiguous portion of the figure. I have been unable to imagine very many verbal-learning analogs of this principle. The few illustrations I have thought up hinge heavily on our verbal ability. The examples in Figure 2 serve

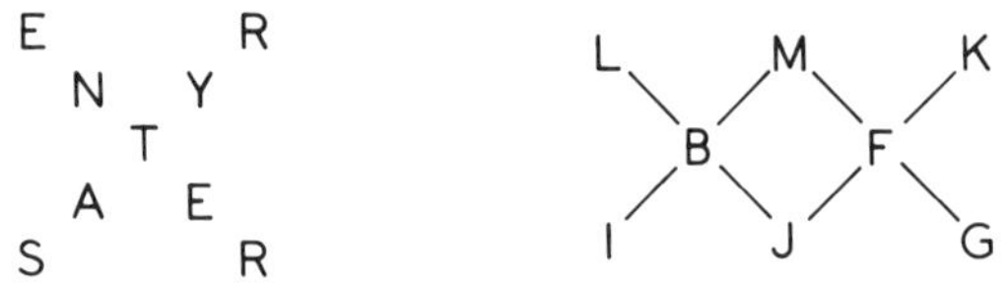

```
E       R           L    M    K
 N   Y               \  / \  /
  T                   B    F
 A   E               / \  / \
S       R           I    J    G
```

Fig. 2. Illustrations of "good continuation" with verbal materials.

to illustrate what I have in mind. In these cases, meaningful letter sequences may be found only if the eye and brain group together the letters along the diagonal. This organization, however, is not immediately apparent, presumably due to our row-by-row scanning habits, and I would not expect the diagonal organization to be noticed in a brief tachistoscopic flash of the letter array.

Wertheimer's other illustrations of "good figure" refer to biases people exhibit in parsing or articulating a visual scene into its component parts, the primitive "good figures." A circle with small triangular spurs at four, eight, and twelve o'clock tends to be described by us as "a circle covering a triangle," although many alternative parses of that pattern are equally plausible. To this kind of coding ambiguity there are, of course, many verbal analogs. For instance, numerous sentences like "They fed her dog biscuits," or "The missionaries are ready to serve," can be ambiguous in several respects—in surface parsing or in deep-structure semantic interpretation (McKay & Bever, 1967). Of course, what one remembers from an ambiguous sentence—as indexed by recall paraphrases, semantic substitution errors, recognition false alarms and the like—are the conceptual relationships or propositions as interpreted by the subject.

OTHER CONDITIONS OF PERCEPTUAL COHERENCE

The discussion so far has illustrated the Gestalt principles of grouping, namely, proximity, similarity, and good figure. We have seen how these can determine the perceptual groupings the person imposes on the material and how those in turn determine characteristics of his recall. There are many other conditions of perceptual organization which determine how easily two features or elements of a field cohere and become associated. Some of these perceptual relations, and their effects on associative memory, have been detailed by Asch, Ceraso, and Heimer (1960) and by Prentice and Asch (1958). When a geometrical figure is composed of several features that "naturally fit together" or exhibit natural coherence, we may call them "unitary" (as contrasted with nonunitary) figures. Examples of unitary figures versus equivalent nonunitary figure pairs are shown in Figure 3, adapted from Asch, Ceraso, and Heimer.

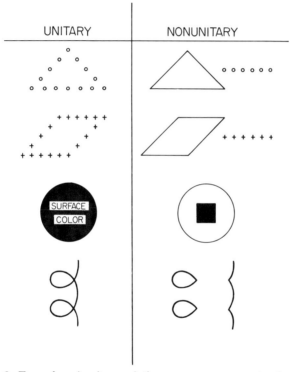

Fig. 3. Examples of unitary relations among components of a figure.

Unitary figures are those in which the two basic components are related by some primitive spatial predicate. Exemplary spatial relations are: X is a *part of* Y, X is the *surface of* Y, Y is *composed of* Xs, X is the mirror image of Y, Y *fits in between* X and Z, and so on. Visual scenes are organized in terms of such spatial relations holding among the primitive objects and properties detected.

The point of the experiments by Asch and his colleagues was that two visual elements have greater coherence (are more easily associated) in memory when they are presented to the subject in a unitary manner. For purposes of our present review, such experiments demonstrate the role of perceptual organization of figural rather than verbal elements upon associative memory for the displays.

FUNCTIONAL RULES

Along with the notions of relations and groupings, the other fundamental notion to be discussed is that of a *function* (see Scandura, 1970, for details). I shall use the term "function" in two different senses, although at an abstract level these usages share common features: first, function refers to a *mapping*, stipulating correspondences (relations) between psychological elements in two different domains; and, second, function may refer to a *decision rule* used for deciding how to classify or characterize something, or telling one how to perform under specified conditions. For example, transposing the letters of all English bigrams, as in BG → GB, constitutes a *mapping*, whereas the set of chess moves of a rook, or the occasions for a driver to stop his car at intersections, constitute *decision rules*.

The usefulness of these concepts for analyzing human memory will be briefly illustrated below. An appropriate beginning is to observe that the adult learner has available a variety of strategies for attacking any material he is required to memorize. The most common and general strategy is to see whether the new material is already "close to" something he already knows. Gestalt psychologists referred to this as the "search after meaning." In formal terms, the person searches for a *function* for converting something known into something unknown, the material to be remembered. A few examples of such functions in standard laboratory learning tasks might be the following tabulation:

In Serial Learning:	Function
The series, R E K A E P S D U O L	is LOUDSPEAKER backwards
The series, P B L R A U N S T H	is PLANT and BRUSH interleaved in alternation
The series 816449362516941	is composed of the squares of the integers in decreasing order
In Associative Learning:	Function
14 → 28	"Response" is the stimulus × 2
DAP → PAD	Interchange 1st and 3rd letters
HAT → MAT	Response is a rhyme of stimulus word
Collie → Dog	Response is the superset of stimulus word

In these paired-associate cases, we can say that the "response" can be generated knowing the stimulus and the functional rule transforming the stimulus into the response.

We have to imagine—organizational theorists are willing to imagine—an internal "executive monitor" or homunculus that examines the material to be learned, and performs two tasks: (a) tries to find a function or relation between what is known and the new material to be learned, and (b) if such a function is discovered, it is then used, together with supporting material, to generate the new material. In the words of Woodworth and Schlosberg (1954), the new material is repre-sented internally as "schema-plus-correction." The point behind all such moves is economy of effort: the learner assimilates the new material with the least effort possible. The state of affairs may be diagramed as in Figure 4:

Fig. 4. Schema illustrating the functional relation or mapping between known and unknown material. In this manner, new information gets assimilated to old.

Some rules are useful for converting one element into another, as in the paired-associate illustrations above. Other rules are useful for describing and generating entire sets of items, as in a serial list of free-recall list. Illustrations of rule-generated lists are (a) all the integers from 34 to 57, (b) all one-syllable words that rhyme with *cat,* (c) all three-letter words formed from C or H as the first letter, A or U as the second letter, and T or M as the third letter, and (d) the set of all concept cards containing blue triangles regardless of their size, number, or location on the display card. In each of these cases, a poten-tially large set of items is implied (e.g., all two-digit numbers, all the r^N concept cards formed by combining r levels of N stimulus attributes). The experimental list is a subset within this larger set. Suppose that this experimental list were the set of to-be-remembered items in a memory experiment. Then, economic description of this subset would serve as a decision rule for classifying and distinguishing which stimuli were on the list and which were not (so-called "recognition memory"). But the rule could also serve as a way to generate the items of the set. The complexity of the rule and the conditions of presentation, etc., would determine how soon the subject discovers it, which in turn would determine how soon he could reproduce the set of to-be-remembered items.

To relate these ideas to concepts of Gestalt psychology, it is clear that the learning and recall of a particular item depends more upon wholistic properties of the entire list, the totality of its relations or its "structure," than upon characteristics of the item considered in isolation. That is, the organization of the whole determines the characteristics (the "meaning," as the old Gestalters would say) of the parts comprising it.

Another common learning or organizing strategy which fits into the schema of Figure 4 is use of "natural language mediators" by clever experimental subjects. Such mediators might be called codes (or translation dictionaries) for the assimilation of unknown to known material. For example, in learning nonsense syllables, the most frequent strategy of adults is to convert or transform the nonsense syllable into a word, then remember the word-plus-the-transformation. In a recent dissertation at Stanford, Prytulak (1971) analyzed the various possible transformations which people try out to convert a CVC into a word. For instance, a frequent transformation is to suffix additional letters to make a complete word, as in BAC → BAC(on) and GOL → GOL(f). Prytulak was able to rank order the transformations according to the priority with which the subject tested them on the CVC. He showed that syllables of low meaningfulness were those which could not be converted into a word except by a low-priority transformation. A plausible reconstruction is that when asked to remember a nonsense syllable, the person first looks for a transformation which converts it to a familiar word; if he succeeds, he then stores that word plus the transformation (as Woodworth assumed with his schema-plus-correction hypothesis). When he is asked to recall the syllable, he tries to retrieve the word-plus-transformation and, if successful, he applies the *inverse* transformation (e.g., delete the suffix) to the word to yield the original nonsense syllable. That is a good example of how a person constructs meaning out of nonsense, and by so doing assimilates new material into his memory.

A few qualifications are in order regarding the encoding of nonsense. First, it would appear that "natural language mediation" of nonsense is a "slow rate" phenomenon; subjects need some time to do it, and the strategy is ineffectual with rapid presentations of the memory list. Second, the more elements (e.g., letters) there are in a nonsense string, the less likely one is to find a natural language mediator (NLM) for the series as a whole. Thus immediate recall of seven-letter strings presented at a rate of two per second is unlikely to be "contaminated" very much by natural language mediation. However, recall of a nonsense trigram or string of binary digits shown for two seconds is liable to be quite affected by the incidence of NLMs (Glanzer & Clark, 1963; Groninger, 1966). Third, the utility of a recoding strategy may depend in a complex way upon the generality and simplicity of the recoding rule for the set of items as well as the criterion memory task.

Such complexities are illustrated in studies on coding by Underwood and Erlebacher (1965); in some of their experiments, subjects had to free recall lists of nonsense trigrams like IXS, AYD, ENM, OBJ, etc. Each trigram could be encoded as a word by permuting the letters, and evidence was obtained indicating that the subjects did so recode and use the words for constructing their recall of the trigrams. The several experimental conditions in the Underwood and Erlebacher studies varied the number of different decoding rules (letter permutations) required to derive the trigrams of the list from the corresponding word. If only a single permutation rule were applicable to all items on the list, as in the 2-3-1 set illustrated above, then the subject's recall was materially aided by the rule; but if two or more rules were required, then many decoding confusions occurred and there was practically no net benefit of having the rules available.

There are several reasons why Underwood and Erlebacher may not have obtained positive facilitation of recall with lists exemplifying two (or more) rules. First, letter permutation rules are generally low-priority transformations for converting trigrams to words (Prytulak, 1971), and this is possibly because the different permutation sequences are so easily confused with one another. Second, in Underwood and Erlebacher's study there was no external criterion by which to select which decoding of a word (ISX or IXS?) was more likely. Therefore, the subject was practically required to remember the exact letter sequence anyway. On the other hand, in other studies (reviewed by Prytulak), this selection could be aided by general class characteristics such as knowledge that the decoding target is a CVC trigram, or knowledge that the code word is a high-priority transformation of the nonsense string.

We have much more to learn about natural language encoding of nonsense material into memory—the several processes and their parameters. However, included among these learning processes must inevitably be a "rote-learning" component to handle the nonmediated learning which subjects so frequently report. That simply means that two events have become associated because they were grouped together (in "belongingness") in appropriate proximity relations, and I see no reason why "organizational" memory theorists should shy away from recognizing such rote learning. In alternate terms, the subject is storing the proposition "X occurred next to Y," "X occurred at nearly the same time as Y," or similar propositions stipulating proximity relations.

RULE-DEFINED CHUNKS

I have been discussing rules for characterizing the unknown materials to be learned in terms of known information. But rules can serve a second function, in defining "chunks" or functional units. The effect of a rule in producing groupings may be seen in recent work by Restle and Brown (1970) on serial pattern learning. In their task, the subject is faced with a row of 6 lights and is asked to learn to predict which light will come on next. He is then exposed to a systematic sequence of lights that recycles many times, with the person trying to predict each one. The nature of the repetitive sequence is varied across subjects. Examples of sequences to be learned (numbering the six lights across) might be 2 3 4 3 4 5 4 5 6 or 5 4 5 4 3 4 3 2 3. The overall speed of learning, and the number and nature of errors at each point in the series, serve as the dependent variables. From investigation of many subjects learning many such sequences, Restle and Brown concluded that subjects were grouping their long sequences into a series of "chunks" and that the two basic chunks were the *run* (e.g., 2 3 4) and the *trill* (e.g., 4 3 4). These basic chunks are themselves generated from elementary rules as illustrated by Restle and Brown. Each systematic sequence can be given a structural description in terms of generative operations on sets. For example, if the set is X = (1 2 3), then the operation "repeat of X" generates the subsequence 1 2 3 1 2 3, the operation "mirror image of X" generates 1 2 3 6 5 4, and the operation "transposition by plus one of X" generates 1 2 3 2 3 4. Restle (1970) illustrates how his systematic sequences can be described by recursive application of such operations. For example, the sequence 1 2 3 2 3 4 6 5 4 5 4 3 has the description M[T(X)]. Such compositions correspond to *structural trees* like those in Figure 5.

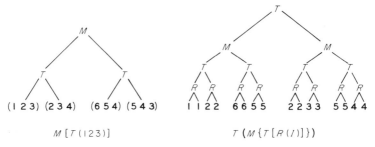

Fig. 5. Structural tree descriptions of the systematic series at the bottom of the tree.

It was hypothesized that subjects would have most difficulty in learning and correctly predicting the highest order transformations in the sequence, and should have the easiest time learning the lowest order transformations. Indexing ease of learning a given transition by the mean probability of errors made right after the transition (which is similar to the TEP statistic mentioned earlier), Restle (1970) found that error probabilities did increase monotonically with the level of the transformation in the tree. For example, in the sequence $M[T(123)]$ in the left panel of Figure 5, this means that the most errors during learning would occur in predicting Elements 6 and 1 (the beginning of the two halves), next most errors in predicting Elements 5 and 2 (the beginning of the minor quarters), and fewest errors in predicting the final two elements in each triplet.

Although Restle shows that a tree structure is a good way to identify relative amounts of difficulty that subjects encounter during learning, he cautiously avoids saying how subjects acquire such compound transformations (i.e., acquisition mechanisms are left unspecified), nor does he assume that the structural tree is the representation (of the sequence) upon which the subject is operating.

A similar development to the Restle and Brown theory is that by Johnson (1970) who has proposed a hierarchical (tree structure) model to explain his results on the learning of serial lists of letters presented in a grouped manner. He proposes that the serial list comes to be represented internally as a hierarchy of "chunks," where a chunk is composed of a subsequence of elements or of lower-level chunks. Thus, the sequence AB CD/EF GH would be represented as chunks $C_1 C_2/C_3 C_4$, where $C_1 = (AB)$, $C_2 = (CD)$, etc., which in turn can be represented as X_1/X_2, where $X_1 = (C_1 C_2)$, which in turn can be replaced by the symbol S. Johnson proposes a particular algorithm by which the person recalls the series, by decoding the hierarchy from top-down, always unpacking chunks with a left-branching priority (see Figure 6). When operating perfectly, the chunk S would be decoded as X_1 and X_2, and X_2 would be placed on a temporary "standby" (memory) list while X_1 is decoded into C_1 and C_2. C_2 would also be placed on the "stand-by" memory list, while C_1 would be further decoded into the terminal symbols A and B (which would then be recalled). This completed, the executive monitor then returns to the next chunk on the stand-by memory list. This would be C_2 in our example. This would be decoded into C and D. Then the next symbol on the stand-by list, X_2, would be fetched and it would be decoded in a manner similar to the X_1 chunk. These rules for traversing a hierarchy are essentially those proposed earlier by Yngve (1960) regarding how sentences might be generated from left to right. Johnson (1970) provides much evidence from recall experiments to support his theory that subjects learn grouped series as hierarchies

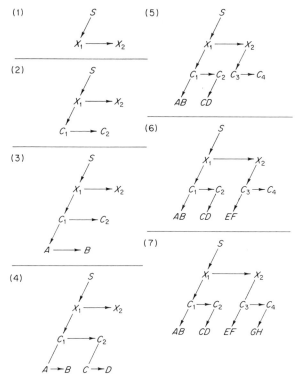

Fig. 6. Successive stages in the decoding of a hierarchy of chunks according to the Johnson-Yngve left-branch priority rules.

of chunks, and that many features of their recall protocols are captured by this hierarchical decoding model (see also Bower & Winzenz, 1969; Winzenz, 1970).

The reason for describing this work by Johnson and by Restle and Brown in this review is that their papers provide some of our clearest demonstrations of organizational effects in learning. A hierarchy is a particular kind of structure, depicting the relations among the psychological units or groups. I began by reviewing some perceptual factors which promoted grouping of elements. But grouping is an operation that can be applied recursively, generating groups of groups. Recursive groupings produce a hierarchy; a hierarchy diagrams the structure of relationships holding among the chunks and terminal vocabulary elements of the series. It is well known that such hierarchical structures are abundant in networks of semantic concepts, e.g., based on the relations of set membership or part-to-whole (Anglin, 1970; Collins & Quillian, 1969). However, I do not wish to leave the impression that hierarchical structures are useful only for representing certain serial lists and a few semantic fields. Recent work in automatic scene analysis and pattern perception (e.g., Miller & Shaw, 1968; Rosenfeld, 1969) is moving in the direction of providing a picture grammar, the output of which is a hierarchical structural description of visual scenes. The total picture decodes into subpictures, which decode into several objects in specified relations, which objects themselves are comprised of subobjects or groups of contours, surfaces, and other primitive elements concatenated by basic spatial predicates (such as those illustrated by Asch's unitary figures—see Figure 3). It is plausible to suppose that people remember pictures of naturalistic scenes in terms of such structural "descriptions" extracted by the visual cortex. Such descriptions in a picture-grammar need not imply the existence of a corresponding verbal description, although the pictorial description would be used for generating simulacrums such as an actual drawing of the scene or the imaginary "drawings" we call mental images (Bower, in press; Simon, in press).

To summarize briefly the ground we have covered, I have indicated some of the main concepts in the organizational approach to problems of human memory. The primitive notions are those of *group* (psychological units segregated by some grouping operation), *relations* among elements, and *functions*, the latter including one-one mappings and decision rules. When confronted with a memory task, the subject first groups the materials into units, then searches for relations among the units or rules for generating the units. Several factors promoting grouping and perceptual unity of verbal and figural information were reviewed, showing their effects throughout several memory tasks. By noting that grouping can be a recursive operation, it was observed that hierarchical tree structures result from repeated grouping of subgroups. Further, we reviewed some evidence that the representation of a person's knowledge in certain limited domains is best conceived of as hierarchical.

Executive Monitor

In the preceding, I have been discussing various forms of organizations, rules, transformations, and the like, which the person may search for in the materials he is to memorize. If one asks "Who or what does this searching, discovering, and applying of rules," he is led immediately to one of the fundamental constructs of cognitive theories, that of an *executive monitor* that controls the internal show of information processing. Miller, Galanter, and Pribram (1960) and Newell and Simon (1963) have provided sustained arguments for postulating an executive that "calls" various programs into action, that monitors how they are progressing towards their goal and that decides when and where to switch control of central processing effort. All simulation programs of any complexity have such executives that oversee, organize, sequence, and run the subroutines. Although the idea of an executive raises for some critics the specter of a shadowy homunculus who dutifully carries out just those behavioral practices which we need to explain, I think it is mandatory that such critics choose their targets in a discriminating fashion to assess the "degrees of freedom" or the numerical differences between the assumptions (assumed abilities of the executive) and the theorems (implied behaviors explained by the theory). In simulation programs, the executive is not a hoary ghost; it is, rather, a well specified piece of program that makes a series of elementary decisions (e.g., does symbol A match symbol B?), each one of which seems to require only a rudimentary ability. However, when tens of thousands of such small decisions are cascaded in a large hierarchially organized program, the operation of the entire system appears complex and intelligent. The humming of the well-tempered computer is proof positive that the executive is not an occult entity.

Surely one feature distinguishing current day information-processing theories of memory from the earlier S-R approaches of Hull, Guthrie, Skinner, etc., is this postulate of an executive monitor. That construct is necessitated by our recognition that the person is a complex machine having available several alternative methods for solving particular problems (such as recalling an arbitrary list of words). To continue our harkening back to the Gestalt tradition, Köhler and especially Koffka (1935) assigned a very significant role to the "self" as an overseer or monitor controlling mental processes, assigning it functions very similar to those discussed above for the executive monitor.

In the context of the discussion of rules and their applications to learning, it would be assumed that the executive examines the material to find whether a given rule applies. If a successful rule is found, it is called into operating memory to transform each stimulus as it is processed. For example, in a list of rhyming paired-associate words, as each stimulus for recall is taken in, the relational rule "rhyme of stimulus" is applied to generate a list of plausible "response" alternatives from which the correct response is chosen (Bower & Bolton, 1969).

Free Recall

PROCEDURAL CHARACTERIZATION

Most of my examples and discussion of principles have covered the areas of serial learning and associative learning. I intend now to shift to discussion of a *procedure*, namely, free recall and the data generated within this paradigm. It has been in this context that many "organizational" phenomena have been found. In fact, the papers in this volume by Wood and Postman seem to consider organizational effects only in free recall. After some preliminary remarks, I will describe an "associationistic" model of free recall and contrast it with some of the organizational phenomena. In that discussion, we will suggest that there is not much substantive conflict between S-R associative versus organizational accounts of free recall.

In free recall, the subject is asked to reproduce all items he knows which fall within a restricted set specified by the experimenter. The query might be to name all current U.S. Senators, all girls he has ever kissed, all novels read or movies seen in the past year, and so on. The typical laboratory experiments specify the restricted recall set (to be given in any order) by an instructed temporal cue to the subject such as "recall the most recently presented list" or "recall the list presented just before this one." That is, the typical retrieval query refers to a temporal (or ordinal list) cue.

The latter methodology is canonized in the technical literature and any procedure deviating significantly from it just is not "free recall." This is unfortunate because there are simply many other ways to specify sets of items besides temporal cues ("the most recent" list). If we adopt as a reference procedure presentation of two lists in succession followed by a cue to recall List 1 or List 2, then a sample of formally comparable procedures would be: present items from Lists 1 and 2 in intermingled order at different locations of the room, then ask for recall of those items presented in Location 1; or present words of List 1 paired with the word *HOUSE* intermingled with those of List 2 paired with *CAR*, then ask for recall of the items paired with *CAR;* or have the words of List 1 spoken by a woman, those of List 2 spoken by a man, then ask for recall of the items spoken by the woman. These correspond to such naturalistic queries as, "What party guests did I see in the *kitchen?*" "What's in the *car?*" and "What did *she* say?"

The reader will note that each of these alternative methods utilizes an implicit "paired-associate learning" procedure in which a single cue is being paired with, and becoming associated to, an entire list of items. This cue then serves as the general entry point for a grand "MMFR" search for the items on the appropriate list. In the context of this more general interpretation, the standard free recall methodology employs a temporal-list cue with the restriction that Lists 1 and 2 always must be presented in blocked (temporal) fashion. With nontemporal cues, of course, the items of the two sets can be presented in any order desired.

ITEM MEMORY AND EVENT MEMORY

The preceding discussion regarding list cues impinges upon a related question regarding what is stored in the subject's memory in the typical free recall experiment. This storage question relates to the issue of list cues because in order for a list-recall query to retrieve anything, that list cue must have been associated with (stored with) at least some of the items to be recalled. So the question is how to characterize what happens when a subject encounters a familiar item, for instance the word *cat*, while studying a list of to-be-remembered words. A variety of hypotheses, metaphors, and analogies have been offered as answers to this theoretical question. Many analogies or metaphorical theories suppose that some specific unit corresponding to a token of the word *cat* is what is stored on this occasion. It is as though a book entitled *cat* were being placed on a circulation shelf of a mental library, or an object labelled *cat* were being tossed into a mental junk box, possibly even a small junk box labelled "List-1," from which recall is to occur by sampling objects and reading off their labels.

Just the converse attitude is my over-all orientation. The mind does not take in or soak up new items as single, isolated symbols like water into a sponge, or new imprints on a wax tablet, or new books deposited in a mental warehouse. I believe that such analogies are systematically misleading. The subject does not enter the item *cat* into his long-term memory when he sees it on the list; he is not learning the item *cat* at all. He already fully knows that item and all its associates. This and many, many other concepts exist already in the person's "semantic memory," which may possibly be represented by a complex graph-structure of relational associations among concepts and properties. The papers in this volume by Collins and Quillian, Kintsch, and Rumelhart, Lindsay, and Norman, attempt to explicate the nature of this conceptual network.

I take as axiomatic the assumption that the information recorded by the mind—"what is stored"—are facts expressible as propositions, which perhaps are only relationships among familiar concepts. For example, a new concept is defined in terms of known concepts and a new word is spelled as a sequence of known letters, etc. The propositions that the free-recall subject is learning are descriptions of cognitive or autobiographical events. At the most elemental level, the subject stores propositions of the form "The word *cat* occurred in that context I have called List-1." This simply links together two known concepts in semantic memory, *cat* and the *List*-1 context (or whatever is the List cue). But presentation of *cat* in the context of List-1 may make the subject think of—may activate associations of—its relations to many other concepts via known propositions. Thus, the subject may think of his Aunt Sarah's cat, what it looked like, how a friend of his was allergic to cat fur, and so forth. I would assume that those several implicit associative responses which are activated by *cat* become connected to a List-1 cue and the fact of the occurrence of such imaginings is "stored in memory" just as is the fact that "*cat* occurred on List-1." The recording of such facts—by the establishment of new linkages between known concepts in semantic memory (including List representatives)—is what Tulving (this volume) refers to as "episodic memory."

At the time of recall, the person may chain associatively from the List-cue to one or more facts surrounding his storage of the fact that the word *cat* occurred on List 1. These several implicit cues may combine to redintegrate the entire complex of propositions thought about when *cat* was seen initially in the List-1 context. Thus, the actual name of the word *cat*, which is all the subject is typically permitted to overtly recall, is probably only a fraction of the relevant propositions he thought about at the time he studied the word *cat* as a to-be-remembered unit. (Study time variables are obviously relevant.) To reiterate my belief, memory is redintegration of our cognitive autobiography, not a literal reproduction of external events.

RETRIEVAL PLANS

As stated before, the criterion task in free recall requires the person to produce in any order all items belonging to a specifically constrained set, and no others (such gaffs are called intrusions). Any scheme that guides the overall conduct of the subject's search through memory may be called a *retrieval plan*. The salient characteristics of a retrieval plan are that it tells the subject where to begin his recall, how to proceed more or less systematically from one unit or group of words to the next. The plan also helps the person monitor the adequacy of his recall, helping him identify where parts are missing and to identify when he has finished.

Retrieval plans vary across tasks and subjects in their elaborateness and amount of detail. I will discuss just four classes of retrieval plans since these seem to cover most of the plans one sees the usual college student using to memorize lists of items. I have called the classes of retrieval plans generative rules, pegword systems, hierarchical systems, and associative chaining. Let us take up each of these briefly in turn.

Generative Rules

This class has been suggested by the research of Miller (1958) and by Whitman and Garner (1962) on free recall of rule-generated lists.

The Whitman and Garner experiments may be taken as prototypic. A typical task of theirs might be to expose the subject to eight of the sixteen possible geometric figures that could be composed by combining all levels of four binary attributes (e.g., one or two, large or small, red or blue, circles or squares). The principle for constructing the population of potential patterns was sufficiently simple that most subjects could probably generate all 16 patterns in the population after only a few exposures to the set. The experimenter chooses a subset of, say, eight of these sixteen patterns to constitute the "memory list" which the subject is to learn to free recall.

The most economic way for the subject to proceed is to try to infer a brief description of the memory set, or to infer a concept or "decision rule" distinguishing patterns which are in versus out of the memory set. Whitman and Garner pointed out the basic similarity between such recall experiments and concept learning experiments, if one identifies the subset presented for free recall with the list of "positive instances" of a concept experiment. A rule for generating free recall of the presented list would have as an essential ingredient the concept characterizing the members of that subset of the total population. Whitman and Garner showed that the difficulty of free recall learning in this situation depended directly upon the complexity of the concept or rule characterizing the subset of presented patterns. For example, learning would be very rapid if the memory set were to occupy an elementary partition of the population (e.g., the eight blue figures), but learning was slower if more stimulus attributes had to be taken into account.

Our conceptual tools may be sharpened by reference to this elementary example in Whitman and Garner's experiment. The concept describing the memory set can serve two functions: first, as a decision rule to decide how to classify (recognize?) a given pattern as having been on or off the memory list; and, second, as a constraint for generation of the memory list in recall, viz., keeping the color at blue, write down the patterns of one or two, large or small, circles or squares. When one goes beyond this elementary context, up to lists using words, then the potential population of relevant items is huge but the subject may nonetheless search for a concept characterizing all or substantial parts of the memory list. For example, a list consisting of ten words rhyming with *frog* plus ten words rhyming with *bat* would doubtless be learned in a few trials with precisely that characterization; similarly, a complete list of instances from four exhaustive categories (e.g., compass directions, silverware, school classes, planets) would be eventually characterized and recalled as "all instances" of those categories.

One may quibble over the dividing line at which concept induction leaves off and specific item memory takes over. Certainly, if the subject detects that all instances of an exhaustive category are on the memory list (which is probable with blocked input), then he need store no specific item information since he can simply generate the category instances out of long-term memory. If, on the other hand, the presented instances do not exhaust the category, then specific item memory is required for the person to distinguish presented from nonpresented members of the category. Presumably, in this case the person implicitly generates instances of the category and checks to see whether they have been seen recently in the list context, and, if so, they are recalled overtly. Kintsch (1970) argues for this type of recognition check before recall of categorized lists.

Pegword Systems

It is a simple matter to show that after exposure to a list of unrelated words the usual subject knows much more than he is able to recall. This can be shown by various cued recall tests (Tulving & Pearlstone, 1966) or by recognition tests following recall failures. The responses in free recall might be described as responses in search of stimuli; what is lacking during recall are cues to remind the person of all the list words he is supposed to recall.

Mnemonic pegword systems are powerful retrieval schemes which directly provide a well-known list of cues for the subject to associate with each word or subjective group in the list to be learned. There are diverse pegword systems. A common one is for the person to first learn a list of pegwords such as one-is-a-bun, two-is-a-shoe, three-is-a-tree, and so on, pairing rhyming concrete nouns with the first 20 or so integers. The person then uses these pegwords as "mental hooks" upon which to hang any new list of words. The person would associate one-bun with the first word of a new list to be learned, two-shoe with the second word, etc., the associations usually being established by mental imagery or by the subject generating sentences linking the pegword and the list word to be recalled. The system is not restricted to placing only one list word per pegword; an earlier experiment of ours (cited in Bower, in press) simultaneously associated several different list words with each pegword (while keeping total list-length constant) without any deleterious effects.

A similar scheme uses a list of geographic locations (Bower, 1970; Ross & Lawrence, 1968) such as "mental snapshots" of a familiar route through a university campus or building. The subject is to place into successive locations images representing the successive words of the list he is learning. Another scheme uses alphabetic pegs (Earhard, 1967) so that list words become associated with their first letter. For example, in a grocery shopping list, one might set up the associates a-means-apples, b-means-bananas, c-means-catsup, and so forth. At the test for recall, the person is to generate his well-known list of pegwords (i.e., the locations or the alphabet) and have these cue recall of the list words.

Such pegword systems can be shown to be exceedingly effective devices for boosting recall, typically doubling or tripling the percentages recalled compared to uninstructed free-recall controls. The advantages of the pegword system in comparison to the usual free-recall condition are several. First, the person using the pegword mnemonic has a definite and consistent learning strategy; he knows what he has to do with each list item as he studies it, viz., pair it up in imagery with its corresponding pegword. Second, he has definite pigeon-holes into which to file the successive response words; alternatively, he has a set of concrete, distinctly imaginable stimuli around which to elaborate an interacting scene incorporating an image of the referent of the response word. Third, the pegword subject has a systematic retrieval plan: he knows where to begin his recall, how to proceed systematically from one unit to the next, and the plan also serves to monitor the adequacy of his recall.

The pegwords of such systems are not determined by the nature of the list to be learned; they are used trans-situationally, are applied automatically to any and all lists to be memorized. Now, semantic category labels, of course, are very effective retrieval cues for recall of their instances that have appeared on an input list which the person was to remember (Tulving & Pearlstone, 1966). Therefore, an optimal set of pegwords should be a known list of semantic categories specifically tailored to characterize the particular list of words which the subject is to learn. When studying the list of to-be-remembered words, the person would then associate each instance-word with its superordinate category; then, at the time of recall the subject would go through his known pegword list of categories, recalling all instances he has associated to that category and which he has tagged as having occurred in the to-be-remembered list (see Wood's chapter in this volume for an example).

In the case above, the experimenter is teaching the person what are the optimal categories he should use for classifying and learning a particular list. If we remove that aspect and simply present the person with a highly categorized list, then we can be reasonably sure the subject is discovering the common categories, associating instance names to these categories, and remembering a temporary "pegword" list of the category names he has discovered to be used as retrieval entries into his memory. The first part of this process, discovery of the common categories exemplified in the list, will vary with the usual "word-concept-learning" variables (Underwood & Richardson, 1956) such as the temporal contiguity (blocking) of similar instances, the probability of implicit arousal of the category name to the list words as indexed by associative norms, and instructions which lead the subject to search for one rather than another kind of common associate, e.g., sense-impression adjectives as opposed to semantic categories. The second phase, linking specific list-instances to the category name, is largely a matter of tagging, for use in retrieval, some associative pathways that already exist, and which are stronger (or more likely to be present) the higher is the normative frequency of the instance-word as an associate in the category norms (e.g., Battig & Montague, 1969). The third phase, remembering a set of category names as cues into the list, will be affected by such variables as how many categories there are, how many times a given category label is implicitly aroused per cycle through the list (i.e., items per category), and whether in successive lists the same or different categories are employed (Shuell, 1968).

The point to be emphasized here, however, is that the implicit category cueing which subjects often use as a retrieval plan is not very far removed from the generative rule and the pure pegword retrieval systems. The categories are like concepts that characterize the word-list in obvious ways and they can be used for generating pieces of that list; and the subject's implicit cueing of his recall by his discovered and remembered categories has all the features of a self-made pegword system. Thus the way people "naturally" perform in free recall with categorized lists bears certain similarities to how they perform with rule-generated lists and with pegword lists, which may be why recall from categorized word lists is also typically quite high.

Hierarchical Retrieval Plans

A list of semantic categories constitutes a first-order retrieval plan, where each cue can retrieve a group of list items. But if there are very many categories (say, seven or more) represented on the input list, then the person has the second-order problem of remembering his list of category cues. As Mandler (1968) has illustrated, an efficient way to proceed, if possible, is for the subject to categorize the category labels into broader but fewer superordinate categories. In this way one would obtain a three-level hierarchical tree: LIST-N would decode into superordinates, say, S_1, S_2, S_3, each one of which decodes into, say, three first-order categories, each one of which cues recall of several instances of the respective category. The power of such superordination schemes to span a field of lexical items can be quite astonishing. The range grows exponentially with the number of levels in the hierarchical tree. For example, a three-pronged tree extending three levels deep can span $3^3 = 27$ items. Such considerations lead one to suspect that a hierarchical organization of the list items should provide an extremely powerful retrieval plan for recall. This is because it provides a simple scheme for recursively generating nested sets of retrieval cues for the to-be-remembered items.

So far as I am aware, relatively little experimentation has been done teaching subjects to search out and utilize a hierarchical organization of free-recall lists. Some early experiments of ours (Bower, Clark, Lesgold & Winzenz, 1969) showed that recall of a large list was greatly facilitated if the experimenter preorganized it for the subject in terms of conceptual hierarchies. That is, it was shown that a subject could efficiently use a conceptual hierarchy as a retrieval plan, beginning his recall at the top node and unpacking it recursively from the top down. Other subjects, presented with the same words, but scrambled in random order, appeared not to recognize the hierarchical organization immanent in the material, nor use it during recall. What is needed are some empirical illustrations of recall facilitation produced when subjects impose subjective hierarchical organization on an arbitrary set of words provided to them. This presumably could be done with Mandler's (1968) category-sorting task, but with instructions suggesting that the subject look for hierarchical relationships among the subcategories he detects.

Associative Retrieval Plans

I save for last my discussion of that class of retrieval plans which I think characterizes most of the population of college-student subjects with whom we deal. The basis of the associative learning strategy is for the subject, as he studies each list-word, to try to search out and mark associative relations between it and other words on the list. This searching out and marking of associative connections among list words goes on continuously during input trials and during output trials. We may represent the individual words of the free-recall list as nodes in a richly interconnected associative network or graph structure. In searching out relations between list words, the subject is metaphorically searching for and marking associative pathways (perhaps of several intermediary steps) existing between the nodes corresponding to the list words. In addition to finding and/or strengthening associative pathways between list words, the person using the associative retrieval plan also needs a few "starters" or "entry points" to recall in the beginning, to start running off his associative chains during recall. By some criterion of subjective optimality, the subject selects a set of good entry points to start his recall tripping down along associative pathways.

What happens over multiple trials of studying and recalling the same list is that (a) longer, more "star-studded" associative chains are marked out to be followed in retrieval, and (b) the person converges upon a more optimal or "associatively pregnant" set of entry-words for starting his recall. The effect of these changes over trials is that it looks as though the subject's recall is becoming progressively organized (stereotyped) in terms of semantic groups (since the associative relations available between two items are most probably semantic ones).

A Simulation Model Embodying the Associative Strategy

For quite some time it has been clear to me that our general ideas about free-recall as related to inter-item associations have some merit, but what was really needed was for someone to explicitly construct and simulate an associative-net model of free recall in order to see what its explanatory powers and shortcomings would be. After various abortive tries by graduate students of mine over the years, including a notable effort by Dewey Rundus and Richard Freund, a reasonably successful and operative model has recently been produced and tested out by John Anderson, a student of mine at Stanford. He has written a long theoretical paper describing his free recall stimulator (Anderson, in press), and that paper should be consulted for details. However, I will discuss a few of the more salient details of the model Anderson has developed.

DESCRIPTION OF THE MODEL, FRAN

The "Data Base"

The model is called FRAN, for Free Recall by an Associative Network. We begin with its semantic association network. At present, FRAN has a vocabulary of 262 concepts (nouns), where a noun is defined in terms of three to nineteen of its associations (determined from Webster's Dictionary) to other words in the network. So we begin with a realistic, multiply connected graph; it is, in fact, possible to trace a pathway from any node (word) to any other node in the network through varying distances.

A free recall list consists of a selection of, say, 24 words from this network, which are to be presented to FRAN one word at a time for

t seconds each. FRAN's routines are divided into STUDY processes and RECALL processes, and each will be described briefly.

STUDY Routines in FRAN

When word i is being studied during input of a free recall list, it is as though a set of activities are going on around node i in the semantic network. During study of word i, FRAN attempts to do two things: (a) to mark node i with an association to LIST, which information is used later for recognition that word i appeared in the LIST context; and (b) to follow out one or more associative pathways stemming from node i, searching for other list-words (i.e., nodes with association to LIST). If such pathways to other list-words are found, then those pathways are marked with a LIST tag. The effect of such marking of pathways is to tell the executive during retrieval to use these marked pathways to get from recall of word i to recall of other list words. The marking of nodes and of useful pathways is assumed to be a probabilistic process, increasing linearly over the study-time per item.

There are three other components to be described regarding the study processes. One of these is a rudimentary short-term memory (STM) which holds on the order of the last two to four items besides the current one it is working on (in the "memory drum window"), plus any of the current working node's list associates it has uncovered. It is recall from this short-term memory that gives the recency effect in free-recall, and which accounts for above average associative strength for items occurring close together in the input list (cf. Glaizer, in press).

A second component to be described is construction of a special set of "starters," which are list words with associations *from* LIST. Along with items in STS, these items are used by the person to begin his recall chains during output. In the program, these starter associates to LIST correspond to a small list we call ENTRYSET (in the current program, it is constrained to be three items or less). The algorithm for placing elements on the ENTRYSET is as follows: at the initial trial, place the first three items on ENTRYSET (this assumption, by the way, produces a "primacy effect" in the serial-position recall curve on Trial 1); if any item in the list is found which leads to more list items in its associative neighborhood than does an item currently on ENTRYSET, then the latter is replaced by the former item; if one item on ENTRYSET is found to lead associatively to recall of a second item on ENTRYSET, then the second one is replaced by that entry-word-candidate having the most list items in its associative neighborhood. The reader should recognize that these are relatively crude heuristics for converging on those items that are most central in the list, that lead to recall of the largest number of associates. With repeated practice on a list, more and more pathways among list items become tagged so that the whole list becomes a single interconnected cluster of marked nodes and pathways. As this happens, the size of ENTRYSET can (does) decrease, since in the limit almost any word will be sufficient to access practically all the other words.

The third learning process requiring mention is the learning that is assumed to go on during output (recall test) trials. Recall of a given word is assumed to provide the subject with another "study" opportunity during which he searches out associative pathways radiating from the recalled node, seeking to find and mark pathways leading to other words of the list. In this way, the subject may learn quite a bit on test trials in the sense of later recalling previously unavailable words, and increasing the probability of stereotypy in recall order across trials.

To summarize, the learning processes which go on in FRAN during study are: tagging of list-words, searching for associative pathways between list words, marking the successful pathways so found, replacing items on the ENTRYSET by items that are associatively more central, and the learning of retrieval pathways during recall itself.

RECALL Routine

In recall, FRAN first dumps out the five more or less recent words in her short-term memory (unless these have been erased by interpolated activity of some kind). These STM items plus the three on ENTRYSET are then sampled, one at a time, and used to commence associative chains for recall. In recalling from word i, the executive examines the several associative branches radiating out from node i to check whether any of them has been marked (with a LIST tag) as a retrieval route to another list word. If such a marked path is found, it is followed to its terminus, which node may be marked with a LIST tag (in which case the corresponding word is recalled), or which may be unmarked. In the latter case, marked pathways radiating out from this intermediate node may be sought; if one is found, it is followed to its terminus; if none exist, then this particular recall chain is terminated and control returns to the executive which then, depending on a time-charge, tries either to find further tagged associations to follow out of node i, or goes on to the next starter and begins associating to it.

FRAN's recall follows a depth-first search of the marked associative network stemming from the starter, going until it hits a dead end (i.e., a node from which no marked pathways arise). It then takes up one of the remaining starters, and in this manner eventually exhausts all the words that can be recalled associatively from the set of starters. When this exhaustion occurs, FRAN's recall protocol comes to a halt, and the output trial has ended. For further information the reader is referred to Anderson's paper.

Figures 7 and 8 are offered in order to give some pictorial imagery to these abstract remarks concerning FRAN's memory structures. Figure 7 diagrams a graph structure representing a mere fragment of FRAN's

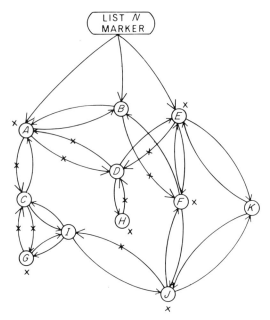

Fig. 7. A hypothetical memory structure that might exist after a study trial. See text for explanation.

pre-existing associative memory. Nodes represent words, and lines between nodes represent pre-existing associations. The diagram is idealized in so far as it depicts nodes only for those items that are on the study list, and associative pathways between them. This snapshot of the memory might be appropriate to the state of the system at the end of one study trial just before a first recall test occurs.

As a consequence of the learning processes, certain words and associations have been tagged; these are marked by X's in Figure 7. The tagged nodes and pathways comprise a subgraph of the original graph. This subgraph is depicted in Figure 8, showing the tagged nodes and pathways of Figure 7. The subgraph is not so connected nor so symmetric as is the original graph. In Figures 7 and 8, items A, B, E are the ENTRY-SET elements as indicated by an association to them from the LIST-N-marker.

FRAN begins her recall on the "left-most" entry word. Any part of the subgraph that is not strongly connected (i.e., by tagged arrows in the correct direction) to an entry word will not be recalled since FRAN will only examine that part of the subgraph which she can reach by following marked associative paths from the entry points. For exam-

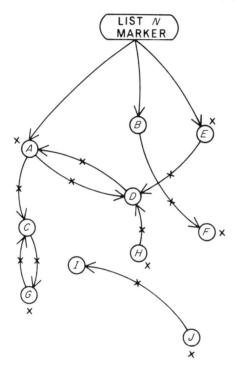

Fig. 8. The marked subgraph that is embedded in the memory structure of Figure 7.

ple, words H and J are marked and would be "recognized," yet they would not be recalled on this test. Furthermore, a list word may be reachable by marked associative pathways and yet not be recalled because the word itself has not been tagged. An example is word C which is unmarked in Figure 8. FRAN would regard C as a mediator in an associative chain, mediating recall of the marked word G in this instance. A final remark about Figure 8 is that in recall FRAN would note that entryword E leads, via marked pathways, to entryword A. Therefore, entryword A would be deleted and replaced during the next study trial by another associatively pregnant entryword.

SOME PROPERTIES OF FRAN's BEHAVIOR

Anderson has run a number of simulations of FRAN's behavior under various experimental conditions. FRAN's behavior is quite variable from one simulation run to the next because the tagging operations are probabilistic, as are important parts of the search-process by which FRAN scans the neighborhood of the word it is studying, looking for other list words. I will give just a few averaged results to illustrate the explanatory powers of such a model before turning to enumerating its deficiencies.

First, in simple multi-trial free recall experiments, FRAN shows the typical exponentially increasing learning curve for recall (cf. Figure 9a). More importantly, measures of stereotypy or subjective organization match those of human subjects (cf. Figure 9b). The data in Figure

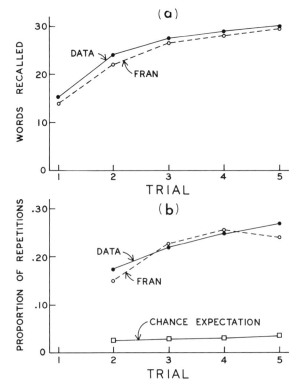

Fig. 9. Comparison of free recall data of FRAN and human subjects.

9 were collected from 18 Stanford students doing free recall of two 32-item lists of unrelated nouns; 36 individual simulations of FRAN were run and their averages are indicated in the figures. In Figure 9b, the measure of sterotypy is the proportion of adjacent pairs recalled on Trial n which are recalled, also adjacently, on Trial $n + 1$. Without any special effort at parameter-estimation or curve fitting, FRAN is seen to fit the data fairly well.

FRAN also shows, on Trial 1 especially, a tendency towards recalling, adjacently, items which were close together in the input list (cf. Glanzer, in press; Kintsch, 1970). This is produced by the short-term memory assumptions: suppose there is an associative link from word n to word n-k; word n-k might not have been tagged, but it is more likely to be in STM at the same time as word n the smaller k is; therefore, it is more likely that word n-k will be recognized, and the path from word n to word n-k will be tagged the smaller k is.

FRAN also shows a proper serial-position curve in recall probability on every trial. The recency effect due to STM is present on every trial. The primacy effect (due to priority of initial items on ENTRYSET) is predicted on Trial 1 only; with random reshuffling of the list items on each trial, the primacy effect disappears on later trials on the list. These predictions fit the results reported by Shuell and Keppel (1968).

FRAN also displays the appropriate relation between words recalled and list-length and study-time (or number of presentations) per item. Figure 10 shows the fit of FRAN to some of Waugh's (1967) data in which free recall was studied as a function of number of distinct word-types (list length) and study time per word-type. Study time per word-type was varied either by presenting a word once for n seconds, or presenting it n times for 1 second, each of its presentations distributed among presentations of other items. In FRAN, increases in list-length increase total words recalled (although proportions decrease) because with more words it becomes somewhat more probable that an associative search from any list-word will come across other list-words, and this relation-bridging is salutary for heightening total words recalled. The effect of study time is simple, direct, and two-fold: increasing the study-time on a word (a) increases the number of pathways that can be searched out from that node, and (b) increases the probability that the node itself will be tagged (associated to LIST N), as well as the probability of tagging pathways between words stemming from the study word. These assumptions suffice to account for the standard effects of list length, study time, and number of repetitions.

The model can also simulate the results of Tulving (1967) on multiple test trials interspersed between study trials. There is a definite "learning

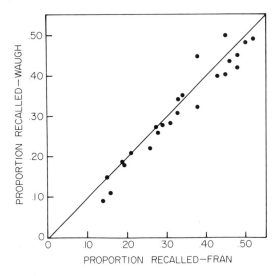

Fig. 10. Observed and predicted proportions recalled from lists of lengths 24 to 120 words long, with each unit presented for 1, 2, 4, or 5 seconds. Data are from Waugh (1967).

effect" from test trials. Moreover, FRAN shows considerable variability in its output on consecutive recall trials without an intervening study trial; as in Tulving's study, many words recalled on one test may be missing in the next consecutive recall test, and vice versa.

Another fact of free recall which FRAN will obviously handle is one reported by Deese (1959), relating recall of a list to the average degree of interitem associations pre-existing among the list words. We have not expended the computer costs to simulate Deese's exact results, but it is obvious that associative retrieval pathways among multiple list-words will be more easily found in a word list having many close associations at the beginning of the experiment. Similarly, the clustering in recall of highly associated word pairs, reported by Jenkins and Russell (1952), is just the kind of result FRAN is designed to explain.

Another implication of FRAN is that it fits the more obvious facts regarding recognition memory in relation to free recall. Kintsch (1970), in particular, has argued that recognition is independent of associative retrieval processes, and has shown this in several experiments. FRAN "recognizes" a test word as having been on LIST-N if an association exists between the corresponding node and the cognitive element "LIST-N." Even assuming the association from word to LIST-N is all-or-none, Bernbach (1967) has still shown how reasonably continuous recognition ratings could be derived from such two-state memory structures. For the moment, what needs to be pointed out is that recognition in FRAN is almost independent of recall in the way Kintsch (1970) hypothesized, but with "recognition monitoring" of items before they are recalled. If recognition fails on an item, then recall will most probably fail; if recall succeeds, then recognition will almost probably succeed. FRAN can also recognize many items it cannot free recall. Recognition of a word depends on marking its corresponding node; however, recall of that same word usually (except for STS) depends on the marking of associative pathways into it from other words of the to-be-recalled list.

As a consequence of these assumptions, FRAN also fits the results on free recall versus recognition measures following intentional versus incidental learning of a set of words (e.g., Eagle & Leiter, 1964). In the model, we suppose that incidental-learning subjects spend their time tagging word-nodes but not searching out or tagging interitem relationships or "retrieval routes," since they are not expecting a retrieval test. On the other hand, intentional learners not only tag word nodes (leading to good recognition performance) but also search out and tag associative pathways between list words. This results in their having significantly higher free recall, despite no difference in recognition between the intentional and incidental subjects.

At present, FRAN has no "encoding" process so it encounters no recognition difficulties due to encoding variability. A word has one corresponding concept node in FRAN's network, and presentation of that word to FRAN always activates that one node. It is fully realized that this characterization is naive: a noun typically has several alternative senses or conceptual encodings, and which of these is activated depends on the context in which the item is experienced. Thus, recognition memory may fail dramatically if the item is tested in a context differing from that prevailing when it was studied (Light & Carter-Sobell, 1970; Tulving & Thomson, 1971). Such results could be represented in FRAN by having several distinct conceptual nodes in long-term memory corresponding to the several senses of a homograph; one of these conceptual nodes would be activated and tagged during the study trial, but, with changed context, a different node may be activated and interrogated for a list-tag during the test trial. Such alterations to FRAN's memory structure could be introduced; but the alteration would be theoretically sterile unless we could specify additional processes regarding how the prevailing context influences the semantic coding of a word. In writing FRAN, Anderson and I were not prepared to do this; perhaps those scientists writing on semantic memory in this volume would be so prepared. In any event, in FRAN we side-stepped this problem despite its importance. One can not try to solve too many problems at the same time; such attempts are usually associated with a state of permanent stupor.

To continue our recital of FRAN's virtues, it will simulate the specific cueing results reported by Tulving and Osler (1968) and Thomson and Tulving (1970). If FRAN studies a to-be-remembered word B in the context of a to-be-associated cue A, then FRAN will (probably) mark node B and the associative pathway it can find from A to B. If tested with word A as a retrieval cue, A is not marked, but the executive examines any pathways from A which are marked, and it is likely to come across that one leading to word B which is itself marked; hence, B would be recalled when A is the cue following A-B study. On the other hand, suppose, following A-B study, one were to try to cue recall of B by presentation of a word C which has a strong preexperimental association to B. But, when started from the test cue C, FRAN is unlikely to come across word B, since the path from C to B has not been marked as relevant to retrieval in this list context, and C probably leads to very many associates to examine before the executive might find one (like B) which is marked (with an association to LIST-N), and therefore recallable. From such assumptions it is clear that FRAN will simulate the Tulving *et al.* results; a given cue will serve as a retrieval cue for a to-be-remembered item only if (or most probably if) that relationship was aroused (and tagged) at the time of input.

A further remark is called for in regard to multiple-list learning. If, after learning List-1, FRAN is exposed to a second set of unrelated items designated as List-2, it will proceed to learn them "from scratch," much as though List-1 had not been learned previously. Items on List-2 and associative paths between them will be marked with a distinct List-2 marker, and the new ENTRYSET will be List-2 words associated to the cognitive element "List-2." In recall of List-2, of course, S would use the List-2 ENTRYSET, would search through only those associative pathways tagged with a List-2 marker, and would recall only those retrieved items associated to a List-2 marker. In brief, the list-marking process keeps the two lists separated in storage and in recall, even if the lists have some items in common.

What is not elaborated at present in FRAN is a specific mechanism to account for forgetting of List-1 during List-2 learning. The presumed losses due to forgetting will be of several kinds: (1) loss of the associations from the List-1 marker to the set of entry words for List-1, and (2) loss or confusion of the list markers that tag words and associative pathways. Losses of the first type cause forgetting of entire chunks or subjective units since an entryword cues recall of a network of associated items. Losses of the second type cause forgetting of items within categories, losses in recognition memory, or list discrimination. Anderson and I have not investigated the consequences of specific forgetting mechanisms in FRAN, although several are plausible. One idea is that the list markers are not in fact distinct, based as they are on sets of internal and external contextual stimuli prevailing during list presentation. To the extent that markers for List-1 and List-2 are similar, then associating "List-2" to its entry words may cause unlearning of the associations from the List-1 marker to its entry words. The situation would be functionally similar to an A-B, A'-C paradigm with different responses and similar stimuli. This hypothesis would then predict the standard results regarding retroactive and proactive interference in forgetting of multiple free-recall lists. It also implies that forgetting mainly involves whole clusters of items, and that probing with the appropriate retrieval cues at the retention test would eliminate much of the forgetting (see Tulving and Psotka, 1971).

I could continue laying out one or another result in the literature which FRAN simulates, but it is more informative to consider its failures.

MISFITS OF FRAN

With an almost uncanny correspondence, the failures of FRAN are almost precisely those which organizational theorists have always considered on intuitive grounds to be the major difficulties for a word-to-word associative theory of free recall. What Anderson has done with his precise simulation model is to explicitly demonstrate the deficiencies of a plausible and explicit associative model of free recall. The deficiencies are instructive insofar as they raise difficulties that can not easily be "hand-waved" aside by proponents of simple associative theories of free recall.

Category Blocking

A first elementary difficulty is that FRAN does not show enough recall nor nearly enough category clustering when she is learning categorized word lists. She particularly lags behind human subjects in these respects when the list items are presented blocked by categories. FRAN does recall and cluster categorized lists more than unrelated-word lists, and she is a bit better on blocked than on randomized lists. But the effects in the simulation are far too small to fit the human data, particularly with respect to category clustering (see Anderson, in press).

What is wrong here? What is wrong is that FRAN uses the instance-to-instance associative strategy, and despite frequent conjectures to the contrary, that strategy simply does not provide the amount of category clustering which adults exhibit in their recall. What is needed is to allow FRAN to use a nonlist word (specifically, the name of the category) as a central entryword into the instances of a category. That would implement the "superordinate" retrieval route which was proposed in Bousfield's (1953) earliest papers on the topic.

Slamecka's Results

FRAN also fails badly in its attempt to stimulate the results of an experiment by Slamecka (1968). Following one or more input trials, some subjects were given half the list on a sheet and told to recall only the remaining half of the list. Their recall of this remaining half was no better (in fact, was frequently worse) than that of control subjects who were trying to recall the entire list. Later experiments by Allen (1969) and Anderson (in press) have shown that with various methodological refinements the half-list "cued" subjects may recall seven to fifteen percent of the unrecalled words of the control subjects. But the fact remains that these effects are very small considering the measures taken to produce positive cueing effects.

FRAN was run on a 40-item simulation of Slamecka's procedure. A study-then-test cycle was done followed by a second study trial, followed by a cued or noncued recall test. The cued condition was simulated by composing FRAN's entry words of the 20 cue (list) words, as well as the usual five from its STS, and the three from ENTRYSET. This takes the hard line that the optimal strategy is for the experimental subject to try to cue recall from the presented half-list. In the control simulation, FRAN recalled all the 40 words she could, then was allowed to study those words recalled for an extra time, trying to stumble across another list word or two to recall. This extra time proved almost completely ineffectual for FRAN as it is, too, for humans. FRAN recalled 14.8 words out of 40 on Trial 1 (7.4 out of each half-list). On Trial 2, on the to-be-recalled half list of 20, FRAN recalled 14.6 when cued, but only 10.6 in the noncued, control condition. So with half-list cueing, FRAN recalled 42% of the words she could not recall without cues. The size of the predicted effect is to be compared to the 0 to 15% improvement observed by half-list cueing under more or less optimal conditions.

The conclusion, much as Slamecka indicated, is that either subjects do not use the half-list cues in the way they should (or there is something inhibiting about its use), or else we are seriously in error, theoretically, in assuming that subjects are using interitem associations as their primary retrieval routes. The conclusion from Slamecka's result, as from FRAN's attempted simulation, is essentially negative: a simple prediction of an associative model is not confirmed. So far as I am aware, there is no compelling theoretical analysis of the significance of Slamecka's findings. It is clear that we could make ad hoc assumptions about how FRAN deals with the half-list cueing procedure, so that we predict no effect. But ad hoc assumptions specifically designed to fit one piece of data are not very satisfying.

Part-to-Whole Negative Transfer

Another failing of FRAN is that, unlike Tulving's (1966) subjects, she does not display negative transfer in going from a part-list to a whole-list of unrelated words. The exact conditions which produce positive as opposed to negative part-to-whole transfer are still being determined. But the standard interpretation is that the negative transfer reflects the persistence of an nonoptimal organization from the part to the whole list. The issue was whether there was any natural way to obtain negative transfer from FRAN.

An appealing method to try to produce negative transfer uses FRAN's differentiation of LIST tags as the mechanism. In studying the part list, FRAN tags word-nodes and useable associative pathways among them with a LIST-1 marker. Suppose that the subject does not understand the construction of the second (whole) list; in particular, suppose he is unsure whether each word of LIST-1 is also in LIST-2. Wishing to avoid intrusions, suppose the person (and FRAN) will recall a whole-list word only if it has a LIST-2 tag on it. The transfer subject may still use as search paths the associative pathways marked with a LIST-1 tag, but his recall is edited for LIST-2 recognition, inhibiting recall of items having only LIST-1 tags on them.

Along with the control condition (irrelevant prior-list learning) and the above condition which required a LIST-2 tag for recall, we also ran FRAN in a third condition which permitted recall of a word if either a LIST-1 or LIST-2 tag were on it. This was supposed to simulate informed subjects who know that all LIST-1 words are in LIST-2, a condition which is alleged by Tulving and Mandler (numerous personal communications, 1968–1970) to produce positive transfer.

The simulation involved 10 Monte Carlos per group on a 12-item part list for four trials, followed by a 24-item whole list for five trials. The simulation results are shown in Figure 11 giving the mean words recalled per condition over the five trials on the whole list. The results are complicated and conclusions depend on what measure one uses to

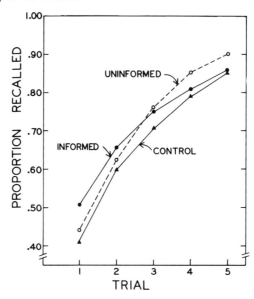

Fig. 11. Mean proportion recalled by FRAN on Whole List 2 under three different conditions.

assess negative transfer. If one examines total words recalled over the five trials, both informed and uninformed conditions show positive transfer with respect to the control condition. Another measure is the learning rate, θ, estimated from the proportionate increase in recall from trial to trial. Assessed in this manner, the uninformed subjects had the highest learning rate and the informed subjects had the lowest, with all pairwise differences statistically significant. This predicted ordering of conditions does not correspond to the facts, regardless of which measure of transfer we take.

Inspection of Figure 11 brings out several curiosities. For instance, the "informed" subjects begin at a higher initial recall level but improve more slowly over trials than the "uninformed" subjects (see Lesgold & Bower, 1970, for a similar cross-over in serial-to-paired associate transfer). It appears that this cross-over is caused by FRAN's algorithms for replacing words on its ENTRYSET. In the "informed" condition, FRAN tends to keep old LIST-1 items on its ENTRYSET since they are not rejected outright because of having the wrong list tag, and they do lead FRAN into recall of many words. The cross-over by the "uninformed" subjects comes about because they must construct practically a new ENTRYSET for LIST-2; and in thus starting over, almost from scratch, FRAN selects new entry words that are more central to the entire list than was true in the "informed" condition.

This reconstruction of the three conditions suggests that negative transfer could be produced by special ad hoc assumptions regarding the persistence of part-list items on FRAN's ENTRYSET when it learns the whole list. However, the problem again is one of elegance; a specific ad hoc theoretical assumption would be adopted merely to fit one disturbing piece of data, and that detracts from the value of the model.

Rule Discovery and Generation

Another deficiency of FRAN is that she can not solve verbal problems that require her to note and keep track of a common *relationship*. For example, if FRAN were to be given a list of 10 words rhyming with *cat*, plus 10 rhyming with *frog*, she would not now "recognize" the common phonemic concepts. Nor is she now capable of using a phonemic concept (or simple classificatory rule) as a rule of generating and retrieving instances of the rule that were presented on the memory list.

This deficiency is somewhat like FRAN's deficiency with categorized lists, wherein she predicts too little clustering because (a) she does not "recognize" or label the categorical structure of the list, and (b) she does not use the category label (a nonlist item) as a retrieval cue on ENTRYLIST.

A beginning towards rectifying these deficits would be to explicitly label the associative relations in FRAN's memory, and have her notice and temporarily record what relations proved useful in finding relations· between items on the memory lists. In this manner, she might discover that "superordinate of X" or "rhyme of X" are useful in reducing search-time to find relations among list-items. Matters would also be helped by permitting FRAN to have nonlist words (like a category name) as elements of ENTRYSET, or by letting a "word-plus-relation" (e.g., "rhymes of *frog*") serve as an element on ENTRYSET.

Linguistic Structure

The other serious deficit of FRAN is that she is not a language comprehender; she does not "understand" sentences in any different sense than she understands random strings of the same words. If the successive words in the list were those of a sensible sentence, FRAN would not treat them any differently than she would a randomized list of the same words, and her recall would be about the same in the two cases. People, of course, recall the linguistically structured lists much better, and the more so the closer the word order approximates grammatical English (Miller & Selfridge, 1950). This failing of FRAN is a serious flaw, but one shared by all explicit models of free recall with which I am familiar. The experiment violates the tacit "boundary conditions" of the usual free recall experiment; it deals with language comprehension and its effect on memory, and models of free recall are simply not addressed to that topic. Models for dealing with comprehension are still in very rudimentary stages. The problem is exceedingly complex; the papers in this volume by Collins and Quillian, by Kintsch, and by Rumelhart, Lindsay, and Norman, illustrate the intricacies and complexities of speculating about semantic memory and sentence comprehension.

As Postman points out elsewhere in this volume, correctly I think, the mass of systematic results from memory experiments have not yet been substantially illuminated by these speculations regarding the structure of semantic memory. The speculators seem more concerned with accounting for certain linguistic distinctions, intuitions, and competences shared by us all than in programming explicit learning models, fitting learning curves, and the like. There are obvious differences among the conference participants in what they consider to be the "important problems" to be solved (e.g., understanding language comprehension versus the data from standard memory experiments), and their strategy for approaching their problems. This issue can be expected to generate more efforts like those of the papers mentioned which try to draw conceptual bridges between the two areas.

FRAN AND FREE RECALL THEORIES

Before closing this discussion, perhaps some final comments are warranted on FRAN and the current state of theories of free recall. In my estimation, FRAN is the most powerful explicit model of free recall now available. In a comparison with current mathematical models of free recall (e.g., Shiffrin, 1970; Norman & Rumelhart, 1970), FRAN is to be favored because it fits some of the most elementary "organizational" facts about free-recall protocols (e.g., increasing SO over trials of unrelated words). Such facts are typically not addressed by those models for the very good reason that those models typically assume that individual list-items are stored and retrieved independently of one another. The item-independence assumption is extremely useful for simplifying mathematical derivations, but, I presume, all of us now believe it to be false. In comparison to a semantic marker theory such as Kintsch's in this volume, the important remark is that FRAN is a going, operative program that, in fact, fits (some) data, whereas Kintsch's speculations about a possible model are, so far as I know, still in the planning stage, and inoperative.

Actually, simulating FRAN has taught us several salutary things. One obvious fact is that, at one level of theorizing, there is not much discriminable difference between an "organizational" and an "associa-tionistic" approach to theory-construction about free recall. In this re-gard, I am in substantial agreement with Postman's comments in his chapter in this volume. There are a few differences, like a preference for labelled (as opposed to unlabelled) associative relations, a preference for selecting superordinate entry-points rather than following a strictly associative strategy, and so forth. But the differences do not strike me as terribly significant at this level. On the other hand, I would take strong issue with those "hand-wavers" who claim that only facts about associations need be invoked to account for free recall data. To draw an analogy, to build a bridge I need steel beams and concrete, but the problem of designing and building the bridge is not solved by simply saying it is some combination of steel beams and concrete. I feel the same about the ubiquitous reference to associatons as explanations of mnemonic facts. We might agree that the "data-base" of the mind is an elaborate graph structure of various relations ("associations"). But there remains the "design" problem, of specifying how an executive oper-ates with and upon that associative graph for the purpose of remembering the material at hand. The inadequacy of the simplistic, associationistic approach to memory has been revealed by its failure to provide a de-tailed specification of those processes and "mental operations."

It is often said that one learns more from one's failures than one's successes. This has certainly been true of our simulations with FRAN. We have essentially learned the limitations of a model which simply operates with associations among list words. It was not obvious to us before we ran the simulations that FRAN would have the specific deficits discussed earlier, especially those where the size of a predicted effect is too small by several orders of magnitude. Those are the kinds of therapeutic demonstrations that prevent our automatic reliance upon simple associative explanations of future results in free recall. The ap-propriate challenge to an associative hand-wave is "show me how, ex-actly." If nothing else, FRAN should at least prove herself therapeutic in legitimizing such sufficiency queries.

Summary

Some principles underlying research on organization and memory were reviewed. Gestalt laws of grouping were illustrated in verbal learning contexts, demonstrating the influence of perceptual variables upon memory units. The Gestalt postulate that subjects "search after mean-ing" was viewed in terms of assimilation of unknown and to-be-remembered material to other things subjects already know. The discovery and application of rules for generating the to-be-remembered material was one illustration used; a second was the production of natural-language mediators for aiding memory of nonsense materials. The use of rules was also illustrated in characterizing what the person learns about systematic serial patterns.

The free recall task was then discussed since it provides some salient evidence for organizational processes in memory. After characterizing list-differentiation cues and the nature of event memory, a set of retrieval strategies used by subjects was enumerated. A computer simulation model for free recall, FRAN, was described. FRAN postulates a set of mental structures and learning processes operating upon an associative "semantic memory." FRAN was shown to be a powerful theory for explaining many of the standard results in free recall. However, its deficiencies were also regarded as informative with respect to claims in the literature and associative versus organizational explanations of results.

References

Allen, M. M. Cueing and retrieval in free recall. *Journal of Experimental Psychology,* 1969, **81,** 29–35.
Anderson, J. FRAN: a simulation model of free recall. In G. H. Bower (Ed.), *The psychology of learning and motivation.* Vol. 5. New York: Academic Press, in press.
Anglin, J. M. *The growth of word meaning.* Research Monograph No. 63. Cambridge, Massachusetts: M.I.T. Press, 1970.
Asch, S. E. Reformulation of the problem of association. *American Psychologist,* 1969, **24,** 92–102.
Asch, S. E., Ceraso, J., & Heimer, W. Perceptual conditions of association. *Psychological Monographs,* 1960, **74.**
Battig, W. F., & Montague, W. E. Category norms for verbal items in 56 categories. *Journal of Experimental Psychology Monographs,* 1969, **80.**
Bernbach, H. A. Decision processes in memory. *Psychological Review,* 1967, **74,** 462–480.
Bousfield, W. A. The occurrence of clustering in recall of randomly arranged associates. *Journal of General Psychology,* 1953, **49,** 229–273.
Bower, G. H. Analysis of a mnemonic device. *American Scientist,* 1970, **58,** 496–510.
Bower, G. H. Mental imagery and associative learning. In L. W. Gregg (Ed.), *Cognition in learning and memory.* New York: Wiley, in press.
Bower, G. H. and Bolton, Laura S. Why are rhymes easy to learn? *Journal of Experimental Psychology,* 1969, **82,** No. 3, 453–461.
Bower, G. H., Clark, M., Lesgold, A. M., & Winzenz, D. Hierarchical retrieval schemes in recall of categorized word lists. *Journal of Verbal Learning and Verbal Behavior,* 1969, **8,** 323–343.

Bower, G. H., & Springston, F. Pauses as recoding points in letter series. *Journal of Experimental Psychology*, 1970, **83**, 421–430.
Bower, G. H., & Winzenz, D. Group structure, coding, and memory for digit series. *Journal of Experimental Psychology Monographs*, 1969, **80**, No. 2, Part 2, 1–17.
Collins, A. M., & Quillian, M. R. Retrieval time from semantic memory. *Journal of Verbal Learning and Verbal Behavior*, 1969, **8**, 240–247.
Deese, J. Influence of inter-item associative strength upon immediate free recall. *Psychological Reports*, 1959, **5**, 305–312.
Eagle, M., & Leiter, E. Recall and recognition in intentional and incidental learning. *Journal of Experimental Psychology*, 1964, **68**, 58–63.
Earhard, M. The facilitation of memorization by alphabetic instructions. *Canadian Journal of Psychology*, 1967, **21**, 15–24.
Glanzer, M. Storage mechanisms in recall. In G. H. Bower (Ed.), *The psychology of learning and motivation*. Vol. 5. New York: Academic Press, in press.
Glanzer, M., & Clark, W. H. The verbal loop hypothesis: Binary numbers. *Journal of Verbal Learning and Verbal Behavior*, 1963, **2**, 301–309.
Groninger, L. D. Natural language mediation and covert rehearsal in short-term memory. *Psychonomic Science*, 1966, **5**, 135–136.
Jenkins, J. J., & Russell, W. A. Associative clustering during recall. *Journal of Abnormal and Social Psychology*, 1952, **47**, 818–821.
Johnson, N. F. The role of chunking and organization in the process of recall. In G. H. Bower (Ed.), *The psychology of learning and motivation*. Vol. 4. New York: Academic Press, 1970.
Koffka, K. *Principles of Gestalt psychology*. New York: Harcourt, Brace, & World. 1935.
Köhler, W. *Dynamics in psychology*. New York: Liveright, 1940.
Kintsch, W. Models for free recall and recognition. In D. A. Norman (Ed.), *Models of human memory*. New York: Academic Press, 1970.
Lesgold, A. M., & Bower, G. H. Inefficiency of serial knowledge for associative responding. *Journal of Verbal Learning and Verbal Behavior*, 1970, **9**, 456–466.
Light, L. L., & Carter-Sobell, L. Effects of changed semantic context on recognition memory. *Journal of Verbal Learning and Verbal Behavior*, 1970, **9**, 1–11.
McKay, D. G., & Bever, T. A. In search of ambiguity. *Perception and Psychophysics*, 1967, **2**, 193–200.
Mandler, G. Association and organization: facts, fancies, and theories. In T. Dixon & D. Horton (Eds.), *Verbal behavior and general behavior theory*. Englewood Cliffs, New Jersey: Prentice-Hall, 1968.
Miller, G. A. The free recall of redundant strings of letters. *Journal of Experimental Psychology*, 1958, **56**, 485–491.
Miller, G. A., Galanter, E., & Pribram, K. H. *Plans and the structure of behavior*. New York: Holt, Rinehart and Winston, 1960.
Miller, G. A., & Selfridge, J. A. Verbal context and the recall of meaningful material. *American Journal of Psychology*, 1950, **63**, 176–185.
Miller, W. F., & Shaw, A. C. Linguistic methods in picture processing: a survey. *Proceedings of the Fall Joint Computer Conference*, Dec. 1968, pp. 279–290.
Newell, A., & Simon, H. A. Computers in psychology. In R. D. Luce, R. R. Bush, & E. Galanter (Eds.), *Handbook of mathematical psychology*. Vol. I. New York: Wiley, 1963.
Norman, D. A., & Rumelhart, D. E. A system for perception and memory. In

D. Norman (Ed.), *Models of human memory*. New York: Academic Press, 1970.

Prentice, W. C., & Asch, S. E. Paired-associations with related and unrelated pairs of nonsense figures. *American Journal of Psychology*, 1958, **71**, 247–254.

Prytulak, L. Natural language mediation. *Cognitive Psychology*, 1971, **2**, 1–56.

Restle, F. Theory of serial pattern learning: Structural trees. *Psychological Review*, 1970, **77**, 481–495.

Restle, F., & Brown, E. Organization of serial pattern learning. In G. H. Bower (Ed.), *The psychology of learning and motivation*. Vol. 4. New York: Academic Press, 1970.

Rosenfeld, A. *Picture processing by computer*. New York: Academic Press, 1969.

Ross, J., & Lawrence, K. A. Some observations on memory artifice. *Psychonomic Science*, 1968, **13**, 107–108.

Scandura, J. M. Role of rules in behavior: Toward an operational definition of what (rule) is learned. *Psychological Review*, 1970, **77**, 516–533.

Shiffrin, R. Memory search. In D. Norman (Ed.), *Models of human memory*. New York: Academic Press, 1970.

Shuell, T. J. Retroactive inhibition in free-recall learning of categorized lists. *Journal of Verbal Learning and Verbal Behavior*, 1968, **7**, 797–805.

Shuell, T. J., & Keppel, G. Item priority in free recall. *Journal of Verbal Learning and Verbal Behavior*, 1968, **7**, 969–971.

Simon, H. A. What is visual imagery? An information processing interpretation. In L. W. Gregg (Ed.), *Cognition in learning and memory*. New York: Wiley, in press.

Slamecka, N. J. An examination of trace storage in free recall. *Journal of Experimental Psychology*, 1968, **76**, 504–513.

Thomson, D. M., & Tulving, E. Associative encoding and retrieval: weak and strong cues. *Journal of Experimental Psychology*, 1970, **86**, 255–262.

Tulving, E. Subjective organization and the effects of repetition in multi-trial free recall learning. *Journal of Verbal Learning and Verbal Behavior*, 1966, **5**, 195–197.

Tulving, E. The effects of presentation and recall of material in free recall learning. *Journal of Verbal Learning and Verbal Behavior*, 1967, **6**, 175–184.

Tulving, E., & Osler, S. Effectiveness of retrieval cues in memory for words. *Journal of Experimental Psychology*, 1968, **77**, 593–601.

Tulving, E., & Pearlstone, Z. Availability versus accessibility of information in memory for words. *Journal of Verbal Learning and Verbal Behavior*, 1966, **5**, 381–391.

Tulving, E., & Psotka, J. Retroactive inhibition in free recall: Inaccessibility of information available in the memory store. *Journal of Experimental Psychology*, 1971, **87**, 1–8.

Tulving, E., & Thomson, D. M. Retrieval processes in recognition memory: Effects of associative context. *Journal of Experimental Psychology*, 1971, **87**, 116–124.

Underwood, B. J., & Erlebacher, A. H. Studies of coding in verbal learning. *Psychological Monographs: General and Applied*, 1965, **79**, (13, Whole No. 606).

Underwood, B. J., & Richardson, J. Verbal concept learning as a function of instructions and dominance level. *Journal of Experimental Psychology*, 1956, **51**, 229–238.

Waugh, N. C. Presentation time and free recall. *Journal of Experimental Psychology*, 1967, **73**, 39–44.

Wertheimer, M. Untersuchungen zur Lehre von der Gestalt, II. *Psychologische Forschung,* 1923, **4,** 301–350.

Whitman, J. R., & Garner, W. R. Free recall learning of visual figures as a function of form of internal structure. *Journal of Experimental Psychology,* 1962, **64,** 558–564.

Winzenz, D. Group structure and coding in serial learning. Unpublished Ph.D. dissertation, Stanford University: Stanford, California, 1970.

Woodworth, R. S., & Schlosberg, H. *Experimental psychology,* Revised ed. New York: Holt, Rinehart and Winston, 1954.

Yngve, V. A model and an hypothesis for language structure. *Proceedings of the American Philosophical Society,* 1960, **104,** 444–466.

Yntema, D., & Trask, F. P. Recall as a search process. *Journal of Verbal Learning and Verbal Behavior,* 1963, **2,** 65–74.

4 | *Organization and Recognition*[1]

George Mandler

Current interest in the relation between organization and memory
has been typically concerned with the organization of long-term storage
and the retrieval of items from that storage. Organization and memory
may be considered as nearly synonymous from one point of view, since
presumably only items that are organized and thus retrievable can in

[1] Preparation of this chapter and the research reported herein were supported
by National Science Foundation Grant GB 20798 and by a grant MH-15828 from
the National Institute of Mental Health to the Center for Human Information
Processing. I am indebted to Marilyn Borges, Richard H. Meltzer, and Karalyn
Patterson for experimental and theoretical collaboration, and to Alan D. Baddeley,
Jean M. Mandler, and Endel Tulving for most helpful criticism and suggestions.
None of these is to be held responsible for any radical, moderate, or conservative
assertions included herein.

fact be recalled (cf. Mandler, 1967). As a result, most of the work
in organization and memory has looked at the free recall task. In that
context, investigators have usually varied the opportunities given to
the subject in organizing material at the time of input. Such variations
have included the presentation of experimenter-organized lists, or giving
subjects some specific opportunity to organize the material prior to recall.
Our own work (Mandler, 1967, 1968, 1970) has stressed maximal opportunities for organizing material by requiring subjects to sort lists of
words into categories of their own choosing. Subsequent to such sorting
and categorization, and when the organization has reached a stable level,
various aspects of recall are used as measures of the effect of prior
organization. We have shown extensively, for example, that under these
conditions recall is in fact a linear function of the number of categories
used during sorting (with a limit of seven categories, i.e., without an
overload on category recall).

It might be useful at this point to state once more in general terms
what we mean by organizational processes and variables. Generally, the
term "organization" refers to mental structures that establish relations
among items, events, features, etc. These structures are, at least, of three
types: categorical, serial, and relational (Mandler, 1970). Any of these
organizations or structures (to use Garner's, 1962, usage) refer to stable
and consistent relations among members of a subset of such items or
events. Such an organization is categorical if the subset refers to a semantic category, for example, serial when some syntax is implied, and
relational when some mnemonic device is used to relate two or more
items to each other. Organizational variables are those variables that
determine the structure of these organizations, their stability and cohesiveness, and the specific relational devices used.

As a corollary to our interest in organizational processes, we are concerned with the organization, or reorganization, of material that is
present in permanent storage. We are not interested, at this time, with
the processes whereby new items enter that lexicon. Furthermore, all
the empirical and theoretical discussions in this chapter deal with recognition out of long-term or organized memory and do not address short-
term or primary memory processes. Finally—except in passing—we are
not going to discuss ordering or syntactic processes. The study of events,
lists, and items has as its primary justification the access to semantic or
categorical structures without significantly involving syntactic structures.

Some five years ago the problem of recognition and organization
seemed to be relatively simple and we entered on what we thought would
be a series of minor experiments to demonstrate what was then conventional wisdom and what is still accepted as a plausible position (e.g.,

Kintsch, 1970; Murdock, 1968). Specifically, it is assumed that while recall depends on the retrieval of items by means of the organization of storage, recognition does not. We believed then, as apparently everybody else did too, that subjects would not use retrieval systems during recognition, whether the task presented them with organized or with unstructured lists of items. What was presumably the case was that we were dealing with two distinct processes in memory—a retrieval process and a decision process. Recognition depended—by that argument—solely on a simple decision process unaffected by organizational variables. Subjects process a word presented in the recognition task, look up that word in long-term storage and, if in fact it had a tag indicating that it had been previously presented, then it would be recognized as an old item. Müller (1913) first made this distinction between retrieval and decision processes and Kintsch (1968) summarized this point of view most emphatically by saying that organization "can have no effect upon recognition, since organization facilitates retrieval and only recall involves retrieval."

Our hunt for that elusive decision process, independent of retrieval processes, is what will concern some of this presentation. We shall describe some of the persistent findings of relations between organization and recognition in extensions of our previous experiments on organization and recall. After a brief review of the relevant literature, we shall move to an elaboration of the conditions under which the decision process, free of organizational variables, might be found. Following the realization that the organization-free decision process can be found—surprise, surprise—only in marginally organized lists, we shall move on to further evidence on the effect of retrieval processes on recognition. Finally, we shall conclude with some suggestions for a theory of recognition and organization and a final advertisement in favor of organization theory.

Our superior hindsight suggests—particularly in light of other developments in information processing—that the search for two different and largely independent processes operating on two such closely related phenomena as recall, or the retrieval of previously presented material, and its recognition when presented again, should be futile. As it will develop, decision processes based on occurrence tags do take place, as does recognition based on retrieval processes. Recognition requires both occurrence information and organization, though there may be different emphases in different situations. One such—to us now obvious—difference deals with the time since presentation. It is intuitively appealing to suggest that the face of somebody met just yesterday is recognized on the basis of occurrence information, but that somebody one has not seen for years is appropriately recognized only after often extensive retrieval and search involving contexts and categories. With this advertisement of our eventual insights, we can return to our tale.

In 1969 we published the first results of our search for a simple distinction between recall and recognition (Mandler, Pearlstone, & Koopmans, 1969). We had discovered, to our dismay, that no simple distinction was possible. We found that recognition (whether measured by hit rate or by discriminability as indexed by d') was in fact related to degree of organization, again defined as number of categories used in the sorting task.[2] Both in immediate tests and in delayed recognition tests, number of categories and recognition scores were positively correlated, though in no case as strongly as the relationship between number of categories (NC) and amount of recall. In that paper we pointed out that a side issue in the recognition task, namely the problem of semantic confusion, also presented us with unexpected results. We were unable to find semantic confusion (specifically between words and their synonyms) in a recognition test of highly organized lists. Thus our initial data suggested that there was in fact a relationship between recognition and organization, and that, in addition, when subjects are presented with well-organized items, they are not influenced by semantic confusion. The issue of semantic confusion is relevant here, because presumably a recognition test based solely on locating a word in long-term storage and determining whether it does or does not have an occurrence tag, would frequently lead to the misidentification of certain words in storage if some type of semantic feature analysis is used. Given a particular item and the fact that its semantic features have occurrence tags, then a similar item would also, because of the overlap of semantic features, be identified as being old. On the other hand, a high degree of organization would identify an item in storage more precisely (as a function of the particular structure used to organize the material), and in that case not only would recognition be influenced by organization, but semantic confusion would be drastically reduced. The organization would help locate an item more specifically than a simple occurrence tag might.

While we were hunting for some evidence for the independence of recall and recognition processes, other research suggested that such independence can in fact be found. Both Bower (1968) and Kintsch (1968) showed that while experimenter-organized lists produced the well-known facilitating effect in recall, they did not show any differences in recogni-

[2] In all of these analyses, recalled items were discounted in the computation of the relation between recognition and organization. Thus, these relationships hold between organizational variables (specifically, the number of categories used in sorting) and the recognition of nonrecalled items. Any other analyses would, of course, only have restated in part the organization-recall relationship.

tion. Bower, Lesgold, and Tieman (1969) sⁱ cifically talked about "occurrence information" which determines recognition and which is "independent of retrieval cues or schemes for accessing (a word) in recall" (p. 492). Other data (e.g., Davis, 1967; Anisfeld & Knapp, 1968; Underwood, 1965) supported the general notion that semantic or associative confusion does exist during recognition, and thus argued against our other discrepant finding.

However, there has been an increasing amount of evidence in the other direction as well. For example, Lachman and Tuttle (1965) showed that when syntactic organization is used, that is, when organization is truly at a very high level, then recognition is in fact better for organized than for unorganized items. In 1969, a paper by Bower, Clark, Lesgold, and Winzenz (1969) also showed that hierarchically organized lists produced recognition superior to that of random organizations, and they concluded that "recognition of list membership of a word depends on the structure of the list as well as the words that were in it" (p. 331). And D'Agostino (1969), in a replication of Kintsch's experiment, with better controls, showed that a blocked categorized list in fact produced better recognition (with a hit rate of .77 and false-alarm rate of .07) than when that list was presented randomly (with a hit rate of .67 and a false-alarm rate of .06). Another attempt to clarify the Kintsch finding was made by Bruce and Fagan (1970) who assumed that by varying the number of categories in a list they were varying degree of structure. They showed that a 42-word list made up of six categories is recalled better than one made up of 42 categories. Such a finding is directly deducible from our previous work on the category-recall relationship (cf. Mandler, 1967, Figure 7, p. 358), but it is unclear why recognition should vary, particularly when, as in the Bruce and Fagan experiment, the test is administered immediately after presentation and is apparently subject to ceiling effects.

Finally, some recent data from our laboratory (Borges & Mandler in press) cast a shadow over the distinction between random and blocked presentations of categories and their effect on recall. We have found that blocked presentation is indeed superior to random presentation, when randomization involves a lag (spacing) between instances of the same category of 4 to 6 items. When that lag is increased to 9 to 11 items, that is, when instances of the category occur at long intervals, then performance is equal to the blocked presentation. Most of the blocked-random differences reported in the literature typically used spacings of the intermediate type. Without going into any explanations of this finding, it does suggest that simple blocked presentation is not the only way to produce high performance in recall.

Recognition also seems to be sensitive to context, an effect that argues against a simple decision process theory. Light and Carter-Sobell (1970) have shown that the recognition of polysemous nouns is affected by adjectival modifiers. They suggested that retrieval or search operations are important for recognition as well as for recall, and also pointed out that a simple occurrence tag explanation seems to imply that words have but a single representation in long-term memory, an interpretation that not only violates the fact that words have more than one "meaning," but also seems to go against any simple theory of semantic markers or features. Similarly, Tulving and Thomson (1971) demonstrated that recognition of an individual item is dependent on other words that accompany it at the time of input or test. They argued that these results disagree with the widely held view that there is no retrieval problem in recognition memory.

The purpose of the present paper is not to argue at length about the proper resolution of discrepant data, nor, unfortunately, to present a reasonable theory of the effect of organization on recognition. Rather, it will present some data which hopefully will suggest the direction in which an eventual theory that relates organization and recognition ought to go. Such a direction will include the importance of retrieval processes for recognition of material from well-organized lists and the acknowledgment of an organization-free decision process which, however, operates primarily for unorganized and thus fairly transient events or items, and which is ordinarily overwhelmed by organizational variables.

At the present time the theoretical notions which restrict recognition to a decision process about the presence or absence of occurrence tags have not been extensively developed. For example, it is unknown whether an occurrence tag is added to a word (or to the semantic features constituting that word) whenever that item is presented. Thus it is unclear whether presentation by itself or some more active process is involved in the allocation of occurrence tags. Since the proponents of the decision-process point of view have been relatively silent on this point, I do not wish to assume that they have implied one or the other position. What I want to do is present the following considerations:

1. An experimental inquiry into the conditions under which confusion of items in the recognition task does in fact occur. This will be presented in the context of a task in which subjects have varying degrees of experience with the input lists and then are required to distinguish, in a recognition test, among old items and several types of new items, including items from another list, semantically related items, and totally new items.

2. An analysis of recognition performance for items which were presented but not recalled, particularly in a context where subjects must make decisions about the category membership of the items.

3. An analysis of recognition performance for items that were never originally presented—and therefore could not have been given occurrence tags during input—but were recalled. Specifically, this analysis addresses itself to the question whether, subsequent to recall, intrusions are recognized as old items, or as something in between.

The theoretical questions that these arguments and data will raise deal directly with the question whether occurrence tags are assigned during presentation only, or whether the active recall process participates and intervenes in the assignment of occurrence tags. Clearly, if nonrecalled items are not recognized as old items and if intrusions are, then, at least at some times, a more active process than simple presentation and assignment of occurrence tags is involved.

Before proceeding with the general plan outlined above, I would like to dispose of one theoretical argument and a couple of dangling issues from our previous work.

The theoretical argument involves a statement made by Kintsch (1970) in which he excludes class recognition as a relevant aspect of recognition memory. He states, "I believe that nothing is gained by confusing recognition on the basis of familiarity (item recognition) and class recognition. The latter is closely related to concept formation and involves very different processes than the recognition of items drawn from a single, homogeneous set" (p. 339). In other words, Kintsch states that when the recognition process involves the acceptance or rejection of an item on the basis of class membership (presumably category membership), this is a different process from what he would like to deal with in handling recognition memory. However, his argument eliminates a priori the possibility of one set of organizational variables affecting recognition, and thus begs the question. I believe that the use of organization in retrieval processes is in fact very close to concept formation, and if such retrieval plans do affect recognition, then a reasonable theory of recognition memory must consider the possibility that conceptual classificatory processes affect recognition memory. To show that the recognition of homogeneous, and presumably badly organized lists that do not involve any class recognition, is independent of any specifiable organizational variables fails to tackle the problem we hope to investigate here. If subjects make judgments not only on the basis of occurrence tags but also on the basis of class membership, then the structure of that class membership will affect recognition.

Organization and Recognition: Some Unfinished Agenda Items

In Mandler *et al.* (1969b) we showed that the false-alarm rate (after a two week delay) for random fillers and synonym fillers was essentially identical at about .25. It was clear that this was not due to any lack of recognition of the synonymity of the filler items with the original items, nor did it depend on the presence of both new and old items within the recognition list; even a list containing only new items showed the same false-alarm rate for synonyms and unrelated fillers. In order to relieve a nagging doubt, we repeated some of these experiments using acoustically similar fillers in order to show the generality of the recognition test (Mandler, Meltzer, & Pearlstone, 1969). We again had subjects sort 100 items and tested the subjects two weeks later on a recognition task in which they were given 200 words and had to make Yes/No judgments as to whether each word was or was not on the original list. The task used both unrelated and homophone fillers. Again, the false-alarm rate was around .25, regardless of whether old items occurred in the recognition list or not. Finally, in order to avoid the possibility that subjects had adopted different strategies by using different sets of features in the recognition task, we conducted one final experiment in which subjects were given *both* homophones and synonyms as filler words in the same recognition task. There was no distinction between the two types of fillers and the false-alarm rate was approximately .20. Thus, with well-organized lists we obtained no greater confusion with semantically related words (synonyms) and acoustically related words (homophones) than with unrelated words.

Finally, in the Mandler *et al.* (1969b) paper we had made the suggestion that subjects use a retrieval check following the decision process during recognition. We suggested that

> During recognition, items that are judged Old are in two states—those items that are initially given a high confidence rating and those about which subjects are less certain. It is the latter that are then subjected to the retrieval check, i.e., are they retrievable by the usual recall system? There are two kinds of items that are subjected to this test—New items called Old and Old items called Old. The low-confidence New items called Old cannot be retrieved and are then placed in the New–New category. . . . For the Old items called Old which are subjected to the retrieval test, we assume that the retrieval system operates just as in recall; it can recover more items the larger the number of categories used. Thus . . . there will be a proportion of low confidence Old–Old items that remains in that category and that proportion will be larger the greater NC. The resulting effect would be a fairly constant level of false-alarms and an increase in hit-rates with increasing NC (p. 421).

Wolford (1971) recently reported a similar observation of retrievability checks.

I would like briefly to present a description of one way in which such a retrievability process might operate. We deal with four types of items—old and new items that are unequivocally recognized, and old and new items that are considered questionable. It is these latter items that are subjected to the retrieval check. The decision is made whether the word belongs to one of the N categories used during the original sorting (and thus part of the retrieval system). If the item does not fit any of those categories it is called "new." Assume that the word is categorized as belonging to category A. The system then goes to category A and selects five words at random from that category, which we will call set A (the selection of five items is based on data not relevant here which suggests that category retrieval is in fact limited to some value near 5 on a single retrieval from a category). If the word being tested is in fact a member of set A, then it is called old; if it is not a member of set A it is called new. We assume that new words will almost always fail this test and be called new. The probability that an old word will in fact be called old as a result of this retrieval check is approximately 5/category size. The larger the category being sampled the less likely it is that the word will in fact be a member of set A, the smaller the category the more likely that it will be a member of set A. Clearly, with constant list length, the larger the number of categories used by the subject, the smaller will be the size of the categories. Thus, with a large value of NC (number of categories) there will be relatively smaller categories and therefore a greater likelihood that a word being checked in this retrieval check is in fact recognized and called old; conversely, the smaller the value of NC the less likely it is that the retrieval check will yield a positive recognition of an old word as old. Since this process only affects a small number of words, and since the check itself depends on the random choice of words from a set, one would not expect a relationship between NC and recognition to be very large and, in fact, as we have shown previously, the correlation between NC and recognition scores, while positive and significant, is not of an impressive magnitude (with a median r of about .48 between NC and d').

Effect of Organization (or Learning) on Occurrence Tags, Recognition and Semantic Similarity

In our previous work we have demonstrated that organizational variables affect recognition at least to some extent in the same fashion in which they affect recall. A related question asks whether recognition covaries with degree of organization. Some of the studies cited above have shown that a high degree of organization does under some circumstances improve recognition memory.

One of the continuing arguments in current studies of long-term recall and recognition concerns the class of variables that determine recall. Traditionally, it has been assumed that this class of variables is best listed under the rubric of "learning," while a recurring theme in the past ten years has been that classical "learning" variables should be replaced by "organizational" variables, that is to say, long-term memory in particular falls under the rubric of "organization."[3] One of the central issues in this discussion has been whether giving subjects additional trials or time with materials to be remembered is a "learning" variable or an "organizational" variable. Clearly the classical view has been that it is the former, while the organizational position is that any additional trials or time give subjects an additional opportunity to organize the material (i.e., to establish or discover organizations or relations among the items to be remembered). The sheer presentation of items as such, under that view, is irrelevant if it is not at the same time accompanied by organizational activity (see, for example, Mandler, 1967, and Tulving, 1966). It is not my purpose at this time to review the evidence for or against these two points of view. Rather, I would prefer to assert my allegiance to the organizational camp and to proceed on that basis.

In the experiment to be reported below, organization was varied by giving subjects increasing opportunities to organize a list of words. Clearly, these subjects also had an increasing opportunity to "learn" the material. However, I am not concerned with controlling for the degree of "learning" in this situation any more than experiments in the learning tradition are concerned with controlling degree of organization when varying classical learning variables such as number of trials or time. I would rather present this material and let the reader who is committed to some variation of an associative strength view reinterpret the data

[3] In using the concept of organization rather than learning in these experiments, no derogation is intended to the importance of learning as a psychological problem. On the contrary, by distinguishing processes of organization, reorganization, retrieval, storage, and structure (operating on the existing mental content) from learning processes which deal with the acquisition of new responses, items, and event structures, we hope to reawaken an interest in the distinction between *what* behavior is available and *when* it is displayed (Mandler, 1954, 1962). Making behavior (or responses) available is the problem of a psychology of learning, dealing with the integration of response sequences, and the establishment and shaping of new repertories. The psychology of organization deals with the accessibility and structure of existing repertories.

as indicating the effect of degree of learning on recognition. The data should be of interest regardless of the choice of interpretation. Specifically, the purpose of this experiment was to examine three aspects of recognition memory. First, we were interested in the degree to which recognition, as measured by hit rate and false-alarm rate for unrelated items, varies with the degree of organization (or learning) of a list. Second, the experiment further investigated the question of semantic confusion and asked whether increasing organization (or learning) defines an item more exactly and thus decreases the confusion between original items and their synonyms. Finally, we wished to investigate further the nature of specific occurrence tags. If an occurrence tag is given to an item whenever it appears, then degree of organization of that item should not influence the validity or strength of such an occurrence tag. The way the following experiment tested this particular proposition was to present subjects with two lists and give them as a task the recognition of one of those two lists. Presumably, items on both of the input lists would have general occurrence tags, and confusions between the target list (whichever it is) and items from the non-target list should give us some clues as to the function of specific occurrence tags. Thus, the occurrence information in these experiments is of two kinds: general and specific; the former is tested by the false-alarm rate to new "unrelated" items, the latter by confusions between the two lists. In the following presentation we give the most salient aspects of this experiment which has been described in detail elsewhere (Mandler et al., 1969a).

GENERAL DESIGN

Four different groups of subjects were tested. The basic variation was in the opportunity to organize two lists of 60 "unrelated" items each. *Group 4-Sort* was given four successive trials of sorting and categorizing the items; *Group 1-Sort* was given one sorting trial; *Group 7-Sec* was given the same amount of exposure time to the items as *Group 1-Sort*, but was not permitted overtly to categorize the items; *Group 2-Sec* was treated like *Group 7-Sec*, except that items were presented for two rather than seven seconds each, and subjects were not permitted to write down the items, as they were in the other three groups. In all groups, subjects were given identical experience with two consecutive lists, designated as List 1 and List 2. Following the presentation of List 2, all subjects were given a recognition task consisting of all the items from the two lists plus synonyms of subsets of the two lists and brand new unrelated items. Half of the subjects were told that List 1 was the target to be recognized; the other half of the subjects were given List 2 as their target.

SORTING TASK

Groups of subjects were seated in a room facing a projection screen. Each subject was given a booklet consisting of five pages: a blank page, and four pages divided into seven columns each. The subjects were shown nine practice words on the screen and instructed to look at each word as it appeared and write it down on the first page of the booklet. The subjects were then told that they would be shown 60 words on the screen, one at a time, and that these would be presented several times in new random orders. Their task was to group the words according to their meaning into any number of categories from two to seven. They were free to change their system of categorization at any time, but they were told to try to use the same categorization on subsequent trials after they had chosen a particular system. On the first presentation of the list, words were projected on the screen at the rate of one every seven seconds. When the subject first saw a word he wrote it down in one of the seven columns of the second page of the booklet. As each succeeding word appeared, he decided whether that word went with one of the groups of words on the page or whether it belonged in a new group. After the 60 words had been presented, subjects turned the page under the booklet and, after the slide tray had been replaced, started the second trial, and so on, for a total of four trials. On trials 2 to 4, words were presented at a four-second rate. *Group 4-Sort* subjects were given four such trials. *Group 1-Sort* subjects were given only the first sorting trial with seven seconds per item. *Group 7-Sec* subjects were not instructed to sort the words, but only to write down each word as it was presented. *Group 2-Sec* subjects saw each item for two seconds but were not permitted to write the words down. All subjects were told that they would be asked to recognize the items later. Following the presentation of the first list, the subjects were given a new booklet and the second list was presented in the same manner as the first as soon as a new slide case was inserted in the projector.

RECOGNITION TASK

Approximately seven minutes after the presentation of the second list, during which booklets had been collected and each subject had been given a deck of 180 IBM cards, the subjects started the recognition task. On each IBM card a word was printed in the upper right hand corner, followed by a pair of parentheses. Subjects were divided into two groups; half were told to put a Y (for Yes) beside all words that they had seen on List 1, and N (for No) for all words which had not been seen on the first list. The other half of the subjects were told to mark Y for items that had been on the second list, and N for all other items. In addition, subjects added a confidence rating, which will not be reported here. After marking each card, the subject turned it over and was told not to look at cards once they had been marked. The subjects were told to mark each card and to guess if uncertain. Each subject's set of cards was arranged in a different random order and contained the 120 items from the two lists, 30 synonyms (15 for each of the two lists), and 30 unrelated fillers.

These data make it possible to investigate hit rates as well as three types of confusion in recognition memory: general recognition errors of new unrelated words, semantic confusions between words and their synonyms, and occurrence confusion between the target and nontarget lists. Given one of the lists as a target in the recognition task, we obtain hit-rate probabilities of calling the old words old, and three false alarm probabilities of misrecognizing new unrelated words, synonyms, or words from the other, nontarget, list.

With four different groups, each given one of the four degrees of organizing opportunities, and with half of the subjects in each group given one of the two lists as the target, there were eight independent groups. Figure 1 shows the results of the recognition task for these eight groups. An analysis of variance was performed on each of the four recognition scores (one hit rate and three false-alarm rates) with four degrees of organization and two target lists as the independent variables. For the hit-rate data, the only significant effect was organization. For the list data (false alarms on items from the nontarget list) only the target effect was significant. For the semantic data (false alarms on synonyms of old words), organization was significant, as was the target effect. For new unrelated fillers, organization was a significant effect, as was targets. Finally, an analysis of d' values for hit rates and false alarms on new fillers showed an organization effect and a target effect. The mean d' values for the four organization groups from highest to lowest degree of organization were 3.35, 2.70, 2.12, and 1.15. For the two target lists the d' values were 1.87 for List 1 and 2.79 for List 2.

Thus the analyses confirm what is evident from Figure 1. Discriminability decreased with a decrease in organization, and List 2 was more discriminable than List 1. There was no effect on the identification of list membership (list tags) as a function of organization. Old items were increasingly confused with their synonyms as organization de-

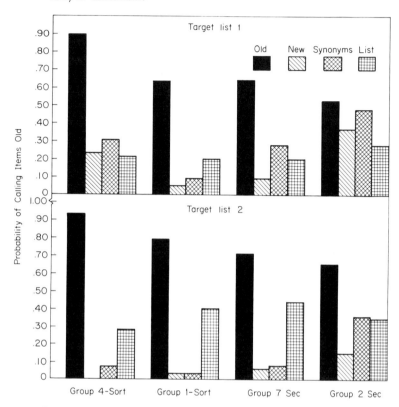

Fig. 1. Probability of calling items Old for four experimental groups under conditions when Ss are asked to consider List 1 or List 2 as their target list. For each set the figure shows the hit-rate for Old items from the target list and the false-alarm rate for New items which Ss had not seen before, for Synonyms which are synonyms of items in the target list, and for List items which are items from the nontarget list (i.e., List 2 items for Target List 1, and List 1 items for Target List 2).

creased and the confusion was greater for synonyms of List 1 than those of List 2. Finally, the hit rate and "unrelated" false-alarm rate showed a decrease in hit rate and an increase in false-alarm rate with decreasing organization (or learning) and a higher false-alarm rate for List 1 than for List 2.

The comparisons among the four organizational groups are most informative for the primary questions of interest here. The identification of a list (or its occurrence tag) is not correlated with organization, but discriminability of a list and semantic discrimination are a function of organization. Thus, in terms of the argument presented by Kintsch and others, the data support their contention that some occurrence tags (in this case list-specific tags) should not be and are not affected by degree of organization. If recognition were purely a function of the identification of such tags, then the notion that recognition depends only on the identification of "occurrence information" which is independent of organization would be supported. However, we have found that discriminability between old and new items, that is, general occurrence information, is affected by organization and so is the distinction between items and their synonyms. In other words, general occurrence information as measured by false alarms of "unrelated" fillers varies with organization, but specific list occurrence does not. Bower and Winzenz (1970) have also shown, in a different paradigm, that recognition (i.e., general occurrence information) increases with degree of relational organization of a set of items.

It was suggested earlier that items about which subjects are uncertain as to list membership are put through a postrecognition retrieval check. During that check, which determines whether the item is in principle retrievable from storage by the structure of the organization, organizational factors operate. The present data suggest that subjects may first check occurrence tags and then use organizational tests on those items that have weak tags. The more such uncertain items are generated, the better the correlation should be between the organization and recognition. This particular analysis of the situation also explains a previously puzzling finding, namely that the correlation between recognition and organization was higher after a two-week delay than during an immediate recognition test. List tags presumably decay markedly over two weeks and more items are thrown into the category of weak or uncertain items.

The amount of experience with the lists needs some further discussion. At the time of recognition, subjects were about 35 minutes removed from the end of List 1 for *Group 4-Sort*, seven minutes for *Group 1-Sort* and *7-Sec*, and two minutes for *Group 2-Sec*. Similarly, subjects in the four groups had, of course, spent variable amounts of time on the material. While we do not believe, as emphasized above, that time per se is the important variable in human learning, the time variable does affect our data when time since List 1 is taken into consideration. The most important such effect is seen in *Group 4-Sort* which had an inordinately long interval. Figure 1 shows the result for that group in List 1, and there is a major discrepancy in the effect of organization on the false alarms and on semantic confusion.

With respect to some of the previous data on recognition and organization, which do not show a difference between lists of varying degree of organization, it is suggested that in those studies the degree of separation of the two groups on the organization variable is relatively slight. Such studies typically fall within the range of the *1-Sort* and *7-Sec* groups, where the absolute difference in recognition (for List 2 in particular) is also slight.

We have now shown that semantic confusion occurs when there is a low degree of organization. Previous findings that semantic discriminability does not suffer significantly under conditions of high levels of organization still hold. Thus, the difference (for List 2 which is uncontaminated by time since exposure) between new fillers and synonym fillers in our experiment was small for the first three groups, but it rose to a ratio of nearly 2.5:1 for *Group 2-Sec.* These data bring our series of experiments in line with previous findings, which typically are studies in which relatively little organizational structure could be imposed on the items by the subjects. More superficially, one might conclude that whenever subjects do not know a list of words well, they are more likely to be confused.

Finally, it is recognized once again that the words "learning" or "practice" may be substituted for "organization" in this account. One puzzling aspect of such a substitution would be the failure of learning or practice to influence the strength of specific list tags. Presumably, under such a point of view, the occurrence tags associated with an item should vary with degree of exposure or practice. In fact, we find that the probability that an item from one list is misidentified as belonging to the other is independent of the degree of practice (or organization) of those two lists.

Recognition Memory for Items That Are Presented But Not Recalled

The data presented above, as well as some suggestions from the literature, indicate that when lists are well organized recognition is superior to that of items from sets that have a low degree of organization. This suggests that the relation of an item to a retrieval system is important. Other evidence (e.g., Lachman & Tuttle, 1965; Light & Carter-Sobell, 1970; Tulving & Thomson, 1971) also suggests that tightly organized systems facilitate recognition, or that recognition is dependent upon the position of the word within the organization, rather than on its occurrence per se.

If we assume that recall is dependent primarily, if not solely, on the operation of an organization, or a retrieval scheme, then the words that are recalled are in fact items that have been organized, while words that are not recalled have failed to enter the organizational schema.

If this is the case, then recalled and nonrecalled items from an input list should behave radically differently in a subsequent recognition test if organization does affect recognition. Recalled words should be recognized with a higher probability than nonrecalled items, which presumably have not been properly organized. There is some prior evidence in the literature that this is in fact the case. For example, Underwood and Freund (1968) gave subjects an input list of 40 words followed by immediate recall and a recognition test 24 hours later. Their data show the following probabilities for calling items old: recalled items were called old with the probability of .90, while nonrecalled items were recognized correctly with a probability of .52. This latter value compares with a probability of .42 of calling related filler words (which are associates of the original input list) old items, and the probability of .32 of calling unrelated filler items old items. Thus, it appears that, in recognition, nonrecalled items which were in the original list are treated more like new items than like old.

In a study addressed specifically to this problem we used a forced-choice recognition task to assess the relative effect of prior recall on recognition memory. The experiment also directed itself to the question whether subjects do in fact make category judgments at the time of recognition.[4]

Ten subjects were given two presentations of a 20-item list at a 1-sec rate. The list consisted of four categories with five items per category. Each of these items came from the first ten items given in Battig and Montague's (1969) category norms. In order to be sure that subjects recognized the categorical nature of the lists, they were given the names of the four categories and asked to repeat these names until the experimenter was sure that they were aware of the nature of the four categories in the list. Following the two presentations of the input lists, subjects were given a free recall test. Immediately following the free recall they were given a forced-choice recognition task. They were presented with IBM cards on each of which two words were listed. They were asked to circle the word which they remembered best as having been on the input list. The words used in the recognition task were:

1. All the words from the input list (which thus included both recalled and nonrecalled words—these will be designated by the symbols R and $\bar{R}$).

2. Categorized items not in the input list—these were items with the same frequency of occurrence in the norms as the original items in the input list, but none of these words had been actually presented. They

[4] This study was carried out by Karalyn Patterson.

did of course represent items from all the four categories, and will be designated by the symbol N.

3. Noncategorized new items—these were words that did not occur in any of the norms for the four categories and of course were not in the original input list. They will be designated by the symbol X.

The recognition task contained all possible pairwise combinations of all four types of words: that is, R, $\bar{R}$, N and X words. Since R, $\bar{R}$ and N words in any pair may be from the same or different categories, the data were analyzed separately for those pairs where the two words came from the same category and where they came from different categories, but no differences even approaching significance were found, and therefore this comparison will not be considered further.

TABLE 1

Two-Alternative Forced-Choice Probabilities for All Combinations of Four Different Types of Items

	$\bar{R}$	N	X
R	.82	.87	1.00
$\bar{R}$		.60	1.00
N			.98

Table 1 shows the proportion of choices of a particular type of word over all other kinds in the forced-choice situation. It shows the proportion of words in the left-hand column chosen over the words in the other three columns. Thus, for example, the probability that recalled words (R) were chosen over new categorized words (N) was .87, and of course conversely the probability that N words were chosen over R words was .13.

The data clearly show a major differentiation between R words which have a high probability of being chosen over all other words, $\bar{R}$ and N words which show great degree of confusability, and X words which are practically never chosen in the recognition task. Ordering of these items can be accomplished rather nicely by using the d' values for forced-choice between two alternatives. Figure 2 shows a simple ordering

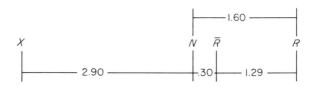

Fig. 2. Distance in d' among four types of items.

of the four types of words on the d' scale. The values of d' for the choice of $\bar{R}$ over X and R over X are, of course, not available because of the perfect choice behavior of the subjects. It might be noted parenthetically that for a .99–.01 choice the d' value would be 3.28, while the data in Figure 2 produce a predicted value of 4.39 for the R–X comparison, and 3.20 for the $\bar{R}$–X comparison.

These data clearly suggest that subjects make two types of distinctions. First there is a distinction between the category membership of a word as against words that do not belong to one of the categories in the lists, as shown in the high degree of discriminability between X words and all other words. Second, subjects distinguish rather well between recalled words and nonrecalled words on one hand, and recalled words and categorized nonlist words on the other hand. Their choice of recalled words was above .80 in both cases. At the same time, subjects seem to have great difficulty in distinguishing between words that were on the list but were not recalled, and words that were not on the list but belong to the same categories used in the list. It is as if the only major clue the subject uses in recognizing an $\bar{R}$ word is its category membership, and any additional information gives him only a slight advantage over categorized nonlist words.

In a subsequent experiment, only briefly mentioned here, we again used the forced-choice recognition task in a list differentiation situation. In that experiment, subjects were given two lists both of which used identical categories but different instances of those categories. They were then given a recognition task using one of the lists as the target list and again including R, $\bar{R}$, N and X words (Mandler & Borges, 1971). The experiment suggested again a division into three groups of words, namely: (1) recalled words from the target list; (2) new (X) words; and (3) nonrecalled words (whether from the target list or not), recalled words from the nontarget list, and N words.

The difficulty of deciding whether nonrecalled words do or do not have occurrence tags suggests a dilemma for the position that organization does not affect recognition. If one assumes that nonrecalled items cannot be retrieved, this should not affect their recognition if recognition is independent of the retrieval scheme. It must be recognized, however, that such an argument assumes that items receive occurrence tags at the time of presentation. It could be argued that only some items receive such tagging at the time of input, and that nonrecalled items are essentially items that do not receive occurrence tags. From the point of view of a general strength model this would be quite attractive since one assumes that an item that does not get an occurrence tag also has a low probability of being recalled. Thus, while we would argue that these data support the importance of retrievability in recognition, an alternative position, though not clearly stated in the available literature, is possible for a two-process recall and recognition model.

There is another body of data on the recognition of nonrecalled items that should be considered. In both of our previous series of experiments on the recall and recognition of well-organized lists (Mandler et al., 1969a; Mandler et al., 1969b) we have presented recognition data for two cases: when the list includes recalled items, and when such items have been removed from consideration. In both cases recognition (hit rate) is at the .90 level. Thus, when lists are well organized recognition is at a high level for both recalled and nonrecalled items. An argument from the point of view of occurrence tagging only for items that are eventually recalled (and recognized) would have to predict practically perfect (.90 recall) under these conditions, which of course is not the case. For the organizational point of view, the lack of perfect recall is of course independent of any strength or tagging notion; rather, recall is limited by retrieval limitations from organized memory which, though not clearly understood at present, have been the subject of some speculation within organizational theory (cf. Patterson, Meltzer, & Mandler, 1971).

The fact that subjects make clear distinctions between items belonging to the categories used in the lists and items that do not belong to such categories is, of course, not novel. As we have pointed out above, Kintsch specifically excluded this case as one not relevant to the organization and recognition argument. What seems to be the case is that subjects make category judgments before making recognition decisions. We would argue, of course, that this is simply one way in which organization influences recognition.

Recognition Memory for Items That Are Recalled But Not Presented

If, as we have shown above, items that are presented but not recalled tend not to be recognized as old items, one might argue that occurrence tags are given to items during the recall test and not during presentation. However, the fact that an item fails to be recognized because it fails to be recalled does not, as we have pointed out, argue that occurrence tags necessarily are ineffective; they may simply not be all-or-none events during presentation.

Another way of asking the same question is to examine items that are recalled but have never been presented. Presumably, such items could not possibly have been given occurrence tags during presentation. On the other hand, they are items that have been retrieved and thus are subject to organizational effects. Hanawalt and Tarr (1961) have presented some data on the recognition of such intrusions that were not presented but were recalled. In their experiments, subjects were required to recall adjectives from 24 phrases and were subsequently given a five alternative forced-choice recognition test. Among the five alternatives were the old words and a synonym of the originally presented word. They found that in some cases subjects recalled the synonym but not the original word. By examining those cases in the recognition phase, they found that in the five-alternative forced-choice situation subjects tested immediately after recall chose the wrongly recalled word (the intrusion) with a probability of .67 as against .33 for the correct response, and .001 for all other words. After 48 hours a test with independent groups showed that the intrusions were chosen with a probability of .74 as against .18 for the correct word, and .08 for all other words. Thus, there is a strong tendency—increasing over time—for subjects to choose recalled words over presented correct words.

We have performed a similar analysis on data from an experiment undertaken for different purposes.[5] Twenty-six subjects were given a 60-word list consisting of 20 categories with three items per category. Category names were presented together with the items. These items (with their category names) were presented at a 3-sec rate in a random order. Following this input, subjects were given a cued recall and, following that, a recognition test with 120 items which consisted of the three old items from each category plus three new items from that same category. In examining the recall, we found that 14 subjects recalled as intrusions one or more items that were used as fillers on the subsequent recognition test. We then analyzed the probability of calling items Old for the data from these 14 subjects, but only for the categories in which these intrusions occurred. Thus, for each of these categories we had some words that were correctly recalled, some words that were not recalled, some words that were intrusions, and, finally, words that were fillers belonging to the category. The probability of calling these items Old were: for recalled words .97, for nonrecalled but presented words .57, for intrusions, that is, recalled but not presented words, .92, and for nonpresented, nonrecalled words (other fillers) .20.

These data clearly go in the same direction as the Hanawalt and Tarr findings. Subjects treat intrusions and recalled words essentially alike responding to both kinds of words as if they had in fact been presented. On the other hand, nonrecalled words, as in our previous

[5] From an experiment by Marilyn Borges.

data, are called Old with a much lower probability, though significantly higher than the false-alarm rate for the new fillers.

It appears that the only reasonable way to assimilate these data to a position that stresses occurrence tags rather than retrieval in recognition is to assume that occurrence tags are assigned during recall, and, thus, when an intrusion is given in recall it is also assigned an occurrence tag. That seems to be appropriate since there is good evidence to believe that recall trials do function as input trials, and intuitively it is also reasonable that a subject would call Old an item he had just recalled as having been on the list.

The difficulty with such an explanation is that it compounds the complexity of an occurrence tag explanation. In the previous section we suggested that an item may or may not receive an occurrence tag during input and, thus, if it is not recalled one may assume it did not receive an occurrence tag. We now have to assume that items that are recalled but did not receive an occurrence tag during input (the intrusions) also receive occurrence tags (during recall). As a matter of fact, the occurrence tag notion seems to be most reasonable if we assume that such tagging occurs at the time of recall. Such a position would accommodate both kinds of findings since nonrecalled items presumably are not tagged and intrusions are tagged. Thus, assigning the occurrence information to the time of recall maintains that position, but of course also supports the organizational position since presumably an item is recalled only if it has been subjected to the retrieval process. If items are tagged subsequently to that retrieval process, organization should, in fact, affect recognition since only organized items would be tagged.

The fact that recognition memory is not only excellent for weakly organized lists but also sometimes independent of the existing organizational structures rules out any such position. Clearly, occurrence tags are assigned both during input and during output. What may be the case is that the probability of such a tag being assigned during the input cycle is lower than the probability of such assignment during output—and subsequent to retrieval. One need only appeal to attentional factors to argue that occurrence tags are more likely to be assigned during recall when items are self-presented, but that they will also be assigned to items during input, though with a lower probability.

Just as a strength model could accommodate somewhat to the differential recognition of unrecalled items, so can it explain the high recognition of intrusions. Whether one assumes that (1) intrusions receive occurrence tags during recall or (2) that items must be at a high strength due to associative or semantic overlap in order to be recalled incorrectly in the first place, both arguments would predict high recognition rates for intrusions. However, I find these exercises primarily demonstrations of my agility in extending the strength model, and obviously prefer an explanatory concept in terms of retrievability which makes better contact with the body of theory with which I am concerned.

Prospect for Recognition

We started off some years ago with the naive assumption that a clear distinction could be made between recognition and recall processes. As we noted above, our early efforts, since we started with highly organized materials, were unsuccessful in that we neither were able to find such a clear cut distinction nor were we able significantly to affect false-alarm rates, even for semantically similar material (synonyms). The outcome for the first set of studies was that we did find a significant impairment in recognition memory when we worked with materials that were of no particular interest to us, namely, essentially unorganized lists of words. In another language what we found was that when subjects had very little experience with a list they were unable to make very clear distinctions as to what had or had not been in the list, either in an absolute sense or in terms of semantic similarities.

But having found that the reason for our initial failure to affect recognition rates significantly was our preoccupation with highly organized material, our attention to the distinction between recognition and recall processes developed a functional autonomy. It turned out that it is possible to demonstrate relationships between organization and recognition, that the effect of organizational processes not only depends on having, in fact, well organized lists, but on other factors as well. The following list suggests the range of phenomena that an adequate theory of recognition should encompass:

1. First of all, as degree of organization (or learning) increases, there is an increasing discriminability of old and new words and a decreasing tendency to confuse conceptually related items (primarily involving semantic relations).

2. Specific occurrence tags, that is, those associated with particular lists are, in contrast, unaffected by degree of organization (or learning).

3. Processes occurring during recall, or mechanisms affecting recall, appear to be more important in determining the recognition of an item than sheer presentation of an item. Thus, unrecalled items, though presented, show a lower level of recognition than recalled items; and, conversely, recalled, though unpresented items (intrusions) show as high a level of recognition as recalled items.

4. The experimental literature suggests that whenever highly organized systems are used, recognition is in fact superior; failures to find effects of organization are associated with low degrees of organization (or learning).

5. The effect of organizational factors on recognition increases over time. This suggests that subjects rely more on categorization and conceptualization at some time after (e.g., at least a day or two) original presentation of the item.

Thus our exploration of recognition memory does not permit a clear distinction between a decision process based on occurrence tags and an independently operating retrieval process based on organizational structures. Both processes affect recognition memory to varying degrees. There is little doubt that occurrence tagging is a powerful factor in recognition. Such a process accounts for much of recognition performance in the laboratory. However, organizational factors also enter into recognition memory, and probably more so in everyday usage. One way in which this effect takes place involves occurrence tags assigned during output. We have suggested that the assignment of occurrence tags to retrieved and self-presented items is probably more likely than the assignment of occurrence tags during input. Thus, retrieved or organized items are more likely to have occurrence tags than presented items that may or may not be recalled. One direction for future research would be the assessment of occurrence tags for items that are potentially retrievable. Does an item in fact have to be actively retrieved in order to be assigned such a tag, or can one distinguish between two kinds of items in the absence of a recall test—those that could be retrieved and those that could not? And is there a distinction between recognition memory for these two kinds of items? In any case, if the suggestion that occurrence tags on recalled items are important determiners of recognition, a theory of recognition must take into account both input and output tagging. And occurrence tags on retrieved items will of course reflect the operation of organizational processes.

The second way in which organizational processes enter recognition memory depends apparently on weak or decayed occurrence tags. Organizational variables become more important the longer the time interval since presentation. Thus, when subjects are uncertain about the prior occurrence of an item, they are more likely to use retrieval processes and to depend on relational cues in order to determine prior occurrence. We have suggested in the introduction one intuitive argument for such a process. In short, occurrence tags preempt the recognition process when items are relatively unorganized and recent, but with increasing organization, as well as with older and weaker tags, organizational processes tend to dominate.

It is also possible that the choice of recognition mechanisms may reflect a difference in strategies. It is possible that one or the other or both processes may be selected as more or less appropriate to the task presented. Some of the data on contextual effects on recognition (Light & Carter-Sobell, 1970; Tulving & Thomson, 1971) suggest that even in the presence of presumably recent and effective occurrence tags, recognition memory operates primarily through the use of organizational or retrieval processes. The experimental manipulation of the preferential use of one or the other of these strategies would shed further light on this question.

At no time do I want to deny the existence of occurrence information being stored with events or with the organization of events. What does seem to be the case is that any reasonable theory of adult mental structures must take into account that such occurrence information or tags play a relatively minor role in the production, retrieval, or recall of organized material. And since most of the recall of interest, that is in daily life and in typical situations involving the human mind, taps organized material, the importance of frequency or recency information will be of minor, and probably esoteric importance. Occurrence tags (and *inter alia* list tags) surely need to be admitted to psychological theory, but other "relational" aspects of recognition usually override these effects. Alternatively, one might assume that in the recognition of highly organized material the human mind depends primarily on organizational, relational information, and only secondarily on occurrence information. Recency or time tagging is probably important when organizational cues are poor or absent; the individual is thrown back onto the only remaining information available—frequency and recency. And it is of course in the laboratory that such conditions are typically produced; they are at least unusual, if not absent, in the daily life of the individual. However, even time or occurrence information may in turn be subject to organizational constraints, and one might, for the sake of theoretical consistency, talk about the organization of time and frequency.

For example, occurrence information is frequently considered to have some frequency or recency information coded with it, though it is rarely stated how such information may be encoded. Much of the time the implicit assumption is some associationistic notion that the co-occurrence of two events provides the markings for the two events—one by the other. Thus, an event occurring at some specific time carries with it the time tag while the time information carries with it the event tag.

Organizational—or cognitive—theory does not rest at that point, but goes beyond it to ask how the relation between the two events is determined and stored. Since it is unlikely that man carries some internal clock, time tagging or recency tagging presumably has as its base some organizational or relational principles. A recent study by Ornstein (1969) has shown how the experience of duration is mediated by a concept of time, dependent on the organization of memory during the time period in question.

Finally, it must be noted that we are talking about recognition memory for items that exist in long-term storage and are tagged for occurrence on specific occasions. In that sense, such a theory should be applicable to the general use of language, since language typically involves at least in part the recovery of items from the long-term lexicon. But, clearly, any hunt for an organization-free autonomous recognition process for such linguistic materials will prove to be futile. For organized lexical items, recognition will always involve some organizational processes.

Summary

The general argument was advanced that recognition of items in long-term memory is a function of organizational variables. The traditional notion that recognition is a function of decision processes relying on occurrence information was examined in the light of available evidence. It was suggested that such dependence on decision processes—and independence from organizational variables—is typically found when lists or items are not well organized. Experimental evidence was adduced to show that occurrence information varies with the degree of organization of a list. Similar evidence was brought to bear on the problem of the discrimination and recognition of semantically similar items. Here too it was shown that as degree of organization increases, so does the rejection of new, but semantically similar items. The argument was then expanded to deal with the effect of retrieval processes during recall on subsequent recognition. It was shown that items that are presented but not recalled tend to be recognized as nonpresented (new) items, while items that are recalled but not presented (intrusions) tend to be treated like presented and recalled (old) items. The cumulative evidence and considerations of organizational theory indicate that organizational and retrieval processes play an important part in the recognition of organized material. While occurrence information is obviously coded with input, it is typically overwhelmed by more powerful organizational variables.

References

Anisfeld, M., & Knapp, M. Association, synonymity, and directionality in false recognition. *Journal of Experimental Psychology*, 1968, **77**, 171–179.

Battig, W. F., & Montague, W. E. Category norms for verbal items in 56 categories: A replication and extension of the Connecticut category norms. *Journal of Experimental Psychology Monograph*, 1969, **80**.

Borges, M. A., & Mandler, G. Effects of within-category spacing on free recall. *Journal of Experimental Psychology*, in press.

Bower, G. H. Organization and memory. Invited address at meetings of Western Psychological Association, San Diego, California, 1968.

Bower, G. H., Clark, M. C., Lesgold, A. M., & Winzenz, D. Hierarchical retrieval schemes in recall of categorized word lists. *Journal of Verbal Learning and Verbal Behavior*, 1969, **8**, 323–343.

Bower, G. H., Lesgold, A. M., & Tieman, D. Grouping operations in free recall. *Journal of Verbal Learning and Verbal Behavior*, 1969, **8**, 481–493.

Bower, G. H., & Winzenz, D. Comparison of associative learning strategies. *Psychonomic Science*, 1970, **20**, 119–120.

Bruce, D., & Fagan, R. L. More on the recognition and free recall of organized lists. *Journal of Experimental Psychology*, 1970, **85**, 153–154.

D'Agostino, P. R. The blocked-random effect in recall and recognition. *Journal of Verbal Learning and Verbal Behavior*, 1969, **8**, 815–820.

Davis, G. A. Recognition memory for visually presented homophones. *Psychological Reports*, 1967, **20**, 227–233.

Garner, W. R. *Uncertainty and Structure as Psychological Concepts*. New York: Wiley, 1962.

Hanawalt, N. G., & Tarr, A. G. The effect of recall upon recognition. *Journal of Experimental Psychology*, 1961, **62**, 361–367.

Kintsch, W. Recognition and free recall of organized lists. *Journal of Experimental Psychology*, 1968, **78**, 481–487.

Kintsch, W. Models for free recall and recognition. In D. A. Norman (Ed.), *Models of Human Memory*. New York: Academic Press, 1970.

Lachman, R., & Tuttle, A. V. Approximation to English and short-term memory: Construction or storage? *Journal of Experimental Psychology*, 1965, **70**, 386–393.

Light, L., & Carter-Sobell, L. Effects of changed semantic context on recognition memory. *Journal of Verbal Learning and Verbal Behavior*, 1970, **9**, 1–11.

Mandler, G. Response factors in human learning. *Psychological Review*, 1954, **61**, 235–244.

Mandler, G. From association to structure. *Psychological Review*, 1962, **69**, 415–427.

Mandler, G. Organization and memory. In K. W. Spence and J. A. Spence (Eds.), *The psychology of learning and motivation*. Vol. 1. New York: Academic Press, 1967.

Mandler, G. Organized recall: Individual functions. *Psychonomic Science*, 1968, **13**, 235–236.

Mandler, G. Words, lists, and categories: An experimental view of organized memory. In J. L. Cowan (Ed.), *Studies in thought and language*. Tucson, Arizona: University of Arizona Press, 1970.

Mandler, G., & Borges, M. A. Effects of list differentiation, category membership and prior recall on recognition. Technical Report No. 16, Center for Human Information Processing, UCSD, 1971.

Mandler, G., Meltzer, R. H., & Pearlstone, Z. The structure of recognition: Effects of list tags and of acoustic and semantic confusion. Technical Report No. 7, Center for Human Information Processing, University of California, San Diego, 1969. (a).

Mandler, G., Pearlstone, Z., & Koopmans, H. S. Effects of organization and semantic similarity on recall and recognition. *Journal of Verbal Learning and Verbal Behavior,* 1969, **8**, 410–423. (b).

Müller, G. E. Zur Analyse der Gedächtnistätigkeit und des Vorstellungsverlaufes. III. Teil. *Zeitschrift für Psychologie, Ergänzungsband,* 1913, **8**.

Murdock, B. B., Jr. Modality effects in short-term memory: Storage or retrieval? *Journal of Experimental Psychology,* 1968, **77**, 79–86.

Ornstein, R. E. *On the Experience of Time.* Harmondsworth, England: Penguin Books, 1969.

Patterson, K. E., Meltzer, R. H., & Mandler, G. Inter-response times in categorized free recall. *Journal of Verbal Learning and Verbal Behavior,* 1971, **10**, 417–426.

Tulving, E. Subjective organization and effects of repetition in multitrial free recall learning. *Journal of Verbal Learning and Verbal Behavior,* 1966, **5**, 193–197.

Tulving, E., & Thomson, D. M. Retrieval processes in recognition memory: Effects of associative context. *Journal of Experimental Psychology,* 1971, **87**, 116–124.

Underwood, B. J. False recognition produced by implicit verbal responses. *Journal of Experimental Psychology,* 1965, **70**, 122–129.

Underwood, B. J., & Freund, J. S. Errors in recognition learning and retention. *Journal of Experimental Psychology,* 1968, **78**, 55–63.

Wolford, G. Function of distinct associations for paired-associate performance. *Psychological Review,* 1971, **78**, 303–313.

5 | On the Relationship of Associative and Organizational Processes[1]

James F. Voss

[1] This paper was supported by the National Institute of Child Health and Human Development (HD 00957-07) and was written with the support of the University of Pittsburgh, the University of California at Irvine, and the National Institute of Mental Health, Special Fellowship, MH-47183. The author also wishes to thank Drs. William Battig, Richard Thompson, and Endel Tulving for their helpful comments pertaining to an earlier draft of this paper.

The purpose of this paper is to consider the relationship of those processes typically considered associative to those processes that have been considered organizational. The paper has three major divisions: associative processes, organizational processes, and associative-organizational relationships.

Associative Processes

NATURE OF AN ASSOCIATION

In recent years the question of what constitutes an association has received considerable attention. The works of three authors illustrate this trend. Tulving (1968) pointed out that the term association, used descriptively, merely means that one event follows another, that is, B follows A with some regularity. Postman (1968), in an effort to categorize the ways in which the term association is employed, delineated six uses of the expression. These included association as a descriptive term, as an indicator of verbal mediational processes or nonverbal mediational processes, and as a statement of pre-existent verbal hierarchies. Finally, in a criticism of associationistic concepts, Asch (1968, 1969) emphasized the importance of conceiving of an association in terms of the relation of two events, A and B.

Two factors emerge from these considerations. First, it is clear that the term association has no single, precise definition that may be stated without qualification. Second, it is important to separate a descriptive usage of the term from an interpretive usage. In a descriptive sense, the term association is used only to show that two events tend to be related in some nonchance manner; an interpretive or theoretical usage, however, either may imply some reason for the nonchance relationship or the relationship itself may be used as an explanation for some other event.

Similarly, the term associative strength, even though sounding like a theoretical construct, has for the most part been used descriptively. Thus, when A is followed by B with a high probability, the strength of A-B is taken to be relatively large; conversely, when there is a relatively low probability that B will follow A, strength is said to be weak. Furthermore, in a response hierarchy, associative strength is considered in terms of the relative probability of occurrence of responses, for example, if given A, the probability of B is greater than C, then A-B associative strength is greater than that of A-C.

ACQUISITION OF ASSOCIATIONS

Associations usually have been considered to be learned via the associative laws, foremost of which is contiguity. Because of its central position and because criticism of the law of contiguity has been extensive in recent years, this law is considered here in some detail.

Classical associationism has been traced to Greek thought (Warren, 1921), although it is probably safe to assume that many of the modern expressions of associationism received their strongest impetus from the British empiricists. In some ways, the most extreme of the empiricists was Hume (1748), who essentially reduced knowledge to the correlation of sensations.

The issue of Hume's philosophy that is of concern in the present context is what may be termed the "out there" versus the "in here" problem. Hume expressed the view that man is only capable of knowing his sensations, and that knowledge of sensations consisted only of knowing that occurrence of sensation A is correlated with the subsequent occurrence of sensation B. Hume's position was regarded as one of skepticism because it essentially denied direct knowledge of anything "out there." Thus, to Hume, sensations may be copies of what is "out there," but we simply do not really know whether, in fact, they are. The point I wish to make in relation to Hume's position is that Hume apparently did not advocate that the acquisition of associations consisted of copying, internally, the occurrence of two environmental events because the environment, in a direct sense, could not be known. We find, therefore, that the empiricist who attempted to reduce mental life to the contiguous occurrence of successive impressions was speaking of events "in here" which were not necessarily correlated with events "out there."

It is of particular interest to note that in the early twentieth century, association-oriented theorists of human learning had reservations about the nature of associations and the distinction of "out there" and "in here." For instance, we find Robinson (1932, p. 7) stating "By *association* we may mean simply the *establishment of functional relations among psychological activities and states in the course of individual experience*" (italics are Robinson's). Robinson (p. 72) states the law of contiguity as follows: "*The fact that two psychological processes occur together in time or in immediate succession increases the probability that an associative connection between them will develop—that one process will become the associative instigator of the other*" (italics are Robinson's). Finally, Robinson notes (p. 73): "It should be kept in mind that mere coincidence in time or more immediacy of temporal succession will not insure the establishment of a demonstrable association between two psychological processes. Thus, even if it could be shown that there cannot be association without contiguity, the presence of the factor of contiguity is not enough to insure association."

Similarly, Key (1926) summarized a substantial amount of research, and pointed out the importance of what she called subjective factors in associative learning, and further provided evidence for the importance of relations between items to both acquisition and recall, including subjective and idiosyncratic methods of organizing.

In view of Hume's position and in view of comments such as Robinson's, we are confronted with the fact that a number of associationists emphasized the importance of considering associative development in terms of "psychological processes" rather than simply being formed by the association of contiguous environmental events. Why then, we may ask, has associationism been criticized so severely in recent years (e.g., Asch, 1968; Deese, 1965, 1968) on the point that the law of contiguity should be rejected because it advocates that what is learned is a copy of contiguous environmental events? As we have seen in our brief account, classical associationists were quite concerned with the question of what is associated, and they did not advocate that the internal is simply a copy of the external.

In this writer's opinion, recent criticisms of classical associationism may be traced to the assumption that what is "in here" is a copy of what is "out there." Furthermore, why this assumption came to be made, despite the contrary positions of individuals such as Hume and Robinson, may possibly be attributed to two primary sources. First, it is obvious that the conceptualization of human learning problems was quite influenced during the decades of 1930–1960 by operationalism, and by the stimulus-response theoretical orientation which was based on the conditioning paradigm. Thus, behavior was conceptualized in terms of S-R units which were acquired via contiguity, frequency, and possibly drive components, and experimentation tended to be focused upon the manipulation of variables which provided information regarding how such S-R units were acquired. Human learning problems also were generally viewed with this orientation, and emphasis was placed upon how the stimulus manipulations influence response acquisition. Such a view, of course, minimized the role of organismic processing, since operationally what was learned was taken to be the S-R units.

The second reason I would offer for the lack of distinguishing "out there" from "in here" with respect to associations is that the two major verbal learning procedures of the earlier decades of the twentieth century, paired-associate and serial learning, did not lend themselves to the study of associative processes; instead, they tended to preclude the existence and operation of the laws of contiguity and frequency (Voss, 1969). Indeed, only recently, when the traditional methods have been modified, such as in the study of stimulus selection, or when other procedures have been used, such as in the use of free recall, have questions been raised pertaining to the role of contiguity and frequency in verbal learning. Thus, it may be argued that the recent criticisms of classical associationism within the verbal learning context may in part be attributed to the emphasis placed upon methodologies which were restrictive, especially when the methodologies were combined with the S-R, operationalism Zeitgeist of the 1930, 1940, and 1950 decades.

That what is "in here" is not necessarily a copy of what is "out there" has, in these days, been recognized by human learning investigators of the associationist tradition. Probably the best example of recognition of the problem is that of the distinction of nominal and functional stimulus, so succinctly phrased by Underwood (1963). The importance of this issue cannot be overestimated, for recognition of the problem suggests that establishing behavioral laws is an even more complex problem than we had imagined. Figure 1 presents a diagram of why the issue has become so complicated, as shown in the context of associative learning.

Row 1 presents the occurrence of an association, A-B. In row 2 implicit reponses to the events are assumed, r_a and r_b respectively. Of extreme importance, however, is evidence which indicates that this response is not simply an identification response such as the RR of Bousfield, Whitmarsh, and Danick (1948), but instead consists of a number of interrelated responses that have reference to a reasonably large number of dimensions. Row 3 depicts this state of affairs by considering r_a and r_b in terms of the components $r_{a1}, r_{a2}, \ldots r_{an}, r_{b1}, r_{b2}, \ldots r_{bn}$, respectively.

Row 4 presents the occurrence of two responses that are identical to the A and B items, that is, overt or covert verbalizations, termed R_A and R_B, respectively. How each of these responses is initiated is not known, but it may be assumed, at least tentatively, that one or more of the component encoding responses of r_a and r_b may be involved with the initiation of R_A and R_B, respectively. Row 5 presents the development of an association, r_{ai}-r_{bi}. In the development of this association, one component of r_a and one of r_b is assumed to be operating, although it should be noted that with both r_{ai} and r_{bi}, more than one component of the respective encoding may be involved. Row 6 shows a developed association with question marks at points where there evidently is a need to explain process.

From the diagram, it would seem that in order to have an adequate understanding of what happens when an association is acquired, it is necessary to have knowledge of at least five processes. The first is the question of how A is encoded, ?1. The second is how B is encoded, ?2. The third is what components of r_a become associated to what component of r_b, ?3. The fourth issue is how the component of r_b that is related to the component of r_a becomes related to a component r_b that initiates a re-

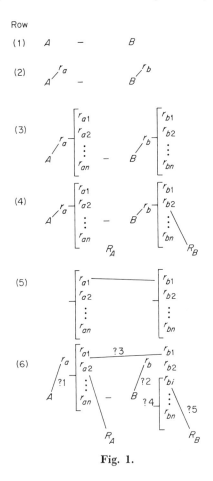

Fig. 1.

sponse, ?4, that is, are these two aspects of r_b the same or are they different and, if different, how they are related. Finally, the last question is how the particular r_i initiates certain responses.

In Figure 2 an analysis of associative processes is presented that is based upon the classical conditioning paradigm. This type of analysis, as is well-known, was especially prevalent during the middle decades of the twentieth century. Row 1 presents the occurrence of A and B. Row 2 presents an implicit response to both A and B, r_a and r_b. Finally, Row 3 presents the associative step of A-r_b, and it is assumed r_b elicits R_B. The only question mark is the line of A-r_b. A modified version appears in Row 4, where the question mark refers to the association of r_a-r_b rather than A-r_b.

What are the essential differences between the more traditional type of analysis shown in Figure 2 and the more recent of Figure 1? It would appear that the increased complexity of Figure 1 is due to the fact that the representation of an environmental event is taken to be something more than a copy of the event, and that the encoding of the

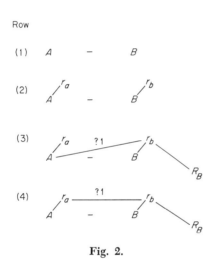

Fig. 2.

environmental event has a complex network of components. In other words, it has become necessary to consider the dimensions that are involved in the encoding of a particular event, and how one or more of the dimensions of r_a and r_b are selected and related in the development of an association. Second, the question of how a response is initiated has become an issue of concern, as shown in Figure 1, rather than simply assuming that event B as it occurs is essentially the same thing as the response, R_b (cf. Greenwald, 1970; Kimble & Perlmuter, 1970).

At this point it should be noted that Figures 1 and 2 are presented as simplified, general statements of the problem. Other individuals undoubtedly would modify Figure 1 and change the issues that require explanation. It also should be mentioned that there have been theories developed within a conditioning framework that have been concerned with the process of representation (e.g., Cofer & Foley, 1942; Osgood,

1952), but the major differences shown by Figures 1 and 2 may be taken to show the divergence between a point of view emphasizing encoding processes and a view primarily based upon a classical conditioning paradigm. Thus, it is argued that one source of the recent criticisms of classical associationism and, in particular, the law of contiguity is that the operationally-oriented thinking of the mid-twentieth century, especially as couched in S-R terms, implicitly led investigators to ignore the problem that what is "in here" may not simply be a copy of what is "out there," that is, what the experimenter presents.

Returning now to the question of this section, the discussion to this point indicates that we must take into account the possible differences that occur between the environmental occurrence of an event and the internal knowledge of the event. In order to do this, a distinction is made between what shall be termed *explicit contiguity* and *implicit contiguity*. The former term shall refer to the simultaneous or immediately successive occurrence of two environmental events; the latter term shall refer to the simultaneous or immediately successive occurrence of the representation of two or more events within an organism. Furthermore, the term *encoding* is employed to denote the representation of an event.

For learning to occur, it is assumed for the purposes of the present discussion that implicit contiguity is a necessary condition. Why implicit contiguity is thought to be important is because it is via the mechanism of implicit contiguity that a new encoding develops. In other words, it is hypothesized that learning takes place by incorporating the new with the old, and that this produces a new or modified encoding. (Whether an encoding is new or modified constitutes an extremely interesting problem, but it is not considered at this time.)

There are also different ways by which implicit contiguity may occur. These include explicit contiguity and the arousal of relationships that exist between the encodings of two items. We will return to this issue in a later section of the paper.

The concept of encoding, although also discussed more fully later in the paper, requires further comment at this point. In particular, the important notion to indicate regarding encoding is that an encoding is not necessarily a copy of an event. Instead, it is the process by which certain aspects or features of the stimulus event are employed in establishing the internal representation of the event. Such features, in this account, are termed *attributes*. Furthermore, two other factors are probably involved which shall be termed *external* and *internal context*. The former refer to contextural events which may be encoded with, or as part of, the particular stimulus event; the latter refer to other encodings which occur with or as part of the encoding of the particular event.

To illustrate, if a pair of verbal units is presented, and the individual is later asked to recognize one of them, the encoding of the first verbal unit may involve not only the unit per se, but the second verbal unit. In addition, other contextual factors related to the experimental situation, such as room, etc., may be included in the encoding. With respect to internal context, an example would be the arousal of a network of items already encoded by the occurrence of a particular item, and the item therefore is encoded not by itself but with the other encodings.

Finally, one more point should be made with respect to these notions, namely, that this general formulation is assumed to hold for verbal material other than associations. As an example, let us take the case of a sentence being read to an individual. The sentence per se may not be encoded, but instead some information is selected or taken from the sentence and encoded. In addition, contextual factors may include other sentences, the speaker, etc., as well as encodings aroused in the individual by the sentence of situation. Thus, it is held that for any set of verbal materials, from a single letter or word to a paragraph, poem, or story, encodings consist of these processes.

In concluding this section, it may be stated that we have argued that acquisition of verbal materials takes place via the implicit contiguous occurrence of encodings, and that such encodings may consist of features or attributes selected from the verbal materials as well as external and internal contextual factors.

Organizational Processes

NATURE OF ORGANIZATION

The term organization has been used in a number of ways. One usage has been to define organization in the framework of sets or classes of events (Mandler, 1967). Mandler stated, "A set of objects or events are said to be organized when a consistent relation among the members of the set can be specified and, specifically, when membership of the objects or subsets (groups, concepts, categories, chunks) is stable and identifiable [p. 330]."

Mandler's definition is useful but limited, for it defines organization only for the case in which objects or events are sorted or classified according to some concept or general criterion. The definition does not, however, state anything about organization that may be based upon such factors as changes in the input-output relationship, that is, the definition does not indicate that an organism may be doing the organizing.

Tulving (1968) distinguished two types of organization as they occur in the free recall type of task. The first, termed primary, refers to effects attributable to task characteristics; the other, termed secondary, refers to organization that is imposed upon the list by the individual. The phenomenon of subjective organization (Tulving, 1962) is an example of this type of organization. It also may be noted at this point that organization in terms of input-output relationships, as found characteristically in the free recall situation, generally has referred to order information (see the chapters by Postman and Wood in this volume), that is, organization occurs if the individual modifies the order of output relative to the order of input.

In the light of the issues discussed thus far, the following definition of organization can now be offered: organization is a process that intervenes between input and output in such a way that input is increased in its systematization and in such a way that there is not a 1:1 input-output relation. This definition emphasizes three points. First, it places the locus of organization within the organism. Second, it stresses that organization leads to greater systematization, not to greater randomness or uncertainty. Third, it suggests that organizational processes may be investigated by studying input-output relationships. In addition, in either the classification or the free recall situation, if an input is highly organized or systematic and the output is identical or similarly highly systematic, this definition asserts that no or little organization has taken place. Although this definition is not ideal, it does emphasize the notion that output measurement may reflect some type of processing on the part of the individual which results in the modification of input. The definition, of course, is neutral with respect to how such modifications may take place.

NATURE OF STRUCTURE

The term structure generally has been used to denote some type of organization of mental processes. Indeed, in the present volume, Greeno refers to the acquisition of mathematical structure, and the subject matter of the chapter by Collins and Quillian could readily be termed semantic structure rather than semantic memory. For our purposes, we are interested in the concept of structure in reference to how verbal material may be organized. We therefore shall define verbal structure as the particular modes or rules by which verbal material is organized.

This definition of structure is obviously quite similar to that of organization. The difference, however, is that the term structure is being used to refer to specific types of organization whereas the term organization is used to note the fact that systematization occurs.

DIMENSIONS OF STRUCTURE

The issue now considered is how verbal units are structured, or, rephrased, what are the dimensions along which verbal units are interrelated?

The problem of delineating structural dimensions is difficult because no criteria have been established regarding the properties of such dimensions. Therefore, the choice of the particular four dimensions that are discussed in the present paper is essentially arbitrary. The sole criterion employed in distinguishing the dimensions is empirical, that is, the dimensions are based upon experimental evidence which suggests that more than one structural dimension is involved in obtaining a given set of data. The four dimensions are formal, associative, semantic, and syntactic, and it is maintained that verbal units are encoded in these dimensions.

The general notion that verbal units are encoded multidimensionally has received substantial support. Bower (1967) provided evidence for a multicomponent storage process via a model which assumed n components of a multidimensional trace. Underwood (1969a) has argued for coding in terms of a number of attributes, specifically mentioning temporal, spatial, frequency, modality, orthographic, and associative components. Modality-specific encoding also has been suggested by Wallach and Averbach (1955) and more recently by investigators of short-term memory (e.g., Baddeley, 1966a,b). In addition, Wickens (1970), relying primarily on work based on the "release from PI" phenomenon, has shown that perceiving a word, in all likelihood, involves coding the item in terms of many categories. Taken as a whole, therefore, multidimensional encoding as a principle may be taken as a widely accepted concept.

Formal Dimension

The formal dimension refers to structure that is based upon the formal similarity of verbal units. In other words, verbal items that sound highly similar or look highly similar are assumed to be encoded in a network according to the set of attributes upon which the similarity may be based.

Evidence for the existence of structure based upon formal relationships comes from a variety of sources. In short-term memory research, Conrad

(1962, 1964) has shown that acoustic confusions are frequent, a finding supported by other investigators (e.g., Baddeley, 1966a,b). That such acoustic processing may involve a complex articulatory-acoustic system has been suggested by Hintzman (1967) and by Wickelgren (1969). Formal similarity also has been shown to be of considerable importance in associative learning tasks, with processes such as intralist generalization shown to be related to the variable of formal similarity (cf. Runquist, 1968). Finally, formal similarity has been found to be the primary type of associative response given to CVCs (Rosen & Greenhouse, 1971).

Associative Dimension

The second structural dimension by which verbal units are encoded is termed the associative dimension. Evidence for an associative dimension is found in recognition studies where, following presentation of a series of words, associates of particular words were falsely recognized as words that had been presented (Grossman & Eagle, 1970; Kimble, 1968; Underwood, 1965). The most frequent explanation for such results has been that the associated words occurred when the list was presented, with such responses being termed implicit associated responses or IARs (Bousfield et al., 1958). Evidence for this interpretation has been presented by Cramer (1970) and by Leicht (1968).

The characteristics of associative structure have been investigated extensively by Deese (1965). His findings as well as other results (cf. Cramer, 1968) indicate that the attributes or bases of associative relations between two verbal units may be quite varied. Indeed, it may be argued that under a given set of circumstances, it is hypothetically possible that any two units in the repertoire of an individual may become associated. Thus, in a sense, it may be maintained that the associative strength of any two verbal units is greater than zero.

Semantic Dimension

The third structural dimension of verbal units is termed the semantic dimension. In the present context, semantic structure refers to the relations of category membership that are implied by the meaning of a single word. That items are encoded semantically is shown by evidence both from short-term memory (e.g., Baddeley, 1966a,b; Henley, Noyes, & Deese 1968; Shulman, 1970; Wickens & Eckler, 1968) and from IAR studies (e.g., Anisfeld & Knapp, 1968; Grossman & Eagle, 1970). Evidence for semantic structure also was found by Bobrow (1970), who showed that adjective and verb presentation which changed the meaning of a noun yielded poorer recall than in conditions in which adjective and noun meanings did not change the essential meaning of the nouns.

Syntactic Dimension

The fourth structural dimension that is postulated is termed the syntactic dimension. The dimension refers to the structure of a verbal unit within its grammatical context. Evidence for syntactic structure may be derived from a number of sources. Epstein (1961) showed that nonsense strings of words presented with characteristic syntactical structures yielded superior recall compared to nonsense sentences without such structures. Marks and Miller (1964) were able to differentiate syntactic and semantic errors. Cofer (1968) found that syntactic encoding may provide one possible way of encoding which may be in opposition to other encoding dimensions. Finally, it may be mentioned that Rohwer (1966) found that recall of a pair of nouns was facilitated when the nouns were presented in a sentence context rather than without the sentence. Extension of this work (Bobrow & Bower, 1969) indicated that self-generated sentences produced superior recall compared to sentences presented that were not self-generated, and that this effect could be attributed to superior comprehension produced by the self-generating sentences. Thus these authors pointed out that syntactic encoding is apparently related to the comprehension of discourse.

Finally, with respect to the four structural dimensions, it should be mentioned that within each dimension there are a large number of attributes by which discriminations within the respective dimension may be made. An account of the specific attributes within each dimension is, however, considered well beyond the scope of this paper.

INTERRELATIONSHIPS OF DIMENSIONS

The question considered in this section is whether the four hypothesized dimensions are independent or whether, in some way, verbal units of one structural dimension are related to the same or different verbal units that are structured in relation to other dimensions.

Evidence suggests that the formal structural dimension is of a somewhat lower level than the other dimensions. Specifically, there are data which suggest the following two hypotheses with respect to the formal dimension: (*a*) the activation of a verbal unit within one of the three nonformal dimensions inhibits the operation of the unit within the formal dimension; (*b*) upon presentation of an item, distraction will reduce or eliminate activation of the highest level of encoding and will activate the encoding of a lower level.

Evidence for the first hypothesis comes from a study by Underwood and Freund (1968). A list of words was presented and prior to particular stimulus words, subjects were forced or not forced to state a word that was adjacent to another stimulus word. In a subsequent recognition task, it was found that associatively related adjacent items occurring during list presentation interfered with recognition performance, but acoustically or formally similar items did not under the nonforced condition. With the forced conditions, however, interference was produced by the items of acoustic and formal similarity. On the basis of these results, the authors suggested that when a higher-ordered encoding process is employed, lower level encodings are likely inhibited. In addition, however, the results suggest that when the lower level encodings are "forced," a process of arousal or possibly disinhibition occurs.

Evidence for the second hypothesis has been produced by Eagle and Ortof (1967). Using a recognition procedure, these investigators found that the use of a distractor at input produced a greater number of "clang" errors rather than higher-level errors such as associative. This result was interpreted as showing that factors which produce inattention at input lead to lower levels of processing.

Thus, it appears that there is some evidence which suggests that the dimension of formal structure is a lower-level dimension, and that the other three dimensions constitute higher levels of organization.

With respect to the nonformal dimensions, it is difficult to argue for anything but a complex interrelationship. Fortunately, the question of the possible independence of structural dimensions is empirically testable. One possible way to pursue this problem is to present words within the context of different structural dimensions and subsequently obtain frequency judgments of the words, as they occur within particular structural dimensions. Whether or not the occurrence of the items within the contexts of noncritical dimensions influences the frequency judgment within the tested critical dimension thus could be taken as a measure of dimensional independence or the lack thereof.

In summary, although there is some evidence that suggests the formal dimension is of a lower order with respect to the other dimensions, how the dimensions may be interrelated is an issue yet to be attacked.

Associative-Organizational Relationships

In the first sections of the paper, the general framework that has been developed consists of the following notions. Acquisition takes place via implicit contiguity. The function of implicit contiguity is to provide a basis for a unitary encoding. Such unitary encodings include not only a verbal unit per se, but also may include what is referred to as external and internal contextual factors. Finally, it was hypothesized that verbal units are structured along four dimensions. We are therefore left with the problem of how acquisition is related to structure. In other words, we have advocated the existence of a learning mechanism and also postulated the existence of particular verbal structure. We have not, however, considered the question of how the learning process incorporates verbal material into the structure. The present section is addressed to this issue.

ORIGIN OF STRUCTURAL DIMENSIONS

Although this topic is not of primary concern to the issues of this paper, the question of the origin of the structural dimensions should receive some consideration. Briefly then, it is maintained that verbal capacity as well as conceptual capacity develop as a function of neural maturation in relation to experience, and thus one may view the development of structure as part of the normal capacities involved in language and intellectual development. Thus, though how such development occurs is an extremely important issue (cf. Lenneberg, 1967), this position at least does not necessitate showing how structural dimensions are derived from implicit contiguity. Instead, the structural dimensions may be considered as given for the purposes of the present paper.

AROUSAL OF DIMENSIONAL NETWORKS

The concept of trace arousal upon stimulus presentation is not uncommon. However, from results such as the IAR findings mentioned previously, it may be argued that not only is a trace of the specific stimulus event aroused upon the occurrence of a stimulus, but the network of encodings that are related to that particular stimulus event is aroused. Furthermore, it is postulated that the network of encodings that tends to be aroused is the dimensional network that is related to the particular occurrence of the event. In other words, if a verbal item had been presented as a unit of an association, subsequent presentation in the associative context would be expected to arouse previous encodings of the same verbal unit that had occurred in the associative context. Evidence for the arousal of the encodings of a network of units rather than only the encoding of the particular verbal unit may be found in recognition studies which suggest the implicit occurrence of related items, as well as studies which have been interpreted in terms of the arousal of related verbal materials (e.g., Henry & Voss, 1970; Kiess, 1968; Prytulak, 1971).

IMPLICIT CONTIGUITY AND STRUCTURE

Within each of the four dimensions, the arousal of related items provides the opportunity for the material that is to be learned to be related to encodings that are aroused. New material therefore is taken to be incorporated into the network of what has been learned by a process which involves the simultaneous or successive occurrence of the encoding of the new material in relation to the internal context, that is, the other aroused encodings. Implicit contiguous occurrence of the aroused encodings with the material to be learned thus produces an encoding which includes the new material. In order to suggest how this process occurs, we shall consider how associative learning may take place under a number of conditions.

ACQUISITION OF ASSOCIATIONS

For the first case, let us consider a pair of dissimilar CVCs of a reasonably low association value. Assuming that the units have been successfully integrated (Mandler, 1954) and, for the time being, assuming they have been encoded (Martin, 1968), it is quite likely that the two dissimilar items do not have similar encoding attributes. Under such conditions, it would seem that associative acquisition would take place via explicit contiguity, that is, by repeated pairings, explicit contiguity produces implicit contiguity (cf. Bruce & Crowley, 1970). Thus, in this case, explicit contiguity is important to acquisition because it is providing an opportunity for implicit contiguity to occur.

In the case in which natural language mediators (NLMs) are used by the individual, one or both CVCs may evoke an NLM, and acquisition is facilitated (e.g., Prytulak, 1971). The possible mechanisms producing such facilitation are of special interest. Specifically, it would seem that the role of the NLM facilitates acquisition by providing a basis for encoding the CVC pair. Without an NLM, there is no such basis. Thus, the NLM provides a means by which the new items may be encoded in terms of items already encoded.

With formally similar CVCs, it would be expected that the pair would be associated in a relatively rapid manner, since there would likely be overlap of attributes and, because of this relationship, it would be expected that NLMs play less of a role in the acquisition of formally similar CVCs than in the case of dissimilar CVCs.

The next case considered is the acquisition of a pair of words. Evidence with respect to the associative dimension indicates that when two items occur and there is any form of associative relationship between the items, acquisition takes place as a function of this relationship. Such a finding seems true with respect to associate norm strength (e.g., Wicklund, Palermo, & Jenkins, 1964), and the degree to which the two items are members of a common network (e.g., Deese, 1959). Furthermore, if there is no associative relationship, there is evidence that subjects try to develop one (Paivio & Yuille, 1969). Such results pose a problem regarding the role of explicit contiguity, for within the associative dimension, explicit contiguity is only of any real importance when the opportunity to establish an associative relationship via the particular attributes of the items is minimal.

The role of explicit contiguity in such instances may be thought to be twofold. First, the explicit contiguous presentation of two verbal units, *A* and *B*, serves what may be termed an "instructional" function for the subject. More specifically, the subject typically is told that he is to learn a pair or a list of pairs, and the subsequent presentation of the pair or pairs provides an instruction which essentially says, "This is what you are to learn." In this sense, explicit contiguity is generally an integral and possibly necessary part of associative learning. However, it is important to realize that although the explicit contiguous presentation tells the subject what he is to learn, it does not follow that he is able to learn the pair or pairs because of their explicit contiguous presentation. The acquisition of an association may be viewed, as Reed (1918a,b,c) pointed out and Bower (1971) has reiterated, as a problem-solving task, and the explicit contiguous presentation of the association may be viewed as defining the problem in the sense of showing what-is-to-be-learned.

The second function of explicit contiguity in cases such as the acquisition of a pair of words is to provide a greater opportunity for a relationship to be established between the words than would be possible if the words were not presented together. In the first case of CVC pairs, it was argued that explicit contiguity leads to implicit contiguity because the major attribute that the two items have in common is the explicit contiguous occurrence. However, when a pair of words is presented, the establishment of a relationship between the words via common attributes may short-circuit this process. Thus, the second function of extrinsic contiguity is to arouse the structural network(s) of one or both items so that the relationship may be established. This relationship then establishes the new encoding because of its implicit contiguous occurrence.

This issue is related to the topic of blocked versus unblocked presentation in free recall (see the chapters by Postman and Wood in this volume), and also to the discussion of contiguity as set forth by Wallace (1970). Basically, Wallace presents the argument that explicit contiguity occurs in the case of random presentation of categorized words via subjects' rehearsal of the items during presentation. Evidence for this view has been obtained (Rundus & Atkinson, 1970; Wallace, 1969). With respect to the semantic dimension, acquisition of a pair of items probably takes place via the attributes of the supraordinate category if the items are members of the same category. If, however, the two items are members of different categories, then acquisition may take place via the attributes common to the categories. At this point, however, it becomes difficult to separate the semantic dimension from the associative dimension.

It is of interest to note, in regard to semantic encoding, that evidence has been found which at least suggests that acquisition of an association in which each item is a member of the same conceptual category may take place not via mediation of the name of the category but via the common relationship of the features of the category (Henry & Voss, 1970).

A cogent theoretical question may be posed at this point, namely, if the acquisition of an association of two semantically related items takes place via the overlapping of similar or identical attributes, what is the role of implicit contiguity? The answer is that, as with the associative case, the development of the relationship, via the attributes, produces a new encoding by implicit contiguity. In other words, although it may seem that the acquisition of the pair may take place via only the relationship, it is argued that the relationship provides for the occurrence of a new encoding.

As previously mentioned, it has been shown (Rohwer, 1966; Rohwer, Shuell, & Levin, 1967) that a pair of words within a syntactic context may be acquired quite readily. This result may be attributed to the high degree of common syntactical encoding in the case of a pair of items when the items are embedded in the same sentence. On the other hand, Wood (1970) has found that embedding nouns in a sentence may retard recall.

The question may be raised of how a pair of items is acquired when one item has been embedded in one sentence and the second item is in a different sentence. In one study of sentence recognition, it was found that subjects apparently extract information from sentences which relate to the meaning of the sentences (Sachs, 1967). It would seem, therefore, that a relationship between a pair of items, each within a different sentence, would be a function of the syntactical relationship of the sentence and perhaps, to a greater degree, of the commonality of meaning of the two sentences. This is noteworthy, for carried one step further, it suggests that, given two sentences with highly similar meanings, it may be possible to develop an associative relationship between two items via the sentences, even though neither word occurred in either sentence. The words, of course, would need to have a strong relation to the respective sentence meanings.

Two factors which emerge from this discussion are as follows. First, within the present framework, the way in which an associative relationship is established between two items varies as a function of the encoding dimension. Second, explicit contiguity of A-B is relatively limited in establishing such a relationship, except for the "instructive" function and the increase in the likelihood of finding a relationship when the arousal of the networks of both items occurs. The exception to this is within the formal dimension, where explicit contiguity is thought to be of greater importance.

ENCODING VARIABILITY

Thus far, the law of frequency has not been considered. The importance of frequency has almost always been emphasized, and today the role of frequency in learning is receiving substantial attention, e.g., in free recall (e.g., Underwood, 1969b), in verbal discrimination learning (e.g., Ekstrand, Wallace, & Underwood, 1966), and in relation to the total-time hypothesis (Cooper & Pantle, 1967). As in the previous discussion, the role of frequency is also discussed only in relation to associative learning.

The fundamental question regarding the role of frequency in the present context is whether successive presentations of a pair of verbal units are encoded in an identical way and accumulate in their "strength," or whether successive occurrences of the same A-B pair are encoded differentially. Another way of phrasing the question is to ask whether repeated presentations of the same pair all "go to the same place" or whether they form a distribution of encodings. Considering a number of factors, mostly nonempirical in nature, the answer to the question that is taken here is that repeated presentations are encoded differentially.

One reason for adopting this view is that within the present formulation, encoding variability is expected to occur with contextual change, and it is reasonable to expect that external or internal context almost always changes. Second, it seems plausible to assume that one occurrence of A-B modifies the organism, so that a subsequent presentation of A-B is acting upon a changed organism. Third, there is the fact that most often other experiences have occurred between two presentations of A-B so that the second presentation is not equivalent to the first in terms of intervening organismic changes. Finally, it would be expected that the organism fluctuates with respect to motivational factors and other organismic processes during repeated A-B presentations. Summarizing, the position is adopted that repeated presentations of A-B are not encoded in an identical manner because of fluctuations both with respect to the external environment and with respect to internal state of the organism. It is interesting to note, incidentally, that John (1967) adopted essentially the equivalent position in proposing a physiological theory of learning.

Given the position of variability with respect to repeated presentations of A-B, it is possible to state how frequency functions within the present framework. Frequency of presentation is important to associative learning insofar that it provides for an increase in establishing a commonality of attributes of A and B. Furthermore, this means that the role of frequency of presentation may vary with the encoding dimension.

At the formal level, where the number of potentially common attributes may be regarded as minimal, it would be reasonable to expect that frequency of presentation would act in conjunction with explicit contiguity in order to provide for implicit contiguity and associative development to take place.

At the remaining three dimensions, the encoding variability that is assumed to occur with repeated presentations is of greater importance.

In general, if attribute commonality does not occur with one occurrence of A-B, it may occur with subsequent presentations because the encodings of both A and B would fluctuate. Moreover, there is the quite likely possibility that A and B may interact so that upon repeated presentations of A and B, encoding variation of one item may change in the direction of the other item.

This interpretation of the role of frequency is especially of importance in connection with the associative and semantic dimensions. With respect to the former, the view suggests that the role of frequency in the acquisition of A-B is a function of the particular attributes of A and of B that occur on any given presentation. Moreover, if the selection of attributes varies in a directional way, that is, one item in terms of the other, then the development of an associative relationship may be viewed as "incremental," in the sense that the attributes of A and B occurring increase in the probability of "finding" a common attribute. Similarly, in the case of the semantic encoding dimension, repeated presentations vary the features or attributes of the two items so that the development of a relationship becomes more likely.

With syntactic encoding, frequency is probably not important when two items occur in one sentence because the common attributes are already there. With one item in each of two different sentences, it would be expected that frequency may be related insofar as repeated presentations of the sentences may provide for some form of commonality to develop between the sentences.

It should, of course, be acknowledged that there is little, if any, direct support for this view or, for that matter, evidence against the position. However, there is a fundamental issue that is raised by this formulation, and the matter should be considered. The problem is that there is a type of dilemma regarding the nature of associative learning: either one must hold that the encodings of A and B are different and are "linked," that is, brought together by some common bond or mediator such as $A\text{-}X\text{-}B$, or one must hold that associative learning occurs because A or B, or both, change. Historically, the former view has been the more popular; it is clear that the position suggested here is the latter. Specifically, it is maintained that although A and B may maintain individual encodings or networks of encodings, the encoded version of A in the establishment of the association $A\text{-}B$ is different than the A that is encoded in relation to another item, as $A\text{-}C$, or even in relation to repeated $A\text{-}B$ occurrences that are not successive.

The role of frequency, as it is described within the present framework, is related to two important concepts of associative theorizing, namely, associative strength and response competition. The former was previously mentioned. The latter states that when there are two or more responses associated with a single stimulus, for example, $A\text{-}B$, $A\text{-}C$, B and C are regarded as competing responses and, the response having the greater associative strength is assumed to dominate and therefore be elicited by A.

Within the present framework, the importance of the concepts of associative strength and response competition is minimized. The reason is as follows. Response competition can only have meaning when the stimulus that is associated with the two or more responses is identical or similar to the extent that discrimination is not possible. However, the present formulation emphasizes that, perhaps with the exception of the formal dimension, stimuli are very seldom, if ever, identical. In other words, the problem faced by the subject in a competing response situation may be primarily one of identifying the appropriate A, that is, discriminating the encodings. Similarly, associative strength of an association, $A\text{-}B$, refers to a particular encoding of A. It is clear, for instance, that if the context of A is varied, as occurring in a sentence rather than as a single item, the response may be modified.

The arguments offered in this section, taken as a whole, suggest that contextual, experiential factors play an extremely significant role in producing a particular response when a verbal item, A, is presented. The emphasis of the present viewpoint is that with the higher encoding dimensions, the response that is elicited is a function of which encoding of A is aroused, in terms of the set of attributes, and that the response is not only a matter of A-B associative strength. Indeed, it would seem that associative strength would be of sole importance only if the encoding of A was identical on repeated presentations. Finally, it should be noted that the present viewpoint reflects an extension of Martin's (1968) concept of encoding variability, with the contention that high-m encoding involves more variability than low-m encoding. The results of Brown and Read (1970), using a free pairing procedure and men's names as the material, support this view in that negative transfer was virtually eliminated in the AB, A-Br paradigm, thus suggesting that A was encoded differentially in the two lists.

THE RELATION OF STIMULUS ENCODING AND ASSOCIATIVE ENCODING

The present formulation rather strongly emphasizes the notion that the encoding of verbal material is not simply a copy of the item. Instead, features of the verbal material are encoded, and external and internal representations are part of the encoding. When these ideas are viewed in the context of associative learning, one of the hypotheses generated is that the encoding of a stimulus item should not be independent of the response encoding. We shall now consider this issue as a specific case developing the notions of the previous two sections of the paper.

Martin (1968) hypothesized that the encoding of high-m items (words) and low-m items (CVCs) is different in that the items are already encoded in the former case, whereas it is necessary to establish in the latter case. Furthermore, Martin argued that this difference produces differential encoding variability in the two cases because the low-m stimuli may be encoded in a variety of ways, but the high-m encoding is fixed. Thus, there is a higher degree of variability that occurs in a low-m encoding, with such variability occurring until a fixed encoding develops. Recently, it may be noted, Williams and Underwood (1970) provided evidence which they interpreted as suggesting that less encoding variability takes place than is suggested by Martin's position.

Martin (1967) employed CCC-number pairs in which the responses were the digits 1, 2, or 3. In one condition, the same digit occurred with a particular response on successive trials, whereas in a second condition the response occurring with a particular stimulus was varied. Using an "Old" or "New" technique of stimulus recognition, it was found that response variation did not influence stimulus recognition performance, a result supported by Royer (1969). This finding suggests that stimulus recognition performance is independent of response consistency or, phrased another way, a consistent response did not facilitate stimulus encoding.

That stimulus encoding is not independent of the response has been reported in two types of studies. Using nonsense shapes and verbal labels as responses, Ellis and his associates have found that the meaningfulness of the verbal labels influences shape recognition (e.g., Ellis, Muller, & Tosti, 1966). They found the effect as a function of association value but not meaningfulness, a result attributed by Ellis (1968) to encoding variability with words scaled via the production method, that is when multiple labels were possible.

Another study (Mavromatis & Voss, 1971) involved presentation of high-m and low-m stimuli, and responses in a 2×2 design. The high-m items were words and the low-m items were CVC trigrams of approximately 50% association value. Following a given number of pair presentations, stimulus recognition and associative recall were measured. The finding pertinent to the present issue is that high-m responses facilitated the encoding of low-m stimuli, but high-m responses did not facilitate high-m stimulus encoding. Thus, the nature of the response influenced stimulus encoding for low-m stimuli.

The problem of the influence of the response upon stimulus recognition also has been pursued within the framework of imagery. Bower (1970), in one condition, instructed subjects to form separate images for two nouns used as the stimulus and response, and in another condition instructed subjects to form an interactive image. In a third condition, no imagery instructions were given. Of importance are two findings: first, stimulus recognition performance was approximately equivalent in all three conditions; second, the interactive instructions produced considerably better associative learning than the other two conditions. These findings indicate that when the stimulus and response are placed in some form of a relationship, associative learning is facilatated and, moreover, such a relationship does not produce poorer stimulus recognition. This latter point is of interest because it suggests that the stimulus did not lose its "unity" when placed in an interactive relation with the response. Also, in the context of imagery research, Paivio and Yuille (1969) found results which suggested that subjects may begin a paired-associate task with one strategy, perhaps with minimal use of the response, but then they may change strategy and employ the response. Although stimulus encoding was not measured in the Paivio and Yuille study, the authors did present evidence indicating that the response item may not have been important initially to the acquisition of the associations, but became important later in learning.

Considering now the role of attributes as proposed in the present formulation, the use of CCC-digit pairs probably were encoded via the formal dimension, without a common attribute except for explicit contiguity of occurrence. However, for the Ellis *et al.* and Mavromatis and Voss results, nonsense stimuli evidently were encoded in terms of the response. Moreover, low-m stimulus recognition performance in the Mavromatis and Voss study varied with response m, thus supporting the notion that the A item is encoded in terms of the B item. Finally, the Bower study suggests that the association may be encoded with the response term influencing associative encoding, but that stimulus encoding per se is not affected. This latter finding suggests a yet more complex encoding process, that of a parallel-type of encoding with respect to the single unit and pair encoding, an interpretation which also suggests why in the Mavromaits and Voss study there was no effect of high-m response upon high-m stimulus recognition.

Although the study of the role of the response in stimulus encoding is quite new, and firm conclusions cannot be readily stated, it would appear that the data and theorizing in the area have already raised a number of significant issues. First, the question of whether properties of the response influence stimulus encoding has been studied; according to the present position, response properties should modify stimulus encoding. Second, with relatively familiar words which have occurred in a number of contexts, is each occccurrence of the word differentially encoded, or perhaps are there parallel encodings of the word per se and the word with the explicit and implicit context.

We have, in the considerations of the last three sections, stayed within the framework of associative learning. However, the general notions go beyond this area, for they suggest that processes dependent on both external or internal context are extremely important, and furthermore suggest that differential encoding of words within different dimensions also is important. Finally, although memory was not discussed, it is clear that the formulations presented imply a redintegrative type of memory system in which we store complex unitary encodings, and memory consists of identifying the appropriate encoding and retrieving the information from it (cf. Horowitz & Prytulak, 1969; Prytulak, 1971).

Summary

This paper presented a discussion of associative processes, organizational processes, and the possible relationships between these two sets of processes. The importance of associative encoding was emphasized, with implicit contiguous occurrence of encodings taken to be fundamental to the development of new encodings. Organizational processes were considered primarily in terms of verbal structure, with four dimensions of verbal structure hypothesized, namely, formal, associative, semantic, and syntactic. The relation of associative processes to structure was discussed primarily within the specific framework of associative learning, and the incorporation of new material into verbal structure was viewed as a process of encoding development which is a function of the arousal of particular encodings of the structural dimensions and the occurrence of the encoding of the new material.

References

Anisfeld, M., & Knapp, M., Association, synonymity, and directionality in false recognition. *Journal of Experimental Psychology*, 1968, **77**, 171–179.

Asch, S. The doctrinal tyranny of associationism: or what is wrong with rote learning. In T. R. Dixon & D. L. Horton (Eds.), *Verbal Behavior and General Behavior Theory*. Englewood Cliffs, New Jersey: Prentice-Hall, 1968. Pp. 214–228.

Asch, S. A reformulation of the problem of associations. *American Psychologist*, 1969, **24**, 92–102.

Baddeley, A. D. The influence of acoustic and semantic similarity on long-term memory for word sequences. *Quarterly Journal of Experimental Psychology*, 1966, **18**, 302–309. (a)

Baddeley, A. D. Short-term memory for word sequences as a function of acoustic, semantic, and formal similarity. *Quarterly Journal of Experimental Psychology*, 1966, **18**, 362–365. (b)

Bobrow, S. A. Memory for words in sentences. *Journal of Verbal Learning and Verbal Behavior*, 1970, **9**, 363–372.

Bobrow. S. A., & Bower, G. H. Comprehension and recall of sentences. *Journal of Experimental Psychology*, 1969, **80**, 455–461.

Bousfield, W. A., Whitmarsh, G. A., & Danick, J. J. Partial response identities in verbal generalization. *Psychological Reports*, 1958, **4**, 703–713.

Bower, G. A multicomponent theory of the memory trace. In K. W. Spence & J. T. Spence (Eds.), *The Psychology of Learning and Motivation*. New York: Academic Press, 1967. Pp. 229–325.

Bower, G. H. Imagery as a relational organizer in associative learning. *Journal of Verbal Learning and Verbal Behavior*, 1970, **9**, 529–533.

Bower, G. H. Mental imagery and associative learning. In L. Gregg (Ed.), *Cognition in Learning and Memory*. New York: Wiley, 1971.

Brown, S. C., & Read, J. D. Associative organization in paired-associate learning and transfer. *Journal of Verbal Learning and Verbal Behavior*, 1970, **9**, 317–326.

Bruce, D., & Crowley, J. J. Acoustic similarity effects on retrieval from secondary memory. *Journal of Verbal Learning and Verbal Behavior*, 1970, **9**, 190–196.

Cofer, C. N. Free recall of nouns after presentation in sentences. *Journal of Experimental Psychology*, 1968, **78**, 145–152.

Cofer, C. N., & Foley, J. P., Jr. Mediated generalization and the interpretation of verbal behavior: I. Prolegomena. *Psychological Review*, 1942, **49**, 513–540.

Conrad, R. An association between memory errors and errors due to acoustic masking of speech. *Nature*, 1962, **193**, 1314–1315.

Conrad, R. Acoustic confusion in immediate memory. *British Journal of Psychology*, 1964, **55**, 75–84.

Cooper, E. H., & Pantle, A. J. The total-time hypothesis in verbal learning. *Psychological Bulletin*, 1967, **68**, 221–234.

Cramer, P. *Word Association*. New York: Academic Press, 1968.

Cramer, P. Semantic generalization: IAR locus and instructions. *Journal of Experimental Psychology*, 1970, **83**, 266–273.

Deese, J. Influence of inter-item associate strength upon immediate free recall. *Psychological Reports*, 1959, **5**, 305–312.

Deese, J. *The Structure of Associations in Language and Thought*. Baltimore, Maryland: Johns Hopkins, 1965.

Deese, J. Association and memory. In T. R. Dixon & D. L. Horton (Eds.), *Verbal Behavior and General Behavior Theory*. Englewood Cliffs, New Jersey: Prentice-Hall, 1968. Pp. 97–108.

Eagle, M., & Ortof, E. The effect of level of attention upon "phonetic" recognition errors. *Journal of Verbal Learning and Verbal Behavior*, 1967, **6**, 226–231.

Ekstrand, B. R., Wallace, W. P., & Underwood, B. J. A frequency theory of verbal-discrimination learning. *Psychological Review*, 1966, **73**, 566–578.

Ellis, H. C. The role of stimulus meaning in generalization gradients of recognition memory: an encoding-variability interpretation. Paper presented at "Perception as Behavior" symposium, Southwestern Psychological Association, New Orleans, 1968.

Ellis, H. C., Muller, D. G., & Tosti, D. T. Stimulus meaning and complexity as factors in the transfer of stimulus predifferentiation. *Journal of Experimental Psychology*, 1966, **71**, 629–633.

Epstein, W. The influence of syntactical structure on learning. *American Journal of Psychology*, 1961, **74**, 80–85.

Greenwald, A. G. Sensory feedback mechanisms in performance control: with special reference to the ideo-motor mechanism. *Psychological Review*, 1970, **77**, 73–99.

Grossman, L., & Eagle, M. Synonymity, antonymity, and association in false recognition responses. *Journal of Experimental Psychology*, 1970, **83**, 244–248.

Henley, N. M., Noyes, H. L., & Deese, J. Semantic structure in short-term memory. *Journal of Experimental Psychology*, 1968, **77**, 587–592.

Henry, N., & Voss, J. F. Associative strength growth produced via category membership. *Journal of Experimental Psychology*, 1970, **83**, 136–140.

Hintzman, D. L. Articulatory coding in short-term memory. *Journal of Verbal Learning and Verbal Behavior*, 1967, **6**, 312–316.

Horowitz, L. M., & Prytulak, L. S. Redintegrative memory, *Psychological Review*, 1969, **76**, 519–531.

Hume, D. *An Enquiry Concerning Human Understanding*. 1748. Reprinted by Regnery, New York, 1956.

John, E. R. *Mechanisms of memory*. New York: Academic Press, 1967.

Key, C. B. Recall as a function of perceived relations. *Archives of Psychology*, 1926, No. 83.

Kiess, H. O. Effects of natural language mediators on short-term memory. *Journal of Experimental Psychology*, 1968, **77**, 7–13.

Kimble, G. A. Mediating associations. *Journal of Experimental Psychology*, 1968, **76**, 263–266.

Kimble, G. A., & Perlmuter, L. C. The problem of volition. *Psychological Review*, 1970, **77**, 361–384.

Leicht, K. L. Recall and judged frequency of implicitly occurring words. *Journal of Verbal Learning and Verbal Behavior*, 1968, **7**, 918–923.

Lenneberg, E. *Biological Foundations of Language.* New York: Wiley, 1967.

Mandler, G. Response factors in human learning. *Psychological Review*, 1954, **61**, 235–244.

Mandler, G. Organization and memory. In K. W. Spence & J. T. Spence (Eds.), *The Psychology of Learning and Motivation.* New York: Academic Press, 1967. Pp. 327–372.

Marks, L. E., & Miller, G. A. The role of semantic and syntactic constraints in the memorization of English sentences. *Journal of Verbal Learning and Verbal Behavior*, 1964, **3**, 1–5.

Martin, E. Relation between stimulus recognition and paired-associate learning. *Journal of Experimental Psychology*, 1967, **74**, 500–505.

Martin, E. Stimulus meaningfulness and paired-associate transfer: an encoding variability hypothesis. *Psychological Review*, 1968, **75**, 421–441.

Mavromatis, J., & Voss, J. F. Frequency and meaningfulness in stimulus recognition and associative learning. Unpublished manuscript.

Osgood, C. E. The nature and measurement of meaning. *Psychological Bulletin*, 1952, **49**, 197–237.

Paivio, A., & Yuille, J. C. Changes in associative strategies and paired-associate learning over trials as a function of word imagery and type of learning set. *Journal of Experimental Psychology*, 1969, **79**, 458–463.

Postman, L. Association and performance in the analysis of verbal learning. In T. R. Dixon & D. L. Horton (Eds.), *Verbal Behavior and General Behavior Theory.* Englewood Cliffs, New Jersey: Prentice-Hall, 1968, Pp. 551–571.

Prytulak, L. S. Natural language mediation. *Cognitive Psychology*, 1971, **2**, 1–56.

Reed, H. B. Associative aids: I. Their relation to learning, retention, and other associations. *Psychological Review*, 1918, **25**, 128–155. (a)

Reed, H. B. Associative aids: II. Their relation to practice and the transfer of training. *Psychological Review*, 1918, **25**, 257–285. (b)

Reed, H. B. Associative aids: III. Their relation to the theory of thought and to methodology in psychology. *Psychological Review*, 1918, **25**, 378–401. (c)

Robinson, E. S. *Association Theory To-Day.* New York: Century, 1932.

Rohwer, W. D., Jr. Constraint, syntax and meaning in paired-associate learning. *Journal of Verbal Learning and Verbal Behavior*, 1966, **5**, 541–547.

Rohwer, W. D., Jr., Shuell, T. J., & Levin, J. R. Context effects in the initial storage and retrival of noun pairs. *Journal of Verbal Learning and Verbal Behavior*, 1967, **6**, 796–801.

Rosen, S. M., & Greenhouse, P. The effect of stimulus type on formal similarity between stimuli and their primary associations. *Psychonomic Science*, 1971, **22**, 66–67.

Royer, J. M. Associative recall as a function of stimulus recognition. *American Journal of Psychology*, 1969, **82**, 96–103.

Rundus, D., & Atkinson, R. C. Rehearsal processes in free recall: a procedure for direct observation. *Journal of Verbal Learning and Verbal Behavior*, 1970, **9**, 99–105.

Runquist, W. N. Formal intralist stimulus similarity in paired-associate learning. *Journal of Experimantal Psychology*, 1968, **78**, 634–641.

Sachs, J. S. Recognition memory for syntactic and semantic aspects of connected discourse. *Perception and Psychophysics*, 1967, **2**, 437–442.

Shulman, H. G. Encoding and retention of semantic and phonemic information in short-term memory. *Journal of Verbal Learning and Verbal Behavior*, 1970, **9**, 499–508.

Tulving, E. Subjective organization in free recall of "unrelated" words. *Psychological Review*, 1962, **69**, 344–354.

Tulving, E. Theoretical issues in free recall. In T. R. Dixon & D. L. Horton (Eds.), *Verbal Behavior and General Behavior Theory*. Englewood Cliffs, New Jersey: Prentice-Hall, 1968. Pp. 1–36.

Underwood, B. J. Stimulus selection in verbal learning. In C. N. Cofer & B. S. Musgrave (Eds.), *Verbal Behavior and Learning*. New York: McGraw-Hill, 1963. Pp. 33–48.

Underwood, B. J. False recognition produced by implicit verbal responses. *Journal of Experimental Psychology*, 1965, **70**, 122–129.

Underwood, B. J. Attributes of memory. *Psychological Review*, 1969, **76**, 559–573. (a)

Underwood, B. J. Some correlates of item repetition in free-recall learning. *Journal of Verbal Learning and Verbal Behavior*, 1969, **8**, 83–94. (b)

Underwood, B. J., & Freund, J. S. Errors in recognition learning and retention. *Journal of Experimental Psychology*, 1968, **78**, 55–63.

Voss, J. F. Associative learning and thought. In J. F. Voss (Ed.), *Approaches to Thought*. Columbus, Ohio: Merrill, 1969. Pp. 83–110.

Wallace, W. P. Clustering in free recall based upon input contiguity. *Psychonomic Science*, 1969, **14**, 290–292.

Wallace, W. P. Consistency of emission order in free recall. *Journal of Verbal Learning and Verbal Behavior*, 1970, **9**, 58–68.

Wallach, H., & Averbach, E. On memory modalities. *American Journal of Psychology*, 1955, **68**, 249–257.

Warren, H. C. *History of the Association Psychology*. New York: Scribner, 1921.

Wickelgren, W. A. Auditory or articulatory coding in verbal short-term memory. *Psychological Review*, 1969, **76**, 232–235.

Wickens, D. D. Encoding categories of words: An empirical approach to meaning. *Psychological Review*, 1970, **77**, 1–15.

Wickens, D. D., & Eckler, G. R. Semantic as opposed to acoustic encoding in STM. *Psychonomic Science*, 1968, **12**, 63.

Wicklund, D. A., Palermo, D. S., & Jenkins, J. J. The effects of associative strength and response hierarchy on paired-associate learning. *Journal of Verbal Learning and Verbal Behavior*, 1964, **3**, 413–420.

Williams, R. F., & Underwood, B. J. Encoding variability: Tests of the Martin hypothesis. *Journal of Experimental Psychology*, 1970, **86**, 317–324.

Wood, G. Free recall of nouns presented in sentences. *Psychonomic Science*, 1970, **18**, 76–77.

PART II

6 | *A Process Model for Long-Term Memory*[1]

David E. Rumelhart
Peter H. Lindsay
Donald A. Norman

[1] This research was supported by USPHS Grant NS-07454 to the authors from the National Institute of Neurological Diseases and Stroke, and by USPHS Grant MH-15828 to the Center for Human Information Processing from the National Institute of Mental Health, by a grant from the Sloan Foundation to the Institute for Advanced Study and by NSF Grant 6B-8587 to D. E. Rumelhart.

Many people have been involved in the creation of the concepts presented here. Properties of the language, especially the definitions of individual words and relations, were performed by Adele Abrahamson, Jim Levin, Marc Eisenstadt, Yaakov Kovarsky, and Steve Palmer. Implementation of a list processing system designed especially for these rules on both the Burroughs 6500 and the PDP-9/15 computers was performed by Donald Blankenship, Mark Miller, and Bob Olds. The list learning program was written by Mark Miller and Randy Gibson.

A Process Model

The nature of a theory must depend on the question it is designed to answer. For the most part, psychological theories of human memory have been closely tied to one particular type of memory function: how people learn lists of words. Yet the retention of a specific sequence of words is but one of the many demands that are placed on human memory. In fact, during the life of the average adult, rote memorization seems seldom to be required.

Long past events are not so much remembered as they are recreated. People can answer complicated questions about the information stored in long-term memory (LTM). They use memory to solve problems, to make logical deductions, to understand ideas, as well as to memorize facts. Even when subjects learn lists of words, they typically attempt to reorganize the input they encounter in terms of their past experience. If we are to expand our understanding of the nature of memory, we must inevitably come to grips with some of these more complex functions of human endeavor.

DATA AND PROCESS

In this paper we examine the nature of the memory system that might underlie these more sophisticated memory functions. We consider two basic aspects of the problem. The first is the structure of the *data base*, the way by which information is represented in the LTM. The second is the nature of the *processes* which operate upon the data base. There need be no formal distinction between that information which is a part of the data base and that which is a process operating upon the data base. One very important aspect of our process model of memory is that processes are stored in the data base. They may be retrieved and used like any other information, or they may be activated and thereby perform their processing operations upon other data. Finally, we propose that there is an *interpretive process* which operates on information contained within the data base, retrieving information when necessary and activating (or interpreting) the processes when that is necessary.

To see how these concepts interact, consider the following query:

Query: In the house in which you lived three houses ago, how many windows were there on the north side?

Most people claim to solve this problem by visualizing the house they now live in, then moving back to each previous house until they arrive at the proper goal. Then they determine in which direction north was with respect to the house, visualize the north wall and mentally traverse the house in a systematic fashion, counting the windows as they proceed. In this retrieval we see several factors operating. First is the determination of a *process* for reaching the solution. Second is the factual information in the *data base* concerning the detailed structure of the house. Third is the *enactment* of the processes in order to complete the task set by the query.

OUR TASK

Once the system has been defined, the memory theorist arrives at a choice point. Just what kinds of cognitive processes should be examined in order to test the robustness of the memory structure? Is it inductive, deductive, or analogic reasoning, or perhaps problem solving (Ernst & Newell, 1969; Newell & Simon, in press), or the formation of belief systems (Abelson, 1968), the evolution of neurotic personalities (Colby, 1967; Colby & Smith, 1969), or the extraction of cause-effect relationships from an external event sequence (Becker, 1970)? Conceivably, one ought simply to study the memory for lists of items. The choice is not easy. To some extent, the power of the memory representation is reflected in the range of processing tasks that it can sustain and the generality of the processing routines underlying different types of cognitive tasks. It is important to keep in mind the variety of tasks that must be supported by the same memory system if we are to identify any common principles in the processes involved in memory function.

Our goal is to develop a memory structure that is capable of encoding and representing a reasonable range of the information it is likely to encounter, that has direct and explicit rules for translating external information into an internal representation, and that is flexible enough to support a variety of cognitive and information-processing tasks. In the first part of the paper we outline a general model for representing the information in LTM and some of the functional components of the memory system. In the second section we describe in more detail the formal properties of the model and a grammar for encoding information.

In the final part we give some examples of how the memory model works. We consider two different types of memory tasks which are at opposite ends of the spectrum of cognitive complexity. The first task is list learning. Here the approach is to try to make contact with the principles of cognitive models that are concerned both with describing understanding and thinking and also with the vast experimental literature that studies memory behavior when the opportunities for thinking and understanding are minimized. The second type of task is a common component of many theories of cognitive processing: the procedures for generalization and discrimination of the information encoded in the data base.

RELATED APPROACHES

Our general approach is related to several other systems. In computer sciences and artificial intelligence, it is closely influenced by two developments: the study of large-scale information retrieval systems and question-answering systems (see Minsky, 1968; Frijda, in press; Simmons, 1970). The idea that processes can both be stored in the data base and operated upon as data and also be activated and thereby actively operate upon other data also appears in several other places. The two most relevant to our model are the systems for problem solving devised by Becker (1970) and the language understanding system of Winograd (1970).

Some of the aspects of the representation of information in LTM are analogous to the case grammar developed by Fillmore (1968, 1969) and the conceptual framework of Schank (1970, 1971). The psychological aspects of the system reflect earlier work on the simulation of human cognitive structures, much of which is nicely summarized in the introductory book by Loehlin (1968) and the review article by Frijda (in press). The papers in this volume that are closely related to our work are the papers by Kintsch, by Collins and Quillian, and by Bower. Though they are similar to one another in various respects, each stakes out a slightly different method of approach and a different area of primary interest.

ON THE DEVELOPMENTAL STATUS OF THE SYSTEM

Before turning to the system, a warning is in order. One of the great virtues of considering specific process models of memory is that it allows us to decide whether our verbal theories are really sufficient to perform a given task or, indeed, whether they are even testable at all. Though our intuitions about what will happen in a given model are usually seductive, they often turn out to be misleading. At the present time, our model is in a developmental stage. Some of the mechanisms have been tested in actual simulation or with experiments, but much is still tentative. We introduce them here in order to raise questions about the kinds of mechanisms that must be considered when attempting to model LTM. There has already been a major change between the paper presented at the conference and the one presented in these pages. We expect more major changes in the future as we learn about the nature of human cognitive processes.

A Structure for Long-Term Memory

The first step in developing a process model of memory is to describe explicitly how information is represented in the memory. In our model, the basic structural element of the data base is a set of nodes interconnected by a relation R, $R[c_1, \ldots ,c_n]$.[2] Nodes represent any cluster

[2] Two equivalent representations are described in this paper. One is a formal language for describing relationships among the information of the data base. The other is a graph structure that allows the information base to be illustrated. The language and the graph representations are formally equivalent (we present the rules for converting one representation into the other). Each has advantages, however. The language is more conducive to formalization and a rigorous statement of the assumptions. It is the format that we use in the computer implementation of the data base. The graph structure is a valuable notational system that allows the user to see the interrelationships of the information structure more readily. We find it easier to think about the graph representation, but more appropriate to state our assumptions in terms of the language notation. Elsewhere in this volume Collins and Quillian use graph notation almost exclusively (quite different from our notation, however). Kintsch uses a language representation exclusively.

of information in the memory. A relation is an association among sets of nodes. A relation has two important properties: one, it is labeled; two, it is directed. That is, the relations interconnecting nodes has distinctive meanings, depending on the direction in which the relation is traversed. Using the relation in the direction opposite to its label is equivalent to using the inverse relation. Relations, then, are bidirectional but not symmetrical. These relations are used by the memory system to encode logical or semantic associations among nodes.

The basic representation of the memory structure, in graph notation, is shown in Figure 1. Here two nodes, named a and b, are shown in relationship R.

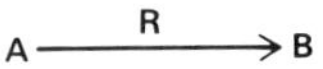

$$A \xrightarrow{\text{R}} B$$

Fig. 1.

It is important to note that the arrowhead simply serves to define the direction in which the relation applies. Thus, the link between nodes can actually be traversed in either direction, yielding the pair of equivalent descriptions of Figure 1:

$$R[a,b] = R\text{-inverse}[b,a].$$

For example, if R specifies a *superset* relation, then $R\text{-}inverse$ specifies a *subset* relation:

$$\text{subset}[a,b] = \text{superset}[b,a].$$

Any number of relations may be attached to a single node, and all relations attached to the same node operate conjunctively. If a disjunctive interpretation is desired, it must be specified by means of a *simple conjunction* (*or, xor, and*).

A relation need not be binary. Thus, we could represent the n-ary relation R in language notation as:

$$R[a,b, \ldots ,n],$$

or in graph notation by means of a circle (in which the relation name is written) and a set of n labeled arrows pointing to the nodes used by the relation. Because the ordering of the arguments (ranges) of the relation is important in determining the meaning, either the labels are designated with names that unambiguously reflect their role in the relation or they are numbered to indicate their place in the ordered set of arguments.

Every definable piece of information in the memory system, then, is encoded in the format of a node plus its relations. The node is the only addressable unit in the memory system and encodes all of the ideas that make up the knowledge of the data base.

Although all nodes are named in the system (i.e., addressable), the names may not have simple natural language equivalents. When a node does have a natural language name, then we distinguish its usage in different contexts by distinguishing between *primary* and *secondary* nodes. A *primary* node is the only node in the memory system that refers directly to the natural language word, and it may contain an abstracted definition of that word expressed in the relational format. *Secondary* nodes represent the concepts as they are used in specific contexts—a *token* use of a primary *type* node. We will illustrate this distinction as we discuss the representation of concepts, events, and episodes in the memory system.

CONCEPTS, EVENTS, AND EPISODES

When examining the kinds of things that must be represented in a model of human LTM, it is convenient to distinguish among three classes of information: *concepts, events,* and *episodes. Concepts* refer primarily to particular ideas. An *event* is action-based, denoting a scenario with its associated actors and objects. An *episode* is a series of events or actions. Although these different classes of information can be logically distinguished, they are all represented in the same memory format. To introduce the main ideas, we will only briefly illustrate the types of relations that are useful for representing concept, event, and episode information.

Encoding Concepts

When it comes to defining concepts in the memory system, three types of functional relations are of primary importance: the classes to which a concept belongs (i.e., its supersets), the characteristics which define it as a member of that class, and the examples or subsets of that concept. We use three labels for specifying these functional relations. *Isa* defines set membership: thus, *John isa person; dog isa animal. Is* and *has* are used to define property relations: *has* for objects, as in *animal has feet; is* for qualities, as in *John is fat.* To specify a subset relation, the inverse of *isa* is used: *animal isa-inverse dog*, meaning a subclass of animals is dog.[3] Although these three relations are neither necessary nor sufficient to define concepts, they provide crucial information needed during the manipulation of the conceptual information in the memory system. An example of their use is shown in Figure 2. In this example, note that

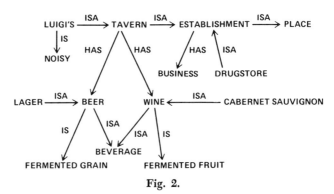

Fig. 2.

we have represented everything in terms of *primary* nodes. In actually encoding this information, most of it would be represented in *secondary* nodes which are designated by angular brackets: ⟨ lager ⟩. The secondary nodes are connected to their primaries by the relation *isa*.

Encoding Events

An event is a scenario with actions, actors, and objects. In general, a verb describes the action that is taking place, so the representation centers around the verb. Our scheme for representing events is conceptually similar to the ideas described in the case grammar by Fillmore (1968, 1969). We treat an action as a relation that can take various arguments. The exact interpretation of the event depends on the arguments of the relation.

For example, consider the observation:

1. The rock rolled down the mountain.

This represents an event centered around the critical action *roll*. The "rock" is the *object* rolling down the mountain (set in motion by some anonymous actor); "down the mountain" specifies the *path* of the action;

[3] The algorithms for encoding information into the data base encode the inverse relation automatically whenever an assertion is made. Thus, for the assertion *dog has feet*, the inverse relation *feet has-inverse dog* is also entered into the memory system.

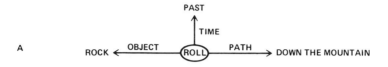

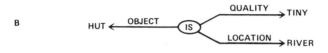

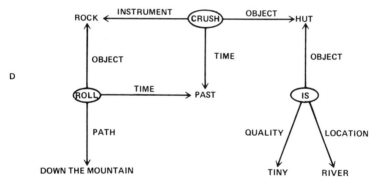

Fig. 3.

the *time* is in the past. The encoding of this information into the memory structure is shown in Figure 3A. Now consider the further information that:

2. The hut is tiny.
3. The hut is at the river.

The action here centers around the relation *is:* in this case, "tiny" is a *quality,* "river" a *location,* and "hut" is the *object* of the relation *is.* This produces Figure 3B. Now consider:

4. The rock crushed the hut.

The "rock" is the *instrument* which acts on the *object* "hut." Hence, the structure of Figure 3C.

The last structure, Figure 3D, shows the complete representation of the event:

5. The rock that rolled down the mountain crushed the tiny hut at the river.

Indeed, when Bransford and Franks (in press) asked subjects to learn the individual sentences 1–4 above and later tested for recognition, they found that it was the full concept, sentence 5, that was recognized even though it had never been shown to the subjects.

As in the case for concepts, most events are actually encoded in terms of secondary nodes. The corresponding primary action is designated by the function label *act*. Thus, the event:

6. John hits the ball with the small bat.

would be encoded as shown in Figure 4. As with concepts, the secondary node represents the usage of the word in a specific context.

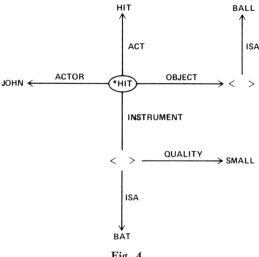

Fig. 4.

The processing system distinguishes between concepts and events by whether an *act* or an *isa* arrow leaves the node. Causal relations can also be encoded, as in:

7. Hearing the growling and snarling, Perrault raises his rifle.

The *then* link in the representation of scenario 7 (Figure 5) illustrates one of the basic mechanisms for connecting events or action sequences into an episode.

Primary and Secondary Nodes

There are problems when a single concept or event must be referred to many times, but in different circumstances. Suppose that we are using the act *hit* in the two sentences:

8. John hits the ball.
9. Peter hits the cat.

The difficulty is shown in Figure 6A. We need to separate the two uses of the act *hit*. We do this by distinguishing between the definitional

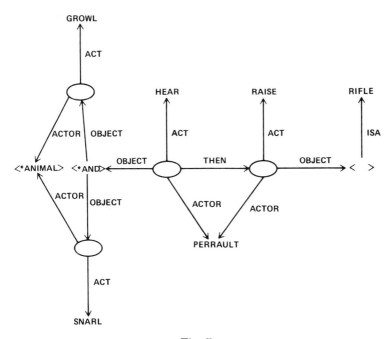

Fig. 5.

node for *hit*, the *primary* (or type) node, and the particular use of that node, the *secondary* (or token) node. We represent secondary event nodes by encircling them. The secondary node for an *event* is connected to the primary node by the relation *act*. When a secondary node is shown in diagram form by a circle, the *act* relation is assumed to exist. Thus, the encoding is shown in Figure 6B.

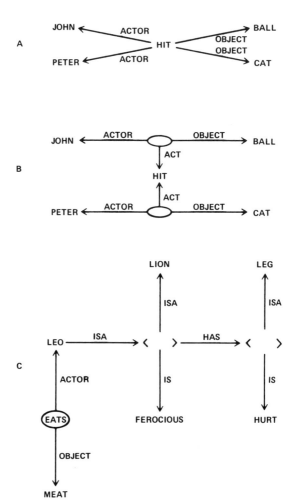

Fig. 6.

Similar problems and solutions arise with concept nodes. As mentioned earlier, secondary concepts are enclosed in angular brackets: ⟨ animal ⟩. This can be read as "this animal" or "token animal." Secondary concepts are connected to their primary nodes by the relation *isa*. Thus, the illustration in Figure 6C depicts the concept:

10. Leo, a ferocious lion with a hurt leg, eats meat.

Encoding Episodes

The representation of an event is centered around a single action. An *episode* is a cluster of events or actions. The interrelations within the event clusters are encoded by special arrows called *propositional conjunctions*. Two of these conjunctions are the *then* relation, which leads to the next event in an action sequence, and the *while* relation, which interconnects events with unspecified temporal order. The *then* and *while* arrows are illustrated in the episode of Figure 7:

11. John murders Mary at Luigi's.

This mechanism for clustering events into episodes has considerable flexibility for representing temporal information in the memory system.

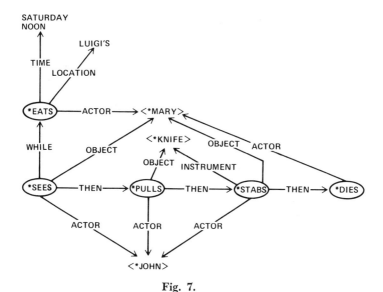

Fig. 7.

Time is defined locally within the context of a specific event sequence. Since any level of embedding is allowed, any level of time scale can be defined.

In general, conjunctions like *then* and *while* provide an organizing principle for events similar to that provided by *isa* in clustering concepts. The "superset" of an event results from the logical grouping of events which may have general properties in common. The *while* and *then* links specify the temporal relations within each example. The examples themselves may be supersets of lower order event clusters.

This conceptualization of event clusters is crucial to the memory model, for it allows us to encode the procedures for retrieving, manipulating, and evaluating stored information—the *processes* of the model—in the same way we encode the conceptual and event information. An event is simply an action or relation among several arguments. An episode is a sequence of events—the equivalent of a subroutine. The *act* relation can be interpreted as the enactment of that subroutine. Thus, the actions involved in internal processing can be represented in exactly the same format as external action sequences that have been observed by the system. The flow of action in an episode is a process of the memory system. The only difference between external event sequences and internal processes is whether the system (person) actually performs operations or simply does them mentally as it follows through the specification of an episode.[4]

The Interpretive System

The ability to encode episodes directly into the data base has important implications, both from a practical and a theoretical point of view. Practically, this means that when we actually simulate this structure on a computer, we can use the process language itself to perform the simulation. This allows us to do most of the programming in a flow-chart form which describes the sequence of operations to be performed at varying levels of generality. The same routines that encode and edit concept and event information will automatically encode the processing routines. Since the language of the simulation is the same as the language of the data base, the system becomes relatively independent of the particular machine or the programming language that is being used. Only the general interpretive system (the executive program) and a relatively small set of *primitive* routines have to be defined outside of the memory structure itself.

Moreover, the process-episode representation has important theoretical implications, for it allows the procedures that operate on concept and event information to operate on itself. Conceptual, event and episode information is completely intermixed in the memory system, and all are represented in this same format. The *then* links are used interchangeably to lead to the next event in an observed action sequence or the

---

[4] It is interesting to note that a number of functions used by the interpretive system during processing can also be used during the actual execution of that same event. When following the events shown in Figure 5, the interpreter treats the *act* relation as a call to the subroutine *stab* and goes to the definition of *stab* to find the arguments required. *Stab* may specify that a *person*, an *object*, and a *pointed instrument* are needed. This provides the plan for searching for specific arguments in the observational sequence or for making inferences about arguments that may be missing in the memory of an event. If it is only "thinking" about the event sequence, then missing arguments do not distract it. But, if it is trying to execute the sequence (that is, if it wishes to stab someone), then it must actually fill in the missing arguments before it can proceed with the action.

next process to be executed by the interpreter. If the action called for can be executed, it will be; if not, the system simply continues evaluating the processing network.

Finally, the overall organization of the simulation system is itself a model of memory function. It consists of a set of primitive operating routines, an executive or interpretive system, and a short-term memory (STM). The primitives of the system are made up of a small set of comparison and counting routines (written in a specific programming language and, thus, outside of the memory model).[5]

The Implications of STM

The interpretive system is intentionally designed to operate with a limited STM capacity. The STM holds the links needed to keep track of the pathway through a process, as well as any temporary results generating during the execution of a process. Thus, if the procedure being executed exceeds STM capacity, the interpreter can get lost and make errors. This feature of the model simplifies tests of a generally proposed assumption: that the complexity of cognitive processes and the selection and development of particular processing strategies may be primarily constrained by limitations in STM capacity.

GENERAL FEATURES OF THE MODEL

To summarize, there are several fundamental aspects of this process model of LTM. The basic element of information in the memory network is the event, consisting of a set of nodes interconnected by a relation. A node is a functional cluster of information that can represent a concept, event, or episode in the system and may have any number of relations attached to it. Secondary nodes may be derived from primary nodes; higher-order nodes may be defined by the concatenation of lower-order ones. The exact constraints on which nodes may be related to which other nodes are outlined in the following section.

Relations among nodes are directed and labeled. Relational labels are the basic means of encoding logical or semantic functions which interconnect nodes. Though a distinction has been made between the representation of concrete concepts, events, and episodes, these three types of information are in fact encoded in identical formats, and completely intermixed in the memory structure. Together they form the total body of knowledge that the system has at any given time.

[5] About 12 primitives are presently defined for the memory model. Only three of these depend on the particular network structure that is used to represent the information in the computer system.

The Formal Character of the Memory System

We presume that information is stored as a network of *concepts* interconnected by *relations*. This assumption has little content. It is only when we are able to specify the way in which concepts, events, and relations are built up and changed as a function of experience that we begin to have a potentially useful model. In this portion of the paper we attempt to systematize and state rigorously and concisely the rules whereby new information modifies the memory system. In the following sections we discuss the two major constituents of the memory system (relations and concepts), introduce some minor constituents (operators and connectives), and define the notion of a proposition (the unit of internal language). In the course of our discussion we introduce several *rules of formation* which explicitly describe the procedures for generating new concepts and relations from old ones. The rules fall into four general categories:

1. Rules of formation for relations;
2. Rules of formation for concepts;
3. Rules of formation for propositions;
4. Rules of formation for operators.

A number of new terms are introduced. Table 1 gives definitions and abbreviations of the most important of these terms and should be referred to throughout the next section.

RELATIONS AND THEIR MEANINGS

Relations are associated with the prototypical events or situations. One useful analogy is to consider relations to be scenarios, with the concepts as the actors and objects playing the roles of the various characters in the scenarios. The general notation for a relation is:

$$R[\text{range}_1, \text{range}_2, \ldots, \text{range}_n]$$

where R is the name of the *relation* and $range_i$ is the name of the *range* of the ith *variable*. Consider a situation in which an actor, A, strolls along a path, P, at some time, T. In this instance we would say that *stroll* is a relation which holds among three concepts A, P, and T. The concept A is a particular instance from the range of *actors* (animate beings capable of strolling), concept P is a particular instance

TABLE 1

Notation and Definitions of Terms

Term	Notation	Definition	Example
Concept	C	The name or description of some definite object, event, or class of objects.	John, Bill, bat
Conjunction, propositional	$P\,conj$	Any of the set of connectives which can hold among propositions. Simple conjunctions (below) are a subset of the propositional conjunctions.	if, then, because, and, or
Conjunction, simple	$Conj$	The logical conjunctions.	and, or, xor
Operator, prepositional	$P(v)$	An operator which applies to concepts of time or location to generate new concepts of time or location defined with respect to the original concepts.	before(noon) under(water)
Operator, relational	$O/$	An operator which applies to relations and certain other operators to generate new relations or operators.	very/big slowly/walk
Proposition	$Prop$	An ordered set of concepts and the relation which ties them together or a conjoined set of propositions.	hit[John,ball,bat]
Qualifier	$Q(v)$	An operator which operates on concepts to produce new concepts with the properties specified by the qualifier.	big(ball) red(balloon)
Quantifier	$\#(v)$	An operator which operates on concepts to produce new concepts. These concepts specify a portion of the original concept, often as a certain number of the original concept class.	many(dog) amount(milk) edge(woods)
Relation	$R[v_1, \ldots ,v_n]$	The name of the associations which may hold among sets of concepts.	hit[actor, object, instrument]
Variable	v_i, x_i	A symbol which can take as values any of a set of concepts.	$R[v_1, \ldots ,v_n]$

from the range of *paths* (on which one might stroll), and T is an instance from the range of *time*. The relation *stroll* always must have the form:

stroll[actor,path,time][6]

and the particular event would be represented by:

stroll[A,P,T].

Notice here that we name the relation for the verb in English to which it most clearly corresponds, although it is not necessary that relations correspond to any single English term.[7]

There are three distinct ways of forming new relations. The first way is by application of a *relational operator, O,* to one relation to generate another. The rule can be expressed as:

Rule 1a. $R[v_1, \ldots ,v_n] \rightarrow O/R[v_1, \ldots , v_n]$

This should be read by using the word "replaces" for the arrow: hence, the *n*-valued relation R *replaces* the *n*-valued relation O/R.

To illustrate, suppose that the relation *walk* is denoted *walk*[*actor, path,time*]. Then we might derive the relation *stroll* from the relation *slowly/walk*.[8] Following Rule 1a, we would write:

stroll[actor,path,time] → slowly/walk[actor,path,time].

Relations which are formed by application of Rule 1a need not have natural language equivalents. Thus:

not/slowly/stroll[actor,path,time]

---

[6] Throughout this section we use the range *actor* to correspond to animate beings capable of initiating actions. If more than one variable has the same range, we subscript them as *actor₁, actor₂*, etc. The range *path* corresponds to any temporally sequenced list of locations. It should be noted, however, that the name of the range need not correspond to any single word in English. Presumably, ranges are learned by induction as experience with relationships is acquired.

[7] Our association of relations with verbs derives directly from Fillmore's (1968, 1969) case grammar approach to verbs. (Kintsch's discussion of case grammar in this volume is a useful reference.) What we are calling *ranges* of our variables is related to what Fillmore calls *cases*. We in general embed less semantic meaning in our labels than Fillmore associates with his. Our treatment of relations also corresponds to the *propositional form* of mathematical logic (*c.f.* Church, 1956).

Although most of our examples employ verb names as relations, the comparative form of adjectives can also serve as relations. Hence, taller [object₁, object₂] is a legitimate relation.

[8] Relational operators are often associated with adverbs, including negation.

is a legitimate relation, although there is no single word in English that expresses that idea.

The second procedure whereby new relations can be formed from older ones is by specification of the variables within the prior relation. We write this as:

$$Rule\ 1b.\ R[v_1,\ \ldots\ ,v_n] \to R[x_1,\ \ldots\ ,x_m]$$

where $m \geqq n$.

We can illustrate Rule 1b by deriving *walk* from the general relation *move*. *Move* is a very general concept, one that is intended to represent the scenario in which an *actor* causes an *object* to follow along a *path* by means of some *instrument* at some *time:*

move[actor,object,path,instrument,time].

We can derive *walk* as a special restriction on *move:*

walk[actor,path,time] $\to$ move[actor,actor,path,I,time]

where I is a concept of an actor who alternately puts one foot in front of the other while allowing at most one foot to leave the ground at any one time. (We discuss the notation for such complex concepts in a later subsection.) Thus, this notation is interpreted to say that the relation *walk* can be said to hold among an *actor, path,* and *time* whenever that *actor* moves himself along that *path* by means of *instrument* I.[9]

The third way of generating new relations is by conjunction of several old ones. Hence:

$$Rule\ 1c.\ R[v_1,\ \ldots\ ,v_n] \to R[x_1,\ \ldots\ ,x_m]\ Pconj\ R[y_1,\ \ldots\ ,y_k]$$

where *Pconj* stands for the class of conjunctions called *propositional conjunctions.* Any number of relations can be conjoined.

[9] The relation *move* is intended to be very general. Hence, many different relations will be derived from it. Move is probably very similar to the concept of *trans* used by Schank (1970, 1971), and a number of the different types of *act's* postulated by him become simple restrictions and specifications on the ranges of our relation *move.* Hence, the action of *fall* denotes a movement whose instrument is gravitational attraction (and, therefore, is almost never needed to be stated explicitly in the description of the event). Moreover, *fall* does not require an *actor* and would thus differ from a relation like *push* which specifies a type of move that obligitorily requires the presence of an actor. The relations *jump* and *walk* are similar in that both require the *actor* and the *object* of the underlying relation *move* to be identical. Hence, upon hearing the statement that Mary was pushed, a normal response is "Who pushed her?" An analogous response of "Who felled her?" is meaningless upon receiving the statement that Mary fell.

Rule 1c can be illustrated by the derivation of the relation *flee* from the relations *quickly/go* and *fear*, conjoined by the *Pconj because:*

flee[actor,object,time] → quickly/go[actor,from[object],time]
because fear[actor,object,time].

In words, we say that when an *actor* goes quickly from an *object* at some *time because* he *fears* it, then we can say that the *actor flees* the *object.*

The three rules 1a, 1b, and 1c generally allow more concrete relations to be defined in terms of more abstract ones. In addition, we presume that there is a process of abstraction or generalization which derives more abstract relations from less abstract ones. We discuss some of these later under the topic of generalization.

CONCEPTS AND THEIR MEANINGS

A concept is a node in the memory system which corresponds to an object or idea that can be named or described. Whereas relations have free variables (ranges) which must be filled, concepts have none. They are complete by themselves. Concepts act as the constants which replace the ranges of relations to generate descriptions of particular events. A relation with a particular set of instances as its ranges is itself a concept (of the type called a *proposition*), which can enter as a constituent in still more complex events.

Concepts are usually designated by the English name corresponding most closely to the meaning of the concept. Thus, the name *dog* denotes the concept of the class of dogs. Similarly, *animal* designates the node corresponding to the concept of the class of animals. Concepts, like relations, need not correspond in a one-to-one fashion with words. In fact, most concepts have no simple natural language equivalent. For example, a particular dog which we might see on the street need have no term which distinguishes that dog from all other dogs. We name such special occurrences with the name of the class to which the object belongs preceded by an asterisk to indicate that it is a particular instance of that class, and followed by a number to distinguish this example from all other instances of that concept which we might observe. Hence, some particular dog might be named *dog4 and some other dog *dog7, etc.

Just as the meanings of relations are not given by the names of the relations, neither are the meanings of the concepts given by their names. The meanings are given through the relations which hold among the various concepts. Thus, for example, suppose we have a concept of a certain dog named *dog1. This concept stands in certain relations to various other concepts in the memory system. For example, $*dog1$ is an element of the class of dogs, hence:

$$isa[*dog1,dog].$$

In addition, suppose we know that this dog belongs to a certain man:

$$belongs[*dog1,*man].$$

The dog may also have bitten a mailman on the leg:

$$bite[*dog1,*mailman,*leg2,past].$$

It is through the set of such relationships in which any given concept participates that the concept has meaning.

Qualification of Concepts

Just as new relations can be formed with reference to old ones, so can new concepts be formed from old ones. The most common means of generating new concepts is by simply *qualification.*

$$Rule\ 2a.\ C \to Q(C)$$

where Q is a *qualifier* of a concept.[10] Rule 2a states that a qualified concept is itself a concept. Thus, for example, we write:

$$lamb \to young(sheep).$$

Quantification of Concepts

A second means of generating new concepts is by application of a *quantifier* (#) to a concept:

$$Rule\ 2b.\ C \to \#(C)$$

Thus we write $two(man)$ to denote a set of men which, among other things, has cardinality two. Similarly, $many(man)$ is a set containing a large but indefinite number of men. In addition to these more usual uses of quantifiers, we consider such notions as:

$$part(Spain),\ unit(measurement),\ amount(milk)$$

to be applications of Rule 2b.

---

[10] Qualifiers usually correspond to adjectives. They behave much like relations except they have only one variable. Church's (1956) identification of the term *property* with a singular propositional form seems similar to our use of qualifiers.

Prepositional Operators

A third operator, the *prepositional operator* (P) is assumed to apply only to concepts of *location* and *time*.

$$Rule\ 2c.\ C \to P(C)$$

A prepositional operator operates on a concept of time or location to produce a new concept of time or location defined with respect to the original concept. Thus:

under(book), before(noon).

Conjunction of Concepts

Conjoined sets of concepts are themselves concepts. Thus, Rule 2d states that the simple conjunction of any number of concepts can be used to replace a single concept:

$$Rule\ 2d.\ C \to Conj(C_1,\ \ldots\ .)$$

We have considered only three simple conjunctions at this time: *and*, *or* (inclusive or), and *xor* (exclusive or). Thus, the concept *dogs and cats* is written:

and(dogs,cats).

Concepts as Propositions

Perhaps the most important class of concepts is the one called *propositions*. All of the concepts we have considered so far are simple in that they denote some particular object or class of objects. Propositions are those concepts which express facts about relationships among concepts. Propositions differ from other concepts in that they can be true or false. Other concepts can only be said to correspond to an existent or non-existent object. Rule 2e expresses the fact that propositions are concepts:

$$Rule\ 2e.\ C \to Prop$$

where *Prop* is our abbreviation for *proposition*.

A proposition is that concept which corresponds to the perceived relation between concepts and which, as a result, has an internal structure which differs from other concepts. Rule 3a states the most frequent structure of a proposition:

$$Rule\ 3a.\ Prop \to R[c_1,\ \ldots\ ,c_n]$$

In words, a proposition is that concept which corresponds to a *relation* in which the free variables have been replaced by appropriate concepts. Thus, we say that:

bite[*dog1,*mailman2,*leg1,past]

is a proposition which corresponds to a particular event.

Propositions are especially important concepts in our system because they function as the units of internal language, just as sentences function as the unit of external language. That is to say, we suppose that all inputs to the memory system are in the form of relationships among concepts in the form of propositions.

Imagine an event in which a person named John is breaking a particular window with a hammer. How does this get stored in memory? It is the task of the executive in our model, called the *interpreter*, to interpret the action and the actors and translate this perception into one or more propositions. These propositions are then sent to another processor, the *structure builder*, which stores the propositions (i.e., interconnects the appropriate nodes with the appropriate labeled relation) in memory as quickly as it can. (More on this in a later section.) In this particular example, suppose the interpreter translated the perceived event into:

break[*John,*window,*hammer,*house,now]

where *break* is a relation of the form:

break[actor,object,instrument,location,time].

The structure builder would have to find the nodes *John, *window, *hammer, *house and *now* and interconnect them by the relation *break*. Those nodes which did not already exist in memory would have to be constructed by the structure builder at the time of storage. The process whereby the interpreter identifies the appropriate action and actors is somewhat mysterious in our system, but the rules whereby propositions are encoded in the memory system are explicit and will be discussed below.

Propositions, when generated by Rule 3a, correspond to what we have previously called events. Conjoined sequences of propositions are also propositions. Propositions can be joined by *propositional conjunctions* (*Pconj*).[11] These complex propositions correspond to what we call episodes or sequences of events. Rule 3b states that the conjunction of propositions is also a proposition:

Rule 3b. Prop → Prop Pconj Prop

[11] Examples of *Pconj* are *then, while, because, in order that, if, as well as, and, or, xor.*

We may have the proposition:

break[*John,*window,*hammer,*house,now] because
want[*John,collect[*John,*insurance]].

OPERATORS AND CONNECTIVES

In addition to the major constituents of the memory system (i.e., concepts and relations), we have introduced four classes of operators (relational operators, qualifiers, quantifiers, and prepositional operators) and two classes of connectives (simple conjunctions and propositional conjunctions). In each case we have described their usage and given at least one example. Certain of these operators themselves have an internal structure and rules of formation. In this section we describe four rules which show how these operators can be formed.

Qualifiers

Qualifiers, like relations, may be modified by relational operators:

$$Rule\ 4a.\ Q(V) \to O/Q(V)$$

For example, we might have:

$$tiny(V) \to very/small(V)$$

and

$$closed(V) \to not/open(V).$$

Of course, not all qualifiers generated in this way have natural language equivalents.

In some instances, qualifiers may have the structure of relations.

$$Rule\ 4b.\ Q(V) \to R[c_1, \ldots ,V, \ldots ,c_n](V)$$

where V is a *bound variable* that must take on the same value in all three places. Hence, the relational qualifier

$$walk[V,through(*doorway),now](V)$$

has the interpretation that V is one who "walks through the doorway now."

In a similar fashion, Rule 4c states that a conjoined qualifier with a specified variable can be considered to be a qualifier:

$$Rule\ 4c.\ Q(V) \to Conj(Q,Q, \ldots .)(V)$$

Relational Operators

New relational operators can be generated by recursive application of a relational operator on itself. Thus:

$$Rule\ 4d.\ O/ \to O/O/$$

For example:

$$\text{partly}/ \rightarrow \text{not/completely}/.$$

SUMMARY

We have introduced 14 rules which describe the permissible operations of relations and concepts. The rules fall into four major categories:

1. Those to be applied in the formation of new relations;
2. Those to be applied in the formation of new concepts;
3. Those to be applied in the formation of propositions;
4. Those to be applied in the formation of new operators.

These rules are summarized in Table 2.

TABLE 2

Rules of Formation

Rule 1. Rules of formation for relations:

   1a. $R[v_1, \ldots, v_n] \rightarrow O/R[v_1, \ldots, v_n]$

   1b. $R[v_1, \ldots, v_n] \rightarrow R[x_1, \ldots, x_m]$ x_i is dependent on v_j

   1c. $R[v_1, \ldots, v_n] \rightarrow R[x_1, \ldots, x_m] \, Pconj \, R[y_1, \ldots, y_k] \ldots$

Rule 2. Rules of formation for concepts:

   2a. $C \rightarrow Q(C)$ *(Qualifiers)*

   2b. $C \rightarrow \#(C)$ *(Quantifiers)*

   2c. $C \rightarrow P(C)$ *(Location* and *time)*

   2d. $C \rightarrow Pconj(C_1, \ldots .)$ *(Conjunctions: and, or, xor)*

   2e. $C \rightarrow Prop$ *(Propositions)*

Rule 3. Rules of formation for propositions:

   3a. $Prop \rightarrow R[c_1, \ldots, c_n]$

   3b. $Prop \rightarrow R[c_1, \ldots, c_n] \, Pconj \, R[c_m, \ldots, c_k] \ldots$

Rule 4. Rules of formation for operators:

   4a. $Q(V) \rightarrow O/Q(V)$

   4b. $Q(V) \rightarrow R[c_1, \ldots, x, \ldots, c_n](V)$ value of x is bound to value of V

   4c. $Q(V) \rightarrow Conj(Q, Q, \ldots .)(V)$

   4d. $O/ \rightarrow O/O/$

We suppose at the outset that our system is equipped with some primitive set of relations, operators, and concepts and that it uses rules such as the ones outlined here to formulate propositions in response to experiential events. The storage of these propositions leads to modifications in and generation of the complex network that characterizes the memory system at any point in time.

The Graph Representation

This section states the rules followed to encode propositions into the graph representation of the data base. The graph structure has already been introduced. Mathematically, the graph representation is a signed, directed graph. Each arc (arrow) has a name and a direction to which that name applies. The arrows connect the nodes of the system. Four different types of nodes are allowed: primary and secondary, concept and event. *Primary* nodes always have corresponding entries in the dictionary. Their names become points of entry into the memory system. *Secondary* nodes have names only as a matter of convenience. Their names play no part in the formal memory processes. Secondary nodes always point to their appropriate referent by an *isa* arrow (for secondary *concept* nodes) or an *act* arrow (for secondary *event* or *episode* nodes).

NOTATION

The general format of the graph is based around nodes and arrows interconnecting them. A node is represented by a dot, with its name printed alongside. Secondary nodes are represented by angular brackets (for secondary *concept* nodes) and circles (for secondary *event* nodes). When the name of a primary node appears within the brackets or a circle name, it is assumed that the relation between them is by an *act* or *isa* arrow between the secondary node and the primary node of that name, even if it is not shown explicitly.

The basic representation of a proposition is a secondary event node with arrows pointing to the concepts which fill the free variables. The arrows are labeled to indicate the order in which the arguments are to be taken. We often label the arrows with the name of the range in which the arguments must fall. Thus, the proposition

hit[*boy,*window,*stone][12]

[12] In this and several other instances we have not specified the location or time of the event. Since all events are assumed to have places and times of occurrence, we reserve the last two arguments of each relation for place and time, respectively. Occasionally for purposes of brevity, as in this instance, we do not specify these variables in our examples.

where *hit* is a scenario in which an *actor* hits an *object* with an *instrument*, has the graphical representation shown in Figure 8A. The circle represents the secondary event node corresponding to the proposition. Arrows labeled by the range names of the various variables of the relations connect the secondary event node to the concept nodes that replace the free variables of the relation. The printed words in the circle and in the angular brackets denote secondary event and concept nodes which are connected to their primary nodes by the *act* and *isa* arrows, respectively.

It is rare that propositions enter the memory out of context. More often, propositions are conjoined and enter the memory as part of episodes. The encoding of sets of conjoined propositions is accomplished by creating a secondary event node corresponding to the entire episode. This node is connected to the conjoined sequence of event nodes with a *while* arrow pointing to the beginning of the episodic sequence. Figure 8B illustrates the encoding of the proposition

hit[*boy,*window,*stone,*school,yesterday] then

scold[*man,*boy,*school,yesterday].

Because the actor, location, and time all were the same for both constituents of the proposition, we specify them only once at the higher level event node. This allows us to gain access to the node event: "What happened to the boy in school yesterday."

As illustrated in the previous section, the concepts which replace the free variables of a relation may be more complex than single lexical entries. Rules 2a–e give five legitimate forms that concepts can take. Four of these are encoded in the following proposition which corresponds to the idea that John and Mary want to have three red balloons (Figure 8C):

want[and(John,Mary),have[and(John,Mary),three (red(balloons))]].

The encoding of a concept generated by Rule 2a is illustrated by the encoding of *red*(*balloon*). The general rule is to construct a secondary concept node which is an instance of the main concept (i.e., the node is connected to the primary node corresponding to that concept by an *isa* relation) and to label arrows which point from the node to the qualifier with *Q*.

The encoding of concepts generated by Rule 2b is illustrated by the encoding of *three*(*red*(*balloons*)). Quantifiers are encoded as a secondary concept node with a labeled arrow pointing to the quantifier in question and an arrow labeled *isa* pointing to the referent set for the quantifier (in this case *red balloons*).

The *object* argument of *wants* illustrates the use of a proposition as a concept as generated by Rule 2e. In this case the object arrow points to the event node for the embedded proposition. This yields a representation very similar in format to that of the propositional conjunction shown in Figure 8B. The applications of Rule 2d are illustrated by the *actor* variable of *want* and *have*. Here we have arrows labeled by the proper simple conjunction connecting the conjoined concepts.

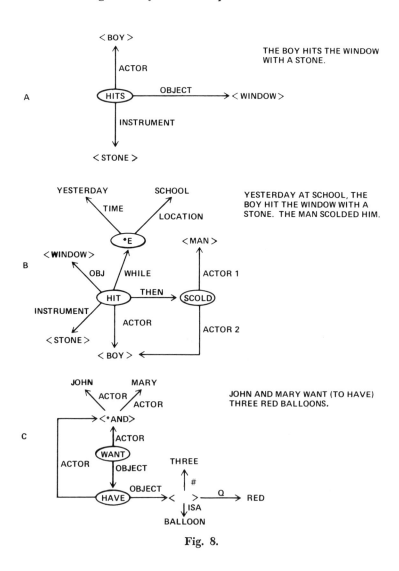

Fig. 8.

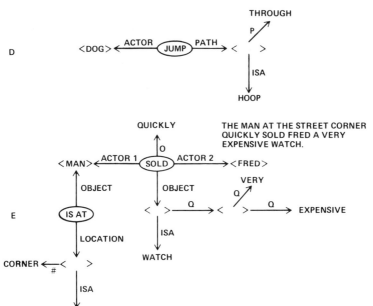

Fig. 8. Continued.

Figure 8D shows the use of a prepositional operator. Its use is much like that of the quantifier or qualifier.

The encoding in graph notation of the relational operator and the relation used as qualifier is illustrated by Figure 8E: *The man at the street corner quickly sold Fred a very expensive watch.*

STANDARD SHORTHAND

Any relation can be used in a shorthand notation when only the first two arguments are specified. This shorthand notation simply involves labeling the connecting arrows with the relation name rather than with the names of the argument classes.

MEANINGS AND THEIR RELATIONS TO STORED PROPOSITIONS

The definitions of relations and concepts—which we shall call the *meaning-store*—are presumed to be derived from experience with repeated appearances of the lexical item in specific uses or by modification of lexical items whose meanings have previously been determined. The exact processes whereby this acquisition of general knowledge takes place is a major unsolved problem for psychology. What we have done for this model is to place certain restrictions on the general format that the meaning-store entries must take, and to specify to some extent the kinds of information which must be stored at the primary nodes. For example, since the usages of concepts require that they can be inserted as arguments for relations, they must follow the format of concepts as outlined in Rules 2a–e. Similarly, the meaning-store representation of relations must be in the form of propositions which have a certain number of free variables, and which label these variables with the class of concepts which may fill them. In the next subsection we illustrate, as examples, possible meaning-store entries for the main categories of constituents that we have considered: concepts, relations, and operators.

Interrelations among Memory Elements

To this point we have discussed the representations for propositions and for meaning-store entries independently of one another. It is useful to see how these various elements stored in memory interrelate to one another. Figure 9 illustrates a section of the memory space which

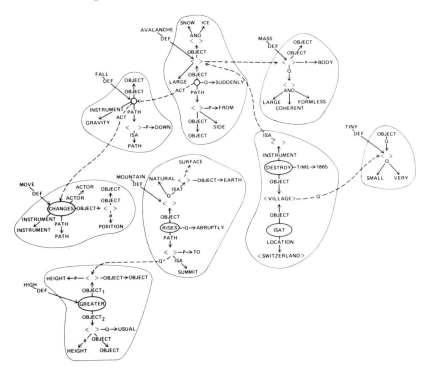

Fig. 9.

encodes the proposition that *In 1865, an avalanche destroyed a tiny village at the bottom of a mountain in Switzerland.* The figure gives the entries for *avalanche, mountain, fall, move, tiny, high* and *mass,* as well as the proposition itself.

The diagram allows us to see how simply the system we are describing allows for paraphrases of the proposition. We can say that:

In Switzerland, an avalanche once destroyed a very small village . . . ,

by inserting the meaning-store entries for tiny. Or, we could say that:

A mass of ice and snow which fell suddenly from the side of a mountain destroyed a . . . ,

by inserting the entry for avalanche. Moreover, we could say:

A large, coherent, formless body of ice and snow which fell from the side of a mountain destroyed a . . . ,

etc. In short, the meaning-store entries of the items can be readily inserted to conclude that falling snow and ice was the instrument of the destruction, as well as a myriad of other facts not stated in the original proposition.

It will be actions that are most often the object of paraphrase. Hence, because *stroll* is defined as *slowly/walk* and *walk* as a special case of *move* (see the earlier discussion on relations), the proposition:

John strolled through the village

might get recalled as:

John moved slowly through the village.

Processing and Retrieval Procedures

The data base we have defined is an organized collection of pathways specifying possible routes through the memory. Retrieving information from such a memory is like running a maze. Starting off at a given node, there is the option of going down any one of a number of labeled pathways. Taking one of these paths, there is then a series of crossroads, each leading off to a different concept. Each path from the crossroads leads to a new maze with a new set of choice points and new pathways to follow. In principle, it is possible to start at any point in the vocabulary of concepts and, by taking the right sequence of turns through successive mazes, end up at any other point. This is what is meant by an organized memory system in which all the information is interconnected. It is a network of potential pathways to be used by interpretive and retrieval processes.

Once the structure of the data base has been defined, then the primary problem becomes one of specifying the processing and retrieval strategies involved in the development and use of the LTM system.[13] Defining and evaluating the processing procedures is a relatively novel exercise for psychological theorists, and as yet there is no systematic procedure for dealing with different possible schemes. The best we can do at the moment is to examine various approaches along several general dimensions to clarify some of the options available in developing a process theory of LTM.

FORMING GENERAL CONCEPTS

The generalization procedure which we have implemented for general concepts from a set of examples involves a relatively straightforward mechanism. Instances of concepts are connected to general concepts by means of the *isa* relation. When operating on a concept, the generalization procedure first retrieves all of the known examples of the concept (i.e., follows the *isa-inverse* arrows) and examines the information associated with them, looking for common characteristics.[14] If a characteristic is found that is common to a sufficient number of examples (and not contradicted by any), that characteristic is added to the general characteristic of the class of concepts under consideration. The number of examples which must contain the same characteristic in order for generalization to occur is a parameter of the routine.

Consider the following example. Suppose that the system first learns about robins, learning that a robin is a bird, has a red breast and wings, eats worms, etc. Then it learns similar things about sparrows and wrens.

[13] Although it is convenient to distinguish between the two aspects of LTM (i.e., the structure of the data base and the processes that operate on it), the distinction is somewhat arbitrary. Frequently, there is an option between storing a particular type of information directly in the data base or specifying the processes to derive that information when it is needed. Moreover, the results of these processes may in turn be stored in the data base, and thus the distinction may be mainly a developmental one. Also, in the system we describe, the distinction is further confused, because the processes are represented in the same format as all other types of information, and thus can operate on themselves.

[14] Two concepts c_1 and c_2 are said to have characteristic R in common if there are two propositions in memory which are identical, except in one case c_2 fills the same variable of R that c_1 fills in the other case.

At some stage, therefore, the memory structure is that shown in Figure 10A.[15]

Now, at some critical point, the system generalizes, realizing all examples of bird *eat* and *have wings,* so that the general propositions *has* [*bird,wings*] and *eats*⌊*bird,*worms*⌋ should be formed.

If now the system is told that a canary is a bird, has wings, and is yellow, it will respond by adding a new node for canary with the relation:

isa[yellow(canary),bird].

But it will *not* add:

has[canary,wings].

(If the system were a five-year-old child, it might respond, "Of course a canary has wings, silly.") Thus, eventually the system would look like Figure 10B, with most general properties only at the highest possible level.

SUBDIVIDING CONCEPTS

If, during attempts to generalize, the system finds conflicting information associated with the example set, then the concept is subdivided. In the version of the generalization routine that has been implemented, the basis of conflict is the discovery of a direct or indirect contradiction. For instance, direct contradiction occurs when the system finds some examples of its people that are *good* and others that are *not good;* indirect contradiction results when it is found that some people are *good,* some are *bad,* and that the definition for *good* contains the information:

good → not/bad.

During subdivision, the network is restructured to insert intermediate level concepts between the general concept and its examples. The intermediate level concepts are entered into the appropriate discriminating relations and the *isa* relations are revised to connect the examples to the appropriate subclass, and the subclasses to the generalized concept.

For example, if the system wishes to add the concept that a *penguin* is a bird, but it cannot fly, to the structure of Figure 10B, it must subdivide its concepts, as shown in Figure 11A.

---

[15] In the figure, lexical items like *wings* are repeated several times. Actually, they are all the same lexical entry, and the arrows should all point to a single location named *wings.* The format in Figure 10 is used for graphical simplicity, with the understanding that if the primary nodes have the same name, they are actually the same node.

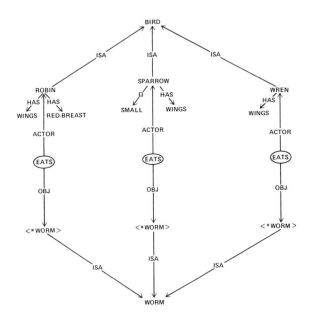

A

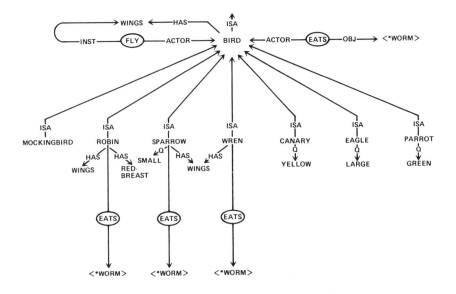

B

Fig. 10.

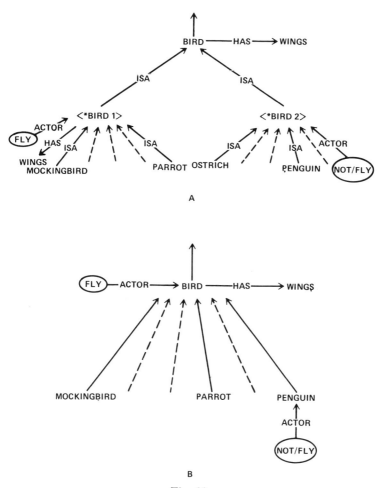

Fig. 11.

Alternatively, if first the system learns that a penguin is a bird, it will assume that a penguin can fly. Later, if it is taught that a penguin *cannot* fly, it is too late for subdivision. The contradictory evidence must simply be added, as in Figure 11B.

ERASURE

A basic axiom followed in the development of the system is that, although new information can always be added to the memory, nothing already present can be erased. Excluding physical or physiological damage, we find no evidence whatsoever to support the notion that the material in LTM can ever be deliberately forgotten. Yes, information in STM can be forgotten (more precisely, through nonrehearsal, it is allowed to fade away). Yes, material might be suppressed through retrieval routines that wish to repress certain regions of the data base, but this material is not truly forgotten, as the resulting neuroses testify.

If material cannot be erased from LTM, then it will contain contradictions and "temporary" structures. The intermediate incorrect steps one follows in solving a complex problem (one that takes a considerable amount of time and thought) will be remembered permanently, along with the final, correct path. The retreival processes must evolve to deal with these contradictions and irrelevancies.

THE IMPLICATIONS OF ABSTRACTION

The net effect of these abstraction procedures is to restructure the information in the memory so that general characteristics of examples migrate up to become attached to the class. Whenever a new example is acquired, only unique properties need be entered, for all general properties will already exist at the superset node. Hence, as more and more is learned, the characteristics that remain attached to a specific concept tend to be only those that uniquely discriminate a concept from other members of the same class. Moreover, a concept may belong (and usually does) to any number of classes—a wife *isa* woman, *isa* mother, *isa* bedpartner—which provide different ways of thinking about the concept. This multiplicity of classes does not in any way affect the generalizing strategy. Following a particular class relation automatically leads to the appropriate examples that should be compared when analyzing the concept of *wife* in a particular context. As it operates on different classes during its analysis of incoming information, the generalizing routine gradually discovers how the concept of wife uniquely intersects any other relevant concepts in the memory.

Note that the memory structure that eventually evolves through the generalization process discussed here is similar to the one Collins and Quillian (1969) propose to account for response latencies in answering certain types of questions. Collins and Quillian argued that the time required to answer a true-false query is related to the distance between the two concepts in the data base. They found that response-time differences in answering various types of true-false questions seemed to suggest a class-subclass organization in human memory. A question of the form *A canary is yellow?*, for example, takes less time to answer than *A canary has skin?* Their results support the notion that unique characteristics tend to be attached directly to an example while general characteristics are associated with the class node to which the example belongs. Meyer (1970) also provides some evidence for a basic class-subclass structure in his study of response times to questions such as *All a are b?* and *Some a are b?*

DEVELOPING THE MEANING OF RELATIONS

The same general mechanism which we have used to restructure concepts in our system can also be used to develop the meaning-store entries for relations. By examining observed events, one can abstract the *free variables* of a relation and the range of concepts which can meaningfully be used to fill a given variable. For example, the principles of abstraction would allow the discovery that *murder* relates two classes of human *actors* and a class of *weapons*. Even subtle distinctions between the classes of *actors* should be discovered by this process (e.g., it might be that the relation hate[actor$_1$,actor$_2$] was required) which would put even more limits on the kinds of elements which can fill the various variables of the relations.

Note also that, for episodes, this abstraction procedure can represent both a generalization from past experience and a prescription of what to look for when subclasses of the abstracted concepts are encountered in the future. Similarly, the same general strategy can be applied to evaluate the crucial components in an action sequence that leads to a given result. The goal here is to induce the importance of temporal ordering of event sequences to weed out irrelevant events which may occur in different contexts (see Becker, 1970, for a discussion).

List Learning

Up to this point our discussion has been primarily oriented toward a specification of operating processes which work on our data base in the normal course of the evolution of the memory system. We have been developing a semantic memory system whose primary support comes from intuitive considerations. In order to make contact with data on memory experiments, we turn to a discussion of theories of list learning and the means of formulating such a theory within our theoretical framework.[16]

[16] In our model, formulating a specific theory of list learning involves specifying the rules employed by the interpreter in formulating propositions in response to the presentation of elements of a list. Note that we suppose these rules to constitute a strategy which is under the subject's control and, thus, can be expected to vary somewhat from subject to subject and with the requirements of the experimental situation.

Although models differ in terms of their detailed specifications, a process model of list learning typically contains three basic elements: a limited STM that can hold a small number of items for a short period of time, an organized or structured LTM in which the informational elements are interlinked according to some defined rules, and a specific search strategy for retrieving and remembering information from LTM during the learning of the list. The primary tests of the model are whether it reproduces the general characteristics of people's learning behavior, such as the serial position effect, the gradual growth of learning across trials, the effects of list length and presentation rate, and the general organizational properties of the subjects' output protocol. Time (i.e., presentation rate) is usually a basic parameter of the model, since it determines how much processing can be performed on a given input item.

Within this overall description, the memory theorist has several fundamental choice points. The first question concerns what is learned. Is list-learning primarily a matter of learning *associations* among list items? In a process model, this type of learning corresponds to a search and retrieval mechanism that follows the relational links attached to nodes in LTM in an attempt to find pathways that interconnect the list items. Or should learning be conceived of as a problem in *reconstruction?* Here the search mechanism attempts to retrieve information associated with a LTM element so that it can later identify that element from an analysis of the remembered characteristics. A second basic question concerns the extent to which retrieval is directed. *Undirected* retrieval corresponds to a search strategy which has nonselective rules for determining which paths to follow for retrieving particular types of information associated with a given element in LTM. For *directed* retrieval, there must be explicit criteria for deciding which particular piece of information attached to a memory element is most likely to be useful and should be investigated first. (Obviously, a directed search strategy is only possible with a structured memory where the links connected to an element carry distinguishing labels.)

Finally, there is the question of how the results of learning are remembered so they can later be used during recall. Does the learning system actually mark or *tag* the specific elements in LTM and later launch a search for these tags? Or does it build a new and separate *structure* for the list which is added to LTM, leaving the previous organization of LTM unaffected by the learning experience?

These dimensions are, of course, not exhaustive, but they do provide a convenient framework for comparing various process models of list learning. Bower (this volume) has described a model proposed by Anderson (1971) in which learning is conceptualized as undirected pathfinding. The heart of the learning mechanism is a routine which attempts to find pathways going between list items, using an undirected breadth-first search. The results of the learning experience are recorded by tagging (on a probabilistic basis) the pathways that have been found to interconnect list items. Collins and Quillian (1969, 1970, see also this volume) use the same general search strategy as a method for disambiguating pronominal references in normal linguistic inputs. Both of these models use an undirected associative search, although the search process in Collins and Quillian's model operates on a semantically-structured data base. (Anderson's data base evidently does contain directed, labeled links, but this feature was not used in the model reported by Bower.)

Norman and Rumelhart (1970) have proposed the alternative of viewing retrieval as a problem of reconstruction. The list item is reconstructed by retrieving characteristics or attributes associated with that item. Each item is represented by a memory vector composed of the attributes of the item, with each attribute being a connection between the item presented and the context of the list. Attributes are added to LTM at a rate determined by the strength of this item in STM. The limitations of LTM for the list result from interactions in the rate at which information can be formed, the length of time an item resides in STM, and the number of items that are being processed at any moment. When the processings of several different items overlap in time, all of them suffer. As a result, the first few items in a list enjoy an advantage over later items in that their processing is more efficient; hence, these first few items are stored better than later ones. The model presented here can be mapped onto the Norman and Rumelhart multicomponent model by identifying the sets of relations in which a concept participates with an attribute of memory.

Figure 12 illustrates how the mapping can be made. Figure 12A is a graphical representation of a possible entry for *dog* which we suppose to be an item on an input list. This illustration shows the concept *dog* entering into six relationships with other concepts. This represents six characteristics (or attributes) of the concept *dog*. There are six corresponding propositions expressing these relationships, namely:

isa[*dog,animal]
barks[*dog]
has[*dog,fur]
eats[*dog,meat]
isa[*dog,pet]
has[*dog,four(legs)].

We suppose that the strategy employed by the interpreter in this case is to formulate descriptive propositions about items on the list. Figure 12B illustrates the form the memory might take for a list with *dog* and *cat* as the first two items.

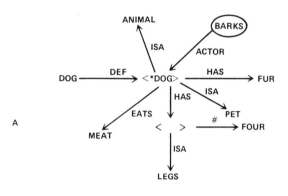

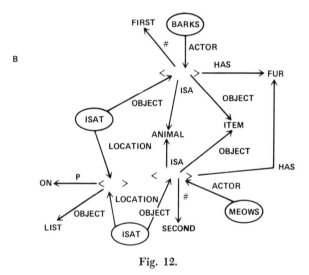

Fig. 12.

Although the learning and retrieval mechanisms are fundamentally different in these two classes of models, they both have had considerable success in reproducing many general features of list-learning performance with unrelated words. The most crucial shortcoming of these models is that storage and retrieval are viewed as undirected. In Anderson's model, the associative links in LTM are unlabeled, and thus there is no basis for conducting a retrieval search for meaningful relations among the input items. In the Norman and Rumelhart model, the attributes attached to a node are treated as a mathematically homogeneous set. Since there are no explicit rules for using the structure of LTM to guide the retrieval and retention of information, these models cannot account for subjects' ability to use semantic information in list-learning experiments.

DIRECTED STORAGE AND RETRIEVAL

Ideally, a learning process which is attempting to find associations or reconstruct an item in memory should be highly selective and store only the most pertinent information about an incoming item. It should make intelligent use of the LTM structure in deciding what information to retain about a particular word within the context of the word list. As an initial attempt to explore some directed storage and retreival strategies, we investigated a model for learning categorized lists using a memory structure of the type proposed here.

Learning Categorized Lists

Since we wished to examine some of the detailed characteristics of learning behavior with organized lists, the experimental paradigm chosen for simulation was the "one plus one" experiment (Mandler & Dean, 1969). In this experiment a list is presented incrementally, one word at a time, with only one list item appearing on each trial. After each additional list item is presented, the subject attempts to recall *all* of the words presented up to that time. The paradigm is particularly useful for analyzing how the subject's organization of the list changes with each successive input.

With categorized lists, perhaps the most striking feature about learning under these conditions is the change in organization of the subject's output on successive recall trials. Typically, a subject starts off recalling items in their input order for the first few trials. For some subjects, after five or so inputs, a transition is made to recalling the items organized in category clusters rather than in their input order.

To simulate list learning under these conditions, we implemented a skeleton version of the memory structure presented here. The memory contained only three primitive binary relations: *isa, is,* and *has.* Moreover, the concepts encoded were selected to be easily classifiable in terms of set-subset relations—animals, vehicles, structures, furniture, etc. The storage and retrieval strategies differed from previous models in that the LTM on which the search process operated was hierarchically organized in terms of class structure, and the search and retrieval mechanisms were explicitly biased to make use of this class information. The general strategy for learning was to start off trying to remember the specific items on the list in STM and to reorganize the STM information whenever STM capacity was exceeded. Reorganization was based on examining the classes to which current residents of STM belonged, attempting to replace specific items with their class names whenever this would reduce the amount of information that had to be remembered. The strategies employed can best be illustrated by following the fate of an input to the system.

On receiving an input, such as *dog*, the learning system first located the LTM element corresponding to *dog*, and with a certain probability, tagged it with a list tag (i.e., the interpretive system formulated and stored the proposition: has [dog,list]). It then retrieved the class name to which *dog* belonged (isa[dog,animal]: hence, *animal* is the class name) and proceeded through a series of tests to decide whether or not to retain the input item to STM. The tests were as follows:

1. Is the class name of the input currently in STM (i.e., is the class name *animal* already in STM)? If so, discontinue processing.
2. Do any of the items in STM belong to the same class as the input (i.e., are there any *animals* already in STM)? If so, replace the STM item with the appropriate class name and discontinue processing the input.
3. Do any STM items belong to the same class (i.e., are there two or more examples of furniture, vehicles, etc.)? If so, replace the example names with the appropriate class name and add the input to the top (most recent) of the STM stack.

If all attempts at reorganizing or categorizing the information in STM failed, the input item was pushed into the top of the STM, and one of the current residents was deleted (allowed to be forgotten): in terms of which information was retained, priorities were given to category names (i.e., items with no list tags) over unorganized items. Although the system we tested used only one level of the hierarchical organization, the same routines could obviously operate on any depth of structuring. The contents of STM simply become more and more abstract representations of the input words as the STM limitations forced the system to higher levels of organization.

A simple directed search model does manage to reproduce many of the more important organizational features of a subject's recall performance under similar conditions. The transition from recalling in input order to recalling by category is triggered in the model by the strategy of waiting until STM is full before attempting to reorganize the information. The actual recall by category is a result of the retrieval mechanism which first looks for list tags directly on the item referenced in STM and, failing this, follows the *isa-inverse* paths to look for list tags associated with subsets of the remembered information. Categories of information will disappear as a whole from successive output protocols whenever the access route to LTM—the category name—is lost from STM. Similarly, the system may recover a whole category of information that has not been recalled for several trials if it regains the access route by reorganizing and retaining new examples when they are presented. Items belonging to the same category are more likely to be reorganized and retained when they appear close together in the input list because of the priorities given to saving organized information as opposed to individual items when STM becomes overloaded.[17]

This directed pathfinding strategy, then, would seem to be capable of handling many of the general features of categorized list learning, as well as some of the anatomical details of a subject's recall protocol. Moreover, the vast majority of learning studies of the organization of memory use lists structured according to these basic types of category classifications. The representation scheme we are proposing, however, contains far more information than class-subclass relations. We need to consider more general retrieval strategies that can make fuller use of the potential power inherent in the memory structure.

RETRIEVAL AS RECONSTRUCTION

The basic approach of the associative retrieval strategies discussed has been to specify a pathfinding strategy for discovering and marking the links that interconnect nodes in the memory system. The alternative approach is illustrated by the Norman and Rumelhart multicomponent model which attempts to retrieve information that can be used to reconstruct the particular items on the input list. That is, rather than learn specific paths among the list items, the semantic characteristics of the items themselves are learned. Recall is a matter of trying to find concepts

---

[17] Although we have not conducted extensive quantitative tests of this model, it is interesting to note that our graduate students could not readily distinguish the simulation's performance from that of real subjects. What is more interesting is that, when confronted with the output protocol from test runs, they had a great deal of difficulty deducing the specific operating principles of the model. For those of us interested in trying to deduce the learning strategies of human memory, it is a sobering experience to practice our skills on simulation models which operate according to well-defined and presumably far simpler principles.

in LTM that match up with these characteristics. Failures in recall occur when the system has not yet acquired enough specific information to uniquely identify an item in LTM rather than when an interconnecting bridge between two list items is lost.

In the recent list-learning literature, there has been more and more emphasis on the importance of retrieval cues and the notion that memory is primarily a problem of reconstruction from partial information, although no explicit process models incorporating these principles have been proposed. Moreover, dealing with list learning as a problem in reconstruction emphasizes the similarities between memory function and the information processing mechanisms involved at other levels in the system. The multicomponent model, for example, is based on a feature extraction scheme essentially equivalent to the Pandemonium model that has been proposed as a scheme for classifying and identifying incoming sensory signals (Selfridge, 1959). We have already noted that the major shortcoming of this model is that it does not explicitly use the structure of LTM as a guide to retrieval and retention during learning.

In terms of pattern recognition systems, the major competitor to feature extraction has been the concept of a *discrimination net.* Pattern recognition based on discrimination networks involves a series of binary tests constructed from an analysis of the properties of the input items. The tests are designed to uniquely classify each item within the context of the specific set to be discriminated, and the network evolves through the addition of new discrimination tests whenever an input item is incorrectly classified. Process models of memory based on such discrimination networks have been applied to nonsense syllable and paired associate learning tasks and have been quite successful in simulating overall learning curves, serial position effects, the effects of intralist and interlist similarity, retroactive and proactive inhibition, and some overlearning phenomena (Simon & Feigenbaum, 1964; Frijda, in press). So far, however, these models have relied exclusively on the physical properties of the input in constructing the discrimination network. We are presently implementing a storage and retrieval strategy that operates on our semantic memory in much the same way. Although the programs have not yet been tested, the design is far enough along that we can outline some of its general characteristics as a learning strategy.

A Semantic Discrimination Net

The basic notion is to build up a semantic retrieval network by comparing each new input against the items currently residing in STM. The interpretive system proceeds by testing a new input against the information that has been stored up to that point and selecting new

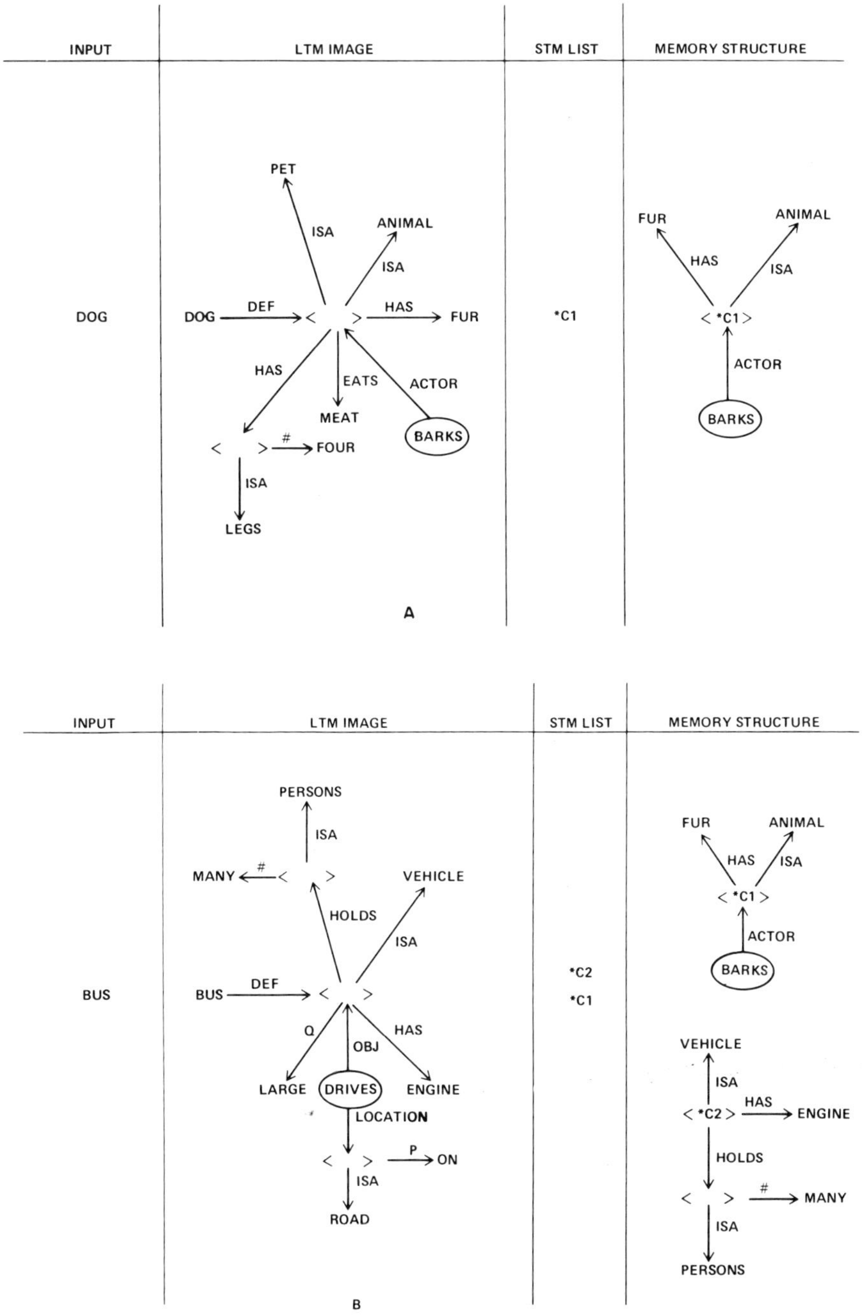
INPUT
LTM IMAGE
STM LIST
MEMORY STRUCTURE
DOG
PET
ISA
ANIMAL
ISA
DOG
DEF
HAS
FUR
HAS
EATS
ACTOR
MEAT
BARKS
#
FOUR
ISA
LEGS
*C1
FUR
ANIMAL
HAS
ISA
< *C1 >
ACTOR
BARKS
A
INPUT
LTM IMAGE
STM LIST
MEMORY STRUCTURE
PERSONS
ISA
MANY
#
VEHICLE
HOLDS
ISA
BUS
BUS
DEF
Q
OBJ
HAS
LARGE
DRIVES
ENGINE
LOCATION
P
ON
ISA
ROAD
*C2
*C1
FUR
ANIMAL
HAS
ISA
< *C1 >
ACTOR
BARKS
VEHICLE
ISA
< *C2 >
HAS
ENGINE
HOLDS
#
MANY
ISA
PERSONS
B

Fig. 13.

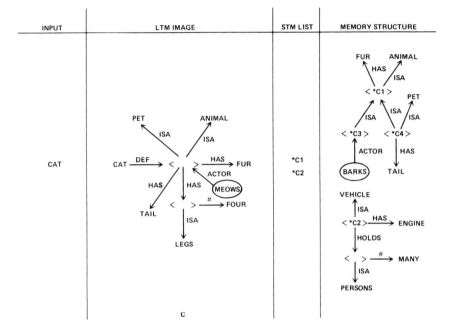

Fig. 13. Continued.

information to be retained on the basis of those test results. Thus, when a new input is presented, the corresponding node in LTM is contacted and the associated semantic information is made available. (This can be considered as activating the image of the concept in LTM.) For the first word on the list STM is empty and the interpreter simply begins forming propositions descriptive of the concept in question and sends these propositions to the structure builder to be stored. (Thus, the first item for this model is treated in the same manner as all items are treated in the multicomponent model.) The name (address) of the newly constructed node is stored on the top of the STM list. For all subsequent items, the interpreter first retrieves the most recent entry on the STM list and begins testing the semantic characteristics of the newly presented item against those stored for the previous item.

In examining the semantic information that is stored about a STM entry, the system deals with the concepts to which the input is directly related and the way in which they are related separately. (That is, is the image in any way related to animal? If so, is the relation a *subset* or *isa-inverse* relation?) If no overlap is found the system retrieves the next concept and tries again. If none of the present concepts are in any way similar to the input image, semantic information about the new input is indiscriminately stored (as with the first item of a list) and the name of the newly stored information is put into STM.

Figure 13B shows a possible result in the memory system following the entry of the words *dog* and *bus* as the first two words in a list. We suppose here that the interpreter formulated and sent to the structure builder the propositions isa[*C1,animal], has[*C1,fur], and barks[*C1] in response to the input of *dog* and that the interpreter sent the propositions isa[*C2,vehicle], holds[*C2,many(person)], and has[*C2,engine] in response to the input of *bus*. Note that at this point in time STM would contain the addresses of *C1 and *C2.

Whenever an input is found to share some semantic attribute with a concept in STM, that input is integrated into that concept so that the STM concept will serve as a retrieval cue for the input. If only some of the attributes are held in common, then the STM concept is subdivided (as in the generalization process) and two new concepts are formed, both of which are subsets of the original STM concept. The original concept retains the common attributes; those unique attributes which originally modified the STM concept are moved down to modify one of the new concepts. The system then stores as many attributes as it has time for or that exist that are unique to the input item with the other newly formed concept.

Figure 13C illustrates the possible effects of adding *cat* to the list in which *dog* and *bus* have been previously presented. First, the concept *cat* would be compared against the last concept in STM, in this case *C2. Presumably there will be no overlap between *cat* and *C2. Then *cat* is tested against *C1. Here we find some common attributes. Namely, *cat isa animal* and *cat has fur*. But the overlap is not complete—cats do not bark. Thus, we want to integrate *cat* into *C1, but in order to do it we must create two new concepts which we will call *C3 and *C4. To *C3 we will attach those attributes of *C1 which are not also of *cat*, and we will delete from *C1 the attribute of barking. Thus, the interpreter would instruct the structure builder to delete the proposition barks[*C1] and to store the propositions barks[isa(X,*C1),*C3] and isa[*C4,*C1]. The interpreter would then formulate and store as many unique characteristics of *cat* as possible with concept *C4. Hence, we might suppose that the propositions isa[*C4,pet] and has[*C4,tail] would be stored in the memory structure as illustrated in Figure 13C.

Whenever there is a complete overlap in the semantic associates at a given level of the STM concept, then the system launches a search for subclasses of the concept. If subclasses are found, testing is continued; if not, the system begins extracting information from the input image, adding it to the STM concept until the next input arrives. If, after proceeding down through several levels of the concept, it fails to find any similarities in the remaining image of the input and the characteristics of the subsets, it adds a new subset to that level.

To recall the list, the retrieval mechanism moves through the semantic network built up during learning, trying to find LTM concepts that are consistant with the semantic attributes specified by the retrieval network. The basic retrieval mechanism is an intersection routine. A concept node is first retrieved from STM, and the associated semantic information is submitted as a query to the memory to retrieve items that have these particular characteristics. Thus, if $isa[X,animal]$ is the first semantic associate of a STM concept, the inverse relation name— isa-$inverse$—is used to activate the memory nodes having this characteristic. If the next piece of semantic information associated with the concept is $has[X,fur]$, then this information is used to further narrow down the set of candidates. Whenever the number of possible items is reduced to one, that item is recalled. Hence, failures in recall occur when the retrieval cues are not sufficient to identify a unique concept in LTM or when information has been lost because of an overload on STM during learning. The priorities for forgetting from STM are similar to those discussed for the category recall system (see section on *Learning Categorized Lists*, p. 237).

In general, this learning strategy would seem to provide a relatively simple, yet powerful mechanism for organizing semantic information into a retrieval network for contacting particular elements in LTM. It provides an intelligent basis for deciding what to remember about a specific input within the context of the list that is being learned. Both the similarities and the critical differences between the items are used to construct the retrieval network. Moreover, any structural characteristic of LTM can be used as a retrieval cue.

The retrieval network discussed here does differ somewhat from a standard discrimination net. The test nodes are not simple binary tests. Tests may be for one of many multiple values on a given dimension, or for one of many multiple relation types from an event, or simply for the presence or absence of a particular semantic associate.

Perhaps most intriguing about this learning strategy is the potential for automatic evaluation and revision of the semantic network as the system attempts to use it during recall. The goal of the network is to provide retrieval cues for rapidly locating particular "areas" in the LTM structure. A given cue in a particular branch of the retrieval network is useful as long as it helps to converge on an appropriate region of LTM. Thus, retrieval cues acquired during learning can be modified if they do not make a significant contribution to recall and, hence, there is an automatic procedure for revising the decision tree as retrieval proceeds. These revisions would, in turn, help subsequent learning, since they would reduce the time spent testing and classifying an input relative to the time available for adding information specifically associated with a list item.[18]

References

Anderson, J. R. Recognition confusions in sentence memory. Unpublished manuscript, 1971.

Anderson, J. R. FRAN: A simulation model of free recall. In G. H. Bower (Ed.), *The psychology of learning and motivation.* Vol. 5. New York: Academic Press, in press.

Becker, J. D. An information-processing model of intermediate-level cognition. Stanford Artificial Intelligence Project Memo AI-119, 1970.

Bransford, J. D., & Franks, J. J. The abstraction of linguistic ideas. *Cognitive Psychology,* in press.

Church, A. *Introduction to mathematical logic.* Princeton, New Jersey: Princeton University Press, 1956.

Colby, K. M. Computer simulation of change in personal belief systems. *Behavioral Science,* 1967, **12,** 248–253.

Colby, K. M., & Smith, D. C. Stanford Artificial Intelligence Project Memo AI-97, 1969.

Collins, A. M., & Quillian, M. R. Retrieval time from semantic memory. *Journal of Verbal Learning and Verbal Behavior,* 1969, **8,** 240–247.

Collins, A. M., & Quillian, M. R. Facilitating retrieval from semantic memory: the effect of repeating part of an inference. *Acta Psychologica,* 1970, **33,** 304–314.

Ernst, G. W., & Newell, A. *GPS: A case study in generality and problem solving.* New York: Academic Press, 1969.

Frijda, N. H. The simulation of human memory. *Psychological Bulletin,* in press.

Fillmore, C. J. The case for case. In E. Bach & R. T. Harms (Eds.), *Universals in linguistic theory.* New York: Holt, Rinehart and Winston, 1968.

Fillmore, C. J. Toward a modern theory of case. In D. A. Reibel and S. A.

---

[18] The retrieval network constructed during list learning is essentially equivalent to a basic component in several theories of problem solving—the subgoal tree (Newell & Simon, 1964; Becker, 1970). According to these theories, a problem is broken down into a hierarchical network of subgoals. Ideally this subgoal tree should be followed using a "progressively deepening" search strategy. That is, the movement down a particular subgoal path should be discontinued whenever the current activities are not making progress or when other subgoal paths become more promising. The main difficulty in attempting to simulate this search pattern has been in determining the criteria that might be used to decide when progress is being made or when other paths are more promising. In the semantic network there is an obvious criterion: the rate at which the given path is converging on a particular memory element.

Schane (Eds.), *Modern studies in English*. Englewood Cliffs, New Jersey: Prentice-Hall, 1969.

Loehlin, J. C. *Computer models of personality*. New York: Random House, 1968.

Mandler, G., & Dean, P. J. Seriation: development of serial order in free recall. *Journal of Experimental Psychology*, 1969, **81**, 207–215.

Meyer, D. E. On the representation and retrieval of stored semantic information. *Cognitive Psychology*, 1970, **1**, 242–300.

Minsky, M. (Ed.) *Semantic information processing*. Cambridge, Massachusetts: MIT Press, 1968.

Newell, A., & Simon, H. A. *An example of human chess play in the light of chess playing programs*. Pittsburgh, Pennsylvania: Carnegie Institute of Technology, 1964.

Newell, A., & Simon, H. A. *Human problem solving*. Englewood Cliffs, New Jersey: Prentice-Hall, in press.

Norman, D. A., & Rumelhart, D. E. A system for perception and memory. In D. A. Norman (Ed.), *Models of human memory*. New York: Academic Press, 1970.

Schank, R. Semantics in conceptual analysis. Stanford Artificial Intelligence Project Memo AIM-122, 1970.

Schank, R. Intention, memory, and computer understanding. Stanford Artificial Intelligence Project Memo AIM-140, 1971.

Selfridge, O. Pandemonium: a paradigm for learning. In D. V. Blake and A. M. Uttley (Eds.), *Mechanization of thought processes*. London: H. M. Stationary Office, 1959.

Simmons, R. F. Natural language question-answering system: 1969. *Communications of the Association for Computing Machinery*, 1970, **13**, 15–30.

Simon, H. A., & Feigenbaum, E. A. An information processing theory of some effects of similarity, familiarity and meaningfulness in verbal learning. *Journal of Verbal Learning and Verbal Behavior*, 1964, **3**, 385–396.

Winograd, T. A program for understanding natural language. *Cognitive Psychology*, 1971, **2**, in press.

7 | Notes on the Structure of Semantic Memory[1]

Walter Kintsch

[1] Preparation of this report was made possible by a grant from the National Institute of Mental Health, MH 15872.

One of the components of language facility is the memory store that contains a person's knowledge about words. This lexicon is organized in various ways, and behavior that involves lexical knowledge reflects this structure. The linguist encounters the consequences of lexical structure in his analyses of language, just as the psychologist can study its expressions in verbal behavior and thinking. The purpose of these notes is to outline some preliminary considerations for a model of the lexical component of memory that may be capable of adequately representing our knowledge about words, and that may serve as a basis for various psychological process models. The inquiry is directed primarily towards determining what general principles apply for such models, rather than the actual construction of a lexicon itself. The main part of the paper is theoretical. However, one fairly direct experimental test of a principal assumption will be described. Furthermore, the model of memory structure may be combined with specific hypotheses about how this structure is employed in certain tasks, and the resulting process models are subject to empirical test. Two such applications, to free recall and judgments of semantic acceptability of sentences, will be reported.

I have tentatively suggested distinguishing three different lexical components (Kintsch, 1970): a matrix **P** of phonetic features which specifies the sound of the word (and how this sound is to be produced),[2] a matrix **I** of sensory features which represents sensory information associated with the dictionary entry (e.g., images), and a list **S** of syntactic-semantic markers which specify the use and meaning of the word. Only the semantic component of memory for words will be studied here.

Unquestionably thought is not entirely verbal, neither in its development nor in its normal functioning. However, the present paper is only concerned with verbal relationships. Furthermore, the subject matter has been limited even more severely by separating semantic and pragmatic factors. We shall be concerned merely with the structure of a person's vocabulary, not his "model of the world." In other words, the empirical truth, falsity, likelihood, etc., of statements are irrelevant for present purposes. In terms of the distinction between pragmatic semantic, and syntactic factors, we are only dealing with the latter two. Without a doubt, pragmatic facts are of overriding importance in many situations

---

[2] **P** is somewhat of a misnomer: it seems likely that there is some rather abstract level of representation from which phonetic, articulatory, and even graphemic cues can be derived. The interrelationships among these cues are not fully understood, but for some interesting remarks concerning the need for an abstract level of representation see Chomsky (1968). The functional components of the various subsystems of **P** and **S**, and their organization have been studied by neurological methods by Luria (1966) and Weigl and Bierwisch (1970).

in which words are used, but by restricting our concern to purely semantic problems, some complexities may be avoided, and a sufficiently rich field of investigation remains. Operationally, we shall make the following distinction: a question concerns a semantic problem if it can be answered on the basis of information available in memory; a question concerns a pragmatic problem if it necessitates reference to the state of the outside world.

Features, Markers, Semantic Relations, or Propositions?

It will help to understand the peculiarities of the proposed model of lexical structure if some alternative approaches are examined first. A look at a conventional lexicon is somewhat disappointing to the theorist. Words are not really defined in the standard dictionaries in any precise way; instead, various means are employed to indicate their meaning more or less vaguely, but these means are usually sufficient for the intelligent, adult user of the dictionary. They may be extralinguistic means (such as diagrams), or linguistic definitions, both explicit and implicit. Neither of these are of much use for the construction of a memory model because of their lack of formal structure. The methods that seem more suitable for formal approaches may be classified into several broad categories: feature systems, systems based upon semantic relationships, and some less restrictive approaches employing logic-like languages.

FEATURE SYSTEMS

Some good examples of how a feature system works have been described by Miller (1969). For instance, Miller shows how some English kinship terms can be defined by using three features, SEX, GENERATION, and LINEALITY, where GENERATION may have three values, while the other features are binary. Features here are abstract dimensions and every definiendum is characterized by a particular value on each dimension. In most cases, however, it is impossible to assign a value on every dimension, for example, the feature SEX is clearly irrelevant if the definiendum is STONE. Thus, words are defined only by assigning them values on relevant dimensions. The term semantic marker is often used in such systems to distinguish them from feature systems proper.

Implicit or explicit in the use of a feature system is the assumption that only a reasonably small number of dimensions will be needed. Indeed, many writers believe it to be an important goal for semantic theory to identify the set of primitive semantic features (e.g. Bierwisch, 1969). Others Katz & Fodor, 1963) distinguish between universal bases for classifying meaning, that is, semantic markers, and features specific to the meaning of a particular word, which they call distinguishers. We shall not use this distinction between markers and distinguishers since compelling arguments against it have been stated by Weinreich (1966) and Bierwisch (1969).

In practice, it seems that any word may serve as a marker in the definition of another word. Certainly there is no very obvious set of basic markers that would be sufficient for purposes of definition, unless one restricts oneself to very artificial word sets (such as kinship terms). I do not believe that it is possible to identify a set of basic markers in terms of which all others can be defined. Certainly it is impossible at this time. Whether there in fact exists such a set of semantic primitives is another question. At this point it seems wisest not to burden the research effort with the search for semantic primitives, which may or may not exist.

SEMANTIC RELATIONS

Another way of defining a word is by specifying the semantic relationships that it enters into with other words. Of course, ultimately this amounts to the same thing as specifying a word's features, but for expository purposes the two approaches may be discussed separately. The most common semantic relationship used in definitions is synonymy. Other semantic relationships that can be and have been used in semantic theory are incompatibility (e.g., the set of *color* terms), antonymy (e.g., *big-small*), hyponymy (e.g., *tulip-flower*), converse (e.g., *buy-sell*), or consequence (e.g., *fire-smoke*), as discussed by Lyons (1968). The linguist may add to these collocations and the psychologist would want to add the familiar association to this list (Deese, 1965, has explored the construction of an associative dictionary where each word is defined by the responses it elicits on a free association test.)

I do not believe that either association or collocation are very useful to the semantic theorist. If two words are connected in an associative net the only thing that is thought to matter is the strength of their connection; for instance, INSECT and WING are about equally likely as responses to BUTTERFLY, and, hence, the associations BUTTER-FLY-INSECT and BUTTERFLY-WING are considered to be equivalent. However, this procedure neglects the intuitively important fact that the first relationship is one of set inclusion while the second is a part-of relationship. BUTTERFLY needs to be defined by two different relationships, one a class relationship, and one a part-of relationship. Thus, semantic relations are like associations, except that the nature of the relationship is specified.

Without denying the facts of association, I believe that "association" would be a poor choice as a basic theoretical concept. Rather, association is a fairly complex phenomenon which needs to be explained in terms of more elementary processes, that is, one will have to show how free associations are generated in the system that is proposed below. It would of course be possible to extend the meaning of the term "association" so that it would subsume all relationships that exist in a lexical system. For instance, Deese (1965) takes a step in that direction when he adds a law of "grouping" to the classical laws of association (contiguity, frequency). However, a new term may be preferable to broadening the notion of association.

Talking about semantic relationships between words has two important implications: first, it makes clear that any word may be related to any other word, that is, there is no set of primitive terms; second, a relationship is a complex expression, unlike a feature or marker. In order to define a word we must state what other word it is related to, and what the nature of this relationship is.

The model of semantic structure that I have proposed earlier (Kintsch, 1970) stresses semantic relations. Each dictionary entry is defined by a list of the semantic relations that it enters into with other words. I called these relationships, perhaps unfortunately, "semantic markers." These semantic markers are complex symbols: they specify which items are related, and what the nature of the relationship is. Katz, in his more recent work (Katz, 1966, 1967), uses the term similarly. This usage differs, however, from the way in which the term marker was originally employed by Katz and Fodor (1963), where "marker" was more nearly equivalent to "feature." Because of this terminological confusion I shall no longer use the term "marker" in this paper.

The question of semantic primitives has already been brought up once in connection with feature systems. The same argument that was presented there can now be repeated. Just as we rejected the notion of a small set of semantic primitives in terms of which everything else must be defined, we find impractical the notion of a small number of primitive semantic relations. There seems to be as little reason to restrict the number of permissible relationships between words as there is to restrict the number of words that may enter into these relationships.

In order to define lexical entries, all relationships that can be expressed in the sentences of a language may be required. In the words of Weinreich (1966, p. 446):

> Every relation that may hold between components of a sentence also occurs among the components of a meaning of a dictionary entry. This is as much as to say that the semantic part of a dictionary entry is a sentence—more specifically, a deep-structure sentence.

Such a system has some very desirable features: word meanings can be made as precise or as vague as required, it is easy to see how meanings can change and how new words are added to the language by expressing their meaning in terms of sentences of that language.

PROPOSITIONAL SYSTEMS

Two considerations are all-important in thinking about the lexical component of memory: economy of storage and linguistic relevance. The first almost certainly means that the lexicon must be a generative one: it is inconceivable that all information about a word is directly stored with that word; instead, only very little information can be stored directly while most of what is relevant to the full meaning of a word must be inferred. Thus, information must be stored in such a way that inference rules can operate upon it. Linguistic relevance means that it is not sufficient to deal with the meaning of individual words, but a way must be shown in which these words can be combined into phrases and sentences.

In order to meet these stringent requirements, some formal language in which lexical definitions can be expressed is needed. The formalism that appears to be best suited for the task is some kind of low-order propositional calculus. I say low-order calculus because the attempt to translate language expressions into something like a fully quantified predicate calculus is surely misguided. Formal logic was developed precisely because language is so sloppy that it is insufficient for certain purposes (such as formal reasoning). To propose formal logic as a model for language only means forcing language into an intolerable straightjacket (though of course it would be nice for purposes of computer simulation and the like if one could translate normal language into predicate calculus). What we need is a greatly less powerful and elegant formalism that permits the operation of lexical inference rules as well as the semantic-syntactic rules that are necessary to produce sentences, but that does not impose more order than there is.

We are not alone, of course, in having noticed how useful logical expressions can be for the representation of lexical information. Many linguists have maintained that sentences must be represented as predicates at the semantic level (e.g., Schmidt, 1962, and the papers by McCawley, Fillmore, & Bach in Bach, 1968). Weinreich at one point used the predicate notation for lexical definitions (Weinreich, 1963), and Bierwisch (1969) has shown how the complex markers of Katz (1966, 1967) may be expressed as logical predications with some gain of both clarity and parsimony. Computer scientists who work on natural language question-answering systems frequently use formal logical structures for their data base.

Simmons (1970) has provided an excellent review of this area. These formal languages range from weak, general, predicate-like expressions to full-fledged predicate calculus formulas. The tendency in much of this work is to regard the latter as ideal, because most of the emphasis has been on theorem proving, rather than representation of large data structures. Very sophisticated methods for theorem proving are in use in some of these programs, but they depend upon higher-level logical languages which necessitate a restriction of the subject matter to a small, manageable area. Thus, the problem of how data structures are organized is more often avoided than solved: it does not seem to matter how a small, restricted memory is organized, as long as it can be scanned easily (e.g., Green & Raphael, 1968). The program that deals most realistically with problems of memory structure is that of Quillian (1967, 1969). A highly sophisticated memory model has recently been constructed by Frijda (1970), based upon the results of several computer simulations.

There may also be some psychological reasons that argue for the use of predication as a data-base language in a model of memory. For instance, Vygotsky has concluded from his analysis of "inner speech" that the structure of thought may be much closer to logical predication than to normal sentence structure (Vygotsky, 1962). Perhaps "thinking" represents operations at the level of the semantic base structure, before it has been transformed into actual sentences through the application of syntactic rules.

Before continuing, a brief discussion of the notion of "lexical item" itself is necessary. Any word or idiom may be a lexical item. How idioms can be handled like simple lexical items has been described by Fraser (1970). A problem arises, however, because of the polysemy of most words. Following the usual practice of standard dictionaries, some theorists let a lexical item correspond to a particular graphemic expression and then list the various "meanings" of that item (e.g., Katz & Fodor,

1963). Elsewhere, (Kintsch, 1970) I have treated different meanings of the "same" word as differet lexical items, following a suggestion by Weinreich (1966). Some items are written in the same way but differ in their semantic descriptions; other items have the same semantic characteristics but are written and pronounced differently, as is the case for synonyms. There does not seem to be any reason to give priority to the written form of words (e.g., one could make homonym units with at least as much justification). It is another question exactly when different meanings of a word should be distinguished. It would seem that different lexical items should be established only in cases where clearly contrastive meanings exist, but not when there is merely a certain vagueness of meaning so that context words are needed to determine the precise sense in which a word is used. For instance, we would not want two different entries for *go*, through *go* clearly means something different in *go by car* and *go by plane*. Many words in a well-developed language like English are depleted of meaning and depend for their interpretation upon other words, but such cases must be clearly distinguished from true ambiguity of meaning.

A Propositional Base for Grammar

The vocabulary of the English language may be divided into two classes: content words and function words. In the present model, function words are introduced into a sentence by the grammar which transforms a propositional base structure into a surface structure, that is an English sentence; content words, on the other hand, appear in the base structure. Thus, it is the latter that are of primary concern for a model of lexical memory, and we shall not consider function words further. Content words will be defined by ordered lists of propositions whose structure will be discussed later (Description Lists for Lexical Entries, p. 262). In the next section (Propositions), the use of propositions as the basic building blocks of the memory model is explained. The following section (Case Grammar) then deals with the sufficiency of such a propositional base as an input for transformational grammar.

PROPOSITIONS

A proposition consists of a relation and one or more arguments. Relations are normally verbs (as in 1,2), adjectives (3,4), or conjunctions

(5) ; arguments are nouns, except in cases such as (5) where other propositions serve as arguments:

(1) *The dog barks.* (BARK,DOG)
(2) *Mother bakes a cake in the oven.*
(MOTHER,BAKE,CAKE,IN OVEN)
3) *The old man.* (OLD,MAN)
(4) *Agnew is critical of intellectuals.*
(CRITICAL,AGNEW,INTELLECTUALS)
(5) *The stars are bright because of the clear night.*
(BECAUSE,(BRIGHT,STARS),(CLEAR,NIGHT))
(6) *A collie is a dog.* (DOG,COLLIE)

Note the notational conventions adopted here for writing propositions: propositions are always written in capital letters and enclosed by round brackets. The order in which the terms are written is significant: the relational term is always written first, and the order of arguments is fixed. In general $(R,A,B) \neq (R,B,A)$.

In (6) a noun appears in the slot normally reserved for relational terms. Such propositions will be called nominal propositions. This anomaly could be avoided, for example, by writing (6) as (IS MEMBER OF, COLLIE, DOG). However, to omit the copula in some cases, for example, in (3) and (4), while retaining it in others, seems inconsistent. In any case, nominal propositions play a very special role in the memory structure, as will be shown later, and they might as well be distinguished notationally. We omit the copula from the propositional expressions in sentences such as (3), (4), and (6) because the copula seems to be a semantically empty dummy item that is used to carry other kinds of information about the sentence (such as tense or modality).[3]

Syntactically, a proposition corresponds to a simple sentence. A surface structure sentence is often a complex form constructed from several propositions, some of which are not transformed into actual sentences, but form potential sentences. For instance, *"The old man drinks mint juleps"* is composed of the actual matrix sentence *"The man drinks mint juleps,"* and the embedded sentence *"The man is old,"* or in terms of propositions (DRINK, MAN, MINT JULEPS) and (OLD, MAN). For convenience of notation we shall write this as (DRINK, (OLD)MAN, MINT JULEPS). The ability to embed one proposition into another is crucial

---

[3] The copula is, in fact, absent in the surface structure of several languages, such as Greek, Latin, and Russian.

for the representation of complex materials. Two more examples should give the reader a better idea of the power of this technique:

(7) *Catching butterflies is dangerous.* (DANGEROUS, (CATCH,BUTTERFLIES)) = σ

(8) *He doubted that catching butterflies is dangerous.* (DOUBT,HE,σ)

In order to be able to denote modification of the relational term of a proposition, higher-level predication can be employed. Suppose one wants to represent the sentence *"Clouds approach rapidly."* Clearly, it is necessary to indicate that *rapidly* modifies *approach*, not *clouds:*

(9)   ((RAPID)APPROACH,CLOUDS)

The only way that even higher level modification of verbs can be expressed in the surface structure is through strings of adverbs, and long strings are probably very rare in the language. As an example, note Lyons' sentence.

(10) *Mary dances extraordinarily well.*
     (((EXTRAORDINARY)GOOD)DANCE,MARY)

The analysis of a complex sentence into underlying simple sentences, each of which corresponds to a proposition, is related but not identical to the concept of syntactic deep structure as used by Chomsky (1965). Lakoff & Ross (1967) have pointed out three important differences between deep structure sentences and semantic base structure formulas in the form of logical propositions: the treatment of quantification and negation, both of which will concern us later, and the absence of the concept verb phrase. The latter point is illustrated by the following example, where the deep structure form and the propositional form of the same sentence are compared:

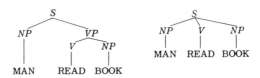

Note that the concept of surface structure applies equally to deep-structure and propositional analyses. In both a sentence is a surface structure which is to be derived by means of transformational rules from an underlying structure. In the case of Chomsky, this is a phrase-structure tree, the so-called deep structure; here it is a proposition which will be referred to as the base structure of the sentence.[4]

Surface structures (i.e., actual English sentences or phrases) and the base structure representating from which they are derived are related in complex ways. Given a particular base structure, many possible surface structures can be derived, as in

(11)   (BARK,DOG)   (i)   *The dog barks*
                        (ii) *The dog is barking*
                        (iii) *The barking dog*
                        (iv) *The dog*

(11-iv) is a somewhat extreme example, but one can readily imagine a situation where this elliptic sentence might be used to communicate the information (BARK,DOG). Exactly what determines whether (BARK,DOG) will be transformed into (11-i), (11-ii), (11-iii), or (11-iv) depends upon syntactic and pragmatic factors. The latter are disregarded here, but some comments about syntax will be made below.

Because the base-to-surface-structure transformation is one-to-many, the case frequently arises that two different base structures are represented by the same surface structure, e.g.,

(12)   *The dog barks*   (i)   ((DEFINITE)BARK,DOG)
                          (ii) ((GENERIC)BARK,DOG)

(12-i) could be translated as *"This particular dog barks,"* while (12-ii) conveys the general information that dogs can bark. The way we have chosen here of representing this difference in meaning is to introduce the base structure elements DEFINITE and GENERIC, plus some obligatory transformation rules which delete these elements from the surface structure. Given this kind of complexity, it is obviously not

---

[4] The question of whether generative semantics is, in principle, different from what Chomsky calls the "standard theory," or whether the two are merely notational variants is controversial. Generative semantics starts with a semantic base (often propositional), to which syntactic and eventually phonological rules are applied. The standard theory on the other hand, generates quadruples (S, P_i, P_n, P), where S is the semantic interpretation of a sentence, P_i its deep structure, P_n the surface structure, and P the phonological interpretation. As Chomsky (1969) has pointed out, there is no precise sense to the question of which of these is selected first if one is talking about competence models, just as it is meaningless to assert that one or the other side of an equation "comes first." However, if one is talking about a performance model, this question is perfectly appropriate. Going from a propositional base to a corresponding surface structure and phonological realization implies that a certain sequence of processes is being performed. Thus, for the purpose of building a model of memory, we must prefer a semantically based approach over the standard theory.

possible, in general, to assign a base structure to an isolated sentence unambiguously. A surface structure of a sentence is just one cue that the listener uses in inferring the base structure of a message. Verbal as well as nonverbal contexts play equally important roles.

CASE GRAMMAR

We have proposed that propositions be used as the building blocks of the memory model. It now must be shown that a model constructed in this manner is capable, at least in principle, of serving as the lexical component of a grammar. More precisely formulated, the question becomes the following: is there a set of syntactic rules that transform propositional expressions, as defined above, into English sentences? A number of linguists are at present working on this problem, such as McCawley (1968) and Fillmore (1968). The purpose of the present section is not to contribute anything to their work; I merely want to show the reader who is unfamiliar with modern work on generative semantics what a grammar that starts from a propositional base looks like. For this purpose it seems best to discuss one particular linguistic theory, although it should be understood that linguistic theories change rapidly these days and that there is no general agreement among linguists about which theory is "right" or even "best." However, our model is not tied to any specific syntactic theory, as long as it employs a propositional base structure or something formally equivalent.

For my purpose, the most suitable linguistic theory is that of Fillmore (1968, 1969). I shall briefly outline Fillmore's system, concentrating upon the relation between his system and the proposed model and omitting all detail about syntactic transformation rules.

The basic concepts of the theory are case categories (C), propositions (P), and sentences (S):

(13) $$S \rightarrow MP$$

where M is a modality component, and

(14) $$P \rightarrow VC_1C_2 \cdots C_n$$

where V is a verb and C_i is a member of $\{A,O,R,I,E,L,P, \ldots \}$, $C_i = C_j$ only if $i = j$.

(15) $$C_i \rightarrow K\,NP$$

where NP is a noun phrase, and K is a morpheme indicating case (prepositions, affixes, be, do, and word order).

The most important case categories that Fillmore used are the following:

agent (A)   the animate instigator of a verb action
instrument (I)   an object causally involved in the verb
experiencer (E) animate being affected by the verb
result (R)   object resulting from the verb
locative (L)   object identifying location or orientation of the verb
object (O)   noun whose role is identified by the meaning of the verb.

A few examples will illustrate the role of these case categories:

(16)   The entrance (O) was blocked by the chair (I).
(17)   The house (R) in the mountains (L) was built by John (A).
(18)   John (A) gave Jane (E) a book (O).
(19)   John (E) received a book (O) from Jane (A).
(20)   The president (A) asked the students (E) to repent (P).[5]

For each case category there exists a set of nouns that can be used in the slot indicated by the category symbol. Note that these sets are not disjoint [e.g. *John* is agent in (18), but experiencer in (19)]. A memory model needs to show how nouns are assigned to the various case categories, and we shall return to that problem in a later section (The Structure of Lexical Memory, p. 262).

If propositions are written in such a way that the case of each argument is indicated, structures are obtained upon which syntactic transformation rules can operate. Actually indicating the case of each argument is not merely a deplorable complexity caused by the peculiarities of Fillmore's grammar, but is, in one way or another, absolutely necessary to make a propositional system work unambiguously. Consider the phrase *"Catching butterflies"* from (7), which was represented by (CATCH,BUTTERFLIES). It is clear that the object role of *butterflies* must be indicated, because *butterflies* could be used in an agent role, for example, butterflies may catch each other. Thus we write

$$(\text{CATCH, } O\text{:BUTTERFLIES})$$

In general, propositions must be written as

(21) $(\text{RELATION, } C_1\text{:}\underline{\quad},C_2\text{:}\underline{\quad}, \ldots, C_n\text{:}\underline{\quad})$.

However, we shall usually omit case categories in the following to simplify notation, except when they are not obvious.

[5] A proposition is used as an argument in (20); we shall label it *P*, rather than *S* as Fillmore does. The embedded element is a proposition rather than a sentence because it lacks a modality component: nothing is implied about whether the students actually repent, have repented, or the like.

Given a particular relational term, certain cases may be required in the surface structure while others may be optional. Consider the following example where the object is required, but the agent is optional:

(22)

> *John repairs the car*
> **John repairs*
> *The car is being repaired*

In the present paper we shall indicate required arguments by underlining:

(REPAIR, A̲: JOHN, O̲: CAR)

We also have dependencies among arguments in the sense that the presence of a particular argument requires the presence (or absence) of another. We shall indicate this linking by appropriate subscripts:[6]

(23)

John drives the truck on the road.
John drives on the road. John drives the truck. The truck is driven on the road.
John drives.   *The truck drives.   *Drives on the road.

(DRIVE, $O_{A,L}$: TRUCK, A: JOHN, $L_{A,O}$: ROAD)

where all arguments are optional, but if an object is present, either an agent, locative, or both must be present, and if a locative is present, an agent or object are required.

Sentences are derived from two components according to (13): a proposition and a modality component. The latter specifies the modality of the sentence as a whole, most importantly tense, sentence negation, mood, aspect, modalization, and perhaps others.[7] For instance, the sentence *John slept* is derived from the proposition (SLEEP, JOHN) and the modality PAST. Fillmore writes base structures in the form of a phrase marker:

---

[6] We cannot use Fillmore's bracket notation, because brackets are already employed for other purposes.

[7] I am thinking about some adverbial phrases that may best be regarded as sentence modalities rather than as parts of a proposition, e.g., *Perhaps John is a radical liberal, Very likely John is a radical liberal.*

Both **K** and the determiner D are empty in the present example. Transformation rules turn this base structure tree into the surface structure phrase marker (25). One of these rules, for instance, is concerned with the subject selection: in this case, the rule that is applied is simply "If there is an agent, it becomes the subject."

In the base structure of the sentence *Boulder is beautiful* the case indicator **K** is not empty. The surface structure of the sentence is

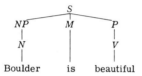

For the corresponding base structure we have the proposition (BEAUTIFUL, *L*: BOULDER), and the phrase marker

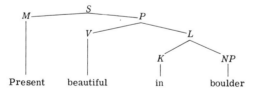

The transformational rules that take (24) into (25) and (27) into (26) are described in some detail in Fillmore (1968). One of these rules turns the modality *present* into *is*.

The last example also illustrates how prepositions are introduced in this grammar. Each case category has its typical prepositions (e.g., *by* or *with* for instrumental, *to* or *for* for experiencer, and ϕ for objective), and there exist rules which allow case categories to be rewritten as *Prep + NP*. However, there may also be some semantically nonempty prepositions which must be introduced directly from the lexicon. For instance, it will not do to identify *ascent* as locative in *"The ascent along the ridge"*: the *along* cannot be introduced by syntactic rules, because the meaning of the phrase depends upon it: *along* the ridge, not *above or below* it! I am not clear how Fillmore handles this problem.

I find it most natural to let such prepositions serve as relational terms of propositions. Thus we have (ALONG, O: ASCENT, L: RIDGE). In fact, one might consider abandoning locative as a case category entirely.

The Structure of Lexical Memory

Two kinds of lexical elements have been described: the definienda (for brevity referred to as words, though they may be phrases), and propositions. The problem that is to be taken up in this section is how these elements are organized. The main features of the proposed model are as follows. First, for each definiendum, a list of propositions that characterize it will be established by connecting appropriate propositions through the operations of conjunction and disjunction (Description Lists for Lexical Entries). Second, we must consider the structure of the set of all propositions. We shall describe two organizational principles, which amount to a classification system for nouns (The Structure of the Noun System, p. 266) and for verbs (The Structure of the Verb System, p. 269), respectively. Third, a system of inference rules will be described that provides a generative capacity and, thus, economy of storage: each lexical entry is directly defined by relatively few propositions, but additional information can be generated through the operations of inference rules. These rules are called redundancy rules because they exploit the inherent redundancy of the lexical system (Generative Properties of the Lexicon, p. 273).

DESCRIPTION LISTS FOR LEXICAL ENTRIES

The operations $\wedge$ and $\vee$ are used to connect propositions that describe a particular lexical entry. As a result of these operations, a *description list* of propositions is obtained. The propositions

$$P_1, \ldots, P_n$$

may be connected through either $\wedge$ or $\vee$, for example, as

$$P_1 \wedge P_2 \wedge \cdots \wedge (P_k \vee P_{k+1}) \wedge \cdots \wedge P_n.$$

For instance, suppose one wants to represent a person's concept of APPLE by means of the following combination of propositions:

(FRUIT,APPLE) $\wedge$ (DELICIOUS,APPLE) $\wedge$ ((RED,APPLE)
$\vee$ (YELLOW,APPLE) $\vee$ (GREEN,APPLE))

I have previously used the term *associative fields* to denote the lists of propositions that are obtained through conjunction and disjunction (Kintsch, 1970). Conjunction has its usual meaning. Disjunction is to be understood as exclusive disjunction, that is, it asserts either one of the disjoint elements, but not both. It is used when there is a choice between alternatives, for example, apples may be either red, yellow, or green.

Note that in the APPLE-example above, higher-level predication has not been employed. The full definition should presumably read:

((DELICIOUS)TASTE,APPLE) $\land$ ((RED)COLOR,APPLE), etc.

However, if a lexicon is organized appropriately and if the appropriate redundancy rules exist, the fact that *delicious* refers to the *taste* of the apple, and *red* to its *color* can be inferred and need not be stored explicitly.

The proposal to define lexical entries through lists of propositions, that is, through other lexical entries that are, in turn, defined somewhere else, is certainly not unconventional. This is exactly what is done in most dictionaries, and Quillian (1967) has used the same procedure for his memory model. In Quillian's terms, each lexical entry is represented by a single *type* node which shows the "associative links" with other nodes that represent the meaning of that word. In addition, each word that is used has a special associative connection (the *token* node) with its type node. In the present system, nodes are not introduced explicitly. To use a computer analogy, the system is content addressable: each word provides immediate access to the list of propositions that represent its meaning in memory.

In Table 1 an example of a lexical entry is presented. This lexical item has been constructed from an encyclopedia entry for *nebula,* and as such it contains much more information about nebulae than most people might possess, but it illustrates the possibilities of the present approach. For clarity of exposition, propositions have not always been decomposed into their elements in that modifiers are often simply written with their corresponding nouns, instead of being introduced by means of a separate expression. The $-sign is used to indicate a free variable, that is, a term that is needed in a proposition to produce a well-formed expression, but which is not specified further (e.g., in line 9 of Table 1 the $ simply indicates an unspecified agent-noun). The only special notation occurs in line 4. The expression in line 4 is to be read as "The class of nebula may be partitioned into N_1 and N_2." The use of such expressions is explained and motivated in a later section of this paper (The Structure of the Noun System, p. 266). The arrangement of propositions in separate lines and the numbering of the lines in Table 1 are

TABLE 1

Sample Lexical Entry for Nebula (N) Together with the Corresponding English-Language Representation[a]

---

1 (LIGHTSOURCE,N) $\wedge$
2 (((RELATIVE)FIXED)LOCATED,N,SKY) $\wedge$
3 ((FUZZY $\wedge$ NEBULOUS)APPEAR,N) $\wedge$
4 [(N_1 $\vee$ N_2) $\rightarrow$ N]$\wedge$
5 (OUTSIDE,N_1,(OUR)GALAXY) $\wedge$
6 (COMPOSED,N_1 $\wedge$ (OUR)GALAXY,STARS) $\wedge$ (GALAXY,N_1) $\wedge$
7 (APPEAR,N_1,CLUSTERS) $\wedge$ ((EVEN)SPACED,CLUSTERS,UNIVERSE)
    $\wedge$ (CONSIST,CLUSTERS,(2–30)GALAXIES) $\wedge$
8 (BECAUSE,α,β) $\wedge$ (((FUZZY)APPEAR,N_1) = α)
    $\wedge$ ((BUT,(SEE,$,$N_1$),$\epsilon$) = β) $\wedge$
9 ((BECAUSE,γ,δ) = ϵ) $\wedge$ (($\sim$SEE,$,(INDIVIDUAL)STARS,EYE $\wedge$ (MOST
    POWERFUL)TELESCOPE) = γ) $\wedge$ ((REMOTE,N_1) = δ) $\wedge$
10 (SEE,$,(3)$N_1$,(NAKED)EYE) $\wedge$
11 (WITHIN,N_2,(OUR)GALAXY) $\wedge$
12 (CLOUD,N_2) $\wedge$ (GAS $\vee$ DUST,CLOUD) $\wedge$
13 (BECAUSE,ϕ,ψ) $\wedge$ ((EVOLVE,(SOME)N_2,STARS) = ϕ)
    $\wedge$ ((EXPAND $\wedge$ CONTRACT,N_2) = ψ) $\wedge$
14 (BECAUSE,τ,σ) $\wedge$ ((GLOW,(GAS)N_2) = τ) $\wedge$ ((LUMINOUS,GAS) = σ) $\wedge$
15 (BECAUSE,ν,μ) $\wedge$ ((GLOW,(DUST)N_2) = ν)
    $\wedge$ ((ILLUMINATE,(NEAR)STARS,(DUST)N_2) = μ)

---

[a] A nebula is any source of light in the sky that has a relatively fixed location in space and looks fuzzy or nebulous. There are two kinds of nebulae. One kind is the nebulae outside of our own galaxy. These nebulae are composed of stars, like our own galaxy is composed of stars. Galaxy nebulae appear in clusters of from two to thirty galaxies. The clusters of galaxy nebulae are spread rather evenly throughout the universe. Galaxy nebulae look fuzzy because the overall nebula is seen, but the nebulae are so remote that their individual stars cannot be distinguished, even with the most powerful telescopes. In fact, with the naked eye only three galaxy nebulae are close enough to be seen at all. The other kind is the nebulae within our own galaxy. These nebulae are clouds of gas or dust. Some of the gas nebulae are evolving to become stars by expanding and contracting. Gas nebulae glow because the gas itself is luminous, but dust nebulae seem to glow because they are illuminated by nearby stars.

introduced merely for convenience of reference; they are not part of the lexical entry.

The description lists produced by joining propositions through conjunction and disjunction are structured lists rather than random strings. From the APPLE-example given above, this important fact is not obvious: it does not seem to make much difference in which order the five propositions that were used to represent the meaning of APPLE are written. However, this is merely a consequence of the poverty of the description list used in that example. In general, the order in which propositions are listed in a description list is not arbitrary. First of all, some structure is imposed upon description lists because propositions may be embedded in other propositions. Line 14 in Table 1 provides an example: the propositions *gas nebula glow* and *gas is luminous* are themselves arguments of the proposition *gas nebula glow because gas is luminous*. A more complex example of embedding is given in lines 8 and 9. Embedding, that is, the use of one proposition as an argument for another proposition, is one of the crucial features of the present system; without it, the system would certainly be insufficient to represent anything but the most trivial semantic relationships. The order of propositions in a description list is likewise crucial for determining possible relationships of subordination.

Subordination is often signaled in the surface structure through special syntactic devices (e.g., dependent clauses), but the present definition of subordination does not depend upon such surface structure features. Subordination determines what I shall call the *range* of a proposition. Statements that appear in description lists are not true in general, but only within a certain range. Subordination indicates this range. Every statement is subordinated to the name of the lexical entry in question. In addition, however, a statement may be subordinated to some other proposition in a description list, which further restricts its range. Consider the second statement from line 7 in Table 1, which says that *clusters are evenly spaced in universe*. This statement is not a general statement about "clusters," but it applies only to the cluster that was introduced earlier, namely by the first proposition in line 7. The second proposition is subordinated to the first proposition, and hence its range is restricted. Subordination in a description list, then, is indicated by order: if a proposition P contains a term A, proposition P', P'', . . . , that occur after it and also contain the term A are subordinated to P. Since propositions always contain more than one term, a complex multidimensional subordination pattern may result. For instance in Table 1, line 7, the last proposition is subordinated both to the immediately preceding propositions, because it shares with them the term CLUSTERS, and to the last proposition in line 6, because GALAXY is shared with it.

The nebula paragraph used in Table 1 has been studied previously for similar purposes by Crothers (1970). Crothers' goals are somewhat different from the present ones: he is primarily interested in determining and explicating the structural relationships that exist within a paragraph. Crothers' paragraph has been used here in order to show that complex material can be represented naturally within the present framework, and that, in particular, the subordination relationships which are present in any complex text and which are crucial for understanding are fully determined in the ordered lists of propositions used to form description lists. Crothers' method makes the "structure of a paragraph" more readily accessible through the use of graphs, while the subordination relationships that exist in a description list are not easily visualized. However, all necessary structural information is implicitly given by the lists of ordered propositions, and no additional principles need be evoked to represent such information in the present model.

Finally, I would like to point out that many changes could be made in the text of Table 1 which would still leave it compatible with the base-structure representation given. Such changes might include changes in sentence and word order, pronominalizations, use of synonyms, and especially omission of some propositions or parts thereof.

THE STRUCTURE OF THE NOUN SYSTEM

Nominal predicates are propositions of the form (B,A) where both A and B are nouns. They are normally read as "A is a B." We want to consider the structure that is imposed upon the set of all nouns by the existence of such relationships. This structure is often referred to as the "set-inclusion hierarchy."

Let $\mathfrak{N} = \{A,B,C, \ldots\}$ be the set of all nouns. For appropriate A and B there exist propositions (B,A). We define a relationship $A \leq B$, A precedes B, which holds whenever the proposition (B,A) exists. We want to study the properties of the system $(\mathfrak{N}, \leq)$. It can be shown that $\leq$ is an order relation, because it is

Reflexive: $A \leq A$ for all $A \in \mathfrak{N}$
Antisymmetric: $A \leq B$ does not imply $B \leq A$ for all $A,B \in \mathfrak{N}$
Transitive: $A \leq B$ and $B \leq C$ implies $A \leq C$ for all $A,B,C \in \mathfrak{N}$.

Thus $(\mathfrak{N}, \leq)$ is a partially ordered set.

An element $A \in \mathfrak{N}$ is said to be a maximal element if $A \leq X$ implies $A = X$. Similarly, we say that an element B, $B \in \mathfrak{N}$, is a minimal element if $X \leq B$ implies $B = X$. $(\mathfrak{N}, \leq)$ has exactly one maximal element, the word NOUN, but there are many minimal elements.

It has sometimes been asserted that the set inclusion hierarchy can be represented by a tree. $(\mathfrak{N}, \leq)$ is clearly not a tree. A tree is a partially ordered set in which each element has a unique successor. This is not the case in the kind of set-hierarchies that we are concerned with. For instance, *dog* may have two immediate successors, *mammal* and *pet*.

For a pair of elements $A,B \in \mathfrak{N}$ an element M, $M \in \mathfrak{N}$, is an upper bound if $M \geq A$ and $M \geq B$. M is a least upper bound (*lub*) if $M \leq X$ for all upper bounds X. The concept of a lower bound is defined similarly: if $A,B \in \mathfrak{N}$, M is a lower bound if $M \leq A$ and $M \leq B$ and $M \in \mathfrak{N}$. M is the greatest lower bound (*glb*), if $M \geq X$ for all lower bounds X.

A partially ordered set is called a lattice if *lub* (A,B) and *glb* (A,B) exist for any pair of elements A and B. $(\mathfrak{N}, \leq)$ is not a lattice for two reasons. Not all pairs of elements have a lower bound. For instance, if

A and B are two different minimal elements, no lower bound exists: there is no word $X \in \mathfrak{N}$ that is a lower bound for *emerald* and *pigeon*, that is, there is no word for the X-slot in (EMERALD,X) and (PIGEON,X). This difficulty could be overcome by introducing a zero morpheme ϕ such that (X,ϕ) for all $X \in \mathfrak{N}$ that is, one could add to the system a unique minimal element. However, $(\mathfrak{N}, \leq)$ still would not be a lattice because for some pairs of elements A and B *lub* (A,B) does not exist. For example, consider the following fragment of a hierarchy that might be encountered as part of someone's memory structure (connecting lines represent the $\leq$ relation):

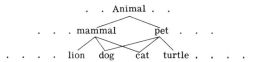

Cross classifications such as those in (28) violate lattice structure: the pair *dog, cat* has two upper bounds (*mammal* and *pet*) but no least upper bound since neither *mammal* $\leq$ *pet* nor *pet* $\leq$ *mammal*, and the pair *mammal, pet* has two lower bounds (*dog* and *cat*), but no greatest lower bound. Other examples may be readily constructed that show that in general pairs of elements in $(\mathfrak{N}, \leq)$ may have more than one lower bound, and more than one upper bound, but no greatest lower bound nor a least upper bound. Therefore, $(\mathfrak{N}, \leq)$ is not a lattice.

It is instructive to inquire which lattice properties are violated in $(\mathfrak{N}, \leq)$. Suppose ϕ is added to $\mathfrak{N}$ as suggested above, so that each pair of elements in $\mathfrak{N}$ has at least one upper and lower bound. A lattice is characterized by the following properties (where $\wedge$ denotes the operation of forming a *glb*, and $\vee$ denotes the operation of obtaining the *lub*):

Idempotence	$X \wedge X = X$
	$X \vee X = X$
Commutativity	$X \wedge Y = Y \wedge X$
	$X \vee Y = Y \vee X$
Associativity	$X \wedge (Y \wedge Z) = (X \wedge Y) \wedge Z$
	$X \vee (Y \vee Z) = (X \vee Y) \vee Z$
Absorption	$X \wedge (X \vee Y) = X$
	$X \vee (X \wedge Y) = X.$

Of these, idempotence, commutativity, and absorption hold for $(\mathfrak{N}, \leq)$. The first two present no problems. Absorption holds because for every $X, Y \in \mathfrak{N}$ there exists at least one *lub* and at least one *glb*, as was shown above. Thus

$$X \vee (X \wedge Y) = X \vee glb\ (X,Y) = X.$$

The first equality follows from the existence of a *glb;* the second equality follows from the definition of a *glb.* Similarly, we can show that

$$X \wedge (X \vee Y) = X$$

because $(X \vee Y)$ exists and is equal to *lub* (X,Y); the *glb* of X and *lub* (X,Y) is by definition X.

Associativity, however, does not hold in $(\mathfrak{N}, \leq)$, as is shown by a counter-example. Consider the structure shown in (28). Associativity is violated because

(lion $\vee$ dog) $\vee$ cat $\neq$ lion $\vee$ (dog $\vee$ cat)
mammal $\vee$ cat $\neq$ lion $\vee$ pet
mammal $\neq$ animal

Similar examples for forming *glb*'s could be constructed in more extensive networks.

There are some further problems posed by the existence of cross-classifications which need to be considered. Suppose the following structure, which is a slight extension of (28), is part of someone's memory:

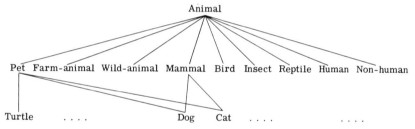

Clearly, (29) misrepresents the actual organization. Supplementary rules are needed whenever a superordinate term is classified in more than one way. We shall say that a set of words form an *antonymous n-tuple* if all words have the same superordinate term and if these words form a partition of the class denoted by that term. For example, *turtle, dog* and *cat* partition the category *pet* in (29); on the other hand, there are three different partitions of *animal* in (29). Whenever a category is partitioned in more than one way, classification rules of the following form are required:

(30) $\{N_1 \vee N_2 \vee \cdots \vee N_n\} \rightarrow C$

where the N_i's are the set of nouns that partition the category C. In (29) the following three rules would be needed:

{pet $\vee$ farm-animal $\vee$ wild-animal} $\rightarrow$ animal
{mammal $\vee$ bird $\vee$ insect $\vee$ reptile} $\rightarrow$ animal
{human $\vee$ nonhuman} $\rightarrow$ animal

The structure of $(\mathfrak{N},\leq)$ can then be described as follows: $(\mathfrak{N},\leq)$ is a partially ordered set with a unique maximal element and it is not associative. Furthermore, special classification rules of the form (30) are needed when a term is subclassified in more than one way.

If $A, B \in \mathfrak{N}$, we shall say A and B are synonymous if $A = B$; A and B are hierarchically related if either $A \leq B$ or $B \leq A$; A and B are members of the same class if they appear both on the left side of a classification rule; and A and B are unrelated if they are not synonyms, hierarchically related, or members of the same class.

THE STRUCTURE OF THE VERB SYSTEM

The organization of the verb-system is somewhat more complex than the structures described in the previous section. The methods used for the classification of nouns cannot be applied in quite the same way. One could introduce propositions of the form (VERB$_1$, VERB$_2$) and construct a classification system like that for nouns. However, that would produce some problems for the kind of transformational grammar that was envisioned in an earlier section and, more importantly, it would be unsatisfactory because verbs must be classified together with the arguments that they take. What needs to be classified are propositions, not simply verbs.

The organization of verbs is obtained in two ways: partly through the set-inclusion hierarchies already discussed, and partly through special rules like (30) which define antonymous n-tuples. The general form of propositions is (RELATION,$C_1,C_2, \ldots ,C_k$) where the C_i are the case categories A(agent), O(object), etc. as explained earlier (A Propositional Base for Grammar). Each case category is a set of nouns. Of course, the same noun may play different roles in different propositions.

Suppose a lexicon would contain only these two propositions involving the verb *operate:*

The surgeon operates on the patient.
The surgeon operates in the emergency room.

The first sentence is an (R,A,E) proposition, the second is an (R,A,L) type. The verb *operate* would therefore be classified as (OPERATE,$\underline{A}$,E,L), that is, propositions involving *operate* must have an agent, may have an experiencer and locative, and cannot have anything else. Of course, this is incorrect, but in a richer memory there would be instances of OPERATE-propositions where the agent is deleted, where an instrumental is present, and whatever else is required for the correct classification of OPERATE-propositions. Note especially that between *surgeon* and the case category agent there will be a whole network of intermediate terms: the *surgeon* is a *doctor,* the *doctor* is a *professional,* the *professional* is a *person,* the *person* is an *agent.* Different meanings of OPERATE constitute branches of this chain: e.g., there will be sentences *The operator operates the machine,* where both operator and machine may have a large number of subordinate terms. Thus, OPERATE-propositions participate in a large network of relationships merely by the fact that the nouns that they take as arguments are themselves members of various lexical structures, primarily the set inclusion hierarchy discussed above, but also various location-networks, and the like.

Complex dependencies may exist among the arguments of a verb, so that a given verb may be characterized not just by its obligatory or deletable cases, but by certain alternative patterns of cases. For instance *grow* may take either a human or nonhuman object, as in *The child grew* and *The corn grew;* the object can be combined with an agent in *The farmer grew the corn,* but not in **The parents grew the child.* What we have here is a restriction on the use of *grow* that prohibits human or animal object in the presence of an agent, but allows them otherwise (Anderson, 1969).

Classification of propositions through the arguments that they take is, however, insufficient in itself. Special rules to establish antonymous n-tuples are needed. These rules are of the form

(31) $[(V_1,X) \lor (V_2,X) \lor \cdots \lor (V_n,X)] \to (C,X)$

where X is a noun (or more precisely, a class of nouns, since nouns in general possess various subordinate terms), and (C,X) is a superordinate proposition. The set of propositions $(V_1,X) \lor \ldots \lor (V_n,X)$ forms a partition of (C,X) in much the same way as the set of nouns in (30) forms a partition of a superordinate noun class. Rules like (31) are needed for similar reasons as those given as a rationale for (30). For instance, objects may be *light* or *heavy* or *red* or *yellow* or *blue,* etc. In order to represent the organization of these propositions correctly, rules like these are required:

(32)
$[(LIGHT,OBJ) \lor (HEAVY,OBJ)] \to (HAVE,OBJ,WEIGHT)$
$[(RED,OBJ) \lor (YELLOW,OBJ) \lor \ldots \lor (BLUE,OBJ)]$
$\to (HAVE,OBJ,COLOR).$

Let $\mathcal{P} = (P,Q \ldots)$ be the set of all propositions. There exists an order relation $\leq$ which holds between two propositions P and Q, $P \leq Q$, if

    (a)   there is a rule $\{P \lor P' \lor \ldots\} \to Q$
    (b)   if $P = (R,N,M)$, $Q = (R,N',M)$ such that $N,N',M \in \mathfrak{N}$, and $N \leq N'$,

where M may be empty, a single noun, or a string of nouns, and R is a relation.

In other words, $\mathcal{P}$ is a partially ordered set like $\mathfrak{N}$: $\leq$ holds if there exists a subordination rule like (31) that establishes an antonymous n-tuple of propositions, or if the arguments of one proposition are superordinates of the arguments of another proposition. Thus, (HEAVY,OBJ) $\leq$ (HAVE,WEIGHT,OBJ), because of (32), and (BARK,COLLIE) $\leq$ (BARK,DOG) because COLLIE $\leq$ DOG in $(\mathfrak{N}, \leq)$.

The structure of $\mathcal{P}$ is essentially the same as that of $\mathfrak{N}$: there exists a unique maximal element (the general form of a proposition, Eq. 21), many minimal elements, and greatest lower bounds and least upper bounds do not in general exist for arbitrary pairs of propositions in $(\mathcal{P}, \leq)$. There are many subsets of $\mathcal{P}$ that form well-defined structures of their own. Just as the relation IS-A-MEMBER-OF produced the set inclusion hierarchy, other relationships produce similar, though more restricted structures. Consider the following statements: *The plate is on the table, The table is in the kitchen, The stove is in the kitchen, The kitchen is in the house.* An order relation LOCATED is implied by these and similar sentences. Several location subsystems may be part of a person's memory structure, because different location hierarchies need not be integrated with each other, except at the highest level.

Quite similar systems are produced by the part-of relationship: it is clear that propositions of the form (PART-OF,A,B) define systems that are formally equivalent to set-inclusion hierarchies, except that we have several different part-of hierarchies that are not related to each other (parts of the body, parts of an automobile). Again, these hierarchies will not be proper lattices because some pairs of elements will have more than one possible least upper bound, for example, one would want to have *joint* and *limb* both as parts of *leg* and *arm*.[8]

---

[8] Since the part-of relation as well as many others give rise to structures that are in many ways quite comparable to the set-inclusion hierarchy, one might question the usefulness of separating the noun-hierarchy from the rest of the system as has been done here. My main reason for making the somewhat inelegant noun-verb distinction here is that it appears necessary to make things work. However, there is some additional evidence for the noun-verb distinction. Both theoretical and empirical reasons can be cited for some kind of noun-priority in the lexicon. For instance, Chomsky (1965), when substituting words into phrase-markers, first inserts the nouns by means of context-free rules, and then selects verbs and adjectives in terms of nouns. In fact, he shows that the converse procedure of choosing verbs independently and selecting nouns in terms of the verbs leads to unacceptable complications of the grammar. Empirically, we have the observations reported by Marshall and Newcombe (1966) about a dyslexic patient who could read nouns quite well (though making many semantic errors, e.g., *thunder* as *storm* and vice versa), performed poorly with verbs and adjectives, and could not read prepositions, adverbs, and the like at all. Weigl and Bierwisch (1970)

Interrelationships among propositions define a large and complicated system of cross-classifications. This system will be used in two principal ways. First of all, it provides a basis for the lexical generation and transformation rules to be discussed in the next section. Given a general proposition such as (BAKE,AGENT:$,OBJECT:$) we can construct many subordinate propositions by filling in the $-signs in the agent and object slots with appropriate nouns. Second, classes of propositions can be established in this way to represent verb features that are important for the syntactic derivations. For instance, verb features, which otherwise would have to be indicated directly with each lexical item, such as *state, process, action,* and *action + process* (Chafe, 1970), can be represented in this manner. In part, these verb classes are defined through the arguments that may be used. Thus, *open* is necessarily used as an *process + action* verb if it takes an agent and object: (OPEN,A:$,$O$:$) as in *Michael opened the door.* However, arguments do not fully determine verb classifications, and rules like (32) must be used to represent the two meanings of (OPEN,O:$) as a *process* and *state* verb, such as in *The door opened* and *The door is open.* Thus, the proposition (OPEN,A:$,$O$:$) would be subcategorized into the three propositions shown below, each of which is a member of a large verb class (arguments other than agent and object have been neglected in this example):

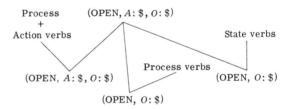

Rules like those in (32) provide a means of dealing with the concept *dimension* within the present framework. Unlike in a feature system, dimension is not a basic term. One can talk about a dimension whenever some propositions are joined by disjunction to form antonymous *n*-tuples. Explicit names (nouns) for the dimension are not required in the present system.

---

report another relevant observation: if a dyslexic patient is told what a sentence is, he is often able to read the sentence if semantically related nouns are substituted, but not if verb substitutions are made. However tenuous this evidence is, it does support the notion that nouns are somewhat more directly accessible in the dictionary than other word types. Thus, the concentration upon nouns in models of memory may not be as unreasonable as it first appears.

Another distinction that is often made by semantic theorists can also be stated within the present framework. That is the distinction between marked and unmarked adjectives. In a feature system *high* is called the unmarked member of the antonym pair *high-low* and low is marked as (-HIGH) (c.g., Lyons, 1968). The reason for this convention is that *high* provides the dimension name: one talks about *height*, not *lowness* or the like, one asks *"How high is it?"* and not, normally, *"How low is it?."* Clearly, this important fact is represented in the present notation, too:

$$[(\text{HIGH}, X) \vee (\text{LOW}, X)] \rightarrow (\text{HAVE}, X, \text{HEIGHT}).$$

(The *light-heavy* example in (32) seems to provide a counterexample; however, note that *heaviness* is a synonym of *weight*, which indicates that *heavy* is the unmarked member of the antonym pair.)

It may also be necessary to distinguish proper antonymy from compelementarity (Lyons, 1968). If two words are complementary, denial of one implies the assertion of the other. For instance, denial of (MALE,X) yields (FEMALE,X), and denial of (FEMALE,X) yields (MALE,X). This, however, is not the case with proper antonyms: denial of (BIG,X) does not necessarily imply (SMALL,X), because BIG and SMALL are not simply opposite properties but are basically comparative terms. (BIG,X), as Lyons points out, is semantically a comparative sentence: *"X is bigger than some norm,"* and denying it may not mean that *"X is smaller than the norm."*

Generative Properties of the Lexicon

Memory structure has been described in the previous sections as though it were a static system, all parts of which exist at all times. However, it appears more plausible that this entire structure is not always actually present, but is generated in part from more basic lexical substructures through the application of inference rules. In the interest of storage economy, a generative capacity appears to be almost mandatory for a lexicon. Because the inference rules that allow one to add to and delete propositions from the lexicon are based upon the redundancy of the system, we shall call these rules redundancy rules.

REDUNDANCY RULES

A redundancy rule permits one to substitute a synonym for a given noun, if one exists, in all expressions in which that noun appears. Synonymity of propositions can be treated analogously, that is, equivalence sets of propositions can be constructed whose members are freely interchangeable. The backbone of the system of redundancy rules are what will be called the hierarchy-deletion and hierarchy-production rules for both the noun-hierarchy and the proposition-hierarchy. Consider the structure of the set of all nouns $\mathfrak{N}$, discussed in an earlier section. Let $N_1, N_2, N_3, \ldots$, N_k, C be specific lexical items. Indices are used here in such a way that Ns with the same subscript always refer to the same lexical item. We shall define a hierarchy-deletion operator **HD** which deletes material from the lexicon given the kind of input shown in (33) and (34); given any other kind of input, **HD** has no effect:

(33) $\mathbf{HD}[(N_2,N_1),(N_3,N_1),(N_3,N_2)] = (N_2,N_1),(N_3,N_2)$

(34) $\mathbf{HD}[(C,N_1), \ldots, (C,N_k);(N_1 \vee \cdots \vee N_k) \rightarrow C]$
$$= (C,N_1), \ldots, (C,N_k).$$

Rule (33) deletes, from storage, nominal predicates that can be inferred. For instance, if the following three propositions are stored in memory, the third one, which is redundant, would be deleted by (33): (DOG,COLLIE),(ANIMAL,DOG),(ANIMAL,COLLIE). Rule (34) deletes statements that a certain set of nouns form a partition of a superordinate term if the term is partitioned in only one way. Thus, suppose someone (a child, to simplify things) has in his memory the propositions (ANIMAL,DOG), (ANIMAL,CAT), (ANIMAL,HORSE) and the rule DOG $\vee$ CAT $\vee$ HORSE) $\rightarrow$ ANIMAL. The latter is redundant and can be deleted by (34). Note, however, that if there were another proposition, say (ANIMAL,PET), with an argument that does not appear in the classification rule for animals (or that appears in a different classification rule), rule (34) does not apply. We assume that (34) is used only after all redundant propositions deletable by (33) have been deleted, and that all propositions of the form (C,N_i) that remain are used as an input. A deletion will occur only if the arguments of the various propositions match precisely the terms inside the classification rule.

Two hierarchy-production rules permit the system to produce the information deleted by the hierarchy-deletion rules:

(35) $\mathbf{HP}[(N_2,N_1),(N_3,N_2)] = (N_2,N_1),(N_3,N_2),(N_3,N_1)$

(36) $\mathbf{HP}[(C,N_1), \ldots,(C,N_k)]$
$$= (C,N_1), \ldots.(C,N_k);(N_1 \vee N_2 \vee \cdots \vee N_k) \rightarrow C.$$

Thus, given (DOG,COLLIE) and (ANIMAL,DOG), we can reconstruct (ANIMAL,COLLIE) by (35), and given (ANIMAL,DOG), (ANI-

MAL,CAT), and (ANIMAL,HORSE), and no other terms of the form (ANIMAL,\$), we infer by (36) that these three terms form a partition of the set of animals:

$$(DOG \lor CAT \lor HORSE) \to ANIMAL.$$

Analogous rules apply to the proposition structure discussed earlier. Let V be a specific verb. Then

(37) $\mathbf{HD}[(V,C),(V,N),(C,N)] = (V,C),(C,N)$

(38) $\mathbf{HD}[(V,N), \ldots ,(V,N);(N_1 \lor \cdots \lor N_k) \to C]$
$$= (V,C);(N_1 \lor \cdots \lor N_k) \to C$$

(39) $\mathbf{HP}[(V,C),(C,N)] = (V,C),(V,N),(C,N)$.

If we know (BARK, DOG), (BARK, COLLIE), and (COLLIE, DOG), rule (37) deletes the redundant (BARK, COLLIE). Rule (38) permits some economy of storage in cases like the following: suppose we have stored (BARK, COLLIE), (BARK, POODLE), and (BARK, SETTER), together with the classification rule {COLLIE $\lor$ POODLE $\lor$ SETTER}$\to$DOG: we can replace the three BARK-propositions with the single generalization (BARK,DOG). Through repeated applications of rule (39) the deletions affected by (37) and (38) can be regained: knowing that (BARK, DOG) and (DOG, COLLIE) we infer (BARK, COLLIE).

Two more rules may be considered in this context, the usefulness of which is perhaps doubtful. In order to write these rules, some kind of quantification must be introduced, which has been studiously avoided up to now. We shall treat the quantifier *some* (and all other quantifiers, too) like an adjective: for instance, *some animals bark* would be written as the verb BARK with a propositional argument, (SOME)ANIMAL.[9] Using this notation one might want to consider rules to produce sentences of the form *Some dogs are collies*, or *Some animals bark:*

(40) $\mathbf{HP}[(C,N)] = (C,N),[N,(SOME)C]$

(41) $\mathbf{HP}[(V,N),(C,N)] = (V,N),(C,N),[V,(SOME)C]$.

Two corresponding deletion rules would also be necessary that take the expressions that appear on the right hand side of (40) and (41) and

---

[9] I have not noted any problems with this procedure as yet on the semantic level. However, it entails a certain complication of the grammar. Quantifiers do not behave like adjectives syntactically, and a distinction between the two must be introduced by syntactic rules.

reverse them, because one would not want such expressions to take up permanent storage space.

While the rules concerned with the noun- and proposition-structures provide a very important part of the generative capacity of the lexicon, they must be supplemented by various other rule systems that are less global. There are many specialized fields of knowledge which require their own rule systems. I shall not discuss any of these in detail, but I can refer to a few examples of this type of system that have been worked out in some detail by others. A particularly good example is Abelson's work on *psychological implication* (Abelson & Carroll, 1965; Abelson, 1969; Abelson & Reich, 1969). For instance, the "purpose module" PURPOSE(Y,A,X) is a semantic subtheory concerned with motivation. *A does X; X causes Y; A wants Y* is a triplet of propositions that imply each other, and a rule system is described by means of which missing members of such a triplet can be filled in on the basis of other information in the memory. Another example that can be cited here is the work of various authors on *kinship systems* and the implication rules that exist within such systems. Raphael's computer program SIR explores the relation *part-whole, ownership,* and *left-to-right* spatial relations, among others (Raphael, 1968). Finally, Piaget's *formal operational schemata* come to mind in this connection: such areas of knowledge as physical equilibrium, conservation, probability, and the like require their own rule systems (Flavell, 1963).

Another rule system is needed to deal with negation. There are a number of important problems here that need to be worked out. For instance, Bierwisch (1969) has provided an interesting discussion of negation of disjunctions in a semantic system. Miller (1969) comments on the role of presuppositions in negation. For example, *It is not a collie* means merely that it may be a *retriever,* a *dachshund,* or a *mutt,* but it is presupposed that "it" is a *dog.*

Some rules introducing various definitions might also be needed. For instance, one would want a rule saying that two members of an antonymous pair are *opposite to* each other, or that two propositions are *similar* to each other. How to handle the latter problem is a topic for further work.

LEXICAL TRANSFORMATION RULES

A second type of rule that is necessary for the operation of a generative lexicon is the group of lexical transformation rules. I am unable to state these rules precisely; that is a task of linguists, but there is reason to believe that sufficiently specific rules for many lexical transformations will become available by the time anyone attempts truly large scale simulations of lexical memory.[10] The basic principle is simple to comprehend: not all words of a language need to be entered separately in memory, but words that are related to each other in certain regular ways may be combined and treated as one lexical unit. I shall discuss two examples, both instances of nominalizations: agent nouns and abstract nouns. Such nouns need not appear as separate lexical entries with their own nets of relationships with other entries, but they can be derived from propositions involving more basic terms.

In English there is a lexical transformation rule that allows agent nouns to be generated from propositions of the form (VERB, AGENT, $). Thus, (42) is derived from (43)

(42)   *Fred is a baker*
(43)   *Fred bakes.*

We need a rule in the lexicon that turns (42), whenever it appears, into the propositional expression (BAKE, *A*:FRED), and that permits substitution of the noun BAKER for (BAKE, *A*:$).

Some abstract nouns can be generated similarly in the lexicon. Rules can be specified (e.g., Bowers, 1969) which turn propositions with an adjective, or a transitive or intransitive verb as relational terms into abstract nouns. For instance,

(44)   (VIRTUOUS, ADA)

may be realized as (45) or, by means of lexical transformation rules as (46):

(45)   *Ada is virtuous*
(46)   *Ada's virtue.*

Similarly, we may obtain

(47)   (LOVE, ADA, KING OF ZEMBLA)
                       → *Ada's love for the king of Zembla*
(48)   (INEPT, KING) → *The king's ineptitude.*

It is clear that these transformations are a highly efficient means of avoiding unnecessary duplication of information in the lexicon.[11] How-

---

[10] The promise of this approach, as well as the unsettled state of affairs, is well illustrated by some recent papers of Bowers (1969) and Chomsky (1970).

[11] If abstract nouns are derived through lexical transformations from certain types of propositions, one might expect it to be more difficult to process such nouns than other nouns which are bona fide lexical entries. There is, of course, a substantial literature that shows that in many learning situations abstract nouns are harder

ever, a number of exceptions to the rule need to be provided for on an ad hoc basis. For instance, the transformation rule must be blocked in the case of *Fred ignores → Fred's ignorance*. Furthermore, not all abstract nouns have verb-or adjective counterparts in English.

In the last two sections, a memory system has been described which has a reasonably small base of stored information, plus redundancy rules and lexical transformation rules by means of which a much larger amount of information can be inferred. It is, of course, by no means necessarily so that everything that can be inferred in the system is actually inferred, rather than directly stored. We have argued that the lexicon must be generative, because otherwise the amount of information to be stored would be too huge to consider; however, inferential work must likewise be limited if a storage system is to be efficient. It makes no sense to save storage capacity on the one hand, only to overburden the system with inferential work. We have tried to show what can be inferred; certainly many propositions that are actually redundant, but which are needed frequently, are stored directly in the human memory. Exactly where the equilibrium point between storage and generation lies is one of the interesting problems that perhaps can be approached someday within a model like the present.

On Acceptability of Sentences

Given the memory structure so far described, which is a set of propositions plus some redundancy rules, we are able to define the notion of a semantically acceptable sentence.

---

to learn than concrete nouns. This result is usually attributed to the facilitating effect of concreteness per se, that is, the higher imagery value of concrete nouns. However, it is conceivable that the need to employ lexical transformation rules in the case of abstract nouns, rather than concreteness per se, may be at least in part responsible for some of the psychological results that have been reported. This is a testable hypothesis: if the need to employ lexical transformation rules plays a crucial role in processing, concrete derived nouns, such as the agent nouns described above, should be no easier to learn than abstract nouns. If lexical derivations are irrelevant for processing but imagery value alone is crucial, agent nouns should be easier to learn than abstract nouns, and in fact just as easy as nonderived nouns of comparable imagery value. It is, of course, also possible that both imagery and transformational complexity play a role. (Agent nouns have, indeed, a higher imagery value on the average than abstract nouns: the mean imagery value of 27 agent nouns that we found in the norms of Paivio, Yuille, and Madigan (1968) is 5.26, while the mean imagery value of the first 50 abstract nouns in the norms that can be derived by the rules discussed above is 3.71.)

Let $\mathcal{S} = \{S\}$ be the set of propositions actually stored in memory (at a particular moment in time). Let ϕ be the set of production rules.

Let $\mathcal{P} = \{P\}$ be the set of propositions that can be generated recursively by applying the rules ϕ to $\mathcal{S}$. More specifically, if all possible production rules are used once to operate upon the set $\mathcal{S}$ of stored propositions, a new set $\mathcal{P}_1$ is obtained, which will be written as

$$(49) \qquad \phi(\mathcal{S}) = \mathcal{P}_1.$$

$\mathcal{P}_1$ consists of $\mathcal{S}$ plus those propositions not contained in $\mathcal{S}$ that were produced by operating upon $\mathcal{S}$. We define similarly

$$(50) \qquad \begin{aligned} \phi(\mathcal{P}_1) &= \mathcal{P}_2 = \phi^2(\mathcal{S}) \\ \phi(\mathcal{P}_i) &= \mathcal{P}_{i+1} \end{aligned}$$

and $\phi^k(\mathcal{S}) = \mathcal{P}$, for $K \to \infty$. $\mathcal{P}$ may or may not be finite.

We are now in a position to define acceptability: for any proposition Q, Q is *semantically acceptable* if $Q \in \mathcal{P}$. Q is *semantically unacceptable* if $Q \notin \mathcal{P}$.

Semantically acceptable propositions differ in the degree of their acceptability:

If $Q \in \mathcal{S}$, Q is a *definitional sentence*.

If $Q \in \mathcal{P}_i$, the value of i provides a measure of acceptability. (Small values of i characterize normal sentences, large values of i unusual sentences.)

The truth value of a sentence is not a semantic but a pragmatic question. However, acceptability and truth value are related. Unacceptable sentences are always judged false. Acceptable sentences may be true or false, depending upon the state of the world.

It is important to realize that a memory system like the one described here is not logically consistent. $\mathcal{P}$ (or $\mathcal{S}$, for that matter) will contain many contradictory propositions. For instance, suppose we have the definitional sentence (EAT, A:CAT, O:MOUSE) $\in \mathcal{S}$. But suppose that we also have in $\mathcal{S}$ another proposition involving eat, (EAT,A:\$,O:\$). Many "unreasonable" sentences can be derived from the latter proposition, among them the contradiction to the definitional sentence given above: (EAT, A:MOUSE,O:CAT). (Actually the O:\$ should somehow be restricted to things small enough to be ingested—one can eat food, sand, or sweaters, but not a mountain, unless in a metaphor).

At this point the degree of acceptability measure which was introduced above comes in handy to avoid utter confusion: if two sentences are contradictory, the memory system has a way of deciding which one to keep and which one to disregard by choosing the one with the greater degree of acceptability.

Note that by defining acceptability as above, no assumptions whatever are implied about the *process* that subjects actually use to decide whether or not a sentence is acceptable. Subjects do not search randomly through memory, but employ criteria of relevance, and they may very well use strategies that involve the detection of contradictions in judging acceptability of sentences. We shall return to the question of a process model for acceptability judgments later.

METAPHORS

Many sentences that people readily understand will be judged unacceptable by the criteria just described. One such class of sentences would be metaphors. Supplementary rules which I shall call analogy rules are necessars to provide the system with the capability to understand and produce metaphors. I shall describe some rather simple rules operating on the lexical structure that permit production and understanding of a certain type of metaphor. No claim is made that these rules are the only ones needed to deal with metaphorical expressions, but the type of constructions that I am concerned with here certainly represents an important case.

Suppose we are given the sentence *The rain drums on the shelter.* The sentence is unacceptable by the rules so far described because the lexicon will inform us the DRUM requires an agent-noun. How do we understand this sentence? We know, presumably, that *rain* may *fall* on a *shelter,* and that in doing so it produces a hollow sound, like someone beating a drum. On the basis of this likeness, the verb *drum* is somehow imported into the original sentence where it replaces *fall* (or whatever the original verb was—there is no need to be specific about that). Thus the meaning of *The rain drums on the shelter* is something like *The rain falls on the shelter and this produces a hollow sound, like someone beating a drum.*

It turns out that if the intuitive argument that underlies the explanation just given is stated more fully and formally, we obtain a rather powerful set of "analogy rules."

Some new notation is convenient at this point. When the symbol @ is used as an argument of a proposition, it refers to the immediately preceding proposition, whatever that was. The $-sign will be used again to indicate arguments that are unspecified except for their case. And if a proposition is identical to one written immediately above it, we shall use the conventional (-"-).

Analogy Rules: Production

Suppose we have two propositions of the form

$$Q = (R,A,B) \wedge (S,@,D)$$

where R and S are relational terms, and A, B, C, D arguments. (Writing propositions in this way, i.e., with exactly two arguments, is merely a notational convenience: B and D may sometimes be ϕ, or they may represent a whole string of arguments.)

A memory search is made for the complex proposition that is related to Q in the sense that the second part of it is identical with the second part of Q, that is,

$$(\$,\$,\$) \wedge (S,@,D).$$

Let Q' be such a proposition:

$$Q' = (T,E,F) \wedge (S,@,D).$$

Q and Q' may be combined to form the new proposition.

$$P^* = (\text{LIKE}, Q,Q').$$

Compression rules are applied to P^* to form the metaphorical expression P. The compression rules will be stated separately because they are surface structure rules. The meaning of a metaphorical expression, that is, its base structure representation, is P^*, not P, the actual metaphor.

The production rules show how the semantically unacceptable, metaphorical sentence P can be generated. Acceptance rules show how such sentences can be "understood," that is, how the corresponding base representation P^* can be calculated from P.

Compression Rules[12]

Given a complex proposition P^* there are some fairly simple rules that transform P^* into P, from which the actual surface structure is then derived by the usual grammatical processes.

---

[12] Compression seems to be a very general semantic phenomenon and is by no means restricted to *like*-sentences. For instance, compression occurs sometimes with complex sentences with the relator *because*: *The heavy damp weight of the forest* seems to be derived by compression from (BECAUSE,(HEAVY, WEIGHT OF FOREST),(DAMP,FOREST)) analogous to *C2*, except that the relator from the first expression is not deleted and the second term is simply added to it.

There is no general principle here, however. Consider the following *because*-con-

Both Q and Q' are reduced by deleting the second (common) proposition, as well as all dummy variables indicated by the $-sign.

Further compression depends upon the nature of Q and Q'. Two cases arise, depending upon whether the verbs in Q and Q' are identical or different.

Case (i): identical verbs:

$$Q = (R,A,B)$$
$$Q' = (R,D,E).$$

Thus,

$$P^* = (\text{LIKE}, (R,A,B),(R,D,E))$$

and *Compression Rule C1* transforms P^* into

$$P = (\text{LIKE}, (R,A,B),(D,E)).$$

Case (ii): different verbs:

$$Q = (R,A,B)$$
$$Q' = (T,D,E).$$

Therefore,

$$P^* = (\text{LIKE}, (R,A,B),(T,D,E))$$

and *Compression Rule C2* yields

$$P = (\text{LIKE}, (T,A,B),(D,E)).$$

A further (optional) *Compression Rule C3* drops the explicit comparison:

$$P = (T,A,B).$$

---

structions which, when compressed by rules analogous to $C1$–$C4$, yield ungrammatical sentences:

  (i) (BECAUSE,(VACANT,HOUSE),(MOVED,OWNERS)) yields
       The moved-owners-vacant house
  (ii) (BECAUSE,(VACANT,HOUSE),(FOR SALE,HOUSE)) yields
       The for-sale-vacant house.

That compression is a surface structure phenomenon rather than a base structure phenomenon is indicated by its language specific character (base structures and rules are presumably universal): The German sentence corresponding to the last example is quite well formed:

Das zum Verkauf leerstehende Haus.

Instances of compression involving quite different grammatical constructions are not hard to find. Take for instance *marble brow*, which is derived from *Brow as white as marble*, or *Tom has a pistol, and Dick a sword* which was discussed by Ross (1970) as an instance of "gapping."

In working with various examples the following supplementary principle has been observed:

Compression Rule C4: like is dropped before a preposition:

(LIKE, $(R,A,B),C$) is transformed to (R,A,B,C)
if C is of the form Prep + Noun.

Analogy Rules: Acceptance

Because of the nature of the compression rules, three different types of inputs must be considered:

(i) $P = ($LIKE$, (R,A,B),(E,F))$, where (R,A,B) by itself is acceptable, but P is unacceptable;
(ii) $P = (T,A,B)$, where (T,A,B) is unacceptable, and similarly
(iii) $P = ($LIKE$, (T,A,B),(E,F))$.

Given this kind of input, memory is searched for two complex propositions Q and Q' which employ, in an acceptable manner, the arguments and relational terms that appear in P and which share a common implication:

$$\begin{aligned}
\text{(i)} \quad & Q = (R,A,B) \wedge (\$,@,\$) \\
& Q' = (\$,E,F) \wedge (-''-) \\
\text{(ii)} \quad & Q = (\$,A,B) \wedge (\$,@,\$) \\
& Q' = (T,\$) \wedge (-''-) \\
\text{(iii)} \quad & Q = (\$,A,B) \wedge (\$,@,\$) \\
& Q' = (T,E,F) \wedge (-''-).
\end{aligned}$$

If the search is successful, we have for all three cases

$$\begin{aligned}
Q &= (R,A,B) \wedge (S,@,D) \\
Q' &= (T,E,F) \wedge (S,@,D).
\end{aligned}$$

P is understood by assigning it the acceptable base structure representation P^*:

$$P^* = (\text{LIKE}, Q, Q').$$

Note that for both the production and acceptance rules, the only lexical items that were used in the first components of both Q and Q' are items actually employed in P. Other terms that need to be introduced in order to form acceptable propositions are indicated merely by their case markers (actually, only the $\$$-sign is used here—we have neglected case markers in order to simplify the exposition). The only new lexical items that have been used appear in the second component of Q and Q': they are needed to explicate the common implication of the two sentences which are to be related by *like*.

Two examples will be given to illustrate the operation of the analogy rules.

(51)   *The fog enveloped the bridge like a moist blanket.*

The part of the sentence, *The fog enveloped the bridge,* is well formed; all that is needed is to find a basis for the comparison with a moist blanket. This is provided by the fact that whatever is enveloped by a moist blanket or fog gets wet. Thus we have

Q = (ENVELOP, FOG, BRIDGE) $\wedge$ (CAUSE,@,WETNESS)
Q' = (ENVELOPE,(MOIST)BLANKET, 0:$)
$\wedge$ (CAUSE,@,WETNESS)

which may be combined to form

P^* = (LIKE,(ENVELOP,FOG,BRIDGE),
(ENVELOP,(MOIST)BLANKET,$)).

By $C1$ this is compressed into P, which is the propositional representation of the original sentence:

P = (LIKE,(ENVELOP,FOG,BRIDGE),((MOIST)BLANKET)).

(52)   *The fog comes on little cat's feet.*

For clarity, case categories will be indicated this time:

Q = ($,$O$:FOG) $\wedge$ (NOISELESS,P:@)
Q' = (COME, A:$ I:ON LITTLE CAT'S FEET)
$\wedge$ (NOISELESS,P:@).

The $ in Q might refer to MOVE; the one in Q' presumably stands for CAT.

P^* = (LIKE,($,FOG),(COME,$,ON LITTLE CAT'S FEET))

which is transformed by $C2$ and $C4$ into

P = (COME,FOG,ON LITTLE CAT'S FEET).

Note that we could have applied $C2$ and $C3$ instead, which would have produced

P' = (COME,FOG).

A Sample Lexical Entry

To conclude this section, we shall present a brief example of how the lexical entry for the verb *bake* might be constructed. The purpose of this example is to show how the various submechanisms function together that were discussed above in isolation. The description list for *bake* will be given first (for convenience of reference only one proposition will be written on each line):

1. ((BAKE,A:HUMAN,O:OBJECT = α,
   L:IN OVEN $\vee$ SUN) = β) $\wedge$
2. (IMPLIES, β, (HEATED,O:α, I:DRY HEAT) $\wedge$
3. (HARDEN,O:α,I:β) $\wedge$
4. (DRY,O:α,I:β) $\wedge$
5. ((γ_1 $\vee$ γ_2 $\vee$ γ_3 $\vee$ γ_4) $\rightarrow$ β) $\wedge$
6. ((BAKE,A:BAKER,O:BREAD $\vee$ CAKE,L:IN OVEN) = γ_1) $\wedge$
7. ((BAKE,A:COOK,O:FOOD,L:IN OVEN) = γ_2) $\wedge$
8. ((BAKE,A:WORKER,O:BRICKS,L:IN OVEN $\vee$ SUN) = γ_3)
9. ((BAKE,A:POTTER,O:CERAMICS,L:IN OVEN) = γ_4)

The four "normal" uses of *bake* are listed in lines 6–9; they specify more or less precisely who bakes what. In the fifth line, these normal forms are subordinated to quite a general proposition; that permits anyone human to bake any object whatsoever. This expression is shown in line 1. In lines 2–4 are listed some general consequences and implications of *bake*, such as that the object which is being baked is heated by dry heat, and is thereby hardened and dried out.

Since none of the arguments in the propositions above are marked as required, all possible deletions are permissible, and we obtain such sentences as

Mother is baking a cake in the oven
Mother is baking the cake
The cake bakes in the oven
Mother bakes (on Tuesdays)
Mother is baking in the oven (perhaps in response to *Who is using the oven?*)

The sentences above obviously have a high degree of acceptability. Through the use of redundancy rules, many sentences of lower degrees of acceptability may be generated. *The desert bakes in the sun* is perfectly acceptable, but so are *The icefield bakes in the sun*, or *The surgeon bakes daffodils in the oven*. A semantic system by itself has no way of telling that only the first one is likely to be true. Examples of unacceptable sentences are *The cook bakes love*, or *The cat bakes meringue tarts*. On the other hand, we understand by analogy what is meant with *A half-baked idea:* the idea was only half done, like a half-baked cake, resulting in an unpalatable product.

A conventional dictionary will show at least half a dozen different meanings for *bake*, depending upon what is baked, whether the verb is transitive or intransitive, etc. We have only one meaning, but several "normal" contexts are distinguished (and quite a number of abnormal uses are permitted), and the intransitive form of the verb is simply obtained by deleting the agent from the complete form.[13]

Psychological Process Models

After having outlined a general model for the structure of lexical memory one can approach the task of studying specific psychological processes within the structural framework. Only by considering specific process models, designed for specific experimental tasks, can one hope to tie the general scheme discussed above to experimental data. To do so, however, seems absolutely necessary: linguistic intuition is sufficient to suggest what problems need to be studied in the first place, and it may even help us to formulate some reasonable hypotheses about these problems. But in order to test these hypotheses in scientifically acceptable ways it is imperative to go beyond one's intuitions and to bring to bear on the problem the standard methodology of experimental psychology.

As yet, this area of research is quite underdeveloped. Even moderately successful experimental paradigms are few and far between. In part this is so, I believe, because in order to ask intelligent experimental questions one must first develop a suitable conceptual framework—the sort of thing I have been trying to do in the first four sections of this paper. However, there are some experimental studies of semantic structure that have yielded interesting results. I shall mention only a few

[13] It is interesting to compare our sample lexical entry with the examples Fillmore provided at the end of his paper (Fillmore, 1969). Fillmore indicates separately case, e.g., (*A*), presupposition, e.g., *A* must be HUMAN, and meaning, e.g., the object is heated by dry heat. Here some presuppositions are implied by the way propositions are written, e.g., (BAKE, *A*: HUMAN), etc., while others, as well as Fillmore's "meaning," are separately listed (lines 2–4 in the example). Some grammatical information that Fillmore lists has been omitted in the present example (e.g., what the appropriate prepositions are, and what normally becomes the sentence subject and object). This kind of information must be added to our lexicon before it can serve as a satisfactory component of a grammar. Other information that Fillmore lists with each entry can be derived in the present system from the organization of propositions. For instance, Fillmore lists such semantic features of verbs as ±Momentary ("whether or not the verb can be used, in the affirmative, to refer to an event that takes place at a specific point in time"). Rules like equation (31) are used to classify verbs for such purposes in the present system. Thus, there is no need to include this information with each lexical entry.

outstanding examples without attempting to review this work systematically. A number of scaling studies (e.g., Miller, 1969) have clearly shown that there is indeed structure in the lexical system, and in some cases have indicated something about the nature of this structure, especially when the set of scaled words was small and homogeneous (e.g., the animal terms of Henley, 1969). Somewhat more indirect experimental techniques have been successfully used to explore the organization of the lexical system. Luria and Vinogradova (1959) employed the habituation of the orienting reflex as a tool to make inferences about lexical organization. Several other studies approached this problem through the study of reaction times: subjects were given various statements, usually concerned with set inclusion, and were asked to tell as fast as possible whether or not the statement was true (e.g., Landauer & Freedman, 1968; Collins & Quillian, 1969; Myers, 1970).

The process models in these studies are relatively simple. If the information structure described above is to be used as a basis for more complex cognitive operations, some means must be provided to supplement it in various ways. For instance, if a person judges the credibility of statements, one must assume that he is able to add evaluation tags to these statements and that there exists some mechanism for changing these tags (e.g., Abelson & Carroll, 1965). In recognition and recall learning Kintsch (1970) found it necessary to introduce familiarity tags, by means of which the subject can keep track of which words he has seen and processed. The activation tags of Quillian (1967) and Colby et al. (1969a, b) serve a similar purpose in a different situation: they permit the subject to determine whether or not he has already searched a particular portion of the system in a question-answering situation. Becker (1969), on the other hand, uses such a mechanism quite differently: he is concerned with pragmatic as well as semantic problems, and in trying to represent situations through a set of propositions he finds it necessary to give each proposition a weight that indicates the relevance of that proposition to the situation under consideration. What all theses cases have in common is that some *meta-information* is appended to an existing information network which permits this network to be used in a task-specific way.

There are numerous problems here for further research. However, any kind of systematic approach to process models in this area seems premature at this time. The degrees of freedom are simply too large for the theorist: given that there is no structural model that is generally accepted among students of memory (given, indeed, that until quite recently even serious proposals were lacking), and given the meagre data base, all that one can hope for are some very tentative explorations of process models and a few hard experimental results to go by. I shall describe three problems that I have worked on recently, involving either some new experimental data, process models, or both.

CASE STRUCTURE OF SENTENCES

It would be most desirable to obtan some evidence concerning the status of propositions as basic lexical elements. Clearly this is a central assumption of the model, and one that is not particularly well supported by experimental data. A study by Fodor, Garrett, and Bever (1968) presents some experimental support for the idea that lexical complexity of words plays a role in processing sentences, which is quite in agreement with the present hypothesis, though not directly relevant to it. Verbs differ in the number of grammatical structures in which they may be inserted. Fodor *et al.* found that it was less difficult for subjects to paraphrase sentences, or to solve anagrams containing verbs that could be used in only one way, than verbs that could be used in more than one way.

We have performed an experiment in order to obtain more direct evidence for the psychological reality of lexical expressions. Since we cannot ask subjects for these expressions directly—people do not talk in base structures—we did the next best thing: we gave subjects simple sentences and asked them to tell us if there is some information that these sentences convey to them that is not explicitly stated. If, for instance, subjects have in their memory something like the example presented earlier (A Sample Lexical Entry, p. 284) for the word BAKE, they should know that, given the sentence *The cake bakes*, there must be an agent, an oven or the like, and that the cake is heated and dried out by baking. Such an experimental task should be very natural. It is not necessary to explain to the subjects anything about base structures or lexical entries at all.

We selected 18 test sentences in an arbitrary and unsystematic way: the only purpose of the experiment was to show that lexical expressions as postulated by the present model are psychologically real. Two types of sentences were selected: fourteen sentences were incomplete in the sense that cases that could and often would be part of these sentences were omitted; in addition, many of these sentences had other implications that could be expected to be part of a lexical entry (such as was the case for the cake-baking example just mentioned). The remaining four sentences were different in that, judging by my intuition, no additional cases could be part of these sentences, but for each sentence there were some more or less specific semantic implications.

Subjects were given detailed printed instructions.[14] The test sentences were printed in random order on pages which were stapled to the instructions. Subjects wrote their responses next to each sentence. No time limit was imposed, and no information was given beyond the printed instructions. Twenty-seven students and staff members of the University of Colorado participated in the experiment.

Table 2 shows the 18 test sentences and summarizes the experimental results. All responses given by at least 20 percent of the subjects are shown, together with the frequency of each response. The first column shows responses that could be classified as "missing cases." For each case category the most common specific response is shown. For instance, 23 subjects are listed as having responded with *knife* to the test sentence *Seymour carves the turkey.* Actually, not all of these wrote down the word *knife;* some subjects made more general responses, such as *a sharp cutting instrument,* which clearly belongs to the same case category as *knife.* In the second column semantic implications are listed. Again, what is shown may in some cases be a paraphrase of what subjects actually said. The number of responses that occurred with a frequency of less than 20% is indicated in the last column of Table 2. Fifteen percent of all responses fell into this category. The mean number of common responses per sentence was 3.2, with a range from 2 to 4. The mean number of infrequent responses was 4.4, with a range from 0 to 12.

No response occurred with 100% frequency; however, for every sentence one or more dominating response existed, many of which could be classified as missing cases. This observation indicates that the propositional expressions that were postulated in the present model are indeed effective functional units in memory. Substantial agreement among subjects also existed as far as the semantic implications of the test sentences were concerned. However, the agreement here was somewhat less than

---

[14] The following instructions were given to subjects: "Sentences sometimes imply more information than is overtly stated. A reader often can infer unambiguously and with complete certainty that some things, events, or conditions are expressed by a sentence, although they are not explicitly referred to. Thus, assuming only normal use of language *John marries* clearly implies that there was some human female that John married. On the other hand, it does *not* imply such things as that the wedding was in a church, or that the bride wore a white gown—these things may or may not be the case when *John marries,* but they are not specifically implied by the sentence. On the succeeding pages there are 18 sentences. Please study each sentence and write next to it anything that you are sure that the sentence implies. Be as specific as possible (e.g., don't write that *John marries* implies "someone"—say that the someone must be a female!), but do not mention things that are merely possible or probable—only cases of clear implications!"

TABLE 2
Test Sentences and the Responses of 27 Subjects

Sentence	Case responses	Semantic implications	Number of infrequent responses
The secretary types.	typewriter (I):21 on paper (L):9 verbal text (O):8	secretary is skilled:6	3
Seymour carves the turkey.	knife (I):23	turkey is cooked:6	5
The hiker doused the campfire.	water (I):23	fire put out:12 hiker camps outdoors:9	5
Peter was shot.	gun (I):24 bullet (I):10 someone (A):10	Peter was wounded:13	0
Fred was murdered.	someone (A):26	Fred is dead:14 no accident, intent:11	3
Gladys was blackmailed.	someone (A):25	guilty secret:23 pay-off:14 to keep quiet:11	4
The book was printed.	press (I):13 by someone (A):6	someone wrote book:8 someone published it:8	8
The house was sold.	buyer (E):22 seller (A):17	money transaction:11 house for sale:6	2
The cake bakes.	in oven (L):22 someone (A):6	cake is heated:11	5
It was impassable.	barrier, route (O):21	failure to go on:9	2
John investigates.	something (O):25	does not know something:15	3
Frances inquires.	something (O):22 from someone (E):16	does not know something:12	1

Mary persuades.	someone (E):25 (to do) something (P):13	Mary influences someone:10	5
		Mary has reason to:7	10
Cecil continued eating.	food (O):15	Cecil had been eating before:17	
		Cecil was hungry:9	12
The lightbulb glows.		electricity:14 turned on:12 emits light:11	4
It rains.		wet:12 clouds:9 water:9 falling:8	
Leo suffocated.		lack of air:20 Leo is dead:17 some obstruction as cause:6	2
The king died.		was alive before:10 successor:6	5

that for the case responses (most of the infrequent responses not listed in Table 2 belonged to that category). Presumably individual differences play a larger role here than for case responses. Nevertheless, the mere fact that all subjects spontaneously mentioned semantic implications among their responses testifies to their importance as lexical components.

An inspection of Table 2 shows that sometimes sentences which are formally rather similar may give rise to quite different response distributions. In part this may have been caused by a response strategy that was observed in several subjects which tended to distort the data: some subjects gave only one response per sentence, perhaps because of laziness, perhaps because they misunderstood the instructions. Since no postexperimental interviews could be given, we cannot be sure whether this was indeed a response strategy, or whether these subjects simply could not see any further implications. However, such a strategy might explain some curious results: e.g., almost everyone said that *Fred was murdered* implies an agent, but only 10 subjects reported that an agent was implied in *Peter was shot;* however, the latter sentence produced two very strong instrument responses (*gun* and *bullet*), and subjects who gave an instrument response may have simply neglected to give a second response.

I conclude from this experiment that lexical memory contains the information postulated by the present model,[15] in particular information about the arguments that verbs normally take. This may be as general as the case of an argument, *someone shot Peter,* but it may also be quite specific, *the secretary types on a typewriter,* or something at an intermediate level of generality, like the *food* that *Cecil continued to eat.* In addition to the case structure of verbs, memory apparently also contains information about the semantic implications of a word which specify and clarify the conditions under which it may be used.

LATENCY OF JUDGMENTS OF SEMANTIC ACCEPTABILITY

If subjects are given a simple subject-predicate sentence and are asked whether the sentence is true or false their response latencies permit some interesting inferences about the way memory is organized and decisions

---

[15] No claim is made that our data support the specific assumptions of the model about how information is stored; it merely shows that certain kinds of information are indeed part of the knowledge about words that naive subjects possess. The present model employs one possible way to represent that information. However, alternative representations are by no means ruled out by these results. More specifically, Chomsky's (1965) "strict subcategorization rules" could do the work assigned here to case structures, while his "selection restrictions" correspond to our semantic implications, as was pointed out by Fillmore (1969).

are made. For instance, if the semantic distance is increased between the subject and the predicate nominal in a sentence, reaction times increase. Thus, it takes more time to process *A canary is an animal* than *A canary is a bird* (e.g., Collins & Quillian, 1969).

We have performed an experiment (Kintsch, Crothers, & Berman, 1970) that applies the reaction time method to sentence material in which semantic distance is varied in a different way than by the number of steps in the noun-hierarchy. For true sentences we distinguish between definitional sentences and contingently true sentences; for false sentences we distinguish between contradictory sentences and nonsense sentences. Furthermore, we varied the syntactic form of the test sentences. Three kinds of predicates were used: copula-noun, copula-adjective, and verb.

Definitional sentences are sentences that might be stored as parts of the description list of the sentence subject. For instance, *The shark is a fish*, or *The shark swims* is part of the description list for the lexical entry *shark*, though the latter could be derived from knowing that sharks are fish, and fish swim. However, as was pointed out earlier, frequently used information is probably stored directly, rather than generated upon demand in order to avoid excessive inferential work. Contingently true sentences are sentences that may be true under certain conditions, but where the predicate is in no way characteristic of the subject, e.g., *The shark escapes*. In terms of the model, judging the acceptability of such sentences would require repeated applications of inference rules. The distinction that was made between nonsense sentences and contradictory sentences is arbitrary, but it does preserve an intuitively important principle: the "semantic distance" between subject and predicate is clearly greater in the former case. Specifically, we called a sentence contradictory if something appropriate for an animate subject was predicated for a subject that was in fact animate, but the particular predicate was inappropriate for the particular subject: e.g., *The shark growls* or *The shark is a frog*. Similarly, we constructed contradictory sentences with inanimate subjects. For nonsense sentences, on the other hand, we combined an animate subject with a predicate that requires inanimate subjects, and vice versa. *The shark ticks* and *The shark is vacant* are examples of nonsense sentences used.

For a detailed description of the learning materials, the procedure, and the experimental results, the reader is referred to the original report. Here I shall merely present a brief summary. Each subject was given 132 sentences. Subjects were asked to respond true or false as fast as possible but to avoid errors. Three experiments were performed, differing in the way the sentences were presented; in Experiment I all sentences were shown with the indefinite article *a: A shark swims;* in Experiment

II the definite article *the* was used: *The shark swims;* and in Experiment III only the two words SHARK and SWIM were shown, one above the other, and subjects were instructed as to the kind of sentences that they could make from these words. This procedure was used to control for the number of words in the sentence—in the first two experiments the three syntactic form classes differed in terms of the number of words. Only words of medium Thorndike-Lorge frequency were used in constructing the test sentences.

The first noteworthy result concerns syntactic form class: in none of the experiments was there a systematic difference between form classes! This finding came as somewhat of a surprise. The reader will remember that in the lexical model presented above much was made of the difference between propositions with a relation word as predicate and propositions with a noun as predicate (see also Footnote 8). The noun hierarchy described earlier plays quite a central role in the model, in the sense that much of the general propositional structure depends upon argument relations, that is, the noun hierarchy. Thus, I had vaguely suspected that nominal predicates might be a little more accessible in memory than other types of propositions. Three negative experiments have convinced me that reaction times to these sentences are no different than reaction times to verb or adjective sentences, if semantic distance as well as word frequencies are controlled.

Reaction times as a function of the acceptability of the test sentences and semantic distance are shown in Figure 1. Disregard, for a moment, the results of Experiment I. For the other two studies the data are entirely consistent. Not surprisingly, it took much longer to respond in Experiment III, but the pattern of results was the same as in Experiment II. Acceptable sentences are faster than unacceptable sentences, but for both kinds of sentences semantic distance plays a role; if subject and predicate are strongly related in an acceptable sentence, reaction times are faster (definitional sentences) than if the relationship is less close (contingent sentences); for unacceptable sentences this relationship is reversed: when subject and predicate have almost nothing to do with each other (nonsense sentences) reaction times are faster than when they are relatively closely related (contradictory sentences). For incorrect responses there was no systematic effect of semantic distance, but, just as for correct responses, acceptable sentences were processed faster than unacceptable sentences. The proportion of incorrect responses is shown with each point in Figure 1. Most errors were made for contingently true sentences. Now consider Experiment I. Apparently, using the indefinite article *a* resulted in an especially high error rate for acceptable sentences, and in a reduction of latencies for unacceptable sentences.

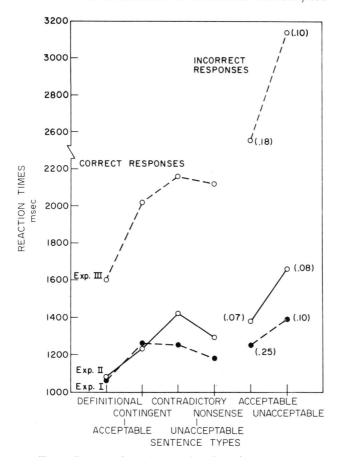

Fig. 1. Response latencies as a function of sentence types.

What kind of model could account for this pattern of results? The first question that we need to consider in building a processing model is what operations are to be included. One of the basic assumptions of the structural model is that given any word W the description list L_W which corresponds to that word in the lexicon is immediately accessible. In addition, we obviously must assume that there exist operations which correspond to the various inference rules that have been discussed. Formally these are rewriting operations. Finally, we need an operation that tells us whether two propositions are identical or not. This is the pattern matching operation. Rewriting and pattern matching may be combined, as, for instance, in determining noun-hierarchy relatedness. Suppose A and B are nouns, and the question is whether A precedes B, $A < B$. For concreteness, let us consider the acceptability of *Collie is an animal.* Suppose (ANIMAL,COLLIE) does not match any proposition in L_{COLLIE}. Also suppose that (DOG,COLLIE) $\in L_{\text{COLLIE}}$. (ANIMAL,DOG). A redundancy rule will let us rewrite the pair of propositions (ANIMAL,DOG), (DOG,COLLIE) as itself plus (ANIMAL,COLLIE). A pattern match will now be successful, and *The collie is an animal* can be accepted. Note that an unacceptable nominal proposition would require considerably more processing but it too would

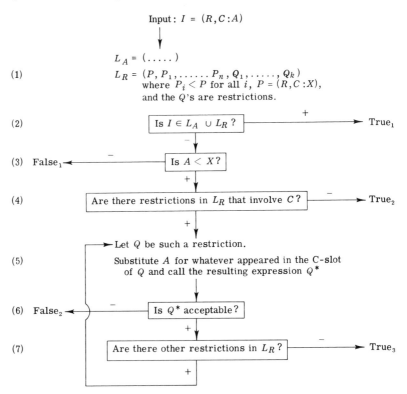

Fig. 2. A processing model for acceptability judgments of simple subject-predicate sentences.

soon come to an end when no more higher order propositions can be generated from (DOG,COLLIE).

Given the access, rewriting, and pattern matching operations described above, and the general structural model, we can construct a simple processing model that will account for the results of Figure 1. The model is outlined in Figure 2. The input is a sentence consisting of a relation R and an argument A which belongs to the case class C. (A corresponding model for nominal propositions presents no additional problems.) Both

R and A are lexical items and hence they have description lists L_A and L_R (1). The first thing a subject does in the model is to see whether the input sentence appears on either one of the description lists (2). If yes, a "true" response occurs, and we assume that these responses have latencies distributed according to a latency distribution $True_1$ which has mean T_1. If the test sentence cannot be located in this manner, the most superordinate proposition involving the relation R is determined from L_R. Suppose this proposition has an argument $C{:}X$, that is, some word X in the same case class as A, the argument from the test sentence. We now ask whether A precedes X (3). If no, the sentence is judged false, with latency distribution $False_1$. As explained above, negative judgments may be quite time consuming here. If X dominates A, we ask (4) whether there are any restriction in the description list L_R that specify certain implications, consequences, causes, etc. of R-propositions (e.g., in lines 2–4 in the sample lexical entry p. 285, are some restrictions on "bake"). If there are no restrictions, "true" responses occur (with latencies $True_2$); if there are restrictions it must be determined whether A is acceptable as an argument in these restrictions (5). Thus, one or more acceptability tests may be embedded in the overall task (6). If any of these acceptability tests are negative, false-responses occur ($False_2$); if all are positive, the sentence will be judged true ($True_3$). From Figure 2 and the comments made earlier about $False_2$ latencies it follows that the mean latencies must be ordered $T_1 < T_2 < F_1 \ll F_2 < T_3$.

Two further assumptions are needed to account for errors in the present model. We assume, first, that errors are slow guesses; if the processing goes beyond some temporal limit, the subject may quit (with some probability) and guess randomly. Thus, error frequencies are made directly dependent upon the latency distributions. Second, we assume, for reasons that will become apparent below, that when a subject locates restrictions at (4) he sometimes fails to process these restrictions and simply answers "false." The latencies of these incorrect responses will be like those of $True_2$.

Since we cannot be sure that all definitional sentences in the present experiment were actually stored in memory (some of our definitional sentences may require inferences, at least for some subjects), the latencies of the definitional sentences are a mixture of $True_1$ and $True_2$. The latencies of contingently true sentences are a mixture of $True_3$ and $True_4$. The latencies of contradictory sentences must be from $False_2$. Nonsense sentences, on the other hand, may be rejected earlier in some cases, but in others they would be processed just like contradictory sentences; hence, their latencies must be a mixture of $False_1$ and $False_2$. Given these response compositions, the rankings of the four sentence types for both errors and latencies shown in Table 3 follows immediately. Clearly $(T_1 + T_2)$ will be smallest. $(T_2 + T_3)$ comes next because there are relatively more T_2's than T_3's (many of the latter will be errors!). The latencies for unacceptable sentences follow from $F_1 < F_2$. Most errors should occur with T_3 and, hence, the highest error frequency is predicted for the contingent sentences; F_2 should also lead to relatively many errors, while F_1, T_1 and T_2 produce the fewest errors.

Incorrect responses for unacceptable guesses are always slow guesses. Hence, their latencies come from the tails of False$_1$ and False$_2$, and should be very large. Incorrect responses for acceptable sentences are in part slow guesses, but in part they occur because subjects give up and say "false" when they find restrictions at Step (4). The latter re-

TABLE 3

Predicted Rank Ordering of Latencies and Error Frequencies for Four Sentence Types

Sentence type	Responses	Latency rank	Error rank
Definitional	T_1 and T_2	1	4
Contingent	T_2 and T_3	2	1
Contradictory	F_2	4	2
Nonsense	F_1 and F_2	3	3

sponses have a latency comparable to True$_2$, so that the overall latency of incorrect responses for acceptable sentences should be considerably smaller than that for unacceptable sentences. The assumption that subjects sometimes give up when they find restrictions also accounts for the results of Experiment I: in that experiment the indefinite article a was used with all sentences, and it seems that subjects interpreted this as *all;* hence, when finding a restriction they responded "false," which led to a very high error rate for contingently true sentences and to rather fast latencies for unacceptable sentences.

The model described here is entirely ad hoc. However, it does illustrate how a process model can be built upon the structural model that was suggested earlier, and, more importantly, what kind of processes need to be considered. Undoubtedly the model will have to be changed in some way before it can fit the data from other experiments. In fact, there is no reason to suppose that given a different experimental situation, subjects employ the same search and decision strategies. However, the basic operations as well as the underlying structure would presumably remain constant across experimental situations. Subjects may, of course, use entirely different strategies in evaluating sentences than the ones described here, for example, strategies that involve the construction of images. As was pointed out in the beginning of this chapter, the failure to consider such possibilities should not be misconstrued as a denial of their importance, but is simply a consequence of my concentration upon purely semantic problems.

A MODEL FOR FREE RECALL

I have suggested earlier (Kintsch, 1970) a model for free recall learning that is based upon the idea that subjects use their knowledge about words and word relationships in this learning task. The data that this model was supposed to account for are the generally observed findings that well organized word lists are easier to recall than unstructured lists, and that related words tend to cluster in recall. I shall briefly review this model here and discuss how the somewhat changed conception of the memory structure that has been presented in the present paper affects the earlier formulation.

The model is based upon the assumption that free recall involves implicit retrieval plus recognition of the learning items. Recognition is thought to be a matter of tagging to be learned items with "familiarity tags" and detecting these tags in the presence of noise. We assume that whenever a word is presented, all information that gets into short-term code for the word ($\mathbf{P}$) will receive a familiarity value increment, as memory (the working memory) is tagged. Thus the phonetic-articulatory well as the members of the corresponding semantic description list. However, since the capacity of short-term memory is limited, not all propositions in a description list may be entered in short-term memory. We assume that propositions which have already been tagged are selected with priority. If a word is not actually presented but enters the working memory in the course of some processing operation, only semantic information is tagged, but not the corresponding $\mathbf{P}$-vector.

A dual storage mechanism is assumed for free-recall learning. Subjects may store words in a rote manner, that is as a new lexical item, called LIST I, of the form

$$(W_1 \cup W_2 \cup \cdots \cup W_n) \rightarrow \text{LIST I},$$

where W_1, W_2, . . . are the to-be-learned words. We also assume that the likelihood that a given word is stored successfully in this way is relatively low.[16] Therefore, subjects may resort to a secondary mech-

---

[16] In order to establish new lexical items as permanent entries, more seems to be required than a few learning trials, but it is not clear exactly what are the necessary conditions for consolidation.

anism that is fast and relatively easy. This consists in the construction of a retrieval scheme through tagging propositions in the description lists of to be learned items that relate these words to each other. Specifically, we assume that whenever a word W_1 is presented, the phonetic features employed in perception plus a sample from L_{W_i}, the description list of word W_i, are entered into short-term memory (and automatically tagged). With some small probability, W_i is rote-learned as explained above. Always, however, the words in short-term memory are scanned and an attempt is made to find (or generate) an acceptable proposition that relates these words. If such a proposition is found, it is added to the description lists of each item involved (and automatically tagged). For instance, suppose GIRL has just been presented, and APPLE is already in short-term memory. A search is made for ($,GIRL,APPLE), which may yield, for instance, (EAT,A:GIRL,O:AP-PLE). This proposition is tagged and included in both L_{GIRL} and L_{APPLE}.[17] If items are presented at a rapid rate this processing may not be completed; in the usual free recall experiment the subject responds to each item as it appears, and therefore processing of previous items will frequently be interrupted unless subjects are given unlimited time.

When subjects are asked to recall the words of a list, the model assumes that they first recall items still in short-term memory and those items that have been successfully stored as parts of LIST I. Of the words already recalled, one is selected at random, and the propositions of its description list are inspected; if none of them have unusually high familiarity tags, another word is selected, or recall is terminated. If a tagged proposition is detected, the words involved in that proposition are scanned. If they are tagged, a recall output occurs. If not, their description lists are inspected for the presence of familiarity tags. This search process continues until some stopping criterion is reached.

Roland Miller, a graduate student at the University of Colorado, has performed a simulation of this recall model with a SNOBOL program. This work was mainly intended to put my informal description of the process into a precise form and to make explicit all properties of the model. Miller has used an artificial memory net of 100 words with rich interconnections in 8 separate clusters. Phonetic features of the words were ignored. Each word was represented as a list of other words and familiarity tags, consisting in part of permanent entries (the semantic memory), and in part of temporary entries which were generated during the recall learning and erased at the end of each experiment. Familiarity

---

[17] Propositions generated in this manner will not clutter up long-term memory forever; deletion rules will sooner or later be used to erase no longer needed redundant propositions from storage.

tags were all set to 0 and only unit increments were made. Several parameters of the model were arbitrarily defined; The size of short-term memory was set to 4. The probability of rote learning was allowed to be .20. The construction of a retrieval scheme was limited by the requirement that only one item pair can be worked on per second of study time. Retrieval processes were controlled by setting arbitrary limits on all recycling loops. However, although much detail and several book-keeping procedures had to be added to the verbal description of the model given in Kintsch (1970), the program is identical with the verbal description when both are expressed as flowcharts.

The program works in the sense that it stores and retrieves items with the mechanisms specified. We have simulated the learning and recall of 10-item and 20-item lists and obtained a complete printout of all the operations involved in the storage and retrieval of each list. Up to now, we have shown that we are able to reproduce the appropriate form of the middle and end portions of the serial position curves for these lists, but not enough of a primacy effect has been obtained. A second problem with the present version of the program is that it has no mechanism that prevents it from entering the same search routine repeatedly; some way of leaving "traces" to avoid this must be included in the program. Finally, we have obtained some encouraging results in simulating recall of lists in which related words were presented adjacently versus randomly ordered lists. A more extensive simulation of recall phenomena is planned.

COMMENTS

Three specific problems have been touched upon in this section. Some fairly direct evidence has been obtained for the psychological reality of propositions as basic lexical elements. Some results concerning latencies of acceptability judgments for simple sentences have been reported, and a model has been outlined that could account for the observed results. Finally, a model for free recall learning was discussed that explains how pre-existing knowledge about word relationships may be employed to reduce the difficulty of the learning task.

The problems posed by these topics are quite different, but one nevertheless may ask whether any common principles have arisen in the course of these investigations. In spite of the sketchy and tentative nature of the work performed so far I believe that one recurring theme can already be identified. All three processing models involve two distinct ways of retrieving information. A given word or proposition is located by means of a pattern match. For instance, given any word, we can

302/W. KINTSCH

locate its corresponding lexical entry, that is its **P**-vector and its semantic description list. Given a description list, we can determine whether any particular proposition is or is not a list member. This direct access to information contrasts with the information retrieval on the basis of a pattern completion operation. Here a proposition in which one or more terms (arguments or relation) are missing (a $-sign has been used to indicate missing terms) may be used as the starting point for a memory search in which an attempt is made to fill in the missing terms in such a way that the completed propositions will be acceptable. This kind of pattern completion process played a crucial role in all of the models discussed here.

The distinction between direct and indirect access to information is not new. Frijda (1970) has noted the significance of this observation in his review article. I have previously summarized some experimental results indicating that performance in recognition learning experiments is qualitatively different from performance in recall experiments, in that only the latter involves a "retrieval" process (Kintsch, 1970). This argument can be strengthened and clarified by noting that, according to the present model, recognition involves pattern matching, but that pattern completion is involved in recall. The distinction between "immediate knowledge production," which I have here called pattern-matching, and knowledge production through pattern completion has originally been introduced by Selz (1913).[18] According to Selz pattern, completion is one of the most important human information processing operations; if the preliminary work reported here is a valid indicator, we have every reason to concur with Selz's judgment.

To end this chapter I would like to remark upon the relationship of the present paper to the other reports presented in this volume. In aim and approach, this chapter is quite similar to the contributions by Collins and Quillian, and Rumelhart, Lindsay, and Norman. Furthermore, there is some overlap with Bower's chapter.

The work of Rumelhart, Lindsay, and Norman, and this work differ in the problems which are emphasized, in the interests of the authors, and in technical detail. Conceptually, however, they are closely related,

---

[18] Selz's term is Komplexergänzung, which Frijda (1970) has translated as "knowledge-unit-completion." I prefer "pattern completion" because it indicates the close relationship with pattern matching, as well as the essential difference between the two operations. Simmons (1970) uses pattern matching in a way that does not distinguish between matching of complete and incomplete patterns. I believe that Selz's distinction is very important psychologically and should be expressed terminologically. However, Simmons agrees in assigning central importance to the matching operation.

and it is not inconceivable that the positive features of both approaches might someday be combined.

Collins and Quillian's model, although still a close relative, differs in some more significant respects. First, the notion of case is quite central in my conception, while Collins and Quillian lack something comparable. Second, the generative capacities of the memory system have been stressed here, and I have tried to describe a model that is sufficiently formal to allow for the operation of powerful and complex rules. Third, and perhaps most significantly, our approaches to the problem of understanding a sentence are fundamentally different. Collins and Quillian use the "intersection method" to find a path between the words of a sentence. If a connecting path is found, the sentence is "understood" and accepted. I have postulated that there are several ways in which a sentence can be understood. Definitional sentences are accepted on the basis of a pattern match; a proposition identical with the sentence input is located in memory. Most sentences are accepted on the basis of pattern completion operations as described earlier. Finally, there are sentences that are not "semantically acceptable," but that still can be given an interpretation as a metaphor. Clearly, this suggestion is less parsimonious than Collins and Quillian's procedure. However, it may be more efficient; the acceptance of normal high-frequency sentences involves very little processing in this way—they are immediately understood, while metaphors must be laboriously interpreted. At this point there is no objective basis for choosing between these alternatives, and it seems best to try to develop the possibilities inherent in both approaches.

The model for free recall and its computer simulation which were described above are closely related to the work presented by Bower, though his computer simulation is far more advanced. The two models agree in many important respects (e.g., both are modelling the two-stage theory of free recall in that both assume that recall is implicit retrieval plus recognition), but there are some interesting differences. For instance, FRAN uses list tags instead of general activation tags, and FRAN has a special mechanism to construct an entry set, while in my model the entry set consists simply of those items that happened to be in short-term memory at the time of testing, or that has been learned by rote. Clearly FRAN is more efficient, but it is not so clear which one more accurately simulates human memory processes.

In what way, though, does the present work relate to traditional experimental work concerning the organization of memory? The only time where contact with this work was made in this chapter is in the discussion of the free recall model. If the sole raison d'être of the model proposed here were to account for free recall data, the whole enterprise would have to be considered as somewhat top heavy with theory. However, there are questions other than how people memorize word lists that need to be asked about organization of memory. Models like the present one are addressed to much broader problems, to questions of how information is stored in the human mind, how sentences are understood and generated, and how inferences are made. In order to obtain an understanding of these problems, knowledge from various sources must be considered, from intuition, from the vast storehouse of knowledge that is linguistics, from the experience of computer scientists constructing artificial intelligence devices, as well as from experimental psychology. The nonpsychological contributions in this paper have probably outweighed those of a specifically psychological nature, though. Until now the main achievement of this and other work concerned with semantic theory has been to provide a broad, speculative framework, consistent with a great deal of nonexperimental information about memory and language, within which certain questions can at last be considered. The next step will be, I believe, not so much an elaboration of this framework, but the development of experimental paradigms that will permit a serious test of the theory. At this point we have a theory without a basis in solid experimental fact—and facts that do not make contact with sufficiently rich conceptions of how people use their memory. Progress will require the two to come closer together.

SUMMARY

In this paper a model for the structure of semantic memory has been outlined. It is primarily concerned with questions of the following kind: What should one choose as the building blocks for a model of semantic memory? What is the relationship between natural language and the semantic structure? What information must a lexical entry contain? Can inference rules be made to operate efficiently in a memory model? How can such a model differentiate between semantically well-formed and meaningless expressions? An attempt has been made to answer these questions in such a way that the resulting model may serve, at least in principle, as a base for language behavior. Since storing all information explicitly may make excessive demands on the storage capacity, inference rules were used to generate redundant information as needed. Thus, language capacity and economy of storage were the two main objectives observed in constructing the model.

It was argued that propositional expressions are the most suitable elements for a semantic model. Some work in generative semantics employing case systems was described which is concerned with finding rules that can derive English sentences from propositional expressions. However, as yet no equally satisfactory solution appears to be available for the converse problem, that of translating English text into a propositional base.

The main part of the paper deals with a proposal for the operation of inference rules in a model of semantic memory and with an analysis of the structure generated by the operation of these rules. A formal analysis of this structure was presented. Two kinds of inference rules were described: redundancy rules, which delete and regenerate redundant propositions, and lexical transformation rules, which are used to derive some words from more basic lexical entries. Problems concerning the equilibrium point between storage costs on the one hand and generation costs on the other were briefly discussed.

Further, it was shown how propositions could be combined to form a lexical entry and how sentences may be understood which differ in the degree of semantic acceptability.

The purpose of the model developed in the present paper is to provide a framework within which knowledge about semantic memory that comes from various sources such as linguistics, artificial intelligence studies, and intuition, can be integrated and form a basis for psychological process models. In the final part of the paper some attempts to use the model for experimental work were described. In one experiment it was demonstrated that a subject given a brief sentence in which some of the arguments of the underlying proposition are missing can infer quite reliably the missing information. A second study explored the time which subjects take to verify or reject sentences of different degrees of semantic acceptability. For acceptable sentences, subjects responded faster when the parts of a sentence were closely related, but for unacceptable sentences semantic relationships between the sentence parts slowed down decision times. These results were found to be in agreement with the assumption that subjects operate upon the memory structure as described by the model using two basic operations: pattern matching and pattern completion. Finally, a model for free recall was described, which also involves the same two operations.

It is hoped that the model will be a further stimulus to experimental work and will guide the application of experimental techniques in the rich field of language and meaning, where experimental psychology has had difficulties in gaining a foothold.

References

Abelson, R. P. Psychological implication. In R. Abelson, E. Aaronson, W. McGuire, T. Newcomb, M. Rosenberg, P. Tannenbaum (Eds.), *Theories of cognitive consistency*. New York: Rand-McNally, 1969.

Abelson, R. P., & Carroll, J. D. Computer simulation of individual belief systems. *American Behavioral Scientist*, 1965, **8**, 24–30.

Abelson, R. P. & Reich, C. M. Implication modules: a method for extracting meaning from input sentences. *Proceedings of the International Joint Conference on Artificial Intelligence*. Washington, D. C., 1969. Pp. 641–647.

Anderson, J. The case for cause: a preliminary enquiry. *Journal of Linguistics*, 1969, **6**, 99–104.

Bach, E. Nouns and noun phrases. In E. Bach & R. T. Harms (Eds.), *Universals in linguistic theory*. New York: Holt, Rinehart, & Winston, 1968. Pp. 91–124.

Becker, J. D. The modeling of simple analogic and inductive processes in a semantic memory system. *Proceedings of the International Joint Conference on Artificial Intelligence*. Washington, D. C., 1969. Pp. 655–668.

Bierwisch, M. On certain problems of semantic representation. *Foundations of Language*, 1969, **5**, 153–184.

Bowers, F. The deep structure of abstract nouns. *Foundations of Language*, 1969, **5**, 520–533.

Chafe, W. L. *Meaning and the structure of language*. Chicago, Illinois: University of Chicago Press, 1970.

Chomsky, N. *Aspects of the theory of syntax*. Cambridge, Massachusetts: MIT Press, 1965.

Chomsky, N. *Language and mind*. New York: Harcourt, Brace, & World, 1968.

Chomsky, N. Deep structure, surface structure, and semantic interpretation. Manuscript. Indiana University Linguistics Club, 1969.

Chomsky, N. Remarks on nominalization. In R. A. Jacobs & P. S. Rosenbaum (Eds.), *Readings in english transformational grammar*. Waltham, Massachusetts: Ginn, 1970. Pp. 184–221.

Colby, K. M., & Smith, D. C. Dialogue between humans and artificial belief systems. Stanford Artificial Intelligence Project, Memo Al-97, August 1969. (a)

Colby, K. M., Tesler, L., & Enea H. Experiments with a search algorithm on the data base of a human belief structure. Stanford Artificial Intelligence Project, Memo Al-94, August 1969. (b)

Collins, A. M., & Quillian, M. R. Retrieval times from semantic memory. *Journal of Verbal Learning and Verbal Behavior*, 1969, **8**, 240–247.

Crothers, E. J. The psycholinguistic structure of knowledge. Technical Report, University of Colorado, November 1970.

Deese, J. *The Structure of associations in language and thought*. Baltimore, Maryland: John Hopkins Press, 1965.

Fillmore, C. J. The case for case. In E. Bach & R. T. Harms (Eds.), *Universals in linguistic theory*. New York: Holt, Rinehart, & Winston, 1968. Pp. 1–90.

Fillmore, C. J. Types of lexical information. In F. Kiefer (Ed.), *Studies in syntax and semantics*. Dodrecht, Holland: Reidel, 1969. Pp. 109–137.

Flavell, J. H. *The Developmental psychology of Jean Piaget*. New York: Van Nostrand–Reinhold, 1963.

Fodor, J. A., Garrett, M., & Bever, T. G. Some syntactic determinants of sentential complexity, II: Verb structure. *Perception and Psychophysics*, 1968, **3**, 453–461.

Fraser, B. Idioms within a transformational grammar. *Foundations of Language*, 1970, **6**, 22–42.

Frijda, N. H. The simulation of human memory. Technical Report, Amsterdam University, March, 1970.

Green, C. C., & Raphael, B. The use of theorem—proving techniques in question-answering systems. *Proceedings of the 23rd National Conference, Association for Computing Machinery*. Princeton, New Jersey: Brandon Systems, 1968. Pp. 169–181.

Henley, N. M. A psychological study of the semantics of animal terms. *Journal of Verbal Learning and Verbal Behavior*, 1969, **8**, 176–184.

Katz, J. J. *The philosophy of language*. New York: Harper & Row, 1966.

Katz, J. J. Recent issues in semantic theory. *Foundation of Language*, 1967, **3**, 124–194.

Katz, J. J., & Fodor, J. A. The structure of semantic theory. *Language*, 1963, **39**, 170–210.

Kintsch, W. Models for free recall and recognition. In D. A. Norman (Ed.), *Models of memory*, New York: Academic Press, 1970. Pp. 331–373.

Kintsch, W., Crothers, E. J., & Berman, L. N. The effects of some semantic and syntactic properties of simple sentences upon latency of judgments of semantic acceptability. Technical Report, University of Colorado, November 1970.

Lakoff, G., & Ross, J. K. Is deep structure necessary? Manuscript. Cambridge, Massachusetts, 1967.

Landauer, T. R., & Freedman, J. L. Information retrieval from long-term memory: category size and recognition time. *Journal of Verbal Learning and Verbal Behavior*, 1968, **7**, 291–295.

Luria, A. R. *Higher cortical functions in man*. New York: Basic Books, 1966.

Luria, A. R., & Vinogradova, O. An objective investigation of the dynamics of semantic systems. *British Journal of Psychology*, 1959, **50**, 87–105.

Lyons, J. *Introduction to theoretical linguistics*. Cambridge: Cambridge University Press, 1968.

Marshall, J. C., & Newcombe, F. Syntactic and semantic error in paralexia. *Neuropsychologia*, 1966, **4**, 169–176.

McCawley, J. D. The role of semantics in a grammar. In E. Bach & R. T. Harms (Eds.), *Universals in linguistic theory*. New York: Holt, Rinehart, & Winston, 1968. Pp. 125–170.

Miller, G. A. A psychological method to investigate value concepts. *Journal of Mathematical Psychology*, 1969, **6**, 169–191.

Myers, D. E. On the representation and retrieval of stored semantic information. *Cognitive Psychology*, 1970, **1**, 242–300.

Paivio, A., Yuille, J. C., & Madigan, S. A. Concreteness, imagery, and meaningfulness values for 925 nouns. *Journal of Experimental Psychology*, 1968, **76**, No. 1, Part 2.

Quillian, M. R. Word concepts: a theory and simulation of some basic semantic capabilities. *Behavioral Science*, 1967, **12**, 410–430.

Quillian, M. R. The teachable language comprehender. *Communications of the Association for Computing Machinery*, 1969, **12**, 450–476.

Raphael, B. SIR: A computer program for semantic information retrieval. In M. Minsky (Ed.), *Semantic information processing*. Cambridge, Massachusetts: MIT Press, 1968. Pp. 33–134.

Ross, J. R. Gapping and the order of constituents. In M. Bierwisch and K. E. Heidolph, (Eds.), *Progress in linguistics*. The Hague: Mouton, 1970. Pp. 249–259.

Schmidt, F. *Logik der Syntax*. Berlin: Deutscher Verlag der Wissenschaften, 1962.

Selz, O. *Die Gesetze des geordneten Denkverlaufs*. Stuttgart: Spemann, 1913.

Simmons, R. F. Natural language question-answering systems. *Communications of the Association for Computing Machinery,* 1970, 13, 15–30.

Vygotsky, L. S. *Thought and language.* Translated by E. Hanfmann & G. Vakar. Cambridge, Massachusetts: MIT Press, 1962.

Weigl, E., & Bierwisch, M. Neuropsychology and linguistics: topics of common research. *Foundations of Language,* 1970, **6,** 1–10.

Weinreich, U. On the semantic structure of language. In J. H. Greenberg (Ed.), *Universals of language.* Cambridge, Massachusetts: MIT Press, 1963. Pp. 142–216.

Weinreich, U. Explorations in semantic theory. In T. Sebeok (Ed.), *Current trends in Linguistics,* Vol. 3. The Hague: Mouton, 1966. Pp. 395–477.

8 | *How to Make a Language User*[1]

Allan M. Collins
M. Ross Quillian

[1] This research was supported by the Advanced Research Projects Agency of the Department of Defense and was monitored by the Air Force Office of Scientific Research under Contract No. F44620-67-C-0033.

We should like to thank the Artificial Intelligentsia at Bolt Beranek and Newman Inc. whose ideas we may have surreptitiously stolen: namely, Joseph D. Becker, Anthony Bell, Daniel G. Bobrow, Jaime R. Carbonell, and William A. Woods. We also want to thank David Meyer and Benson Schaeffer for their comments on an earlier draft of this paper.

The Psychology of Computers

INTRODUCTION

When computers first set out to humble man, they thought it would be good fun to read, and talk, and answer questions. Well, by now they have gotten over their cockiness about reading and the like, though, in consequence, man has not gotten over his. Their failure was not for any lack of cleverness though. Their basic mistake probably was in thinking they could skip over evolution, that their adeptness at artificial intelligence would let them fake their way past us in natural intelligence. Now, with humility written all over their inscrutable faces, computers are trying to revive their egos by imitating man.

One of the things computers missed out on in evolution is how to deal with similarity. They just never developed very good strategies for generalizing what they know about one situation to similar situations. Somehow, the simplest of organisms can do this, but computers do it only in ad hoc ways when they do it at all. Even the language ability that evolution worked so hard to produce appears to rely on this phylogenetically primitive ability. Having missed out on evolution, the problem as computers see it is to take apart a language user without losing any pieces, to see if they can sort out how everything fits together. If they can do that, then they can pretend to read and talk just like people. Although their approach is dissembling, still, what is studied and artificial at first gradually becomes second nature.

THE METHODOLOGY OF COMPUTERS

When looked at from the point of view of computers instead of people, the problems of psychology appear quite different. Computers' interest in psychology stems from their desire to copy the way people think. They analyze people in terms of the way they themselves, at present, work: that is, in terms of strategies, routines and subroutines, pointers, lists, etc. In these terms, they feel they can imitate any kind of process from a chemical reaction to a confrontation between ego and id. It is not so important to them whether this is the best way to try to describe how different processes work, because it is the only kind of description that is of use to them.[2] Put in philosophical terms, their approach is one of nominalism rather than realism.

In general, computers are more interested in the simple, straightforward human abilities rather than in exotic phenomena like perceptual illusions and learning nonsense syllables. This is because computers are, to a man, practical types. They want to walk before they try to run. So they focus on the common stuff of human existence like identifying what a figure is, comprehending what a sentence means, answering simple questions.

Computers also are not too fussy as to how they get their information about people. They think that if it works even partially, it is good enough for the present and they can always improve it later. Not only are they unscrupulous about their method, they willy-nilly make all sorts of arbitrary decisions about how different aspects of human processing might work. These assumptions are forced on them by the fact that for them everything must be spelled out in exquisite detail, or they cannot function at all. It is no good for them to try to understand human language comprehension or question answering, for example, without making any assumptions about the structure of semantic memory, as psychologists try to do (Meyer, 1970; Schaeffer & Wallace, 1970). In order to store any information in their data bases at all, they have to make many arbitrary decisions about how different pieces of information are represented and interrelated. The best they can hope for is to make all these assumptions as realistically as possible. Thus, they are perfectly willing to assume a complicated structure rather than a more parsimonious structure (Bobrow, Fraser, & Quillian, 1967) if they think the more complicated structure will extend their ability to converse with people. They simply do not see as much virtue in parsimony as mathematicians or psychologists do.

For computers, the question of whether a theory is correct is answered in an entirely different way than for psychologists. Psychologists call this the question of validation. Elsewhere in this volume, Postman quite rightly asks how "rational reconstructions of the mechanisms of memory" can be validated. Computers, who like to indulge in just such rational reconstructions, do not feel it is important that their theories predict experimental results for psychologists. What they regard as the true test of a theory is how well it allows them to talk to people in people's own terms. For the time being, it is no more difficult to tell how well

---

[2] This is not to say that computers may not in the future function in different terms.

a computer is doing at learning language than it is to tell how well a child of two or three is doing.

A case can be made that most computers are not really interested in the way people work, but are just taking any ideas they get from watching people and twisting these ideas to their own ends. According to this view, there can be two kinds of computers: those that are interested in the process of copying people for its own sake, and those that are interested in copying people only so far as it is necessary to talk to people. While computers do have such differing attitudes about learning natural language, even those with the latter attitude will have to copy people quite carefully and extensively. Language evolved to suit the human brain, and anything less than a thorough imitation will surely fail. Hence, computers must correctly interpret the way people work, or it should be readily apparent that they have not.

How to Interpret This Paper

There are many things computers would do if they could deal with language in a human way. Two of the things we have tried to help them with are comprehending English as embodied in the Teachable Language Comprehender (Quillian, 1969) and tutoring students about geography as embodied in Scholar (Carbonell, 1970). In this paper, we will try to describe what we have learned from working with them on these problems. Some of our knowledge has been acquired from experimenting with people, some from asking people what they thought about in answering questions, and some from merely trying to reach some mutually satisfactory resolution to the problems facing our computer friends. Frankly, they are more fastidious about details than we would like, and we will not burden the reader with these details; but, in general, it is probably good that they are so demanding.

This paper is meant to describe how some of the major pieces of a language user fit together. The description is wide ranging, but many pieces still are left out. The framework provided describes the human language user as viewed from the perspective of a computer. Hence, both the way people work and computers work are inextricably tied together in the theory. In just the same manner, both the way people work and mathematics work are intertwined in mathematical models of psychological processes. Sometimes it is clear what is done to please the computer or the mathematics, but usually it is not.

The paper is broken into two major sections, one about the structure of semantic memory and one about processing on that structure. With regard to the structure of memory, we discuss the nature of concepts and their relation to words and images, the kind of semantic information people learn and do not learn, and the kinds of inference-bearing relations that form the basis for the organization of semantic memory. With regard to processing, we discuss the semantic search during comprehension and retrieval, the tacit processing which this search implies, the pervasiveness of identifying similar concepts with each other in language processing, the decision rules that are applied to the results of a semantic search in order to decide whether two similar concepts can be identified, the role imagery plays in language processing, and the way people induce what properties to store with what concepts. Our ideas are presented as a loosely-constructed theory of how people function as language users and how computers will have to function to become language users.

Notions about Memory Structure

Computers suffer no qualms in thinking about ideas. They are, after all, in the business of making mechanical what smacks of vitalism to most scientists. Finding a way to represent ideas and concepts in their own terms is one of their first concerns. Their interest stems, of course, from their desire to copy us.

MEMORY FORMAT

There are many different ways semantic information might be represented in a computer. What is done usually is to store information in lists of properties or features about a concept; for example, father might be represented as male, adult, married or widowed, with children. This list can be thought of as the concept "father" to which words or printnames such as "father" or "père" may be attached.

Instead of being lists of words, the lists can be made up of pointers to other lists, those that correspond to each of the words. That is to say, concepts can point to other concepts rather than the names of other concepts. Thus, a concept would be a set of interrelationships among other concepts. There is no reason why lists have to have words or printnames attached, so there can be concept lists without printnames. What such a memory looks like from outside is a whole set of interrelated lists, with pointers to words found on many of the lists. For words with two different meanings, there can be two different lists, both attached to the same word. Where another concept list refers to one of these meanings, it will point to one list and not the other. An interesting aspect of such a network is that within the system there are no primitive or undefined terms in the mathematical sense, everything is defined in terms of everything else so the usual logical structure of mathematical systems does not hold. In this respect, it is like a dictionary.

An important aspect of property lists is that a property can be expanded to as much detail as is desired. This is done by embedding. For example, a father can have children, or two children, or two children both male, and so on, to as much detail as is appropriate. Embedding makes it possible to describe in a property anything that can be expressed in English. Property lists then are indefinitely expandable. For these reasons Quillian (1968, 1969) has used property lists rather than feature lists; but for psychology the distinction is not too important, since in many respects these two forms of representation are equivalent. We will talk about properties from here out, but they can be interpreted as features if that is more agreeable to the reader.

THE NATURE OF CONCEPTS

Concepts are represented by lists in computers because present day computers are serial processors. If parallel machines were built, then the necessity for ordering properties in a list would disappear. In fact, human concepts are probably more like hooks or nodes in a network from which many different properties hang. The properties hanging from a node are not likely to be all equally accessible; some properties are more important than others, and so may be reached more easily or quickly. In such a representation, going from one concept to another does not involve scanning a list, but rather activating a path via some property from one to the other.

Considering both accessibility and number of nodes in a path, it is possible to define in explicit terms the notion of semantic distance between concepts. If numbers are assigned to accessibilities such that lower numbers reflect more accessible properties, then semantic distance is the sum of these numbers along the path between the concepts. The greater the sum, the greater the distance. Under this definition, it is possible for one concept to be closer to a given node than another, even though the first is two steps removed and the second is one step removed. This happens when the sum of the two accessibilities for the first is less than the accessibility of the second. It is important to keep in mind that semantic distance between concepts is not simply proportional to the number of nodes along the path between the concepts.

So far, this just describes an association network of concepts which we think is a thoroughly plausible way to start building a computer memory to mimic human memory. Giuliano (1963) has indicated how such an association network could be represented in an analog computer. The trouble with a simple association network is that it does not specify the relation of properties to concepts. Worms are related to birds because birds eat them (though they are undoubtedly related in other ways too), and to dogs because worms live in a dog's coat of hair. The particular relation is as important to the property as the concepts that are related. Any memory structure that sloughs over these differences could never deal very intelligently with human language.

The relations between concepts are as varied as concepts themselves; indeed, relations are concepts and can be handled in many of the same ways as concepts that correspond to nouns or adjectives. Even adjective concepts such as red or square differ in their relation to different concepts they modify. For example, green is related to grass in a different way than yellow is to canary, since the green penetrates the grass and the yellow is only superficial to the canary. Both relations are different from the relation of blue to sky, since the blue is only in the atmosphere of earth during the day. These examples illustrate that relations can be quite complex, even though the question of "What color is grass?" can be answered without getting into these complexities. Any representation of relations in a computer must permit them to be as detailed as necessary; in other words, the description of a relation must be embeddable.[3]

There is no reason why a semantic memory should consist only of a network of descriptive properties. Concepts are built up out of sensori-motor experience as well as language use, and there is every evidence that people utilize imagery extensively. (See, for example, Paivio, 1969; Bower, in press; Begg & Paivio, 1970.) In computers, the work of Gelernter (1963) and Baylor (1971) suggests that it would be helpful to project concepts on a display screen where they can be manipulated as geometric forms rather than property lists. This could be done within a semantic memory by an image generation routine which uses descriptive properties as *stored variables* for constructing a visual image. For a concept like canary, the color attribute would produce a light yellow color in the image, whereas, for bird, the lack of a specific color value would produce a color-vague image like those shown in a dictionary. These same descriptive properties of a concept can also be treated as

---

[3] Properties are made up of two parts: relations and objects. For adjectival properties, relations are called *attributes* and objects are called *values*. Red and square are typical values, and they refer to concepts. Usually red is said to be a value of the attribute color. We are arguing that, in general, both attributes and values are more complex than this. Thus, for the concept "canary" the attribute color may have embedded the fact that it is only on the surface, and the value yellow may have embedded that it is light yellow, or one of the several yellows that people can distinguish in memory.

feature tests in the recognition of the concept. Hence, one test for a canary is the specific yellow color stored in memory. If this view is correct, then the current debate as to whether meaning (or semantic memory) is composed of imagery or something else such as deep structure (Begg & Paivio, 1970; Chase & Clark, in press; Simon, in press) will end in a draw.

On this theory, people must have several different concepts that have the name yellow. These concepts can also have more complicated names such as canary yellow, or lemon yellow, or mustard yellow. There must also be concepts of sounds like the sound a rooster makes. The name for this concept is "cock-a-doodle-do," but that is different from the image of the rooster's crowing. A person can probably answer the question "Does a rooster say cock-a-doodle-do?" without imaging the concept of a rooster crowing just by referring to the name of the concept. To confuse things more, there must also be a concept of the name "cock-a-doodle-do" distinct from the concept of the sound a rooster makes. The image of this name concept, which sounds like the words "cock-a-doodle-do," is what sounds different from the image of the actual rooster crowing. The point here is that we regard names as concepts, just like any other properties are concepts in their own right. The relation of a word to a concept is the "name" relationship. We would also argue that connotative or emotional properties of concepts, like visual and auditory properties, are tied to affective sensory systems in the same complicated way.

Within this framework it would even be possible to image concepts that involve a time-lapse sequence such as a swinging door or a race. The concept of a door swinging back and forth would be projected by the image-generation routine as the image of a door moving through a decreasing oscillation. The idea of a generation-routine can also be extended into the motor domain. For the concept of addition, the method of counting up the total can be projected onto fingers or matchsticks or whatever else comes to mind. In sum, we would argue that semantic memory refers to a mix of concepts and realizations of those concepts by sensori-motor generation routines.

CONCEPTS ARE NOT QUITE WORD-CONCEPTS

We mentioned earlier that concepts need not have names, and that the same name can be applied to more than one concept. This means that there is no one-to-one or many-to-one correspondence between words and concepts. Of course there are many cases, though, where concepts can be identified with particular words. Hence, it is often expedient to pretend that a word refers to a particular concept, and proceed to talk about the concept "father," for example, as opposed to the word "father."

There is another important case where a point-to-point correspondence between words and concepts breaks down. Often the same concept has more than one name. This is the case with synonyms. An even more common occurrence is when the two names are not synonyms but map onto the concept in different ways. For example, the words "buy" and "sell," to use Simmons' (1966) example, can be handled most easily if they refer to the same concept.[4] The conceptual identity of "buying" and "selling" can be seen in the following sentences: "He sold the girl two chairs. One of the chairs she bought was broken." The mapping of the two words onto the major elements of the concept is very different, however. The concept consists of at least four major elements or properties: the vendor, vendee, the goods given, and the remuneration received. "Buy" takes the vendee as agent and the vendor as the object of the preposition "from." "Sell" takes the vendor as agent and the vendee as indirect object. The goods and the remuneration are treated the same by both verbs. Sorting out which element in memory goes with which word in a sentence is handled most easily in translating from word to concept or from concept to word. In this case, the "name" relationship must be quite complicated, as specified by embedded subrelations.

Noun and verb forms of the same word also must refer to the same concept (e.g., "They *walked* along the coast. The *walk* took over an hour."), and should be treated similarly. Such cases abound in English, and it makes semantic processing difficult if the different words do not refer to the same concept. In the two sentences about walking, use of the article "the" implies that "the walk" was referred to earlier, and the earlier reference cannot be determined without a conjunction of noun and verb at the conceptual level. Recent work of Rubenstein, Lewis, and Rubenstein (1971) supports the notion of the conceptual identity of noun and verb forms.

THE SEMANTIC CONTENT OF CONCEPTS

Not only are concepts not words, they are not definitions of words. Definitions in dictionaries tell only the most important properties about

---

[4] The conceptual identity of buying and selling could be tested by a modification of Koler's (1966) technique. He showed that presenting a word and its translation at different places in recall lists given to bilingual subjects improved recall of the word as much as presenting the same word twice. If buy and sell refer to the same concept, they should reinforce each other in a similar way. However, a recent study of Johnson-Laird and Stevenson (1970) suggests that the two words must refer to the same concept.

a word, or the concept it refers to. Human concepts are much more encyclopedic. As a first approximation, it makes sense to assume that the content of a concept is everything that has been heard or read or seen about that concept.

A few examples can illustrate what we think a person is likely to learn at some time, and other things he is not likely to learn. These are shown in Table 1. Without going into detailed justification at this point, a few comments might be helpful.

TABLE 1
Examples of Information People Learn and Do Not Learn

Information a person may learn at some time	Information a person is *not* likely to learn
1. People can see Aristotle was a man.	Aristotle could see.
2. A vest does not have sleeves.	A vest does not have a brim.
3. Birds can fly. Birds have wings. Penguins can't fly.	All birds can fly. Most birds can fly. All birds have wings. Most birds have wings.
4. Roses are red. Roses are yellow. Not all roses are red.	Not all roses are yellow.
5. Unmarried men are also called bachelors. Young dogs are also called puppies. A car is also called an automobile.	
6. Sheep are herded in flocks. Sheep are kept on farms.	
7. A toad is like a frog. A frog is an amphibian. A wolf is like a dog, but is wild. A dog is a canine.	A toad is an amphibian. A wolf is a canine.

Example 1. Much of what people know (e.g., that Aristotle could see) is never learned directly. If one considers all the properties one knows about people, and all the people one knows, then it becomes evident how economical it is not to store each of the properties with each of the people.

Example 2. A person sometimes learns a negative fact when it contradicts something that might be inferred by mistake or that is true for a similar concept. But, most negative facts are never learned.

Example 3. Most information is not learned in quantified form. Thus, a person usually never learns whether all birds or most birds can fly or have wings (though a person might learn that not all birds can fly). The exceptions are usually learned as special cases.

Example 4. This is a variation on *Example 3.* That roses are yellow might be learned from a song or from seeing one. Assuming that a person already knows roses are red, the relation of the two facts may be noticed and stored, or it may not be. It may sometimes even be learned directly that not all roses are red, because of the direct nature of the contradiction.

Example 5. What are called logical truths are usually cases where the same concept is referred to by different labels. Sometimes one of the labels is a descriptive phrase, as with "young dog." "Middle-aged dog" is probably not a separate concept, even though "young dog" appears to be. This raises the question of when, in the course of learning, "young dog" becomes a separate concept. The solution we propose is to set up a new concept whenever information is to be stored that cannot be derived from the descriptive label (e.g., "young dogs are frisky" or "young dogs are called puppies"). On this basis, for example, "South American countries" would be set up as a separate concept when it is learned that they generally speak Spanish or that they tend to be underdeveloped economically and overdeveloped militarily.

Example 6. These two pieces of information about sheep are subtly contradictory with respect to whether sheep are kept fenced in and whether they are farm animals. It is doubtful that this contradiction would be noticed unless such a question is asked.

Example 7. Very often what is learned is not what superordinate category a concept belongs to, but what other concept it is like.

This set of examples is certainly not meant to exhaust all the possible kinds of semantic information people learn. We will return to these examples from time to time in later sections to illustrate various points about structure or processing.

THE HIERARCHICAL ORGANIZATION OF CONCEPTS

Among the semantic properties of concepts, there are several special property relations that are commonly found. They are special because they permit certain kinds of inferences to be made. A frequently used kind is the *superset* or superordinate relation. All properties of a superset (e.g., people can see) also hold for the instances of that superset (e.g., Aristotle) unless otherwise indicated (e.g., Helen Keller could not see). In many cases, the superset is the most accessible property of a concept,[5] though not always (e.g., it is probably not the most accessible property of a nose that it is an appendage or a body organ). In contrast, the subsets of a concept are not easily accessible properties in general (e.g., when thinking about cows, a person is not likely to consider the fact that one kind is a Guernsey). This asymmetry between supersets and subsets probably stems, at least in part, from the asymmetry in inference, since properties of a subset do not usually hold for a concept.

There is often more than one superset of a concept; in many cases, there is a frequently used superset and one or more lesser supersets within the frequently used superset. A hawk is a bird, but it is also a bird-of-prey; a dog is an animal, but it is also a mammal, and within that group a canine; Paraguay is a country, but it is also a Latin American country, a South American country, an underdeveloped country, and a military dictatorship.[6] Occasionally, there are other supersets that do not lie within the frequently used superset (e.g., a canary is a bird, but also is commonly a pet). There are clearly large differences in accessibility between these different supersets.

Superset is a transitive relation so that concepts form chains where each concept has a more general concept as its superset. For instance, a hawk is a bird and a bird is an animal, so that indirectly animal

---

[5] This, we think, is partly the reason why our results (Collins & Quillian, 1969) in a true-false reaction time task show people to be faster in deciding that "A canary is a bird," for example than they are in deciding that "A canary can sing." We assume that both the superset "bird" and the property "can sing" are stored directly with canary in most people's memory.

[6] This raises the problem of whether all properties should be stored as supersets, since this makes inferences easier. It is easier to retrieve the properties of military dictatorships (e.g., they imprison dissidents) for Paraguay, if Paraguay is stored as a military dictatorship rather than as having a military dictator. Similarly, it would be easier to retrieve properties of hot objects (e.g., they burn hands) for an oven rack, if oven rack is stored as a hot object rather than as being hot. We don't know where to draw the line in setting up supersets, but it seems a bit much to have supersets such as hot objects or objects on Gorky Street. More likely, a person infers that oven racks will burn hands by analogy with the fact that irons (or whatever object he has learned about) burn hands. In the same sense though, canine and marsupial may not generally be supersets either, except to zoologists. If asked whether marsupials hop, people who know kangaroos are marsupials will probably answer "yes," but they must get the property from kangaroos and not from marsupials. That is to say, the property is inferred from an example just as with the iron.

is a superset of hawk. It is also possible to find superset chains among verbs. For example: to sprint→ to run→ to go→ to do; to speed→ to drive→ to go→ to do. A rather long superset chain is: mallard→ duck→ bird→ animal→ living thing→ object. (If this is the longest such chain, it puts mallard squarely at the bottom of memory.) Generally though, these chains do not seem to be more than about three or four steps long, so that semantic memory must be rather shallow on the whole.

Supersets are frequently used in the formation of questions like those in Table 2. For example, if a teacher wants to quiz a student about

TABLE 2
Examples of Superset Use in Formulating Questions

Information	Question about the Information
He *sped* to the hospital.	How did he *drive* to the hospital?
He *drove* to work.	How did he *go* to work?
He *went* to the movie.	What did he *do*?
He killed a *mallard*.	What kind of *duck* did he kill?
She liked *ducks*.	What kind of *birds* did she like?
He saw a *doctor* he knew (*person*).	*Whom* did he see?
He saw a *camel* (*animal*).	*What* did he see?
He put it on the *desk* (*thing*).	On *what* did he put it?
He went to a *football game* (*event* or *activity*).	*What* did he go to?
He saw it in the *sky* (*place*).	*Where* did he see it?
He saw it in *September* (*time*).	*When* did he see it?

information he should have learned, then, the teacher will usually formulate the kinds of questions shown in Table 2. The first two groups show that appropriate questions can be phrased in terms of the superset of the concept sought for both verbs (group 1) and nouns (group 2). By trying to formulate questions of this sort, it is possible to determine the superset(s) of a concept. The last group of examples in Table 2 show that the distinction between who, what, where, and when rests on high-level supersets (in parentheses). We think people use superset chains to reach these high-level supersets every time they formulate these kinds of questions.

As alternatives to the structure described, at least two other kinds of structures might be proposed. One possibility is that all the supersets of which a concept is a member are stored directly with the concept. The five supersets listed above for mallard would all be direct supersets of mallard, just as canine, mammal, and animal are, according to our suggestion, direct supersets of dog. The other possible extreme is that the memory is rigidly hierarchical such that each higher-level superset can only be reached indirectly via a lower-level superset. For example, dog would have animal as an indirect superset via some chain like: dog→ canine→ mammal→ animal. Either of these alteratives is much tidier than the proposed structure.

The latter of these alternatives can be ruled out, we think. Reaction time data (Collins and Quillian, in preparation) indicate that it takes longer to decide that mammals, such as dog, are mammals, than to decide they are animals. This cannot be due to a difficulty in retrieving the concept "mammal" from the word "mammal" as compared with "animal," because the category name was given in advance and a series of trials used the same category. This is opposite the finding that it takes longer to decide birds such as hawk are animals than to decide they are birds. The finding about mammals and animals is not possible if a person decides a dog is an animal via a path through mammal.

On the other hand, the first alternative hypothesis, namely that all the supersets are stored directly with the concept, is not ruled out by the above experiment. The fact that it takes longer to decide a hawk is an animal than to decide it's a bird agrees with our earlier suggestion that deciding a hawk is an animal involves the path through bird. But on the first alternative hypothesis, animal might merely be a less accessible superset stored with each bird name. Against this possibility, we would point out that if a person is told what a mallard is, he only is told that it is a duck. It is very unlikely he would be told directly it is an animal, a living thing, or an object. When he learns a mallard is a duck, he may possibly infer from his previous knowledge that it must also belong to the higher level categories and store that information directly with mallard. However, all the evidence to date (Collins & Quillian, 1969, 1970a; E. E. Smith, personal communication), though not conclusive, indicates that the inference is made each time it is needed.[7]

SEMANTIC ORGANIZATION AND INFERENCE

One possible misinterpretation of the last section is that mammal is stored as a superset directly with most mammals. In our view, it is not likely that many animals would have a pointer to mammal other than odd cases such as whale, bat, maybe kangaroo, and a few of the most obvious examples, such as dog. We think this is so because people

[7] There is a complication here that will be discussed in relation to induction (see Induction and Learning).

learn when they are children that beavers and seals are animals, but it is rare that they learn that a beaver or a seal is a mammal. Furthermore, while canine may be stored as a superset of dog, it probably is not for wolf, though wolves are canines. There are various kinds of information that can be used to decide whether a wolf is a canine or a beaver is a mammal, so such facts need not be stored directly. We will discuss how people make such decisions in a later section, but one kind of information that people may use depends on the *similarity* relation. Like the superset relation, this has implications for the structure of memory.

The similarity relation is one of the class of relations that permits inferences of the type where properties of one concept are applied to the related concept. It allows the same set of inferences as superset, but with less certainty. An example of concepts linked by the similarity relation was shown in Table 1, Example 7. If one knows a toad is like a frog and that a frog is an amphibian, then one can infer with some uncertainty that a toad is an amphibian. Likewise, one might infer that a wolf is a canine since it is like a dog, even though wolves are wild and dogs domesticated. Usually, the similarity relation is qualified by specifying either the basis for distinguishing (e.g., a pony is like a horse only smaller) or the basis for grouping (e.g., a sheep is like a cow in that it chews a cud). Distinguishing characteristics are given when the concepts are alike in most respects, whereas similar characteristics are given when the concepts are different in most respects. When the similarity relation is qualified in either way, it helps to determine what inferences can be drawn across the relation. Nevertheless, there are cases where people learn about the similarity of concepts without learning the basis either for distinguishing or for grouping them, as when a child is told "A toad is like a frog" during the reading of a story about a toad.

There are several other relations that permit whole classes of inferences to be drawn. The class of allowable inferences is specific to the particular relation and is much smaller for each of the other relations than for superset (Carbonell, 1970). A very important relation in some subject areas (e.g., geography, anatomy, architecture) is the *part* relation. One of the most accessible properties of the nose is that it is part of the face. The kinds of inferences possible with the part relation are best illustrated with an example from geography (Carbonell, 1970). To learn that Katmandu is part of Nepal, implies something about its maximum size in area and population, and about its location, climate, and topography. The *proximity* (or *adjacency*) relation carries some of the same implications, such as about location, climate and topography, but with less certainty. Grouping of concepts, which in many cases is done on the basis of the superset and similarity relations, occurs in anatomy and geography on the basis of the part and proximity relations. Grouping on the latter basis does not preclude grouping on the former; witness the fact that hands and feet, or arms and legs are grouped on the basis of similarity, whereas eyes and nose, or neck and shoulders are grouped by proximity.

In the realm of events, about which history and science are largely concerned, the *consequence* (*causality*) and *precedence* relations function to carry inferences (Becker, 1969). There are also many other relations that permit certain inferences but which are only used in limited contexts (e.g., the *parent* relation).

The essential assumption of this section is that the relations that carry inferences always form the basis for organizing any semantic information or subject matter. That is to say, grouping of concepts is almost always along the structural lines imposed by relations such as superset, similarity, part, proximity, consequence, precedence, parent, etc. Often these relations apply in different ways to the same set of concepts and so there are overlaying organizational structures imposed on a set of concepts. This suggests that the reason why organization occurs in memory is to permit inferences in storing and retrieving semantic information. It is by using inference that people can know much more than they learn.

Notions about Memory Processing

With enough assumptions about structure, it become possible to consider how computers might process semantic information in order to function like people.

COMPREHENSION AND RETRIEVAL

When comprehension and retrieval are looked at from the point of view of implementation in a computer, it is useful to treat them as involving the same underlying process. In comprehension, people read a string of words and attempt to construct an *interpretation* based on a configuration of paths in memory between the various concepts referred to by the words in the string. Because, in most cases, each word points to several concepts and any two concepts are connected by a variety of paths, building an interpretation must involve an extensive search to determine how the words can be interrelated within the constraints of syntax and context. The same search takes place in retrieving answers to questions, only the constraints (discussed later) on what constitutes an acceptable configuration of paths are usually more restrictive. [Comprehension is described in considerable detail in Quillian (1969) and retrieval in Collins and Quillian (in press).] In effect, comprehension can be regarded as retrieval with the implicit question, "Is there an interpretation under which the sentence could make sense with respect to what I already know?"

To take a simple example, suppose a child is comprehending his father's statement that "A toad is like a frog." The syntactic constraints in the sentence will dictate that he interpret "like" as meaning "similar to," and so a path between the concepts of "similar to" and "frog" will constitute his interpretation of the phrase "is like a frog." The child also will look up the word "toad" in memory. If the child finds no concept that could correspond to the word "toad," then any interpretation he has found for "like a frog" is possible, and so he sets up a new concept "toad" with the information "like a frog." Suppose, though, that the child had previously learned that a toga is a kind of clothing people used to wear. Suppose, further, that he did not store enough features to differentiate the word "toad" from the word "toga." Then "toad" will get him to the concept for "toga." Comparing the two concepts, one "like a frog" from the sentence and the other "a kind of clothing" from memory, the child will likely discover the contradiction by a process described in a later section (also in Collins and Quillian, in press). The contradiction means that his interpretation of the sentence involving "toad" is not possible with respect to information he already has stored. His response might be something like, "I thought a toad was something people wear." Responses like this, which question the assertion made in a piece of text, are quite common, especially in reading about a subject one already knows something about, such as psychology or language. That such responses occur gives away the fact that people, to a greater or lesser extent, evaluate everything they are told. However, people's evaluations may differ markedly depending on what has been stored previously and how much effort they are willing to spend searching for connections and contradictions.

SEMANTIC SEARCH AND SYNTACTIC CONSTRAINT

The locating of paths between concepts, then, is basic to both comprehension and retrieval. Quillian's (1968, 1969) program searches for paths between concepts using what is called an *intersection technique*. This systematically proceeds outward along all the pointers or paths leading from each concept which is referred to by the words in the sentence. Where a word can refer to several different concepts, the search proceeds outward from all these possible concepts (though a less likely meaning of a word starts off more slowly). At each concept encountered as the search proceeds outward, a tag is left indicating where the search originated. Because many different branches are taken at each concept encountered, the search continually widens like a harmless spreading plague. When the search originating from one word encounters a tag originating from another word, a path linking the two concepts has been found. As the search goes on longer, more paths will be found. The later in the search a path is found, the longer the path will be. Because the length of paths reflects semantic distance in memory, such a search produces semantically probable paths first. The use of tags in the model is a way to implement in a computer the idea of activation, either in terms of priming concepts or in terms of spreading to related concepts. These are very old ideas in psychology.

Quillian's search, as implemented in a serial computer, is an ordered serial search (though it simulates a parallel search), but several aspects of our results on human question-answering (Collins & Quillian, 1969, 1970a) imply that people search for connections between concepts in parallel. What appears to be serial processing in evaluating the paths found, occurs only after locating intersections (Collins and Quillian, in press). We think it is possible that a search using the intersection technique could be implemented in a machine with fairly simple active elements that operate in parallel. A parallel machine to which one can add nodes and paths is not available, but if language processing demands it, then possibly such a machine could be developed.

We implied, above, that although the search for connections is parallel, the evaluation of the connections found is largely serial. People often report in "retrospecting" about their processing of questions that they have considered more than one interpretation of a question (Collins and Quillian, in press). Thus, the evaluation phase appears to enter into consciousness. Whatever consciousness may be, it seems to focus on the processing which is done serially, perhaps in a unit akin to the central processing unit (CPU) of a serial computer.

One of the kinds of evaluation that occurs is whether the semantic path found is compatible with the syntax of the sentence. We currently would argue that syntactic processing takes place in a parsing network (Thorne, Bratley, & Dewar, 1968; Bobrow & Fraser, 1969; Woods, 1970) parallel with the semantic search. When a complete path is found in either network, an interrupt occurs in the CPU, though the search in the semantic network probably continues to look for other paths which can be used if the first fails. If paths are found in both networks, then the semantic and syntactic paths are compared to see if they are compatible (see Quillian, 1969). If a path is found in only one network after some predetermined amount of searching, then this path may be used to guide the search for a corresponding path through the other network.

We can illustrate some aspects of the semantic-syntactic tradeoff described above with a sentence such as "Zebras like horses." Some readers might misread this or decide there is a typographical error leaving out the word "are." Others will make sense of it in the way that dogs like people, but nobody will understand it the way that cats like mice. What we are saying happens is that for the people who misread it, the semantic connection of similarity is found well before the syntactic connection. When this happens, the response may be to force the syntax to fit the semantic connection. For other people, the syntactic connection is found first and the semantic connection can be forced to fit it. Where both connections are found, then the person will compare the two paths and find that they are not compatible. He then will have to choose between the two interpretations on some meta-basis.

TACIT KNOWLEDGE AND PARALLEL PROCESSING

The kind of parallel search outlined and the capability of interrupting the CPU when a connection is found implies that a vast amount of stored knowledge can be tacitly considered in processing natural language. This is illustrated in a passage from Quillian's forthcoming book on media:

> At one time, I was trying to get a computer to be able to read sentences from pre-school children's books. My aim was to have the computer relate these sentences correctly to some body of information it had stored, its memory or "knowledge of the world." One such book, which described crossing a street, contained the sentences, "The policeman held up his hand and the cars stopped." Now, suppose one asks what is the minimum amount of information a mechanism must have stored to relate this sentence to, if it is to comprehend it in a reasonably human-like way? In particular, consider whether the machine must have stored the fact that moving cars usually have drivers? One's first thought might well be no, since drivers aren't mentioned or directly involved in the sentence. But, suppose the sentences preceding this one in the book had said that there had just been an earthquake, and that two cars, parked on a hill, had started to roll down it. Then comes the sentence above, "The policeman held up his hand and the cars stopped." Virtually every adult reader of this will wonder: just how did the policeman manage that? In other words, in understanding the initial sentence, it seems that there indeed *was* some tacit use of the knowledge that

cars ordinarily have drivers. If there were not, how can it be that, once a reader is led to believe that a moving car lacks a driver, he will then recognize that something is strange about a policeman being able to stop it just by holding up his hand?

Similar arguments can be adduced to show that in understanding the sentence above the reader also seems to tacitly take account of information to the effect that: cars ordinarily have brakes, wheels, and tires, that their drivers control these cars, have a knowledge of traffic signals, are able to see out of their windshields, and so on. So, readers must have a large amount of such knowledge mentally stored. The processing done of such knowledge during reading may be fairly minimal, but something has to be done with it or to it, or a reader could not recognize whenever something he reads fails to make sense on the basis of such knowledge.

There is ample evidence that a similar tacit use of sizable amounts of stored information underlies all our visual perception, motor activity, problem solving, and so on (Bruner & Minturn, 1955; Polyani, 1966). Therefore, it has seemed best to me to define the *full meaning*, for any particular person, of anything he reads, sees, thinks, or does, as all the information (stored in his head) that is in any way activated or processed when he deals with that thing (Quillian, 1968). If we define meaning in this way, then the full meaning of even simple stimuli or actions becomes very large indeed, and very large amounts of this meaning are always being tacitly processed as the person proceeds through the world. In other words, consciousness is analogous to the focal awareness one has when a complex scene covers his visual field. There will, at any one moment, be only a very tiny amount of the overall visual field in close focus, a little more of it sufficiently close to the focal point to be fairly clearly observed, which the great majority of it is processed only peripherally, most of this processing being tacit, outside the person's awareness. This peripheral processing will be able to thrust something it discovers into the focus of consciousness if such a thing seems worthy of more explicit consideration, just as an unexpected, rapid movement at the edge of our visual field will be thrust into our attention by our peripheral visual processing. In reading, thinking, talking, and other forms of activity, information is continually drawn from our memory and processed as information in our overall visual field is processed. Thus, the fact that cars are normally controlled by drivers is part of the large amount of stored information that is processed tacitly every time we see or read about a moving car, but which has an effect on our consciousness only if it seems especially pertinent, as when we are told that driverless cars are stopped by a policeman's hand signal.

DECIDING WHETHER CONCEPTS CAN BE IDENTIFIED WITH EACH OTHER

The process of identifying similar concepts with each other arises in many different aspects of language processing. It appears in several different guises, among them reasoning by analogy and use of metaphor. Often the attempt to identify similar concepts turns into a question of whether the two concepts can be identified with each other in this particular case. This happened in an example given in the section on Comprehension and Retrieval where the question arose for the child "Could a kind of clothing be like a frog?" Because anything like a frog is probably an animal, this becomes a question of whether "clothing" and "animal" can be the same thing. We will give a number of examples in the next section to illustrate how frequently the process of identifying similar concepts occurs in language processing. We only want to point out here that it is quite basic to the understanding of language processing to find out how people decide whether two concepts can be identified in a particular case.

There has been a series of reaction-time studies recently on the processing involved in comparing pairs of concepts. Landauer and Freedman (1968) and Collins and Quillian (1970b) have used a categorization task where subjects had to decide whether an object named was in a predesignated category or not. Collins and Quillian (1969, 1970a) used a reaction-time task in which sentences like "A canary is a bird" or "A canary is an animal" were displayed, and subjects decided if they were true or false. Meyer (1970) had subjects decide whether sentences like "All thrones are chairs" or "Some thrones are chairs" are true or false. Schaeffer and Wallace (1969, 1970) used a same-different reaction-time task, where subjects had to decide whether or not two words shown were both members of the same category. In the task, one or several categories were prespecified. These studies are all looking at the processing involved in deciding whether or not two concepts are identifiable with respect to a set of constraints imposed by the task.

We can best explain how the constraints of the task affect the decision about identifying concepts by an example from Meyer. In a sentence like "Some chairs are thrones," the question is whether the syntax of the sentence and the nature of the task (here explicitly defined by "some") permit a subject to identify chair and throne. The answer in this case is "yes." In a sentence like "All chairs are thrones," the answer would be "no," because the syntax does not permit the "all" kind of identification to be made. If the sentence were turned around to "All thrones are chairs," the superset or superordinate relation in memory linking throne to chair could be used as the basis for saying "yes." The same question can be asked in a categorization task. For example, the word chair might be prespecified as the category, and when throne appears as the stimulus word there is an implicit question "Are all thrones chairs?" From these examples it should be clear that the appropriate decision strategy (or decision rule) varies in different cases, depending on syntax and task instructions, and even the range of stimuli used. In this section we will limit our discussion to decision strategies that are appropriate for the "All thrones are chairs" kind of sentence or the equivalent categorization task described. Other tasks may involve some of the same decision strategies, but there will also be differences in the decision strategies that are appropriate.

We have argued (Collins and Quillian, in press) that comparing concepts involves a semantic search proceeding outward in parallel from both the concepts to all associated properties, including superset properties. Any connection found must be checked to see if the relation between the concepts meets the constraints of syntax and context (including the task instructions). In other words, whenever an interrupt occurs during the tacit, parallel search of memory, the connection found is explicitly considered with respect to syntax and task instructions. Reaction-time data can reflect either the length of the search or the evaluation of the path involved in applying a particular decision strategy.

In deciding whether a "canary" is an "animal," the connection that would be used would go through "bird," given our structural assumptions. (See The Hierarchical Organization of Concepts.) Hence, the search that finds this connection should take longer than the one that finds a connection between "canary" and "bird." Reaction time should reflect the length of the underlying search process, and indeed both we and Meyer have found a difference in reaction time in the predicted direction. But, as Meyer has pointed out to us, the difference in reaction time could also derive in part or primarily from evaluating the path found, because an inferential path may take longer to evaluate than a direct superset connection. Therefore, the reaction time differences found in these studies probably reflect both search time and evaluation time.

According to our theory, rejecting the identifiability of two concepts involves finding a path that contains a contradiction. What constitutes a contradiction depends upon the kind of connection found: sometimes it may involve negative information that is stored directly in memory (e.g., bachelors are not married men), but usually it seems to involve finding different values for equivalent semantic properties (i.e., properties where the attributes are the same; red and green are contradictory values of the attribute color). For example, a lime is not a lemon because a lime is green and a lemon is yellow. Apparently, this decision strategy sometimes is based on imagery (see Two Uses of Imagery) and sometimes is not. We are still in doubt as to whether people always find some contradiction on which to base their rejection, even when the two concepts appear unrelated. For example, if asked whether a cafeteria is a dog, people may compare equivalent sensory properties (e.g., a cafeteria is big and spacious and a dog is small and solid) and find different values. On the other hand, they may merely search for a given amount of time or to a given semantic distance without finding a connection, and then reject on the basis of not finding a connection.

The semantic search, however, often turns up connections that cannot be used, and checking these out acts to slow down a person's decision time. For example, if a person were asked to decide whether a "canary" and a "banana" are the same, a connection might be found through their light-yellow color (i.e., a property they have in common). If so, then the person would have to check if this permits him to accept or reject the identification of the two concepts, which it does not. This is a case where a "false" or "no" response is slowed down, but the same thing can happen for a "true" or a "yes" response. For example, deciding whether a submarine is a ship might be slowed down if the property that submarines go under water and ships go on top of water is found before a connection is found that allows the person to say "yes." Subjects report that they do, in fact, find such misleading connections before deciding. As another example, deciding that a "penguin" is a "bird" could be slowed down, if the connection were found that a penguin cannot fly even though birds can. However, since the superset relation from penguin to bird is much more accessible for most people than the fact penguins cannot fly, it is possible that the superset connection would be found and checked out before the other connection would cause an interrupt and thus be considered.

Finding misleading connections is the reason we think that subjects are relatively slow in deciding that two similar concepts (i.e., two concepts with common properties) are not identifiable, a result that both Schaeffer and Wallace (1969, 1970), and we (Collins & Quillian, 1969, in press) have found. Though Schaeffer and Wallace (1970) argue that this result contradicts our theory, they, in fact, have misinterpreted our theory. We argue (Collins & Quillian, 1970b) that it is also the basis for Landauer and Freedman's (1968) finding that to decide an object (e.g., tulip) does not belong to a category takes longer with a large category (e.g., animal) than with a smaller nested one (e.g., dog). This is because a tulip is a plant, and plants are more similar to animals than they are to dogs, as evidenced by the fact that plants and animals are frequently grouped together in language discourse. Wilkins (1971) points out that, by excluding animals that were not dogs from their stimulus sets, Landauer and Freedman inevitably omitted stimuli, such as cats, that were most similar to dogs, while they did not exclude any stimuli, such as plants, that were at all similar to animals.

To complicate the picture further, consider the comparison of two concepts where there is not likely to be a direct superset link stored between the concepts, as, for example, between rat and mammal, or sheep and farm animal, or stagecoach and vehicle. When there is no superset relation available, it is necessary to use a more complicated decision strategy to decide that two concepts are identifiable. It should be emphasized that finding a common property with the same value is not an appropriate decision strategy for saying "yes," as is exemplified by the fact that both clouds and vehicles move, even though clouds are not vehicles. But there is an asymmetry in the "no" case, because people often reject the identifiability of two concepts on the basis of one common property with different values. This is exemplified by two subjects who reported that for "Badminton is volleyball," they rejected the sentence as false because badminton uses a birdie and volleyball uses a ball. The asymmetry between "yes" and "no" decision strategies is one of logic, but the logic gets into trouble because of cases like a submarine and ship, where one property with different values is not grounds for rejection. In such cases we think that people rely on the fact that they will find a connection that allows them to say "yes," thus overriding any mistaken rejection.

Returning to the question of decision strategies for saying "yes," it is logical to say "yes" if all the equivalent properties of one of the concepts (whichever one) are common to the other. If all a person knew about a bat was that it has wings, flies, and is an animal, then it would make sense to say a bat is a bird. Similarly, if all one knows about mammals is that they are animals that bear their young alive and breathe air, then it would make sense to say a rat is a mammal, even without knowing whether rats bear their young alive. People may apply this kind of decision strategy in some cases, such as deciding if a sheep is a farm animal. They can use the strategy by treating a few properties as if they are defining properties. The defining properties for farm animals might be that they are animals and are kept on farms. But people know much more about farm animals than these two properties (e.g., they are raised, fed, domesticated, bought and sold, etc.). Now, in deciding if a sheep is a farm animal, a connection may be found through the fact that sheep were once seen on a farm. Alternatively, a connection may be found through the fact that sheep are herded in flocks out in fields by shepherds, that is to say, not on farms. Depending on which connection is found, a person will respond "yes" or "no." If both connections are found before responding, then he will need to apply some higher-level strategy. But even though he may treat these two properties as if they are defining properties, we would argue that he is tacitly considering the other properties of farm animals as well. Thus, if asked if a mink or a cat is a farm animal, he is likely to consider the fact that minks are not domesticated and cats are not raised, even though both may be kept on farms. What tacit consideration means is that the parallel search will interrupt if any property is found where the two concepts have properties with matching attributes and contradictory values. We do not know what subjects would decide about sheep, minks, or cats, but we suppose it depends on how accessible the various properties are for both of the concepts being compared.

There is another strategy we think people sometimes will use for deciding whether two concepts are identifiable or not when superset information is lacking. We call it the Wittgenstein (1953) strategy. Wittgenstein argued that a concept such as game need not have any set of properties which all games have, and only games have (i.e., defining properties). Instead, he implied that people will call something a game if it bears a close "family resemblance" to a number of activities people call games. In our terms, bearing a close family resemblance would involve some kind of evaluation of the number of common properties.

The use of this strategy is a little clearer if we consider the case of deciding whether something is a vehicle or not. People must have stored a number of instances of vehicles such as trucks, cars, and busses, and for these the superset relation will allow them to decide that they are vehicles. Now, if an object is similar to a car, truck, or bus, then with some uncertainty one can infer that it is a vehicle. For example, such an inference applies to taxicabs; if a car is a vehicle and a taxicab is like a car, then a taxicab is probably a vehicle too. This is inference by analogy in its simplest form. Where the information is not stored directly as to whether something is like a truck, or a car, or a bus, then the Wittgenstein strategy can be applied. The more properties found in common with any of these three vehicles, the more likely will a person conclude that the thing is a vehicle. For example, he is more likely to conclude that a stagecoach or a tank is a vehicle than that a horse or a ski lift is a vehicle.

An important aspect of the Wittgenstein strategy is that the properties a stagecoach has in common with a car count just as much as the properties for which they are different. In other words, the asymmetry in logic that applied when one concept was compared directly with another, disappears when the one concept is compared with an instance of the other. To illustrate this point, consider the question of whether a stagecoach is a car. It is logical to conclude a stagecoach is not a car because a car has a motor and a stagecoach does not. But even though a stagecoach is not a car, it may still be a vehicle. Hence, it makes sense in applying the Wittgenstein strategy to use a less stringent criterion in comparing a stagecoach and a car.

All these strategies we have cited would be applied to the semantic connections that are found during the parallel search of memory. The particular decision strategy that is applied depends on two things: (a) the constraints imposed by the sentence or the task (see The Pervasiveness of Identifying Concepts with Each Other and Induction and Learning), and (b) what connections are found. Notice that the intersection technique, if applied to two concepts such as "stagecoach" and "vehicle" will find connections through properties of busses, cars, and trucks, if these instances are fairly accessible from the concept "vehicle." These connections will have to be used, if that is all that is stored with "vehicle." Such a poverty of knowledge about vehicles and other concepts may be quite common, but there must also be many higher-level concepts, like "game," where people have learned or inferred some properties which are stored directly with the concept. For the concept "game," it seems likely that the property of having rules, for instance, must be stored directly with game. But as Wittgenstein says, properties are never defining properties. That is to say, there will be instances of a concept that do not have all the properties of the concept (e.g., birds fly but penguins cannot), and non-instances of the concept that have some of the properties (e.g., planes fly but planes are not birds).

To conclude this section we would briefly like to mention what we consider to be the major differences between this theory and the models of Meyer (1970) and Schaeffer and Wallace (1970). Though Meyer talks about these processes in very different terms, we doubt that our differences with his model are very substantive except in one respect. He considers several different decision strategies, some of which we have mentioned here. But he treats decision strategies as if people use one of these strategies consistently, at least in any given task, whereas we are arguing that the decision strategy will depend on the connections found. Our position weakens the kind of experimental predictions that can be made, but we think that is unavoidable.

While we are uncertain about some aspects of Schaeffer and Wallace's model, one major difference derives from their idea that concepts are compared in their entirety to determine a threshold for making a decision. One of Quillian's (1968) original arguments was that a concept has no entirety, that the meaning of a concept is the entire network of paths and concepts as accessed from the node of that concept. Activating a concept is a process that takes place over a period of time as paths are followed from the node of the concept. In Quillian's theory, it is possible to compare concepts with respect to the number of properties that have the same value (i.e., properties in common) or that have different values. In this respect, it is like Schaeffer and Wallace's model. But, in Quillian's theory, these are processes that require a search to locate intersections, and hence must take place over a period of time. Perhaps Schaeffer and Wallace's model could be translated into these terms, in which case this difference would disappear.

THE PERVASIVENESS OF IDENTIFYING CONCEPTS WITH EACH OTHER

In order to illustrate how pervasive the process of identifying similar concepts is, we will enumerate several examples that arise in comprehension and in answering questions. In different situations, the decision rule as to whether two concepts can be identified often changes, but we would argue that the processing involved is largely the same.

One very common problem in language comprehension is that of anaphoric reference (Olney, 1964; Quillian, 1969). This is the problem of identifying a noun or pronoun with previous words in the text. For example, consider the sentences:

1. The woman finally hired a lawyer. He was quite charming and greatly pleased his new client.

In the second sentence, "he," "his," and "client" refer to words in the previous sentence, and the problem is to decide which ones. There are often syntactic clues to help determine the proper referent, but the major part of the judgment must rest on concept identifiability: whether or not a "male person" ("he" or "his") can be a "woman," whether or not a "male person" can be a "lawyer," whether or not a "client" can be a "lawyer," and whether or not a "client" can be a "woman," in particular one who hires a lawyer. In anaphoric reference, concepts can be identified for precisely the same set of cases that are identifiable in Meyer's (1970) task, when the sentence starts with "Some." In other words, concepts are anaphorically identifiable whenever the concepts overlap in Venn diagram terms, as do thrones and chairs, or mothers and writers. In a sense, then, Meyer is studying the question of how people make anaphoric references.

Deeper into comprehension, concept identifiability plays an even larger role, especially in dealing with novelty. It is one of the basic processes that allows people to construct an interpretation of a new idea out of pieces of old ideas they have stored in memory. To take an example that may have some novelty left in it, suppose a person hears sentence (2) for the first time:

2. Dumbo the elephant could fly.

To make sense of this a listener will identify Dumbo the elephant with the first flying thing he can think of. This probably will be a bird rather than, say, a plane or a blimp, because in starting from "elephant" and "flying," the shortest applicable path usually will go through "bird" (though not for lovers of flying squirrels). Since having wings is crucial to a bird's flying, the listener will probably provide some sort of bird-like wings for Dumbo. The wings will come out of the sides somewhere, probably from the shoulders because they correspond to where birds' wings are located. In fact, by Disney's design, Dumbo used his very large ears as wings. This example illustrates that comprehension of new concepts is often based on identifying them by way of analogy with old concepts. The comprehension process in this case rests upon the identifiability of the concepts "elephant" and "bird." We think that the process by which "elephant" is identified with "bird" is the same process we described in the previous sections.

There are other examples of how comprehension often involves identifying two concepts by way of analogy. Metaphor is one example, as shown in (3).

3. The boy's brother is a hippopotamus.

A person can decide by the rules of anaphoric reference that a person's "brother" and a "hippopotamus" are not the same thing. Because the metaphoric reference equates them, it is necessary to identify them analogically. Thus, just as Dumbo the elephant was given wings which are the most applicable property for flying that birds have, so, for this case, will the brother be given the most applicable properties of hippopotami. One can infer that his brother must be a large and languorous sort of chap. In fact, with the earlier example of Dumbo, the elephant's flying was treated essentially as a metaphor. Metaphor is really just the case of identifying two concepts that are not identifiable anaphorically.

But the process of identifying concepts with related concepts in comprehension is not restricted to farfetched examples like flying elephants and hippopotamus brothers. It occurs in everyday language in various ways, as seen in (4) and (5):

4. An old knob was fastened on the gate.
5. He hung his coat on the freshly painted door.

In dealing with (4), a person may never have seen or heard of a knob on a gate, but he can readily identify the gate with a door, or the knob with a latch on a gate to make sense of the sentence. In (5), there is an even more common use of identification of concepts. The reader can identify the door in the sentence with a door in memory (either a specific door or a composite door) that he has seen a coat on. The door in memory that he identifies it with need not have been freshly painted, nor need he ever have seen a freshly painted door. He can apply the paint in the same way he has seen it applied on other objects. Thus by identifying the door in the sentence with both a door in memory and a freshly painted object in memory, a person can construct an interpretation of a situation he has never witnessed.

In this last example, we have slipped back to the case where comprehension is a matter of identifying new concepts with old concepts that have the same name. But treating an elephant like a bird, or a brother like a hippopotamus, are not very different from treating a gate like a door, or one door like another door. The first two cases are only farther fetched. In other words, the semantic distance is greater between an elephant and a bird than between one door and another.

The problem of concept identifiability comes up in question answering as well as comprehension. Suppose a person is asked a question like (6) or (7):

6. Does a leopard have stripes?
7. Can a canary quack?

For questions like (6), where there is a similar concept with the property mentioned (in this case tiger), we have found (Collins and Quillian, in press) that people take a relatively long time to decide the answer is "no." This result is understandable because subjects tell us they think of the fact that a leopard is similar to a tiger, which does have stripes. Our structural assumptions make the basis for the difficulty fairly clear. While people learn and store that tigers have stripes and leopards have spots, we doubt that they would ever learn or store that tigers do not have spots or that leopards do not have stripes. Thus, we would expect the fact that a tiger has stripes to be much more accessible starting from leopard than the fact that a leopard does not, inasmuch as the latter involves an inference: leopards have spots, and spots are not stripes. We will examine the nature of this inference further with example (7).

For (7), a person is likely to tell you the answer is no because it is ducks that quack and canaries aren't ducks. If so, the person has explicitly considered the question of whether canaries and ducks can be the same thing. We would argue that probably he has also tacitly considered whether singing, which is the sound canaries make, and quacking are the same. Thus, the question of concept identifiability comes up twice in both (6) and (7).

In this case, the reasoning involved in the above inference is quite illogical, even though it sounds plausible. Just because a seal is not a dog is no reason to conclude that a seal doesn't bark. Similarly, just because a dog can bark does not mean that it can't howl or whine. In other words, maybe canaries quack when they aren't singing even though they are not ducks. The inference that spots contradict stripes was of the same type, but slightly more logical in that there are no animals that have both stripes and spots. The illogic of the inference used to decide that a canary doesn't quack could be made logical if people had the information stored that only ducks can quack. But that cannot be the case, since a person will be in doubt as to whether a goose can quack unless or until he realizes that a goose honks. The thing about geese is that they are so similar (i.e., have so many properties in common) to ducks that they might just quack if one isn't careful. But if the person knew that only ducks quack, there should be no hesitation about geese once it is decided that geese aren't ducks. As another example, suppose people have stored that only dogs and seals bark. If they do, then of course they can infer that wolves do not bark, since wolves are neither dogs nor seals. We think people who know how similar wolves and dogs are will be in doubt, unless, of course, they have heard of a wolf barking. A wolf is similar enough to a dog that, even if one knows they howl, there is no reason to suppose that they do not bark.

These examples suggest that there is a tradeoff in people's use of this kind of inference. For the case of quacking, the more different an animal is from a duck (e.g:, a kangaroo), the more willing people are to conclude that the animal can't quack without knowing anything about the sound the animal makes. The reason why knowledge about the properties of the animal in question enters into this tradeoff probably is based on a principle such as: "The more I know about the animal, the more likely I would know about its quacking if it did in fact quack." In any case, this kind of inference is basic to the way people answer questions, and we fear that computers will have to give up their past insistence upon rigor, if they want to be able to answer the range of questions people can answer.

There is another way that people obtain inferential power from this process of identifying a concept with a similar concept in question answering. Suppose a questioner needs information about the cost to ship tea to Boston from England, or information about the estimated number of schools in Boston. When the direct information on such questions is lacking for Boston but available for other cities, people often rely upon a type of analogical inference for an answer. They identify a city that is like Boston in relevant respects and then infer the answer for Boston from the answer for the other city. For the question of costs of shipping tea to Boston, the strategy is to pick a nearby city (say New York or Providence) for which a figure is available. For the question about the number of schools in Boston, the strategy is to pick a city the same size as Boston, (say St. Louis) for which a figure is available. Then the answer for the other city may be adjusted to accommodate any difference between Boston and the other city on the relevant dimension. As Copi (1961) points out, analogy is at the basis of most of our ordinary inferences from past experience into the future, as when one reads a book because he enjoyed the author's previous books. But we would argue further that analogy, in fact, underlies every aspect of our inferential reasoning.

In this section, we have enumerated a number of different examples from natural language where the processing involved identifying one concept with a similar concept or, on the other hand, finding a basis for distinguishing one concept from a similar concept. To psychologists, this is an old process in a new guise. From the first point of view, it is the process of *generalization;* from the other point of view it is the process of *discrimination.* Surely Pavlov would think it a great joke to find us caught in this web.

Knowing the new uses that evolution makes of old organs, it is not too surprising to find such a primitive capability put to heavy use in the most sophisticated of man's talents. This may be an area where linguists might utilize psychological knowledge for a change instead of the other way round. As Brown (1970) points out, this would probably be the first time in the history of psycholinguistics.

Generalization and discrimination do not come naturally to present-day serial computers, but by using tags to simulate spreading activation, we think it is possible to develop generalization and discrimination processes in computers. The strategies outlined in the last section were examples of such processes.

Two Uses of Imagery

This work started out by investigating structure and processing in a semantic network (Quillian, 1968, 1969) of interconnected concepts. Imagery was happily ignored in order to keep the problems down to a manageable size, though there was an unspoken assumption that images could be generated from concepts. In this section, we will not try to deal with imagery systematically, but only mention where it fits in the scheme of computer-language processing. Imagery has intruded into our experimental studies of question answering because subjects usually give some reason based on imagery for rejecting false sentences (Collins and

Quillian, in press). While imagery probably has many uses, we want to mention two that are particularly relevant to the relation between imagery and concepts.

When imagery intruded into our subjects' reports in rejecting false sentences, it turned out to be used in a way that Quillian had developed to handle the problems of anaphoric reference within his semantic network. In other words, the strategy that people reported using with images was the same strategy Quillian planned to use with semantic properties. In particular, the strategy was to reject the possibility of identifying two concepts whenever the concepts had properties where the attributes (or relations) matched and the values were different. In the anaphoric-reference example of the last section on page 335, "he" did not refer to "woman," because even though they have a common superset ("person"), one has the value "male" and the other "female" on the attribute "sex." The use of this strategy with sensory properties is exactly the same. To take one example, a subject rejected the identifiability of a pearl and a bean after comparing them in imagery. He noticed they appeared to be the same size, but that they were different in shape and color, which formed the basis for his rejection. Imagery may be an efficient way to compare concepts to find a mismatch, because images can be manipulated in a way that properties cannot. Perhaps interactions between separately stored concepts and their properties can be evaluated more readily if the concepts are generated together in imagery. Such an interaction can be illustrated by an example from an earlier paper (Collins and Quillian, in press). Several subjects reported that they rejected "A limousine has a rudder" as false by imaging the rudder on the back of a limousine. It is an imagined interaction that produces a mismatch with memory.

The second aspect of imagery we want to mention makes it seem as if there is much more information in internally generated images than there need be. We would argue that images (not eidetic images, however) contain much less information than pictures. What appears to be richness in images, we think, derives from changing images by changing the concepts from which they are generated. For example, if a person thinks back in memory as to where he left his keys in his office, the procedure might be something like the following:

1. Generate an image of the office and pick the most likely piece of furniture there (say a desk) where the keys might be.
2. Generate an image of the desk top, and scan that for the keys.
3. If not found, then generate the image of the inside of the desk drawer and scan that for the keys.

4. If still not found, regenerate the image of the office and pick the next most likely piece of furniture.
5. etc.

The ability to change from imaging one concept to imaging another would give a computer system the kind of power that a zoom lens on a camera provides. The difference is that, unlike the camera picture, not all the information about the desk top and the drawer, obtained by changing images, is in the original image of the office. This kind of manipulation of internally-generated images from a concept network is still only a gleam in some computer-mind's eye.[8]

INDUCTION AND LEARNING

How information is put into memory obviously has much to do with how it can be retrieved. Until now we have only dealt with inferences in retrieving information as opposed to inferences in storing information. Generally, the inferences made in the process of storing information are referred to as inductions. For example, if a child sees red flowers on several occasions that people refer to as roses, he may well induce from this experience the information that roses are red (i.e., that particular pinkish-red most roses are) as a property which can be evoked by the concept "rose." The fact that the property of redness comes to be evoked by the concept of rose is noncommittal, as to whether all roses are red, most roses are red, some roses are red, or only a few roses are red (though in the latter case redness probably would never come to be evoked). To evaluate whether all, or most, or some, or a few roses are red, given that a person has not learned the answer directly, would require a search of memory starting at "color" and "rose" to find connections through colors other than red. Depending on how many nonred instances of roses are found (with a given amount of effort or as compared to red ones), some estimate about the correct answer can be made.

The importance of induction to language processing lies in the fact that most properties of concepts are not learned directly, but are derived from specific instances of the concept. A person probably stores the fact that birds have wings, because he sees many instances of birds with wings. Once he stores by induction from cases that birds have wings, he can then deduce that a new instance he knows to be a bird, say a mudlark, must therefore have wings.

---

[8] Such a capability for maps is now being developed by Jaime Carbonell at BBN.

The fundamental question about induction is how to decide which properties of specific instances should be stored with the superset? The problem has been attacked for computers by Becker (1970) and Winston (1970). Both deal with the problem in terms of generalization and discrimination; apparently Pavlov has ensnared them as well. Both their systems are designed to learn concepts from graph-structure descriptions of visual scenes, and so both deal with the problem in terms of visual properties rather than symbolic (i.e., nonimageable) properties. If concept learning is in terms of verbal inputs, as might be the case with "vehicle," then the problem would arise in terms of symbolic properties. For instance, if a person is told that cars, buses, and trains are all vehicles, then he may induce from these instances which of their properties apply to the concept vehicle. Again, we would argue that the problem is fundamentally the same whether posed in visual terms or symbolic terms, though visual concept learning is prior developmentally. We will outline the process (for more detail, see Becker or Winston) with an example from the world of birds where we feel relatively safe from flights of fancy.

Suppose that one sees a cute little red feathery creature with wings and a beak, etc., and that it is referred to as a "bird." Next, imagine, maybe, a larger (by a factor of three) black feathery creature with wings and a beak that is referred to as a "bird." Next, maybe a little yellowish feathery creature with wings and a beak that is referred to as a "bird." Each time a person hears a repetition of the word "bird" in the sequence, it leads him to those properties he had stored previously with bird. If a semantic search starts with "bird" on the one hand, and the instance he is looking at on the other, then the connections found will be through properties that the bird in memory and the bird at hand have in common. Therefore, it is precisely those common properties that will be made more accessible (i.e., wings, feathers, and beaks) and the others will not (i.e., color and size).[9] The process as described is pure generalization. Winston (1970) points out that when learning "arch" in this way, the top piece of the arch may be a rectangle one time and a wedge the next time. The strategy he uses is to assume that, when such a difference is found, the top piece can be any instance of the lowest common superset (in this case, block) of the top pieces seen so far. This is exactly the way we would have it.

Suppose, instead of each instance being referred to as a "bird" in

---

[9] Increasing accessibility will also produce forgetting. As some properties become more and more accessible, the likelihood of retrieving properties that do not becomes smaller and smaller. This is in line with Shiffrin's (1970) recent finding which suggests that forgetting is purely a failure in retrieval.

the preceding sequence, the first was referred to as a "cardinal," the second a "vulture," and the third a "canary." When a person sees the canary in this sequence, he will search his memory for a concept that has the properties he sees the canary to have. If we assume he does not have the concept "canary," then he will intersect with the concept in memory most like a canary, that is, the one with the most properties in common with the canary he sees. If he has already formed the concept for bird, then he will find the concept "bird." If he only had learned "cardinal" and "vulture," then he would probably find the concept "cardinal," because it is more like a canary than a vulture is. Thinking of the concept "bird" or "cardinal" when presented with a canary is like thinking of a tiger when asked "Does a leopard have stripes"? [Example (6), page 337]. Whether he locates the concept "bird" or "cardinal" in his search, the name will be different from the name "canary" given to the thing he is looking at. Because the names are different, this forces him to locate those properties that are different (e.g., color). It is the distinguishing properties that are then stored with the concept "canary." In Winston's terms, a bird or cardinal is a "near miss" for the concept "canary." As we described it in this example, the process is pure discrimination learning. Generally though, a person would see several positive instances of canaries in forming the concept "canary." Hence, the course of true learning will be both a generalization and discrimination process. But in learning the concept "bird," we doubt that there are any of the "near misses" that Winston's program seems to rely on. That is to say, people don't look at bats in order to learn the concept "bird."

There are several nonobvious implications of this view. One important implication is that higher-level concepts[10] like bird are learned mostly by generalization, and lower-level concepts like canary mostly by discrimination. Of course, to the degree that people relate birds to other animals in learning the concept "bird," obviously they will have to discriminate birds from the other animals. But if one considers the relative similarity between birds and dogs, say, as opposed to the similarity between canaries and cardinals, it should be clear why we think that learning the concept "bird" will involve much less discrimination than learning the concept "canary" will. And if one considers the relative variability in properties among birds as opposed to the variability among canaries, it should be clear why we think that learning the concept "bird" will involve more generalization than will learning the concept

---

[10] Of course, there are probably exceptions such as mammal. Mammals, though a higher-level concept, may be learned mostly by discrimination from reptiles, amphibians, fish, and birds.

"canary." Anglin (1970), in recent monograph, conducted several experiments with children to find out whether the learning of word meanings was a generalization process or a discrimination process. He concluded that it was a generalization process, but the lowest-level concepts he used were boy and girl. In our view, his selection of words would prevent his finding the discrimination learning that takes place at lower levels, such as between canaries and cardinals.

It turns out that when negative properties are stored in memory (such as "Penguins cannot fly" or "A vest does not have sleeves," in Table 1) it is because learning depends on discrimination. Hence, there is always some similar concept (a confusable concept) which has the given property. In retrieval, the confusability will slow a person down so that it will be difficult to decide, for example, "Does a vest have sleeves?" That is to say, in starting at "vest" and "sleeves," the semantic search is likely to turn up "suit jacket" or some other similar concept with sleeves. Because a concept like "bird" is learned mostly by generalization, there are not likely to be any negative properties stored with it, e.g., "Birds do not have antlers."

As Becker points out, properties never become defining properties by either generalization or discrimination. This is the general semanticist's old argument (Korzybski, 1933) that there is no essence of "chairness" or "pencilness." To take Winston's example of arches, people can still identify Roman or Greek arches as arches, even though the top piece has been knocked down and is lying on the ground. The lack of defining properties in this world makes life much harder for computers.

As the process of learning the concept "canary" was described, it was mostly a discrimination process, but partly a generalization process. To the degree it was a discrimination process, the fact that canaries have wings and feathers would be ignored, since wings and feathers do not differentiate canaries from cardinals or birds. However, to the degree that it is a generalization process, wings and feathers would always co-occur with instances of canaries, and hence would be stored as properties of canaries. Then the question arises as to why our data show (as argued in The Hierarchical Organization of Concepts) that people decide about a sentence like "A canary has wings" by inference from the fact that a canary is a bird and birds have wings. We think the finding has two bases.

First, for many kinds of birds (and other things as well) most people do not have stored much more than the fact that they are birds. This is because a person does not form concepts like mudlark by a process of generalization and discrimination. Instead, he may be told, or he may infer from something he reads, that a mudlark is a bird. When some psychologist asks him to decide if "A mudlark has wings" is true or false, he responds true, because he knows a mudlark is a bird. In constructing sentences for our study (Collins and Quillian, 1969), we made an effort to choose instances (e.g., wren) where the superset property (e.g., has wings) was not particularly associated with the instance. Hence, by design the sentences used were ones likely to be decided by inference. There is nothing in the theory, however, that prevents storing superset properties with particular instances, and we certainly think it is a common practice.

Second, even if a superset property is stored directly with an instance, it may be faster to retrieve it by inference from the superset. This might happen if the property is fairly inaccessible from the instance, but highly accessible from the superset. The learning process we described would tend to produce such a difference in accessibility because generalization of the property (having wings) for the superset (bird) makes the property more accessible, and discrimination for the instance (canary) does not make the property more accessible. As we argued earlier, learning the superset is mostly a generalization process and learning the instance is mostly a discrimination process. Similar differences in accessibility can produce a wrong response to the question, "Can a penguin fly?" If the person thinks first that a penguin is a bird, and birds fly, before he retrieves the fact that penguins can't fly, he may well give an incorrect "yes" response to the question.

One final comment about generalization and discrimination in computers. In The Pervasiveness of Identifying Concepts with each Other, we talked about generalization and discrimination in comprehension and retrieval. There it was necessary to identify a concept with a similar concept in order to comprehend a sentence or answer a question. In this section we have been discussing generalization and discrimination in learning. Here it is necessary to identify the object at hand with a similar concept in memory. Whether the concepts that are identified in this way are treated similarly (generalization) or differently (discrimination) is imposed in either case not by the nature of the concepts identified, but by the constraints of the task. In our example of metaphor, the hippopotamus and the boy's brother are treated similarly by the way the sentence forces them to be identified. In generalization learning, a cardinal and a canary are treated similarly because they are both called birds. In discrimination learning, on the other hand, a canary would be distinguished from a cardinal, and in anaphoric reference, a boy's brother would not be identified with a hippopotamus. The importance of generalization and discrimination to learning, comprehension, and retrieval makes it imperative, we think, that these processes be treated by any computer implementation in the same terms.

ANALOGY AS A LINGUISTIC CONSTRUCT

Linguistic approaches to semantic theory, which are at least partially reflected in Kintsch's paper in this volume, typically specify human semantic knowledge in terms of selection restrictions. Therein lies a major difference between our proposed theory and linguistic-based theories. The difference can be illustrated with an example from Kintsch's paper where he points out that it is permissible to say "The child grew," "The corn grew," and "The farmer grew the corn," but not "The parents grew the child." He explains this in terms of a selection restriction on the use of grow that prohibits a human or animal object in the presence of an agent. Agent and object in this description are *cases*, which are special kinds of relations used in describing verb concepts. In our thinking, cases function for verb concepts much like inference-carrying relations function for noun concepts, in that they are used extensively in language processing, and there are a small number of them that are used quite frequently. On this we are in agreement with Kintsch.

The disagreement can be illustrated by a setting from one of the Oz books by Baum (1908). In the story, Dorothy falls into the earth during an earthquake and lands in a city where apparently there are no children among the people. As the story progresses, she finds out that the people are vegetables and that they have a special garden just outside the city. It turns out that the adults grow children in the garden until they are ripe and then the adults pick them from the garden to become members of the community. Now, in this setting, talk of adults growing children sounds quite natural and, of course, it is because the people are vegetables and it is quite easy to analogically identify vegetable children with plants. Even without such an elaborate plot, it is perfectly easy to understand what is meant by "A farmer grew sheep on his ranch" or "The parents grew their child in isolation."

Everybody has heard of people growing corn, or flowers, or grass and, from these examples, a person might induce the concept of plant as the object of grow in the presence of an agent. Then when a person hears that a lazy man grows rocks in his garden or a scientist grows a theory during his coffee breaks, these can be understood by analogy with how people grow plants. Kintsch postulates special metaphor rules to deal with such cases, but in our view that merely sets up two processes where only one process is necessary. In comprehending such sentences, we think people will always try to find a meaning by identifying the object of grow in the presence of an agent with the concept plant, or whatever object concepts are learned or induced for the verb grow. The more farfetched is the analogy, or, in other words, the more distant is the object concept from plant in semantic memory, the more odd the sentence will sound, that is, the more semantically anomalous it will be. But the point is that there need be no switch or line on one side of which is semantic acceptability, and on the other side of which is metaphor or anomaly.

In our view, there is a continuum from semantic acceptability to metaphor to anomaly, depending on how removed the given object (e.g., trees, horses, children, rocks) is from plant. If you ask a person whether a particular sentence is a metaphor or not, he can answer, but we think he must specifically evaluate the sentence to do so. The test he would probably apply is whether the given object is acceptable as an instance of plant (i.e., whether there is any overlap in Venn diagram terms between the given object and plants). If it is, then he will say it is semantically acceptable, and if not he will call it a metaphor. But if you ask a person whether "He grew oysters in his pond" is a metaphor or not, he is likely to have trouble seeing that it is, because oysters, though animals, are so plant-like. The fact that there are hard cases to decide argues quite strongly that there is a continuum rather than a switch.

It is possible to think about selection restrictions in terms of storing negative information rather than positive information in memory. For example, one might store the information that grow prohibits a human or animal object in the presence of an agent, rather than the information that grow takes plants as the object in the presence of an agent. We are not sure whether Kintsch thinks that negative information is stored or not. As we argue in the preceding section, it seems to us that negative information is only stored in the process of discrimination learning. There is nothing about the process of hearing sentences where people grow flowers, or corn, or grass that would produce discrimination learning. Hearing such sentences would be a case of pure generalization learning, unless children learn that saying something like "The farmer grew the horses" or "The mother grew children" is wrong. We seriously doubt that they are told such sentences are wrong. Should they utter such sentences (if they do at all), we doubt that they would ever be corrected for doing so. But unless they learn such sentences are wrong, our position means that children would never form the negative property that animal or person is prohibited as the object of grow in the presence of an agent. They would only learn the positive property that plants are often the object of grow in the presence of an agent.

One aspect of the learning process is worth pointing out. Suppose all a child knows about growing is that children grow up. Then if he hears the sentence "The corn grows in the field," he can understand it by identifying corn with children. But this use of corn is a metaphor for the child. Suppose later he hears that "flowers grow." He is more likely to relate the flowers to corn than children, and so that child is likely to understand the flowers growing by analogy with corn growing. This too is a metaphor for the child, because clearly flowers are not corn. In general then, depending on what one has heard before, one man's semantically acceptable sentence is another man's metaphor.

The Theory and Experimental Psychology

The theory we have outlined is not designed specifically to yield clear-cut predictions about experiments. Nor did it arise as an explanation of results found in experiments. It started out as a strategy for dealing with language in a computer, and much of the shape it is growing derives not from watching people perform, but, instead, from what programmers figure out about people when they try to build parts of a language-using machine. The theory's main function is to provide guidelines for how to go about building a memory. Hence, it contains descriptions of internal structures and processes, rather than input-output transfer functions for various stages of processing. The processes we are hypothesizing can be put together in too many ways, depending on the strategies of the subject, to always yield output predictions from various input conditions. However, we have tried to show that it leads to some hypotheses that can be tested experimentally.

We think psychology can profit from trying to build a language-using machine, just as the theory of flying has profited from trying to build a flying machine. Think of all the useless experiments on flying that could have been done with birds.

Summary

The first section of the paper considered the philosophical and methodological implications of viewing psychology from the point of view of building computer systems that simulate human language processing. The second section discussed the structure of semantic memory: in particular, the nature of concepts and their relation to words and images, the kind of semantic information people learn and do not learn, and the kind of inference bearing relations that form the basis for the organization of semantic memory. The third section dealt with the processing of information in semantic memory. We discussed the semantic search during comprehension and retrieval, the tacit processing this search implies, the pervasiveness of identifying similar concepts with each other in language processing, the decision rules that are applied to the results of a semantic search in order to decide whether two similar concepts can be identified, the role of imagery in language processing, and the way people induce what properties to store with what concepts. Our ideas were presented as a loosely constructed theory of how people function as language users and how computers will have to function to become language users.

References

Anglin, J. M. *The growth of word meaning.* Research Monograph No. 53, Cambridge, Mass.: M.I.T. Press, 1970.

Baum, L. F. *Dorothy and the wizard in Oz.* Chicago, Illinois: Reilly and Lee, 1908.

Baylor, G. W. *A treatise on the mind's eye.* Institut de Psychologie, Université de Montreal, 1971.

Becker, J. D. The modelling of simple analogic and inductive processes in a semantic memory system. *Proceedings of the International Joint Conference on Artificial Intelligence,* D. Walker and L. Norton (Eds.), 1969.

Becker, J. D. An information-processing model of intermediate-level cognition. Ph.D dissertation, Stanford Artificial Intelligence Project, 1970.

Begg, I., & Paivio, A. Concreteness and imagery in sentence meaning. *Journal of Verbal Learning and Verbal Behavior,* 1969, **8**, 821–827.

Bobrow, D. G., and Fraser, J. B. An augmented state transition network analysis procedure. *Proceedings of the International Joint Conference on Artificial Intelligence,* D. Walker and L. Norton (Eds.), 1969.

Bobrow, D. G., Fraser, J. B., & Quillian, M. R. Automated language processing. In C. A. Cuadra (Ed.), *Annual review of information science and technology,* Vol. 2. New York: Wiley, 1967.

Bower, G. R. Mental imagery and associative learning. In L. W. Gregg (Ed.), *Cognition in Learning and Memory.* New York: Wiley, in press.

Brown, R. *Psycholinguistics.* New York: Free Press, 1970.

Bruner, J. S., & Minturn, A. L. Perceptual identification and perceptual organization. *Journal of Genetic Psychology,* 1955, **53**, 21–28.

Carbonell, J. R. Mixed-initiative man-computer instructional dialogues. Ph.D dissertation. M.I.T., 1970. Also BBN Report No. 1971. Reprinted in part as: AI in CAI: An artificial intelligence approach to computer-aided instruction. *IEEE Transactions on Man-Machine Systems,* 1970, **MMS-11**, 190–202.

Chase, W. G., & Clark, H. H. Mental operations in the comparison of sentences and pictures. In L. W. Gregg (Ed.), *Cognition in Learning and Memory.* New York: Wiley, in press.

Collins, A. M., and Quillian, M. R. Retrieval time from semantic memory. *Journal of Verbal Learning and Verbal Behavior,* 1969, **8**, 240–247.

Collins, A. M., & Quillian, M. R. Facilitating retrieval from semantic memory: The effect of repeating part of an inference. *Acta Psychologica*, 1970, 33, 304–314. (a)

Collins, A. M., & Quillian, M. R. Does category size affect categorization time? *Journal of Verbal Learning and Verbal Behavior*, 1970, 9, 432–438. (b)

Collins, A. M., & Quillian, M. R. Experiments on semantic memory and language comprehension. In L. W. Gregg (Ed.), *Cognition in Learning and Memory*. New York: Wiley, in press.

Collins, A. M., & Quillian, M. R. Category and subcategories in semantic memory. In preparation.

Copi, I. M. *Introduction to logic*. New York: Macmillan, 1961.

Gelernter, H. Realization of a geometry-theorem proving machine. In E. A. Feigenbaum & J. Feldman (Eds.), *Computers and Thought*. New York: McGraw-Hill, 1963.

Giuliano, V. E. Analog networks for word association. *IEEE Transactions on Military Electronics*, 1963, MIL-7, 221–225. Reprinted in part in D. A. Norman, *Memory and Attention*. New York: Wiley, 1969.

Johnson-Laird, P. N., & Stevenson, R. Memory for syntax. *Nature*, 1970, 227, 412–413.

Kolers, P. A. Interlingual facilitation of short-term memory. *Journal of Verbal Learning and Verbal Behavior*, 1966, 5, 314–319.

Korzybski, A. *Science and Sanity*. Lancaster, Pennsylvania: Science Press, 1933.

Landauer, T. K., & Freedman, J. L. Information retrieval from long-term memory: Category size and recognition time. *Journal of Verbal Learning and Verbal Behavior*, 1968, 7, 291–295.

Meyer, D. E. On the representation and retrieval of stored semantic information. *Cognitive Psychology*, 1970, 1, 242–300.

Olney, J. C. Some patterns observed in the contextual specialization of word senses. *Information Storage and Retrieval*, 1964, 2, 79–101.

Paivio, A. Mental imagery in associative learning and memory. *Psychological Review*, 1969, 76, 241–263.

Polyani, M. *The tacit dimension*. Garden City, New York: Doubleday, 1966.

Quillian, M. R. The teachable language comprehender: A simulation program and theory of language. *Communications of the ACM*, 1969, 12, 459–476.

Quillian, M. R. Semantic memory. In M. Minsky (Ed.), *Semantic Information Processing*, Cambridge, Massachusetts: M.I.T. Press, 1968.

Rubenstein, H., Lewis, S. S., & Rubenstein, M. A. Homographic entries in the internal lexicon: Effects of systematicity and relative frequency of meanings. *Journal of Verbal Learning and Verbal Behavior*, 1971, 10, 57–62.

Schaeffer, B., & Wallace, R. Semantic similarity and the comparison of word meanings. *Journal of Experimental Psychology*, 1969, 82, 343–346.

Schaeffer, B., & Wallace, R. The comparison of word meanings. *Journal of Experimental Psychology*, 1970, 86, 144–152.

Shiffrin, R. M. Forgetting: Trace erosion or retrieval failure? *Science*, 1970, 168, 1601–1603.

Simmons, R. F., Burger, J. F., & Long, R. E. An approach toward answering English questions from text. *AFIPS Conference Proceedings*, Vol. 29. Washington, D.C.: Spartan Books, 1966.

Simon, H. A. What is visual imagery? An information processing interpretation. In L. W. Gregg (Ed.), *Cognition in learning and memory*. New York: Wiley, in press.

Thorne, J. P., Bratley, P., & Dewar, H. The syntactic analysis of English by machine. In D. Michie (Ed.), *Machine intelligence*, Vol. 3. New York: American Elsevier, 1968.

Wilkins, A. J. Conjoint frequency, category size, and categorization time. *Journal Verbal Learning and Verbal Behavior*, 1971, 10, 382–385.

Winston, P. H. Learning structural descriptions from examples. Ph.D thesis, M.I.T., Project MAC, MAC TR-76, 1970.

Wittgenstein, L. *Philosophical Investigations* (Translated by G. E. M. Anscombe). Oxford: Blackwell, 1953.

Woods, W. A. Context-sensitive parsing. *Communications of the ACM*, 1970, 13, 437–445.

9 | On the Acquisition of a Simple Cognitive Structure[1]

James G. Greeno

The analysis of mental structure is one of the original problems of experimental psychology. It was the central problem of introspective psychology, or "structuralism." However, during the period in which behaviorism and functionalism dominated theoretical work in psychology, most attention in the psychology of learning was given to the acquisition of entities thought to be relatively simple, such as single response, stimulus discriminations, and associations between verbal units.

[1] This research was supported in part by the U.S. Office of Education Grant No. OEG-0-9-320447-4194 (010), and by the Advanced Research Projects Agency, Department of Defense, monitored by the Air Force Office of Scientific Research, under Contract No. AF 49(638)-1736 with the Human Performance Center, Department of Psychology, University of Michigan.

During recent years, an increasing number of psychologists have returned their attention to the analysis of cognitive structure. Psychological analyses have been both stimulated and enriched by theoretical developments in linguistics, and computer science, as well as by new awareness of theories of which we in America were only dimly aware. The strong interest in and use of the ideas of Chomsky, Simon, and Piaget by American psychologists may be a salient signal that we are entering a new era of structuralism in psychology.

Recent investigations of cognitive structure have used a variety of materials, ranging from lists of words that can be grouped in categories to the game of chess. If word lists are relatively low in structural complexity, and chess is relatively high, then the studies that I will describe use materials with an intermediate amount of structural complexity. In our laboratory at Michigan, we have begun a program of investigation in which our subjects learn a small portion of elementary probability theory. In this paper, I will present some information about how the binomial formula is acquired.

The binomial formula and other simple mathematical ideas are modest cognitive structures, to be sure. Our hope in using this structure is that its acquisition may be simple enough that useful general properties of the process of acquiring cognitive structures can be discerned, where they might be more difficult to discover in situations where the process of acquisition is more complicated. A simple mathematical formula may have a number of advantages in this connection.

First, and perhaps most obviously, analysis of the process of acquiring a simple formula has more hope of being a manageable theoretical and empirical task than is, say, the analysis of acquiring skill in chess. It is in order to keep the task within bounds that we hope will be manageable that we have concentrated on a single conceptual structure—the binomial formula—rather than taking on the task of analysing the learning of a more general topic, such as statistics.

A second advantage in studying acquisition of a simple mathematical structure is that the material being learned by the subject is organized in a way that is well-understood. In this respect, the choice of elementary mathematics as an experimental material allows us to avoid a problem encountered in studying processes of sentence comprehension and memory for sentences. There is considerable disagreement among linguists as to how a sentence is organized. For a psychologist, this lack of agreement on a theory about sentences means that there is no trustworthy description of the stimuli that are used in studies of sentence comprehension and retention. (Perhaps it would be better to say that there are many descriptions, and we cannot determine which one to trust.) On the other hand, there is no disagreement among mathematicians about how the binomial formula is organized. There is a certain comfort in studying the psychology of a situation, knowing that the structural description of our materials is not likely to change very much in the near future.

A third advantage that we see in the materials we are studying is that the structure is complicated enough to impose rather strict constraints on the subjects who learn the materials. We know with near certainty what a subject must learn in order to acquire the cognitive structure corresponding to the binomial formula. This makes our situation somewhat less uncertain than the situation of investigators who use materials that are more simply structured. It is now clear that even in learning a list of unrelated words, a subject finds relationships among the words, thereby organizing the words in some pattern or structure. A major difficulty in analysis is that with material that can be organized in many different ways, subjects acquire structures that are quite heterogeneous; hence the label, "subjective organization" (Tulving, 1962). The problem is analogous to one mentioned by Hilgard (1951) who remarked that if the experimenter does not provide instructions, subjects will provide their own and these will be variable, rather than absent. In relation to the present problem, it seems likely that if the experimenter does not provide a set of materials that are organized coherently, subjects will provide their own principles of organization and these will be variable, rather than absent.

To summarize these methodological remarks, we have chosen to study acquisition of a single mathematical concept with relatively simple structure. Hopefully, the structure we have chosen is simple enough to make the analysis manageable, but sufficiently complex in organization that subjects will all organize it in essentially similar ways. The choice of a mathematical structure allows us to be confident that the structural description of the material that we have is the correct one.

Individual Differences in Learning and Generalization

The first study that I will report was carried out by Dennis Egan. Egan was interested in a straightforward pedagogical question: is it possible to find measuring instruments that would allow subjects to be assigned to teaching methods in helpful ways? He chose to study two instructional methods that have been very much in the news lately— learning by discovery and rule learning. These labels do not refer to entirely homogeneous procedures, but Egan discerned a component of common meaning among characterizations in the literature. If material

is taught using the discovery method, the learner engages in more problem-solving activity than when a more expository method is used. Egan
hypothesized that the most relevant characteristic of discovery learning
from the point of view of psychology might be the demands made by
the discovery procedure on the subject's skill and knowledge about the
material. In the discovery method, subjects learn as they solve problems.
In order to solve problems, they must have some knowledge and skill
that is probably prerequisite to the material being taught, but that must
be accessible to a subject if he is to be able to proceed through the
material in the lesson.

This argument leads one to expect an interaction between the ability
of the subject and the effectiveness of a teaching method. On the hypothesis that a discovery method demands more of a subject, one would
expect the ability of subjects to make more difference if they learned
by the discovery method than if they learned by a method in which
the subject is less active. One of the surprising aspects of the literature
on discovery learning is that this interaction has not been demonstrated.
Corman (1957) and Tallmadge (1968) have compared discovery and
rule-learning methods with subjects whose ability was measured. Their
findings were that bright subjects learn better than duller subjects, and
their versions of discovery learning were more effective than their rule-
learning procedures. But no reliable interaction was observed.

Undaunted, Egan proceeded with his experiment. He gave three tests
to his subjects, who were undergraduates who had not studied probability
or statistics, and asked them for their scores on the Mathematics Scholas-
tic Aptitude Test (MSAT). The MSAT scores, provided by 43 of the
58 subjects, give data comparable to those of earlier studies where measures were of relatively general ability. One test that Egan gave measured subjects' familiarity with some general concepts in the theory
of probability of a joint event, the probability of an event's nonoccur-
rence, and the probability of either of two events. A second test measured
the subjects' skill at some arithmetic operations involved in calculating
binomial probabilities. Problems were given involving computation and
multiplication of factorials, addition of fractions, and raising fractions
to powers. The third test given by Egan was adapted from a task used
by Leskow and Smock (1969). Subjects were asked to write out as many
of the permutations of the numbers 1234 as they could. Instructions
for this task included remarks about the need for a systematic plan
to ensure the inclusion of all possible orders with no duplications. Scores
on this test were based on how closely a subject approximated one of
two strategies: (1) holding initial digits constant and changing digits
on the right, or (2) rotating the preceding permutation.

The idea behind these three tests was to measure knowledge and skill that might be particularly relevant to the learning task to be used. The relevance of the arithmetic skills and the probability concepts is self-evident. The reason for giving the permutations test had to do with a Piagetian idea about learning in general, and in probabilistic concepts in particular. Piaget and Inhelder (1951) has hypothesized that a prerequisite for understanding probabilities is the aspect of formal operations having to do with a person's ability to deal systematically with a set of possibilities. Piaget's experiments suggest that the understanding of probability depends on the ability to systematically count the elements in an outcome space. The permutations test seems to relate closely to that cognitive skill. We felt that this test might be especially relevant to the learning of probability concepts in the discovery method, because there the subject is required to generate hypotheses about the correct answer, and the differences between subjects on the permutations test might reflect differences in their abilities to develop ideas about general relationships in a situation that has important aspects in common with the learning material.

Three subgroups were formed on the basis of each of the measures of ability. For the MSAT, a low score was less than 600, a medium score between 600 and 699, and a high score was 700 or greater. The test of specific concepts had 14 items; scores of 10 or fewer were low, 11 or 12 was medium, and 13 or 14 was high. The arithmetic test had eight items: 0–4 was low, 5–7 was medium, and 8 was high.

Egan devised a sequence of the ideas involved in the binomial distribution that could be presented either as a discovery method, where the ideas were implicit in problems the subject solved, or as a rule method, where the ideas were presented explicitly. The sequence is presented schematically in Figure 1, where the ideas are represented by their symbols in the formula. The general procedure was to present a problem, starting with a problem involving the whole formula (or concept) but usually involving some component of the formula, and see whether the subject knew how to solve it. This was tested by a multiple choice question at each stage. If the subject missed the problem, the concept or formula involved at that level was parsed, providing more detailed problems and instruction. When the subject succeeded in a component, he moved on to another concept at the same level, or returned to a more complex concept that he had missed earlier.

This sequence of ideas was presented in two general ways, with 29 subjects in each condition. Egan's version of discovery learning involved presenting a question at each stage, stated in ordinary English (that is, not in an algebraic formula), as nontechnically as possible. On the

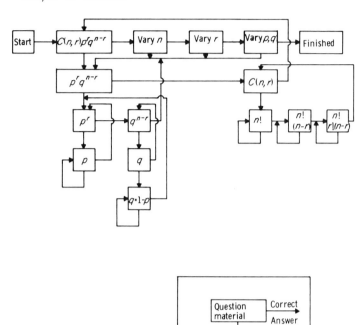

Fig. 1. Flow chart showing the sequence in which concepts were presented in Egan's experiment.

other hand, subjects in rule learning received problems stated as formulas, along with brief definitions of the variables in the formulas. Each step in rule learning had the character of showing the subject how to calculate something, and giving a numerical example, while in discovery learning the items had the quality of an algebra word problem, with the content having to do with the probability of something, or the number of ways something could happen, and so on.

Three dependent variables were measured. One was the amount of time taken by each subject in completing the learning program. A second was the number of errors made by the subject during learning. And the third was the proportion of errors made on a 10-item test following the completion of instruction. The problems on the post test were all multiple choice questions involving calculation of binomial probability in different situations.

Some general findings can be mentioned to begin. First, subjects committed significantly more errors in the discovery method than in the rule method $(p < .01)$. However, there was not a reliable difference between the methods in the amount of time taken by subjects in completing the instruction. The difference in errors is a straightforward result of the difference in methods; the discovery method was intended to require subjects to infer principles from the problems, and had subjects not made more errors in discovery than in rule learning the intended difference between the methods would have been suspect. On the other hand, the lack of a sizable difference in time required for the instruction is a comforting result. It suggests that there was not a substantial difference in the overall difficulty of the two teaching programs.

A third finding was that performance in the post test did not differ significantly between subjects who received the two kinds of instruction. This, like the lack of difference in instruction time, is a pleasant finding since it suggests that differences between the methods probably were not produced by any overall difference in effectiveness of instruction.

A fourth general finding was that the groups formed on the basis of MSAT scores, as well as on the tests of specific concepts relating to probability and arithmetic skills, all differed significantly on all of the dependent variables $(p < .01)$. Brighter subjects learned faster and with fewer errors, and also learned more, than subjects who were not as bright. More to the point, perhaps, the tests of concepts and arithmetic measured characteristics that were relevant to the learning task.

Recall that the main point of the experiment had to do with interactions between ability of subjects and instructional method. First, consider the number of errors made during learning. The data are given in Figure 2. The gist of the results is that in rule learning, few errors were committed by any subjects, while in discovery learning, more errors were committed, and the number of errors was related to subjects' ability in the expected direction. The interactions were reliable $(p < .01)$ in the case of MSAT scores and the arithmetic test.

Next, consider the time taken for learning. The data are shown in Figure 3. For subjects of medium or high ability by any of the tests there was practically no difference between the time taken for discovery learning and the time taken for rule learning. (Recall that the main effect of method of learning time was not significant.) However, for subjects in low ability groups the discovery method required more time than the rule method. This was reliable for the grouping by MSAT scores $(p < .01)$, the test of concepts $(p < .05)$, and the arithmetic test $(p < .05)$.

Finally, consider performance on the test given after instruction had been completed. The results are in Figure 4. First, consistent with Corman (1957) and Tallmadge (1968) we can claim no evidence for an interaction between instructional method and general ability as mea-

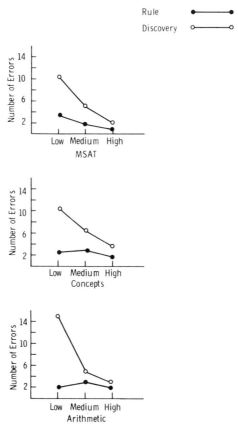

Fig. 2. Mean number of errors in rule and discovery learning for subjects with differing levels of ability on three pretests.

sured by the MSAT. However, substantial interactions were found between the methods used and the tests that measured abilities and knowledge that were specifically involved in the learning task. The effects were at least marginally reliable for both the test of concepts ($p < .05$) and the arithmetic test ($p < .10$).

Unfortunately, performance on the permutations task did not result in reliable effects. The data showed trends in the direction of interesting interactions, and we are exploring the relationship between performance in this kind of task and performance during and after instruction in our current experimental work.

By way of conclusions, the subjects of high ability learned quite a bit by both methods, and it took them a relatively short time to do it.

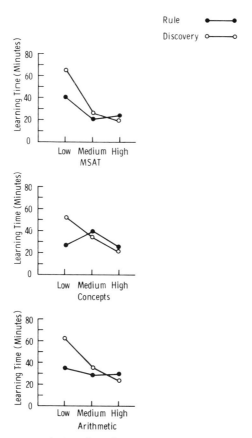

Fig. 3. Mean amount of time in rule and discovery learning for subjects with differing ability on three pretests.

Subjects with low degrees of ability were considerably better off if they were taught by rule method than by the discovery method. Low-ability subjects took longer to accomplish the discovery learning task than the rule-learning task, and they learned less in the process, as indicated by scores on the post test. This relationship seems to have been strongest in the case of arithmetic skills, but it is also true for the tests of concepts and the MSAT.

Subjects whose ability scores were intermediate provided the results of greatest interest. If these subjects are identified by the MSAT, their performance in discovery and rule learning is practically indistinguishable. However, when we use the scores obtained in tests of background concepts and arithmetic skills, the method used makes quite a difference

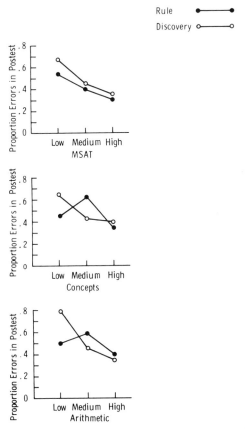

Fig. 4. Mean proportion of errors in post test following rule and discovery learning for subjects with differing levels of ability on three pretests.

to subjects with intermediate ability. Especially when the division is made using the test of concepts, the two procedures required about the same amount of time but subjects apparently learned more from the discovery procedure than from the rule procedure.

A second set of conclusions involves implications for the conduct of research relating abilities or other individual differences to instructional methods. First, the results obtained using tests that are specifically relevant to the learning material may be quite different from those obtained with measures of general ability. Second, data about what happens during the learning period can provide important information about interactions between ability and instructional method. And, finally, regression analyses can mask important effects. Regarding the last point, if the

relationships in these results had been measured with correlation co-
efficients, the interesting interaction in the center panel of Figure 3 would
have appeared as just a higher correlation between ability and performance after discovery than after rule learning, and it would appear
that the concept test was not useful in predicting performance after
rule learning.

The most interesting but least firm conclusions to be taken relate
to the process of acquiring cognitive structures. The least to be said
is that acquisition proceeded differently under the rule and discovery
methods of instruction that were used in Egan's study. An analysis of
the difference would begin by identifying the component processes involved in learning under the two methods, and using differences in the
component processes as possible explanations of differences in the learning outcomes.

First, consider the rule method. Subjects were given information and
solved illustrative problems. To solve such a problem, a subject might
carry out the following steps, not necessarily in a serial fashion.

1. Read the problem text.

2. Select information from the text pertaining to the values of relevant
variables, and coordinate this information to the coded representations
of variables in memory. For example, from the phrase, "the chances
of success were 1/4," subjects could extract information in the form,
"$p = .25$." This would be likely if subjects were interpreting the problem
in relation to some previously learned structure or rule in which "p"
occurred as an element, known to be a probability value.

3. Select a rule or formula for using the variables whose values have
been taken from the text. This might be looked up in available information, or retrieved from memory. Perform any transformations needed
to make the rule applicable to the information.

4. Calculate the answer.

The instruction given in the rule method would be expected to result
in the skills needed for solving the problems given during that instruction. This makes it reasonable to suggest that under instruction by the
rule method, subjects acquired a list of variables (N, r, p, and q) and
the rule for calculating the binomial probability corresponding to a set
of values for the variables. "Acquiring the rule" almost certainly involved more than memorizing a pattern of letters and punctuation that
represents the formula, although it probably involved that. In addition,
if the subject acquired the rule of calculating binomial probability he
became familiar with the sequence of operations including substituting

values for variable names and carrying out the arithmetic operations in a proper sequence to obtain the answer.

Now consider the discovery method. In the discovery method, subjects had to solve problems for which they had not learned an algorithm that would permit them to obtain the answer with a straightforward series of calculations. Problems were stated in terms of concepts that subjects understood or had learned during the learning period. The sequence of steps involved in solving would have to be much the same as in the case of rule learning, but important differences would be present.

1. Read the problem text.

2. Interpret the information in the problem in relation to concepts that are understood. The discovery method did not provide a well-specified list of variables as did the rule method. Therefore, interpretation of information in the discovery method probably had more of the properties of understanding a sentence than in the rule method, and less of the character of filling in values of variables in a list.

3. Search for or generate relationships among concepts used in the problem, particularly relationships that seem to move in the direction of relating the given information with the unknown. This is the kind of process that has been investigated in classical studies of problem solving such as those of Duncker (1945), Polya (1962), and Wertheimer (1959). A subject might find relationships that involved his understanding of the concepts in the problem, or he might apply a more general relational structure that fit the needs of the problem, or he might find a set of concepts in memory whose relationships seem to provide an analogy to the situation in the problem.

4. Carry out any calculations needed to obtain the answer.

If a subject is not able to find a way to solve the problems given in discovery learning, the method may produce more confusion than learning. However, if a subject was able to find a solution to the problem, it had to be on the basis of something he already knew. Of course, a solution of a problem can be achieved without understanding, arriving at the correct sequence of operations by chance. But if a true solution was found, in which the subject genuinely discovered a new relationship among concepts, then the learning that resulted would necessarily be meaningful in Ausubel's (1968) and Katona's (1940) sense. According to this view, when discovery learning occurs, it leads to reorganization of cognitive structure, with new relationships among concepts known by the subject.

In the rule learning, the subject's cognitive structure would be altered primarily by adding new components. Relationships among components of original structure might be altered by the subject's own efforts to incorporate new material into his previous knowledge, but this was not demanded by the learning materials. A pictorial representation might have the new structure on a different plane from the knowledge that the subject brought to the learning situation, with a connection representing the association between some of the components in the new structure and corresponding concepts known earlier. According to our hypothesis, the main difference between rule and discovery learning is that with rule learning new structure tends to be added to prior knowledge, while with discovery learning there is more integration of new information into existing cognitive structure.

To summarize these conclusions, I think that in Egan's results we have some information that begins to show a relationship between what a person knows and how he acquires a new cognitive structure. I will state some hypotheses in a very general way that would not be very helpful were it not for the more detailed information in Egan's experiment. If a person has an appropriate set of background knowledge and skill that is relatively specific to the learning material, he can be given an instructional procedure in which he learns through solving problems. This can result in an acquired structure that is integrated with the learner's prior knowledge and is therefore superior to the outcome of learning that is added to earlier knowledge in a less meaningful way. However, if the person lacks the requisite skills and concepts, the acquisition of a new structure occurs more readily by an instructional procedure in which the component ideas and their relationships are presented to the learner, rather than being inferred by him. The emphasis we place on prerequisite skills and knowledge that is specific to the material to be learned is like that found in Gagné's (1965) theoretical analyses. Egan's results add specific information about what kinds of prerequisites are relevant to acquiring the particular kind of structure used in this study, and highlight the exceptional importance of the prerequisites in discovery learning.

Structural Variables in New Learning

Egan's study provided information about a way in which instructional methods can vary in effectiveness, and we think the reason for the difference is in the degree to which the methods cause new material to be integrated with the subject's prior cognitive structure. The next study that I will describe, carried out by Richard Mayer, gave information about differences in the nature of learned structures—what kind of learning rather than how much. The main variable in these experiments was the sequencing of information given to the subject.

Mayer used two basic instructional sequences, called Formula and Concept. The Formula sequence began with a statement of the binomial formula and proceeded through a sequence in which various components of the formula were explained. The Concept sequence began by introducing the component variables to the subject in relation to general concepts, and then proceeded to show how they are combined in the formula, finally showing the formula at the end.

The two instructional sequences were incorporated in teaching booklets. Both groups learned the formula for binomial probability with the notation

$$P(X = r|N) = \binom{N}{r} p^r (1 - p)^{N-r}.$$

The teaching booklets were of about equal length, and material in both was presented in a series of pages, each containing a brief exposition, followed by an example using the ideas just explained, and an exercise for the subject to work out.

The ideas given in the booklet with the Concept sequence were as follows:

1. Introduction of terms "trial," "outcome," and "event."
2. Notion of a success introduced as some designated event.
3. The probability of a success explained as the proportion of possible outcomes leading to success, or as expected frequency of success over a long series of trials.
4. Use of notation: N for number of trials r for number of successes.
5. Coordination of N, r notation to a specific sequence.
6. The number of ways to get r successes in N trials given as $\binom{N}{r}$, with an explanation of how to calculate the value of this coefficient.
7. Presentation of the fact that probability of a specific sequence is the product of the probabilities of individual outcomes, and calculation in terms of p and $(1 - p)$.
8. Probability of r successes in N trials given as the product of the probability of a specific sequence by the number of such sequences, and presentation of the binomial formula.

The ideas given in the booklet with the Formula sequence were:

1. Presentation of the formula, and definition of its terms: $P(X = r|N)$ as the probability that a certain outcome occurs r times in N trials, r as

the number of times the thing happens, N as the number of times we try to get it to happen, and p as the chance of the thing happening on each trial.

2. Instruction that $P(X = r|N)$ is found by multiplying three quantities: $\binom{N}{r}$, p^r, $(1 - p)^{N-r}$.

3. Instruction that to find $\binom{N}{r}$, use a formula given in terms of factorials, and explanation of these terms.

4. Presentation of the fact that p^r is p multiplied by itself r times.

5. Instruction in obtaining $(1 - p)^{N-r}$ from the quantities p, N, and r, and in finding the value of this term.

6. Instruction that to find $P(X = r|N)$, first find the three component terms given above, and multiply them to obtain the result.

As can be inferred from the outline of the materials, the Concept sequence included more discussion of concepts, while the Formula sequence had the character of a set of instructions and could be likened to a computer program for finding the formula.

After subjects worked through their respective teaching booklets, they received a test containing 12–15 items, depending on the experiment, with at least three items in each of four categories. Examples of the test questions are:

Familiar: $N = 6$, $r = 3$, $p = 1/2$. Find $P(X = r|N)$.
Transformed: $p = 1/3$, $N - p = 2/3$, $N - r = 0$. Find $P(X = r|N)$.
Unanswerable: $N = 2$, $r = 3$, $p = 1/2$. Find $P(X = r|N)$.
Question: Can r be greater than N?

In each of these four categories of test items, there was a question stated in N, r, and p (like those given), an item about flipping coins, and an item about rolling dice.

Mayer began by giving subjects a pretest in which he asked whether subjects had studied statistics or probability in courses, and gave problems to test subjects' skills in the arithmetic needed to carry out the task. Pretest problems included the following

$$\frac{5 \cdot 4 \cdot 3 \cdot 2 \cdot 1}{2 \cdot 1 \cdot 3 \cdot 2 \cdot 1} = \underline{\quad} , \left(\frac{1}{4}\right)^3 = \underline{\quad} , \frac{2}{3} \times \frac{1}{4} = \underline{\quad} .$$

After the pretest, each subject was given a teaching booklet, which he was instructed to read silently. Subjects were given blank sheets of paper on which they could answer sample problems that were included in the booklets. Up to 30 minutes was allowed for completion of the teaching booklets—all subjects finished in that time.

Subjects were run in groups of two to four, and when all subjects were finished with their teaching booklets the test was given. In the instructions for the test, subjects were told to write "no answer" if they felt a question could not be answered.

EXPERIMENT I

In Mayer's first study, ten subjects were tested using each of the sequences. The subjects were women recruited from the subject pool during the fall term. Four subjects had to be rejected because they had studied the binomial formula in a class. All subjects answered at least seven of the ten pretest questions and none were excluded for insufficient calculating skill.

The test results are summarized in Table 1. Note that when all test items are considered, the two methods produced about equal overall

TABLE 1

Proportion of Correct Response by Type of Item and Instructional Method: Experiment I

Instructional sequence	Type of item			
	Familiar	Transformed	Unanswerable	Question
Formula	.75	.57	.43	.43
Concept	.48	.40	.63	.83

achievement. However, there is a noticeable interaction in the data, and it was reliable $(p < .025)$. Subjects receiving the Concept sequence did better at identifying unanswerable questions and at answering questions than subjects who received the Formula sequence, but the Concept sequence produced worse performance in the items that were like the sample problems used in the teaching booklet. Using Lehrer's (1965) apt phrase, subjects who received the Concept sequence understood what they were doing, rather than being able to get the right answer.

Relating this result to the data from Egan's experiment, it should be noted that the problems included in Mayer's instructional materials served to illustrate ideas that had been presented. In this way, both of Mayer's sequences had the general character of Egan's rule-learning method. I am inclined to think, then, that we should consider the structures acquired by Mayer's subjects as being primarily added to their prior knowledge, rather than being integrated into it, in the sense described earlier in connection with Experiment I. On the other hand, new knowledge probably has to be connected to what was known previously for learning to work at all. And because of the differences between the two presentation sequences, Mayer's two groups of subjects probably linked the new material they were learning to different aspects of their previous knowledge. In the case of the Formula sequence, subjects probably connected the material about binomial probability with their prior knowledge about arithmetic—multiplying, raising to powers, and so on. Subjects who received the Concept sequence probably connected the material they learned about binomial probability with their prior knowledge and experience with tossed coins and some general properties of physical systems with random outcomes.

Our interpretation of the effects of the difference involves an hypothetical structural property of acquired knowledge. The components of a cognitive structure have to be connected, but they can be connected more or less strongly. Also, I take it that something about a structure has to be connected with other things that a person knows in order for the structure to be part of his knowledge, but these connections can either be weak or strong. The implication is that we can talk about the connectedness of a structure, with at least a weak analogy to the concept of flow in graph theory (Berge, 1962, Ch. 8). But two aspects of connectedness must be distinguished. One may be called internal connectedness, and refers to the extent to which the components of a structure are connected to each other. And the other may be called external connectedness, referring to the extent to which components of the structure are connected to other contents of the person's mind.

Our interpretation is that the subjects receiving the Concept sequence tended to acquire structures with relatively strong external connectedness, but rather weak internal connectedness, while the opposite held for subjects receiving the Formula sequence. This interpretation uses the idea that in simple mathematical structures connections between components may consist of the arithmetic operations that link the variables. If this is reasonable, then the emphasis on using the formula given in the Formula sequence would produce relatively strong connections between the components of the structure—that is, strong internal connectedness. On the other hand, the Concept sequence gave less emphasis to calculation and more to the meanings of the various components. This should have produced stronger connections between concepts in the new structure and other concepts the subject knew about—that is, strong external connectedness.

The notions about internal and external connectedness come to mind because of the kinds of questions on which the two groups differed. Subjects who received the Formula sequence excelled on problems that were essentially the same as those used during the learning period, and these involved simple calculations involving the formula. Subjects in the Concept sequence excelled in answering questions about the formula. It is an interesting and reasonable possibility that the ability to talk about a structure depends on having information in memory that relates the structure to other concepts and propositions. According to this view, the ability to answer questions about a cognitive structure that one has acquired would depend strongly on just the kind of property that I have been calling external connectedness.

EXPERIMENT II

In this study, subjects were 32 male and 32 female students in the summer term. Eight male and eight female subjects each were tested using the Formula sequence and the Concept sequence, the Formula sequence followed by the Concept sequence, and the Concept sequence followed by the Formula sequence. The experiment was conducted according to the procedures described earlier, with the obvious exception that in the conditions involving two teaching booklets, subjects were given more time—in fact, they had 60 minutes to work through the booklets.

No subjects had to be rejected because of knowing about binomial probability. The female subjects apparently had less mathematical skill than the male subjects in this experiment and the female subjects in Experiment I. Two female subjects were rejected for getting fewer than five correct pretest items out of ten, and the mean score of subjects whose data were used was 8.4. No male subjects were rejected on the basis of the pretest, and their mean pretest score was 9.3, virtually the same as the mean pretest score for the female subjects in Experiment I. In addition, eight subjects, seven of them female, were rejected on the basis of responses to a postexperimental questionnaire indicating that they had not followed instructions or learned the material during the learning phase.

Results obtained in the test are given in Table 2 for the male subjects, and in Table 3 for the female subjects. My discussion will focus on some interactions whose reliability may be of interest. They include Method × Type of test item ($p < .001$), Type of test item × Sex of subject ($p < .005$), and Method × Type of test item × Sex of subject ($p < .005$).

TABLE 2
Proportion of Correct Response by Type of Item and Instructional Method: Experiment II, Male Subjects

	Type of item			
Instructional sequence	Familiar	Transformed	Unanswerable	Question
Formula	.88	.71	.71	.58
Concept	.29	.17	.79	.79
Formula, then Concept	.67	.54	.96	.71
Concept, then Formula	.83	.67	.83	.71

TABLE 3
Proportion of Correct Responses by Type of Item and Instructional Method: Experiment II, Female Subjects

	Type of item			
Instructional sequence	Familiar	Transformed	Unanswerable	Question
Formula	.71	.46	.46	.58
Concept	.29	.38	.54	.54
Formula, then Concept	.67	.33	.50	.50
Concept, then Formula	.75	.38	.50	.50

For the male subjects, performance after the Formula sequence or the Concept sequence alone agreed nicely with the results of Experiment I. Our best guess about the groups receiving both teaching booklets is that they achieved a simple combination of the knowledge acquired in the two booklets. An unvarnished version of this idea would imply that each two-booklet group would do about as well as the better of the two single-booklet groups on each question category. This did not happen, but the deviations from that prediction are relatively small and most are in the direction that could be explained on grounds of recency. The group receiving the Formula sequence first did a little less well on questions involving the formula, and the group receiving the Concept sequence first showed performance in rather good agreement with the combination hypothesis.

The female subjects in this study, whose data are in Table 3, showed generally poorer performance. Recall that these subjects had lower scores on the arithmetic pretest than the other subjects whose data have been discussed. Also recall that Mayer's procedures were similar to Egan's rule-learning method. These two facts make it reasonable to use the data of Table 3 to make further inferences about the effects of rule learning in relation to subjects' ability to perform relevant operations. One interesting result is that performance on items of the Familiar type was virtually as good for these subjects as for the others. This fits with the conclusions from Egan's data that low-ability subjects can learn as well from a rule method as other subjects.

However, this conclusion is supported only as long as we consider just the items that are essentially the same as those used in training. First, if a problem requires an algebraic transformation before its data can be fit into the formula, these subjects appear to do less well than their counterparts whose pretest scores were higher. This could be a straightforward result of a lower level of arithmetic skill, since subjects had to apply arithmetic operations in the test that had not been required during the training.

But of great interest is the lower performance shown by female subjects in Experiment II on the unanswerable problems and the questions. Our interpretation of these questions is that they mainly test the strength of external connectedness of the acquired structures. The test results that we have for these subjects involve arithmetic operations, which we believe are related to acquisition of internal connectedness. The apparent relationship could be due simply to a correlation between abilities of subjects. Perhaps if we had scores on a test like Egan's test of concepts, we would find that the low performance on items of the Unanswerable and Question types was due to low degrees of familiarity with the relevant concepts in the situation. However, it is also possible that there is an interesting interaction between the kinds of abilities we have been thinking about so that the ability to handle the operations involved in a structure is a prerequisite to the acquisition of external connectedness for the structure.

EXPERIMENT III

This study was like Experiment II with two exceptions. First, subjects were like those used in Experiment I—female students in the regular academic year (winter term). Second, the teaching booklets were modified in a way that placed greater emphasis on the subjects' solving of problems. Following each page of instruction there were three pages added. Each new page gave the answer to the question shown on the preceding page, and gave an additional question. The subject was instructed that if his answer to the preceding question was correct, he should go on to the next instructional page, but if he was wrong he should go back to the previous instructional page, reread it, and then try the new question. In addition, an answer sheet was prepared containing a specific place for the answer to each question. (In Experiments I and II, subjects had written answers on a blank sheet of paper—if they wanted to.)

No subjects were rejected for previous familiarity with binomial probability or for insufficient skill in arithmetic. The mean pretest score was 9.2, comparable to the score for Experiment I and male subjects in Experiment II.

The test results are summarized in Table 4. It is possible to see the kind of interaction observed in Experiments I and II, but this takes an eye biased by the preceding results, and the Method × Type of item interaction was thoroughly insignificant ($p > .20$). It can be safely said that the interaction was greatly decreased in this situation. One reason

TABLE 4

Proportion of Correct Response by Type of Item and Instructional Method: Experiment III

	Type of item			
Instructional sequence	Familiar	Transformed	Unanswerable	Question
Formula	.67	.57	.60	.57
Concept	.45	.50	.47	.63
Formula, then Concept	.63	.37	.50	.63
Concept, then Formula	.50	.53	.63	.63

for confidence is that after the results in Table 4 were obtained, a few subjects from the same source were tested using the booklets with the extra pages removed. The Formula sequence gave proportions of correct response of 1.0, .67, .67, and .50 for the four types of question. The corresponding data for the Concept sequence were .50, .33, .67, and .92. These results were obtained with four subjects per condition, and the apparent interaction was reliable ($p < .05$). One possible reason for the reduced effect is that the additional problem solving activity produced increased similarity between the two teaching booklets, causing the outcomes to be less distinct.

A Preliminary Study of Insight

The final result that I will describe is a rather dramatic one, and, although it seems quite clear, we need to do further work to pin down its explanation. The result was obtained by Douglas Stokes.

In his experiment, Stokes taught subjects some facts about a mythical substance called quirnon. Quirnon emits two kinds of particles, called alpha and beta particles, and does so with fixed and constant probabilities. Stokes gave a rather stiff pretest, relatively speaking, in which about one-half of the subjects who arrived were rejected from the experiment. Then he taught subjects two separate facts about quirnon.

One fact had to do with the number of different sequences that would have the numbers of alpha and beta particles. In this instruction, subjects learned to compute

$$\binom{N}{r} = \frac{N!}{r!(n-r)!},$$

and they seemed to know what it meant.

The second fact had to do with the probability of a particular kind of sequence of particles. After completing this training, subjects could solve problems like calculating the probability of a sequence aababa: $p^4(1-p)^2$, if p is the probability of an alpha particle.

Having taught these two facts separately, Stokes gave a test problem to see whether the subjects would combine the facts. The problem was to calculate a binomial probability, and its wording turned out to make a sizable difference in subjects' performance. One wording was, "If a quantity of quirnon emits eight particles what is the probability that four of them will be alpha particles and four of them will be beta particles?" Of eight subjects in the final version of the experiment, none solved this problem. The other wording was, "If a quantity of quirnon emits eight particles, what is the probability that any one sequence out of the set of all sequences that contain four alpha particles and four beta particles will occur?" Seven of eight subjects correctly answered that one, despite its syntactic complexity.

The study of insight has always involved the idea that two ideas or structures had to be put together more or less spontaneously by a subject. Köhler's (1927) study of insightful behavior by chimpanzees is the best known example. Stokes' result suggests that the binomial formula is a structure in which the bridge needed to connect two ideas is a rather specific one. Apparently, for someone who has just learned the components of the binomial formula, an important condition for seeing the relationship is some mention of a set of sequences. Lacking this, the two components seem to bear no relationship to each other at all. However, with an appropriate link subjects seem to perform almost perfectly. We will be conducting further experimental work to see whether we can show that with appropriate pretraining, subjects supply this bridge for themselves. In any case, we apparently have an especially clear case of insightful behavior to work with, and we may have evidence that, in general, insightful behavior requires some sort of linking or bridging between the component ideas that are brought together in the process of solving a problem.

Conclusions

When a person learns new concepts, his cognitive structure is modified in some way. The process of learning, as well as the outcome, will necessarily depend jointly on the learner's existing cognitive structure, properties of the new material to be learned, and the way in which the new material is presented to the learner. The work reported in this paper has involved observations of subjects engaged in learning new concepts, and we have obtained some findings that appear to give information about the process of acquiring new structures. Egan's result shows something about the way in which the subject's existing knowledge and the method of presentation interact in influencing the effectiveness of learning. Mayer's findings show something about the kind of learning outcome that can be produced by different methods of presentation. And Stokes' finding apparently informs us about the importance of having explicit connections between parts of the material being learned.

The studies reported here probably fit more closely with analyses of semantic memory than with memory of events. The papers by Collins and Quillian, by Kintsch, and by Rumelhart, Norman, and Lindsay in this volume provide important general analyses of the way in which knowledge is stored in the mind. These papers dealing with semantic memory have dealt primarily with linguistic knowledge and knowledge about the world that is described by sentences. However, there is a sense of the term "semantics" that refers to conceptual structures in a general way. And if we consider semantics in this general sense, involving relationships among concepts, the studies reported in this paper are mainly about the modification of semantic memory. We have chosen to study modification of semantic structures that involve mathematical concepts, primarily because of their relatively unambiguous structure. However, I am entirely hopeful that the processes involved in modifying cognitive structure when mathematical concepts are learned must be fundamentally the same as processes involved in the acquisition of conceptual structures of other kinds. A substantial beginning has been achieved in the understanding of the nature of semantic memory, and this advance is represented well in the papers dealing with semantic memory in this volume. The understanding we have achieved regarding modification of semantic memory involved in acquiring new cognitive structures is much more modest, but perhaps it is sufficient to justify some degree of optimism for further progress.

Summary

Studies are reported dealing with the learning of a simple mathematical structure, the binomial formula. Dennis Egan has found that subjects' knowledge of concepts specifically involved in the formula and of arithmetic operations involved in calculating with the formula interact with the method of presenting new material. Specifically, subjects having more familiarity with the relevant material learned better in a discovery procedure where subjects learned by solving problems, while subjects having less familiarity learned better in an expository procedure where the new concepts were explained explicitly. We infer from this that the discovery procedure engaged the subject's existing cognitive structure more than the expository procedure, and that therefore the newly acquired structure was probably integrated more into existing structure when it was learned by the discovery procedure.

Richard Mayer compared the outcomes of learning achieved by subjects who received information about the binomial formula in different sequences. Subjects who received a sequence beginning with individual concepts and emphasizing intuitive explanations did better on questions about the formula and worse on problems where the formula was used for calculation than subjects who received a sequence beginning with the formula and emphasizing the operations used to calculate with the formula. We infer that newly acquired cognitive structures vary on two dimensions involving strength of connection among component concepts. One of these—internal connectedness—involves the strength of connection among the elements of the structure. The other dimension—external connectedness—involves the degree to which elements of the new structure are connected with existing cognitive structure, and we suggest that the variable of external connectedness probably has a lot to do with the subject's general understanding of the new structure that he has learned.

Finally, Douglas Stokes has found an instance of insightful behavior that apparently can be manipulated dramatically in a laboratory situation. He taught two subparts of the binomial formula separately, then gave a problem requiring the subject to combine them. The subject's success on the problem depended strongly on whether the problem statement included mention of a concept that provides a conceptual connection between the two parts of the formula.

It is proposed that these studies can be interpreted as contributing a modest beginning toward understanding processes by which semantic memory is modified during the learning of a new cognitive structure.

References

Ausubel, D. P. *Educational psychology a cognitive view.* New York: Holt, Rinehart & Wilson, 1968.

Berge, C. *The theory of graphs.* New York: Wiley, 1962.

Corman, B. P. The effect of varying amounts and kinds of information as guidance in problem solving. *Psychological Monographs,* 1957, **71**, Whole No. 431.

Duncker, K. On problem solving. *Psychological Monographs,* 1945, **58**, Whole No. 270.

Hilgard, E. R. Methods and procedures in the study of learning. In S. S. Stevens (Ed.), *Handbook of experimental psychology.* New York: Wiley, 1951.

Gagné, R. M. *The conditions of learning.* New York: Holt, Rinehart & Winston, 1965.

Katona, G. *Organizing and memorizing.* New York: Columbia University Press, 1940.

Köhler, W. *The mentality of apes.* New York: Harcourt Brace, 1927.

Lehrer, T. New math. *That was the year that was.* Reprise Records, 1965.

Leskow, S., & Smock, C. D. Developmental changes in problem solving strategies: permutation. Research and Development Center in Educational Stimulation, University of Georgia, Athens, Georgia. Research Paper #15, March, 1969.

Piaget, J., & Inhelder, B. *La genèse de l'idée de hasard chez l'enfant.* Paris: Presses Universitaires de France, 1951.

Polya, G. *Mathematical discovery.* New York: Wiley, 1962.

Tallmadge, G. K. Relationships between training methods and learner characteristics. *Journal of Educational Psychology,* 1968, **59**, 32–36.

Tulving, E. Subjective organization in free recall of "unrelated" words. *Psychological Review,* 1962, **69**, 344–354.

Wertheimer, M. *Productive thinking.* New York: Harper & Row, 1959.

PART III

10 Episodic and Semantic Memory[1]

Endel Tulving

One of the unmistakable characteristics of an immature science is the looseness of definition and use of its major concepts. In experimental psychology, a discipline less than a hundred years old, we can measure our progress by the number and generality of empirical facts and the

[1] This work has been facilitated by Grant No. 24171X from the National Science Foundation.

power and scope of our theories, and we can assess the lack of progress by the degree of ambiguity of our most popular terms.

The concept of memory is a good case in point, although perception, learning, motivation, emotion, and thought could serve as equally relevant illustrations. What exactly do we mean by memory?

The question is worth raising, at this time and in this volume, for at least two reasons. First, the term "memory" has recently been permitted to return from the limbo into which it was swept by the tide of behaviorism some thirty or forty years ago. Since it shows every promise of remaining with us for some time to come, we may be excused for exhibiting some curiosity about its meaning. Second, this book, as its title implies and contents show, is all about memory. But the reader who works his way through all the chapters in their numerical order may experience an abrupt shift in the meaning of the term between Chapters 5 and 6: memory of the later chapters may appear to be not quite the same thing as memory of the earlier chapters. And the reader may wonder, too, exactly what we mean by memory. Raising the question about the meaning of the term "memory," and consequent analyses, one version of which is presented in this chapter, might even make a modest contribution towards the reduction of the degree of ambiguity characterizing one of the most popular concepts of contemporary psychology.

Categories of Memory

In a recent collection of essays on human memory edited by Norman (1970) one can count references to some twenty-five or so categories of memory, if one is willing to assume that any unique combination of an adjectival modifier with the main term refers to something other than any of the referents of other such unique combinations. The list extends from "acquisition" memory, "active" memory, and "auditory" memory near the beginning of the alphabet to "short-term," "very-short-term," and "working" memory near the end. Since this list is only an incidental by-product of the combined efforts of the contributors to the volume, it probably represents a rather incomplete listing of different kinds of memory. Although it may be difficult to determine the exact number of items in a complete list of categories of memory, we would probably be not far off the mark if we doubled the number found in Norman's volume.

Most terms referring to different kinds of memory serve the function of dividing some larger domain of memory, however we conceive of it, into smaller areas within which empirical observations and theoretical propositions are thought to be generalizable. Such divisions frequently take the form of a dichotomy: two complementary categories exhaust a superordinate category. For instance, we can think of the "whole" memory as consisting of short-term memory and long-term memory. Within the category of short-term memory we can distinguish between auditory and visual memory, and within auditory short-term memory we can create a further dichotomy between articulatory and acoustic memory.

Such dichotomies are among useful heuristic devices for furthering our understanding of mental processes. Almost all of them increment the signal-to-noise ratio in the literature, many of them suggest new experimental questions, and quite a few of them hold the promise of becoming important entries in more permanent taxonomies of cognitive processes. The development of such taxonomies is no less essential in the field of memory than it is in other scientific disciplines. In discussing the importance of the development of propaedeutic categories in a field not far removed from human memory, Melton aptly summarized the problem as follows:

> The noting of the similarities and differences of things and events is the first step in organizing knowledge about nature. These observations are then the basis for classifications of things and events and the formulation of criteria of inclusion and exclusion. This is essential to the generality that is the goal of a science, as well as to efficient communication among scientists [Melton, 1964, p. 328].

A new kind of memory that has recently appeared on the psychological scene is "semantic" memory. As far as I can tell, it was first used by Quillian (1966) in his doctoral dissertation. In the present volume, three chapters are primarily concerned with semantic memory: papers by Rumelhart, Lindsay, and Norman, by Kintsch, and by Collins and Quillian. The question, therefore, naturally arises as to the relation between semantic memory and other kinds of memory.

If I understand the ambitions of the authors of the three chapters correctly, they go considerably beyond merely creating yet another category of memory. All three chapters reflect the orienting attitude of a "unitary" memory system. The authors seem to think of their work as differing from the traditional investigations of human memory and verbal learning mainly in extent rather than in kind. Rumelhart, Lindsay, and Norman, for instance, see as their objective that of developing and describing a memory structure that is capable not only of memorizing facts, but also of solving problems, making logical deductions, and understanding ideas. Kintsch thinks of semantic memory as an organized internal lexicon that represents a person's knowledge of language and that can serve as a basis for processing information in a variety of memory tasks, including free recall. Collins and Quillian's semantic memory, too, is a highly structured network of concepts, words, and images, capable of making inferences and comprehending language. Although they make no explicit reference to more traditional memory experiments, Collins and Quillian probably would want their "language user" to be able to remember lists of unrelated words.

Despite these explicitly stated or implicitly conveyed intentions of theorists concerned with semantic memory, one may wonder about the term they all use, "semantic memory." A useful concept in science frequently is one whose definition not only makes very clear what it includes, but also what it excludes. For instance, we understand that short-term memory is not long-term memory, auditory memory is not visual memory, and acoustic memory is not articulatory memory. What do we contrast with semantic memory? Semantic memory is not . . . what other kind of memory?

In this chapter I discuss the possibility that semantic memory, among other things, is not the kind of memory that psychologists have been studying in their laboratories since the time of Ebbinghaus. I will suggest that there are sufficiently fundamental differences between the two forms of memory to recommend that we consider, at least for the time being, the two categories separately. To facilitate subsequent discussion, I will refer to this other kind of memory, the one that semantic memory is not, as "episodic" memory. I will refer to both kinds of memory as two stores, or as two systems, but I do this primarily for the convenience of communication, rather than as an expression of any profound belief about structural or functional separation of the two. Nothing very much is lost at this stage of our deliberations if the reality of the separation between episodic and semantic memory lies solely in the experimenter's and the theorist's, and not the subject's mind.

The distinction between episodic and semantic memory systems should not be construed as representing the beginning of some new theory of memory. Rather, the point of view of the two as separate systems represents an orienting attitude or a pretheoretical position whose major usefulness may turn out to lie in facilitating theory construction, without in any way circumscribing the nature of possible theories. In some sense, the distinction parallels that between sensory and perceptual processes, or between transformations of stimulus energy and stimulus information in perception (Gibson, 1966). No one will seriously want to deny that both sensory and perceptual processes are involved in an organism's awareness of its environment, that sensory processes may be influenced by perceptual processes and vice versa, and that, nevertheless, it frequently makes good sense to talk about laws and principles governing one set of phenomena independently of those applicable to the other. I envisage a similar status for the distinction between episodic and semantic memory.

The notion that memory takes different forms which must not be confused in analyses of phenomena of memory has a long history in the philosophical literature. Thus, the concepts of episodic and semantic memory are by no means new, although the traditional terminology has tended to vary from writer to writer and although the philosophical categories of memory have not had any influence on psychological research.[2] A recent notable exception to this general rule can be found in the monograph by Reiff and Scheerer (1959) who draw a clear distinction between *remembrances* and *memoria,* that is, memories with and without the experience of an "autobiographical index" (p. 25).

Episodic versus Semantic Memory

Let us think of episodic and semantic memory as two information processing systems that (a) selectively receive information from perceptual systems (Gibson, 1966) or other cognitive systems, (b) retain various aspects of this information, and (c) upon instructions transmit specific retained information to other systems, including those responsible for translating it into behavior and conscious awareness. The two systems differ from one another in terms of (a) the nature of stored information, (b) autobiographical versus cognitive reference, (c) conditions and consequences of retrieval, and probably also in terms of (d) their vulnerability to interference resulting in transformation and erasure of stored information, and (e) their dependence upon each other. In addition, psychological research on episodic memory differs from that on semantic memory in several respects.

Episodic memory receives and stores information about temporally dated episodes or events, and temporal-spatial relations among these events. A perceptual event can be stored in the episodic system solely in terms of its perceptible properties or attributes, and it is always stored in terms of its autobiographical reference to the already existing

[2] Munsat (1966) refers to "non-episodic" memory, but I am not aware of anyone who has used the term "episodic" memory. It seems to fit well for our purposes. The term "episode" is a somewhat loose synonym of "occurrence," and one of its dictionary definitions is that of "an event that is distinctive and separate although part of a larger series." Episodic memory is about occurrence of such events.

contents of the episodic memory store. The act of retrieval of information from the episodic memory store, in addition to making the retrieved contents accessible to inspection, also serves as a special type of input into episodic memory and thus changes the contents of the episodic memory store. The system is probably quite susceptible to transformation and loss of information. While the specific form in which perceptual input is registered into the episodic memory can at times be strongly influenced by information in semantic memory—we refer to the phenomenon as encoding—it is also possible for the episodic system to operate relatively independently of the semantic system.

Semantic memory is the memory necessary for the use of language. It is a mental thesaurus, organized knowledge a person possesses about words and other verbal symbols, their meaning and referents, about relations among them, and about rules, formulas, and algorithms for the manipulation of these symbols, concepts, and relations. Semantic memory does not register perceptible properties of inputs, but rather cognitive referents of input signals. The semantic system permits the retrieval of information that was not directly stored in it, and retrieval of information from the system leaves its contents unchanged, although any act of retrieval constitutes an input into episodic memory. The semantic system is probably much less susceptible to involuntary transformation and loss of information than the episodic system. Finally, the semantic system may be quite independent of the episodic system in recording and maintaining information since identical storage consequences may be brought about by a great variety of input signals.

Before expanding on this thumbnail sketch of the two systems in a somewhat greater detail, we should consider some examples of episodic and semantic memory tasks. We must remember, however, that the exercise of identifying various memory situations with episodic or semantic memory is neither simple nor particularly informative, since many tasks contain both episodic and semantic features. The assignment of a task to one or the other category depends upon the kind of memory query addressed to the person, the exact nature of the information to be retrieved, or the nature of the memory claim made about the retrieved information by the person retrieving 'it. Nevertheless, a short list of examples may help the reader to follow the subsequent arguments in this essay.

The following memory claims are based on mnemonic information stored in episodic memory: (a) I remember seeing a flash of light a short while ago, followed by a loud sound a few seconds later; (b) Last year, while on my summer vacation, I met a retired sea captain who knew more jokes than any other person I have ever met; (c) I remember that I have an appointment with a student at 9:30 tomorrow morning; (d) One of the words I am sure I saw in the first list I studied was LEGEND; (e) I know the word that was paired with DAX in this list was FRIGID.

Each of these statements refers to a personal experience that is remembered in its temporal-spatial relation to other such experiences. The remembered episodes—whether they be as amorphous as "meeting a retired sea captain" or as precisely circumscribed as "seeing a flash of light"—have no necessary extra-episodic reference of any kind. They are autobiographical events, describable in terms of their perceptible dimensions or attributes and in terms of their temporal-spatial relations to other such events.

Now, consider some illustrations of the nature of information handled by the semantic memory system: (a) I remember that the chemical formula for common table salt is NaCl; (b) I know that summers are usually quite hot in Katmandu; (c) I know that the name of the month that follows June is July, if we consider them in the order in which they occur in the calendar, or March, if we consider them in alphabetical order; (d) I know that uncertainty of an event having five equiprobable outcomes is 2.322 bits; (e) I think that the association between the words TABLE and CHAIR is stronger than that between the words TABLE and NOSE.

Although some of these statements refer to the speaker's "knowledge" rather than his "remembering," all of them can be regarded as memory statements in that their content clearly depends upon information entered into the semantic memory at some earlier time. Unlike episodic memory claims, these statements do not refer to personally experienced unique episodes. Rather, content words in these statements represent linguistic translations of information retrieved about general concepts and their interrelations.

We can now proceed to compare and contrast episodic and semantic memory.

THE NATURE OF STORED INFORMATION

Episodic memory is a more or less faithful record of a person's experiences. Thus, every "item" in episodic memory represents information stored about the experienced occurrence of an episode or event. Whether we think of each event, or its representation in memory, as "an ordered list of attributes with their corresponding values" (Bower, 1967, p. 233), as "a collection of attributes which serve to discriminate one memory from another" (Underwood, 1969, p. 559), as an organized pattern of activity involving vast numbers of cortical cells (Lashley, 1950), or in terms of some other analogue, it can be reasonably completely described in terms of (a) its perceptible properties, and (b) its temporal-spatial relation to other experienced events.

A subject in a laboratory experiment is, at least in principle, equally capable of remembering the occurrence of a highly meaningful and familiar word, a meaningless nonsense syllable, a photograph of a person's face, a line drawing of an unfamiliar figure, or a 2-second 764 Hz pure tone. The subject may find it easier to reproduce some of these events from memory than others, and, indeed, the experimenter may find it convenient to test the subject's memory for some of these events by a recognition test, but no extra-episodic cognitive reference seems to be necessary for registration, storage, and retrieval of such episodic information.

Each experienced event always occurs at a particular spatial location and in a particular temporal relation to other events that already have occurred, events occurring simultaneously with it, or events that have not yet occurred. These temporal relations among experienced events are also somehow represented as properties of items in the episodic memory system. To ask a person about some item in episodic memory means to ask him when did event E happen, or what events happened at time T. Retrieval of information of this kind from episodic memory is successful if the person can describe the perceptible properties of the event in question and more or less accurately specify its temporal relations to other events. Temporal coordinates of an event and its representation in episodic memory of course need not be specified in terms of the clock and the calendar. They could be recorded in terms of temporal occurrences of other events in some as yet little understood manner.

Unlike the relations among items stored in episodic memory, the relations among items in semantic memory are of much greater variety. Some relations among concepts in semantic memory are indeed spatial and temporal, but the large majority of them clearly are not.

Input into the semantic memory system has two sources, perception and thought. When input is perceptual, perceptible attributes of stimulus events are important only to the extent that they permit unequivocal identification of semantic referents of the events. These properties themselves are not recorded in semantic memory. We also know that many perceptual events, in presence of other appropriate input or instructions to this system, result in identical changes in the semantic system. We know very little about the "language" of semantic input generated by thought. It would be entirely useless, therefore, to speculate about the fate of "attributes" of these internal stimulus events. However, it does not look as if it might be useful to insist on temporal sequence of thought elements as an important determinant of resultant changes in the semantic memory system.

AUTOBIOGRAPHICAL VERSUS COGNITIVE REFERENCE

Let us next briefly consider the question of denotative reference of input signals. A person's episodic memories are located in and refer to his own personal past. Most, if not all, episodic memory claims a person makes can be translated into the form: "I did such and such, in such and such a place, at such and such a time." Thus, an integral part of the representation of a remembered experience in episodic memory is its reference to the rememberer's knowledge of his personal identity. William James' conception of memory was that of episodic memory: "Memory requires more than mere dating of the fact in the past. It must be dated in *my* past" (James, 1890, p. 650). Reiff and Scheerer (1959), in describing the distinction between remembrances and memoria, placed particular emphasis on the presence or absence of autobiographical reference: "The important distinguishing characteristic between these two primary forms of memory is that remembrances are always accompanied by the experience of personal continuity through time, while in memoria this experience is absent" (p. 25).

Inputs into the semantic memory system are always referred to an existing cognitive structure, that is, they always have some cognitive reference, and the information they contain is information about the referent they signify rather than information about the input signal as such. Information stored in the semantic memory system represents objects—general and specific, living and dead, past and present, simple and complex—concepts, relations, quantities, events, facts, propositions, and so on, detached from autobiographical reference. If a person possesses some semantic memory information, he obviously must have learned it, either directly or indirectly, at an earlier time, but he need not possess any mnemonic information about the episode of such learning in order to retain and to use semantic information.

Information in episodic memory of necessity must be recorded into the store directly, while semantic memory information can, although it need not, be recorded indirectly or in a piecemeal fashion. For instance, for a person to remember that he experienced an event E_2 after another event E_1, he must have originally experienced those two events in this temporal order. No other possibility exists for entering information about the temporal order of two autobiographical events into episodic memory. On the other hand, it is quite feasible for a person to learn, for instance, that Napoleon was defeated by Wellington at Waterloo, and then learn, on a subsequent occasion, that Napoleon undertook a futile campaign against Russia, and yet have no difficulty remembering the historically correct sequence of the two events referred to by the two earlier statements, provided he receives appropriate additional information about the sequence.

Consider now a typical memory experiment in which a subject is asked to study and remember a list of familiar words or pairs of words. This is an episodic memory task. The occurrence of a verbal item in a given list, at a particular time, and in specified temporal relation to other items in the list is an autobiographical episode having no necessary extra-episodic denotative reference. The subject has successfully retrieved information about this episode when he responds to the retrieval query with the reproduction of an appropriate copy of the input item.

In experiments where to-be-remembered units are meaningful words that refer to concepts stored in semantic memory, the information in semantic memory may be used at the time of the input of the information into the episodic memory store. We will have more to say about such "encoding" later on in this chapter. While such encoding of a perceptual event frequently facilitates its subsequent retrieval, it does not appear to be a necessary condition for the storage and successful retrieval of episodic information.

CONDITIONS AND CONSEQUENCES OF RETRIEVAL

Some of the relevant retrieval characteristics of the two memory systems follow from our discussion of the relation between input and storage in the two systems. For instance, information can be retrieved from episodic memory only if that information had been entered into the store on an earlier occasion. The episodic memory system does not include the capabilities of inferential reasoning or generalization. Inferential reasoning, generalization, application of rules and formulas, and use of algorithms, on the other hand, represent important methods of utilization of information stored in semantic memory. By relying on his semantic memory, it is literally quite possible for a person to know something he did not learn. Thus, for instance, a person may have never learned that March follows June in the alphabetical listing of months, and yet be able to retrieve this bit of knowledge upon an appropriate query.

The consequences of retrieval also appear to differ for the two systems. While retrieval operations can be considered neutral with respect to the contents and structure of semantic memory, in the sense that they do not change the system, the act of retrieval from either system may, and usually is, entered as an episode into episodic memory. Retrieval as feedback into the episodic system may lead to changes in the contents, and the retrievability of these contents, of episodic memory.

INTERFERENCE AND ERASURE OF INFORMATION

Episodic and semantic memory systems probably differ in their susceptibility to transformation and loss of stored information. While in both systems it is very much simpler to record information in the memory store than to eliminate it from the store, forgetting appears to be more readily produced in the episodic than in the semantic system.

We know a fair amount about conditions of forgetting in episodic memory, but almost nothing about how stored semantic information becomes unavailable or inaccessible. It is probably not entirely unreasonable to assume that loss of information from the episodic memory frequently takes the form of some sort of transformation of that information as a consequence of interference with the temporal coding of stored events. Since information in episodic memory is always temporally dated, and since it can only be retrieved if its temporal date is sufficiently accurately specified by the retrieval cue, interference with temporal coding may render access to the to-be-retrieved material difficult or impossible.

Information in semantic memory, on the other hand, is usually encoded as part of, or assimilated into, a rich multidimensional structure of concepts and their relations, and such embeddedness protects the stored information from interference by other inputs. Postman and Parker's (1970) distinction between substitution habits and accretion habits in paired-associate transfer could be used to describe the effects of new inputs into the episodic and semantic system, respectively.

INTERDEPENDENCE OF THE TWO SYSTEMS

Our knowledge about the interdependence between episodic and semantic memory is meager. Theoretical thinking about problems of memory have been strongly influenced by the assumption of continuity of memory, and it is not surprising that under these conditions questions about the relation between the two systems did not make any sense and hence were not raised. One of the heuristic advantages of the distinction between the two systems may lie in the necessity it reveals for exactly these kinds of questions.

We know, of course, about the importance of semantic variables in determining retrievability of material learned in episodic memory experiments of many different kinds—the first five chapters of this volume describe and refer to many such experiments—and these effects can be regarded as evidence for the important role that the semantic system plays in storage and retrieval of episodic memory information. The processes and mechanisms involved in semantic encoding of perceptual events, however, are not at all well understood. Why, for instance, is it easier to remember that word B was seen at the same time as word A, as members of a to-be-learned pair of words, if the concepts corresponding to the words in semantic memory are closely related?

Answers to this and many other similar questions in the literature have often been deceptively simple. For instance, many investigators, adopting the implicit assumption of continuity between episodic and semantic memory, would explain the subject's facility in remembering that B occurred simultaneously with or next to A in terms of an association between A and B, an association that may already be quite strong prior to the experiment and that may be even further strengthened when the two words occur side by side. The probability of retrieval of B, given A, according to this view, is simply a function of the strength of the association between the two items.

If we accept the distinction between episodic and semantic memory along the lines of the present essay, this explanation of the effect of pre-experimental associations on the memory for co-occurrence of the two items at the same time in close spatial contiguity is inadequate. Certain predictions from this explanation also run counter to the encoding specificity principle (Postman, this volume, p. 16; Thomson & Tulving, 1970) that questions the general utility of the "associative continuity" hypothesis. The encoding specificity principle emphasizes the importance of encoding events at the time of input as the primary determinant of the storage format and retrievability of information in the episodic memory system, and points to the necessity of further study of the process of encoding, including semantic encoding.

Although the semantic system frequently influences encoding of perceptual events and, hence, the nature of information stored in episodic memory, there are probably many situations outside the laboratory in which recording and retention of episodic information is relatively independent of information stored in the semantic system. Sensory impressions, such as seeing a flash of light, a person's face, or hearing a fragment of a melody, can probably be remembered quite well without the intervention of the semantic system.

It is not unreasonable to assume that the semantic memory system can also function quite independently of episodic memory. Consider, for example, a situation in which a person reads or hears a short story. Information about the episode of reading or hearing the story is entered into episodic memory, and the contents of the story are registered in semantic memory, in the code of the semantic system and disregarding the specific input events and their perceptible properties. Retrieval of information about the story from semantic memory may take the form of translation of the "internally stored thematic surrogate" (Dooling & Lachman, 1971) into natural language. The product of this translation process may have only an accidental resemblance to the set of original input events. In a recent experiment reported by Howe (1970), for instance, subjects heard a 160-word passage and were tested for its recall two minutes later. On the average, they produced 81.5 words in recall, of which 29.8 were "correct," in that they corresponded to input words, and 51.7 words were "additions," words that had not occurred in the original input passage. This large number of intrusions contrasts starkly with the very low frequency of intrusions in experiments in which input lists consist of unrelated words. Since it is reasonable to assume that a sizable proportion of the 29.8 "correct" words were in fact unidentifiable intrusions, the correspondence between the subjects' output and the original input, scored by episodic memory measures, was rather slight, although the subjects in this experiment could reproduce more than 40 percent of the "idea units."

Relatively little is known about the role that the perceptual system and episodic memory play in the storage of information into semantic memory. Problems of acquisition of semantic information, and problems of modification of existing semantic structures, have not yet been studied by students of semantic memory. The paper by Greeno in the present volume is concerned with the problem of acquisition of a cognitive structure. Although Greeno deals with a highly specific situation, learning of the binomial theorem, his general approach may well help guide future research into the development and growth of an individual's semantic memory.

LABORATORY STUDIES OF EPISODIC AND SEMANTIC MEMORY

In typical episodic memory experiments, the subject must remember that such and such an item—the equivalent of a discrete perceptual event or experienced episode—occurred at such and such a time, in such and such a temporal relation to other items and other kinds of auto-biographical events. These experiments almost invariably are concerned with "accuracy" of the subjects' performance. Thus, the subjects' responses in episodic memory experiments are usually classified into "correct" and "incorrect" ones, depending upon correspondences and discrepancies between the experimental input and the subjects' output. The whole tradition of research in episodic memory strongly reflects this concern with how accurately the subject remembers the material presented to him, rather than, say, what he remembers. Studies of clustering and subjective organization, in addition to earlier research on "qualitative changes in retained activities" (McGeoch & Irion, 1952, pp. 363–367), constitute conspicuous exceptions to the general preoccupation with accuracy or some other measure of power of performance.

To the extent that semantic memory has been studied experimentally at all, two lines of research can be discerned. One is directed at the elucidation of the structure of semantic memory, while the other is represented by attempts to study retrieval processes in semantic memory.

The structure of semantic memory must be almost exclusively inferred from characteristics of the subject's output alone. Since input conditions responsible for the existing semantic structure are usually not known, at least not to the extent they are known and can be specified in studies of episodic memory, the experimenter simply cannot be concerned with correspondences and discrepancies between input and output. One consequence of this state of affairs is that experimenters are much less likely to rely on purely experimental observations for their inspirations and insights about the structure of semantic memory, and much less likely to do the same kinds of experiments that have become traditional in the field of episodic memory in those cases where they do seek guidance for their theorizing from empirical observations. Quite apart from the fact that they seldom raise questions about when any particular fact, concept, or some other item of information in semantic memory was perceived, learned, or somehow else acquired by the subject, they usually make no attempt to classify subjects' responses in studies of semantic memory into correct and incorrect ones. For instance, when inferences about semantic structure are made on the basis of subjects' free associations (e.g., Deese, 1965), all responses subjects make in response to a given stimulus word are accepted as equally useful data by the experimenter. In these studies there is no good and bad performance, and subjects never make errors. Similarly, in studies in which the experimenter wishes to draw inferences about the structure of semantic memory from the way in which subjects sort a set of lexical items into categories on the basis of "similarity of meaning" (Miller, 1969), subjects' behavior is not evaluated with respect to accuracy or some other measure of goodness of memory.

It is true that in investigations of semantic memory that have relied on reaction times as indices of structural characteristics of semantic memory (e.g., Collins & Quillian, 1969; Schaeffer & Wallace, 1970) some responses subjects make are regarded as "incorrect" and excluded from consideraton, but in these studies incorrect responses are attributed to sources other than subjects' semantic memories.

Studies concerned with retrieval from semantic memory, on the other hand, do use accuracy as a criterion of subjects' performance. In these experiments the subject is asked to complete a meaningful word—to "find" it in the mental lexicon—on the basis of a fragment of the word as a cue (e.g., Horowitz, White, & Atwood, 1968), or to tell exactly what and how much he knows about a word whose definition he is given when he cannot quite produce the word itself (Brown & McNeill, 1966). Experiments on tachistoscopic identification of words can also be thought of as relevant to the problem of retrieval from semantic memory, as are studies in which subjects are asked to decide whether a particular string of letters is or is not a meaningful word, and their reaction times observed (Rubenstein, Garfield, & Millikan, 1970).

Utility of the Distinction

In this section of the chapter we will briefly consider some recurrent problems in the study of human memory whose solutions may be affected by the pretheoretical point of view about the distinction between episodic and semantic memory.

ASSOCIATION AND CONTIGUITY

The core of all definitions of the concept of association, as Postman (1968; also this volume) has pointed out, is the sequential order of verbal units. Sequential order of units has received a great deal of attention in the past work on verbal learning, primarily in the context of paired-associate and serial-anticipation list-learning experiments. Consideration of the broader range of episodic memory situations—including free recall, recognition memory, verbal discrimination, the Brown-Peterson paradigm, recency judgments, and others—reveals that memory for the sequential order of input items is always an important ingredient of the subjects' task. The concept of association, therefore, can be used in descriptions of the subjects' accomplishments in episodic memory situations.

The use of associative language is admittedly easier in some situations than others. It is perfectly acceptable, for instance, to say that the subject learned an association between A and B if the subject remembers that events A and B occurred at the same time. And whether we think of A as a part of the retrieval query that specifies the time at which another event occurred whose name the subject is expected to retrieve from memory, or as a stimulus that elicits the associated response B, may indeed be simply a matter of preference. It is probably more difficult to recast in associative terms the subjects' memory claim that he remembers events A, B, and C having occurred in a longer series of events, and that the temporal interval between A and B was approximately twice as long as that between B and C, but a determined association theorist may be able to manage this one, too. By and large, then, there is nothing wrong with the concept of association as a purely descriptive term in the study of episodic memory.

Difficulties do arise, however, when the concept is pressed into service as an explanatory tool. Its shortcomings become apparent especially clearly in the course of examination of the proposition that contiguity is necessary for learning or for association formation. Both Postman and Voss elsewhere in this volume have again emphasized the important role that contiguity plays in learning.

If learning means the subject's memory for the temporal co-occurrence or immediate succession of two events, A and B, then obviously contiguity is necessary. If learning refers to the subject's memory for the occurrence of three events, A, B, and C, and his memory for the temporal interval between A and B as approximately twice as long as that between B and C, then it would seem to be more appropriate to talk about stored information about temporal relations among events rather than contiguity. Contiguity is a temporal relation, and a special kind of temporal relation at that, but there are other aspects of temporal relations that the episodic system is capable of handling. If we explain learning as association-formation based on contiguity, the explanation would apply only to some aspects of the operation of the episodic memory system. Recourse to the concept of implicit contiguity, or functional contiguity (Voss, p. 182; Wallace, 1970) does not provide an entirely satisfactory way out, since it is difficult to imagine how the proposition that associations are built up through implicit contiguity could be denied by any experimental data. The conservative conclusion at this time seems to be that the utility of association as an explanatory concept in episodic memory has not been demonstrated. This is why it may be preferable to describe subjects' behavior in episodic memory tasks in terms of storage and retrieval of information about events and their temporal relations. Such description leaves the problem of explanation of the behavior wide open, as it should be.

Sequential associations and ordering of verbal units has been regarded as highly critical for the production and comprehension of language. For this reason one might think that the concept of association figures prominently in the study of semantic memory. This does not appear to be the case, however. Contiguity of input does not seem to be an important determinant of the structure of the mental thesaurus. Input events widely separated in time may become closely related when they are coded into semantic memory. Invocation of implicit mediators or implicit contiguity, as Postman hints on p. 40, here, too, is not likely to be effective because of impossibility of experimental rejections of such claims.

While the precise order of input events is sometimes important for distinguishing between subtle differences in the meaning of a sentence, and while it always determines the grammaticality of the sentence, a person can pick up a good deal of semantic information from awkwardly ordered and ungrammatical sentences. An ordinary language user, as Collins and Quillian (this volume, p. 346) point out, does not usually go around analyzing grammaticality of sentences, but rather tries to understand them. The role that sequential ordering of input plays in recording information into the semantic memory, therefore, is not yet exactly known, although it seems likely that the concept of association, as it has been used in the more traditional work on episodic memory, will be largely dispensed with in studies of semantic memory. In describing the structure of semantic memory, for instance, the authors of the three relevant chapters in this volume rely heavily on labeled and directed relations among the nodes of the network representing semantic memory. These labeled and directed "associations" in semantic memory contrast with unlabeled and nondirected relations among words in models of episodic memory, such as Anderson's FRAN model described by Bower elsewhere in this volume.

ENCODING AND ORGANIZATION

The concepts of encoding and organization both refer to the possibility that the internal representation of a given perceptual input may assume different forms depending upon certain operations performed on the input, or on its representation in the memory store. (In the latter case it may be more appropriate to refer to recoding and reorganization.) The two terms differ in that encoding implies the transformation of the input independently of other perceptual inputs, while organization carries the implication of changes in the memory trace of an event that are influenced by the presence of certain other traces in the episodic memory store. Thus, for instance, temporal encoding of an input implies the registration of the date of an episode without regard to other episodes, although it may be more appropriate to assume, as I mentioned earlier, that this may not represent the way the system works, and that the temporal date of a stored event may be determined by its organization in relation to other events with their temporal dates. Similarly, semantic encoding of a verbal item in episodic memory implies that the trace of the item is influenced by the information already available about its referent concept in semantic memory, while semantic organization refers to the grouping of items in a given set that somehow reflects the semantic relations among the corresponding concepts.

The most primitive form of organization is based on temporal and spatial proximity of elements in perceptual inputs and displays. Both Bower and Postman, in this volume, discuss the contributions of Gestalt psychology to the understanding of the principles of perceptual unitization. Since episodic memory is a more or less faithful record of temporally organized perceptual episodes, the first two of the four points in the Gestalt argument Postman considers (pp. 4–5)—that mnemonic organization mimics the initial perception of the events to be remembered, and that this organization is determined by proximity relations among component units—would seem to be quite appropriate even today, provided we are talking about the episodic memory system. The relevance of these two points to semantic memory is quite questionable. It also seems rather obvious that this kind of primitive organization need not depend on semantic memory.

Information in the semantic system plays a role in organization of verbal material, the extent of its involvement being dependent upon the basis of organization. If, for instance, three words in a list of to-be-remembered words are HAT, CAT, and MAT, they may be organized into a higher-order unit in terms of either their pronunciation or similarity of letter sequences. While in both cases the rules for organization may originate in semantic memory, organization of the three terms does not depend on semantic relatedness of the words. On the other hand, if the three words were CAT, LION, and TIGER, the encoding of each in terms of its semantic referent provides the basis for their organization into a higher-order unit. A person not familiar with English is likely to organize HAT, CAT, and MAT into a group, but not CAT, LION, and TIGER. Since acoustic coding is less dependent upon the semantic system than is semantic coding, it can be considered to be more direct. The fact that acoustic coding requires less time than semantic coding (Shulman, 1970) thus may reflect different degrees of involvement of the semantic system in the two types of coding and organization. A similar parallel lies in the distinction between primary and secondary organization in free recall (Tulving, 1968). Primary organization depends much less on the semantic system than secondary organization. Indeed, recency effect in free recall as a manifestation of primary organization can be regarded as a consequence of ready accessibility of terminal list items through their distinctive input positions or acoustic traces as retrieval cues.

FREQUENCY AND REPETITION

The distinction between episodic and semantic memory influences one's attitudes towards frequency and repetition of events in memory. Consider a simple experiment in which the subject's task is to remember common English words. How do we interpret a situation where one or more items are presented more than once in the same list (e.g., Waugh, 1967)? In his well-known paper on attributes of memory, Underwood (1969) suggests that one of the attributes of memory is frequency. In recall of a single list with repeated items, the frequency attribute manifests itself in subjects' capabilities of making reasonably accurate judgments about the frequency with which each one of the presented items occurred in the list. This capability is assumed to be based on different values of the frequency attribute of items. This conception is logically similar to the notion of "occurrence information" that is thought of as being "stored in memory for each word" (Bower, Lesgold, & Tieman, 1969, p. 492; also Mandler, this volume), and that presumably is different for words that occurred in the list twice, once, or not at all.

This conception of frequency seems to require the assumption that an identical event occurred n times in a list, with $n \geqq 0$. In the world of perceptual events this something, of course, is the nominally identical physical stimulus, and in the semantic memory system it might be its corresponding concept. The point of view of frequency attribute, or occurrence information, then is that a given item A is one and the same item, regardless of where or when it occurs, and that the frequency attribute of the internal representation of the item is updated every time the item occurs in the list.

From the point of view of episodic memory, however, each event a person experiences is always unique in the sense that in all of his previous autobiographical history there has not been another experience exactly like the present one. An event that occurs now, of course, can be perceived and encoded as similar or somehow else related to other events, but there can be no dichotomy between repetition of one and the same item and presentation of different items. There is no particular reason, according to this point of view, to single out nominal identity of stimulus events as a basis of classification of events into categories whose size the subject is asked to judge. We can ask how many times word A occurred in the list, but we can also ask about the frequency of animal names in the list, or words containing letter "o." If we assume that the subject can estimate the number of occurrences of word A in the list on the basis of its frequency attribute or occurrence information, what is the "memory" or the entry in some permanent memory store whose frequency attribute or occurrence information permits the subject to make estimates about the number of animal names or words beginning with "o"?

The adoption of the point of view of the distinction between episodic and semantic memory (a) permits us to avoid some of the conceptual difficulties inherent in the assumption of frequency attribute or occurrence information attached to some earlier representation of the perceptual event in some permanent memory store, (b) leaves open the possibility of asking questions about the effects of repetition in situations in which the relation between "repeated" events is something other than nominal or physical identity, and (c) suggests that in experiments in which items are repeated within a list the subject be asked not to report what words occurred in the list, but rather tell what events occurred in the list, that is, report repeated occurrences of nominally identical items.

SOME OTHER PROBLEMS

The scope of the present work does not permit us to consider some other problems in the study of human memory for which the proposed distinction between episodic and semantic memory has implications. In this final section, however, I would briefly like to at least mention some of them.

The problem of exactly how to interpret subjects' responses that may represent "guessing" rather than memory, for instance, may appear in a new light if we realize that in episodic memory experiments we are testing subjects for their memory of specific events. Correspondence between a word in an input list and the same word in the subject's recall protocol, therefore, cannot always be regarded as evidence for subject's remembering the occurrence of that word in the list. The possibility that the subject retrieves information from his semantic memory in an episodic memory experiment should not be overlooked, particularly in those experiments in which the number of intrusions is large. Consider again Howe's (1970) experiment referred to earlier (p. 393). A typical subject in that experiment recalled 80 words, 30 of which were "correct" and 50 "incorrect." In describing that experiment I briefly mentioned the possibility that some of the 30 "correct" words may have simply represented accidental correspondences between the subject's translation of the semantic information about the story into natural language on the one hand and the presented list of input items on the other hand. How could we test the subject for "true" episodic information in this case? One possibility would be to give the subject the 80 words he produced in recall, tell him that 30 of these occurred in the input passage and 50 did not, and ask him to select 30 words out of 80 that he in fact remembers from the input. This is not the place to go into computational details of such a test, but it should be clear that the procedure would permit assessment of the degree to which specific words recorded by the subject in his output represented remembered episodic units.

The distinction between episodic and semantic memory may also be quite useful in understanding data such as those reported by Thomson and Tulving (1970) in support of the encoding specificity principle. In absence of the distinction, it would be more difficult to explain why subjects cannot take advantage of strong preexperimental associations between words that serve as retrieval cues and words that occurred in an earlier input list. The remarkable precision with which "selector mechanism" works, as well as the problems posed by the "interference paradox" (Underwood & Schulz, 1960) also may become somewhat clearer and comprehensible if we keep in mind the distinction between episodic and semantic memory.

Finally, we have heard frequent and justified complaints that many decades of research and study by psychologists interested in human learning and memory have not yielded many significant insights that could be used for the improvement of education and for the betterment of learning in classrooms. If it is true that past research in human learning and memory has been concerned primarily with episodic memory, and if it is true that classroom learning has little to do with students' remembering personally experienced events, then it is not surprising that empirical facts and theoretical ideas originating in the verbal learning and human memory laboratories have little bearing on theory and practice of acquisition of knowledge.

Summary

In this chapter I have tried to present a case for the possible heuristic usefulness of a taxonomic distinction between episodic and semantic memory as two parallel and partially overlapping information processing systems. Episodic memory refers to memory for personal experiences and their temporal relations, while semantic memory is a system for receiving, retaining, and transmitting information about meaning of words, concepts, and classification of concepts.

I argued that the two memory systems differ from each other (a) in the nature of stored information, (b) with respect to the denotative reference of input events, (c) in terms of conditions and consequences of retrieval, and possibly (d) in their susceptibility to interference and erasure of stored information. In handling mnemonic information for verbal materials the two systems frequently interact, but the extent of dependence of one system on the other may vary with the particular task.

Laboratory studies of human memory and verbal learning have almost exclusively been concerned with phenomena of episodic memory. The large majority of typical memory tasks reduce to the requirement that the subject remember what particular perceptual event occurred in what temporal (sometimes also spatial) relation to other events. The relatively scant literature on semantic memory consists primarily of studies of free association to, and classification of, word stimuli, as well as studies of retrieval times for semantic information.

The possible range of advantages of the distinction between episodic and semantic memory has not yet been explored. Some illustrative cases were briefly considered in the chapter by relating the concept of two memory systems to problems of association and contiguity, encoding and organization, and frequency and repetition. It is not entirely inconceivable that the adoption of the distinction—at least until such time that experimental and theoretical developments dictate a more parsimonious taxonomy—could aid in the solution of a number of outstanding problems of human memory.

References

Bower, G. A multicomponent theory of the memory trace. In K. W. Spence & J. T. Spence (Eds.), *The psychology of learning and motivation.* Vol. 1. New York: Academic Press, 1967. Pp. 229–325.

Bower, G. H., Lesgold, A. M., & Tieman, D. Grouping operations in free recall. *Journal of Verbal Learning and Verbal Behavior,* 1969, **8**, 481–493.

Brown, R., & McNeill, D. The "tip of the tongue" phenomenon. *Journal of Verbal Learning and Verbal Behavior,* 1966, **5**, 325–337.

Collins, A. M., & Quillian, M. R. Retrieval time for semantic memory. *Journal of Verbal Learning and Verbal Behavior,* 1969, **8**, 240–247.

Deese, J. *The structure of associations in language and thought.* Baltimore, Maryland: Johns Hopkins Press, 1965.

Dooling, J. L., & Lachman, R. Effects of comprehension on retention of prose. *Journal of Experimental Psychology,* 1971, **88**, 216–222.

Gibson, J. J. *The senses considered as perceptual systems.* Boston, Massachusetts: Houghton Mifflin, 1966.

Horowitz, L. M., White, M. A., & Atwood, D. W. Word fragments as aids to recall: The organization of a word. *Journal of Experimental Psychology,* 1968, **76,** 219–226.

Howe, M. J. A. Repeated presentation and recall of meaningful prose. *Journal of Educational Psychology,* 1970, **61,** 214–219.

James, W. *The principles of psychology.* Vol. 1. New York: Holt, 1890; New York: Dover, 1950.

Lashley, K. S. In search of the engram. In *Symposia of the Society for Experimental Biology.* No. 4. London & New York: Cambridge University Press, 1950. Pp. 454–482.

McGeoch, J. A., & Irion, A. L. *The psychology of human learning.* New York: Longmans, 1952.

Melton, A. W. The taxonomy of human learning: Overview. In A. W. Melton (Ed.), *Categories of human learning.* New York: Academic Press, 1964.

Miller, G. A. A psychological method to investigate verbal concepts. *Journal of Mathematical Psychology,* 1969, **6,** 169–191.

Munsat, S. *The concept of memory.* New York: Random House, 1966.

Norman, D. A. *Models of human memory.* New York: Academic Press, 1970.

Postman, L. Association and performance in the analysis of verbal learning. In T. R. Dixon & D. L. Horton (Eds.), *Verbal behavior and general behavior theory.* Englewood Cliffs, New Jersey: Prentice-Hall, 1968.

Postman, L., & Parker, J. F. Maintenance of first-list associations during transfer. *American Journal of Psychology,* 1970, **83,** 171–188.

Quillian, M. R. Semantic memory. Ph.D. dissertation, Carnegie Institue of Technology, 1966. Also in M. Minsky (Ed.), *Semantic information processing.* Cambridge, Massachusetts: Massachusetts Institute of Technology Press, 1968.

Reiff, R., & Scheerer, M. *Memory and hypnotic age regression.* New York: International Universities Press, 1959.

Rubenstein, H., Garfield, L., & Millikan, J. A. Homographic entries in the internal lexicon. *Journal of Verbal Learning and Verbal Behavior,* 1970, **9,** 487–494.

Schaeffer, B., & Wallace, R. The comparison of word meanings. *Journal of Experimental Psychology,* 1970, **86,** 144–152.

Shulman, H. G. Encoding and retention of semantic and phonemic information in short-term memory. *Journal of Verbal Learning and Verbal Behavior,* 1970, **9,** 473–486.

Thomson, D. M., & Tulving, E. Associative encoding and retrieval: Weak and strong cues. *Journal of Experimental Psychology,* 1970, **86,** 255–262.

Tulving, E. Theoretical issues in free recall. In T. R. Dixon & D. L. Horton (Eds.), *Verbal behavior and general behavior theory.* Englewood Cliffs, New Jersey: Prentice-Hall, 1968. Pp. 2–36.

Underwood, B. J. Attributes of memory. *Psychological Review,* 1969, **76,** 559–573.

Underwood, B. J., & Schulz, R. W. *Meaningfulness and verbal learning.* Chicago, Illinois: Lippincott, 1960.

Wallace, W. P. Consistency of emission order in free recall. *Journal of Verbal Learning and Verbal Behavior,* 1970, **9,** 58–68.

Waugh, N. C. Presentation time and free recall. *Journal of Experimental Psychology,* 1967, **73,** 39–44.

Author Index

Numbers in italics refer to the pages on which the complete references are listed.

Garrett, M., 288, *306*
Gelernter, H., 315, *350*
Gianutsos, R., 8, *45*
Gibson, E. J., 34, *45*
Gibson, J. J., 384, 385, *403*
Giuliano, V. E., 314, *350*
Glanzer, M., 8, 10, *45,* 103, 118, 123, *135*
Gorfein, D. S., 53, *88*
Graf, S. A., 84, *90*
Green, C. C., 253, *307*
Greenhouse, P., 178, *193*
Greenwald, A. G., 173, *192*
Groninger, L. D., 103, *135*
Grossman, L., 178, *192*
Gruneberg, M. N., 85, *88*

H

Hanawalt, N. G., 159, *165*
Handel, S., 78, *89*
Hasher, L. A., 22, 24, 28, *45, 46*
Hauser, G. K., 76, *89*
Heimer, W., 99, *134*
Henley, N. M., 178, *192,* 287, *307*
Henry, N., 181, 184, *192*
Higgins, J., 62, *88*
Hilgard, E. R., 355, *377*
Hintzman, D. L., 178, *192*
Horowitz, L. M., 190, *192,* 395, *403*
Howe, M. J. A., 50, 58, *88,* 393, 400, *403*
Hudson, R. L., 67, 71, *88*
Hume, D., 169, *192*

I

Inhelder, B., 357, *377*
Irion, A. L., 394, *403*

J

James, W., 389, *403*
Jenkins, J. J., 124, *135,* 183, *194*
Jensen, A. R., 26, *44*
John, E. R., 186, *192*
Johnson, N. F., 105, *135*
Johnson-Laird, P. N., 317, *350*
Jung, J., 33, *45*

K

Katona, G., 364, *377*
Katz, J. J., 250, 251,. 253, 254, *307*
Keppel, G., 24, 26, *46, 47,* 123, *136*
Key, C. B., 169, *192*
Kidd, E., 76, *88*
Kiess, H. O., 181, *193*
Kimble, G. A., 173, 178, *193*
King, D. J., 84, *88*
Kintsch, W., 20, 33, *45,* 71, *88,* 113, 123, 124, 125, *135,* 141, 142, 145, *165,* 248, 251, 254, 263, 287, 293, 299, 301, 302, *307*
Knapp, M., 143, *165,* 178, *191*
Koffka, K., 108, *135*
Köhler, W., 4, 5, 30, *45,* 94, *135,* 374, *377*
Kolers, P. A., 317, *350*
Koopmans, H. S., 5, 9, *46,* 142, 146, 158, *166*
Korzybski, A., 344, *350*

L

Lachman, R., 33, *45,* 143, 154, *165,* 393, *402*
Lakoff, G., 256, *307*
Landauer, T. K., 287, *307,* 329, 331, *350*
Lashley, K. S., 388, *403*
Laughery, K. R., 33, *45*
Lawrence, K. A., 113, *136*
Lehrer, T., 368, *377*
Leicht, K. L., 178, *193*
Leiter, E., 125, *135*
Lenneberg, E., 181, *193*
Lesgold, A. M., 26, 27, 35, 36, *44,* 55, 71, 82, *87, 88,* 116, 130, *134, 135,* 143, *165,* 399, *402*
Leskow, S., 356, *377*
Levin, J. R., 184, *193*
Light, L. L., 125, *135,* 144, 154, 163, *165*
Loehlin, J. C., 200, *246*
Long, R. E., *350*
Luria, A. R., 248, 287, *307*
Lyons, J., 250, 273, *307*

M

McCawley, J. D., 258, *307*

Subject Index

A

Abstraction, 232–233
Accessibility
  availability and, 5, 13, 15, 65–66
  cueing and, 12–13
  in Gestalt theory, 5
  of higher-order memory units, 66–68,
    80
  organization theory and, 5–6
  of properties of concepts, 314
  semantic distance and, 314
  of supersets, 320–322, 331
Access operation, 295–296
Accretion with new inputs into semantic
  memory, 391
Accuracy in episodic memory experiments, 393–394
Acoustic coding
  in short-term and long-term memory,
    83–86
  semantic coding and, 298
Acquisition
  of associations, 182–185
  of associatively related words, 182–185
  of semantic information, 393
Acronyms, 97
Activation tags, 287
Adjectives, 273
Ambiguous words
  attributes of memory and, 80–83
  as links between memory units, 72–73
  as retrieval cues, 80

Analogy
  comprehension by, 336–339, 346–348
  identification of similar concepts by,
    328
  inference by, 333, 338–339
  as linguistic construct, 346–348
  metaphor and, 346–348
  semantic distance and, 347
Analogy rules
  acceptance, 283–284
  production, 281
Anaphoric reference, 335–336, 340
Aptitude-treatment interaction, 356, 359
Arithmetic operations test, 356–357, 359,
  361–362
Artificial intelligence, 200
Association
  acquisition of, 169–175, 182–185
  contiguity and, 169–175, 395–397
  descriptive usage, 168, 396
  development of, 171
  explanatory tool, 396
  interpretive usage, 168
  list learning and, 234
  nature of, 168
  organization and, 38–41, 58–59
  pre-experimental, 392
  as relation of two events, 168
  semantic memory and, 397
Association network, 314–315
Associationism, 170–171, 174
Associationistic model of free recall, 109
Associative continuity hypothesis, 392

in perception and memory, 93–107
primary and secondary, 176, 398–399
primitive form of, 398
priority for new items and, 34
as products of organizational processes, 39
proximity based, 398
quality or pattern of, 25
recognition and, 139–164
retrieval processes and, 162
retroactive inhibition and, 64
semantic, and inference, 322–324
as source of transfer, 25–32
state of learning and, 34
in storage versus retrieval, 11–16, 78–79
structure and, 176–177
as systematization, 176–177
as theoretical construct, 39–40
trace interaction and, 13–14
two processes of, 68–71
Organizational processes
associative processes and, 167–191
attributes of memory and, 80, 85–86
control mechanisms and, 18–19
definition, 139–140
experimental isolation of, 34–38
free recall and, 50–51
grouping operations and, 78–79
labeled set of associations and, 78–79
limited capacity and, 6–11
marker model and, 20–21
in paired-associate learning, 30
retrieval and, 11–13
retrieval plan formation and, 78–79
schemata and, 9–10
Organizational structures, 324
Organizational variables, 140
Orienting reflex, 287
Output consistency, as index of organization, 22–25

P

Paired-associate learning
associationism and, 170–171
cued recall and, 16
transfer
from free recall to, 31–32
to free recall from, 29–31, 58

Paradigmatic responding, 61
Parallel processing, 327–328
Parallel search, 325–328
Part relation, 323–324
Paths, 326–327
Pattern completion process, 302
Pattern matching operation, 295–296, 302
Pattern recognition, 240
Pegword systems, 113–115
Perception
organization and, 398
organization in, 93–107
Perceptual coherence, 98–100
Perceptual systems, 385
Polysemy, 253–254
Precedence relation, 324
Predicate calculus, 253
Pre-experimental associations, 392
Pre-experimental organization, 35–38
Prepositional operators, 218
Prerequisite skills, 365, 372
Presentation, blocked versus unblocked, 12, 115, 143, 183–184
Presuppositions, 276
Primacy effect in free recall, 118
Primary and secondary nodes, *see* Nodes
Primitive semantic features, 250–251
Priority for new items, 34
Proactive interference, 177
Probability, 356–357, 359, 361–362
Problem solving, 356, 364
Processes operating on data base, 198–199
Processing and retrieval operations, 227–233
Properties
accessibility of, 314
concept identification and, 330–335
image construction from, 315–316
knowledge of, and inference, 338–339
network of, in semantic memory, 315–316
relation to concepts, 315
semantic information and, 313–314
tacit consideration of, 332–333
Propositional systems, 252–254
Propositions, 254–258
in case grammar, 258–262
definition and examples of, 213
rules of formation for, 212